HEALTH CARE MANAGEMENT ISSUES IN CORRECTIONS

by Kenneth L. Faiver, MPH

FOUNDED 1870

American Correctional Association
Lanham, MD

American Correctional Association Staff

Reginald A. Wilkinson, President
James A. Gondles, Jr. , Executive Director
Gabriella M. Daley, Director, Communications and Publications
Leslie A. Maxam, Assistant Director, Communications and Publications
Alice Fins, Publications Managing Editor
Michael Kelly, Associate Editor
Mike Selby, Production Editor

Cover design by Mike Selby.

Printed in the United States of America by United Book Press, Inc.,
        Baltimore, MD.

ISBN 1-56991-070-7

This publication may be ordered from:
American Correctional Association
4380 Forbes Boulevard
Lanham, Maryland 20706-4322
1-800-222-5646

For information on publications and videos available from ACA, contact our
worldwide web home page at: http://www.corrections.com/aca.

Library of Congress Cataloging-in-Publication Data

Faiver, Kenneth L.
    Health care management issues in corrections / by Kenneth L.
Faiver.
        p.   cm.
    Includes bibliographical references and index.
    ISBN 1-56991-070-7
    1. Prisoners—Medical care—United States. 2. Prisoners—Mental
health services—United States. 3. Prisoners—Health and hygiene—
United States. 4. Prison administration—United States.
    I. Title.
    HV8843.F35   1997
    365'.66—dc21   97-17919
                                                             CIP

TABLE OF CONTENTS

A Spectrum of Care
Factors That Should Not Influence the Decision
Factors Influencing the Decision to Intervene
Other Factors
Conclusions

by Kenneth L. Faiver, MPH

Basic Principles
Tuberculosis
Human Immunodeficiency Virus and Hepatitis B, C, and D
Other Sexually Transmitted Diseases
Other Infectious Diseases
Public Health Function of Jails
Discharge Planning
Some Legal Considerations

by Kenneth L. Faiver, MPH

Unimpeded Access
Segregation and Lock-down
Intake Screening
Clinic Appointments
On-call Arrangements
Copayment—a Strategy to Limit Access

by Kenneth L. Faiver, MPH

Aging of the Population
Some Practical Considerations

by Kenneth L. Faiver, MPH, and Dean P. Rieger, M.D., MPH

Intake and Periodic Screening Activities
General Outpatient Considerations
Additional Reproductive Issues
Aging
Cosmetic Concerns
Health Education
Job Assignments

by Kenneth L. Faiver, MPH

FOREWORD

Increasingly, the law is mandating that correctional institutions provide medical services for inmates that at least meet community standards. They must do this with an eye on both the level of care and its cost as well as its security implications. With the growing number of elderly inmates in prisons, the cost of health care is expected to escalate because older individuals need more health care and more costly care than others. Many additional systemic features have an impact on the cost and treatment of inmates, including the spread of antibiotic-resistant tuberculosis, costly medical management for HIV/AIDS patients and other concerns.

Health Care Management Issues in Corrections provides administrators and students of corrections with a clear starting point. Kenneth Faiver, an experienced correctional medical administrator, describes major management concerns and suggests approaches that not only are cost-effective but meet relevant correctional health care standards.

This book successfully describes the situations that corrections professionals need to face regarding special populations, including the disabled, the elderly, women, those with infectious diseases, the mentally challenged, as well as issues in the general inmate population. For example, with the graying of the correctional population, additional health care needs to be provided — and although this can be very costly, Faiver suggests ways to offer the service at far reduced costs. Similarly, while mental health concerns and treatment are an increasing issue, two chapters provide guidance, including the use of restraints and psychotropic medication.

Faiver shares a perspective on the privatization of health care that will enable those considering it to understand some of the central concepts and concerns and be able to make educated choices that are relevant for their particular situation. Also included in this chapter are details on how to write RFPs and contracts that protect the facility or agency and may lead to heightened understanding and more effective monitoring.

ACA's customer service staff report that information addressing medical concerns in corrections is one of the leading areas of interest within our membership, and we are pleased that we now can offer such well researched but practical answers to some of these queries. Soon, if not already so, correctional systems will be the largest health care providers in the nation. It is vital that they be managed with concern for both security and quality medical care for the confined. Faiver strikes this balance-and teaches us how to understand the medical issues and codes of ethics in light of the realities in our correctional systems.

James A. Gondles, Jr.
Executive Director
American Correctional Association

PREFACE AND ACKNOWLEDGMENTS

Not that anyone ever told me it would be easy to write this book. But sometimes it was. In fact, there were times when it really felt good to "have my say" on a subject about which I hold very deep convictions. At other times, it seemed like a never-ending project—much bigger than I had imagined.

Bits and snatches of the work were written on airplanes and in airports. But the real composition took place at an idyllic cabin on a beautiful wooded lake in central Michigan. Here, in solitude and far from distractions, it was possible to combine and arrange the material, research the literature, and bring the text together. For the generous and repeated provision of this space, without which there would have been no book, I shall be forever grateful to my sister, Mary Therese, and to her husband, Marvin Dennis Swanson.

I have no regrets. The topics addressed in this book are, I believe, of great importance. In a sense, it sums up a lifetime of work. It gathers and borrows from all that I have encountered during my life, but especially from my work in various correctional health care systems. I have benefitted from many, many people. Other than those who directly assisted with preparation of this book, I will mention only two: Perry M. Johnson, who invited me to come to work for the Michigan Department of Corrections in 1975 when he was director of the agency, and Robert H. Scott, former chair of the Michigan Parole Board, a career correctional worker, scholar, and a friend. Both have inspired and shaped my thinking about how the confined ought to be treated. Perry, who completed his term as President of the American Correctional Association (1993-1994), used to keep on his desk a quotation of Dostoyevsky indicating that the quality of a society can be judged best by inspecting its prisons. Perry often said that prisons were places *of* punishment, but not *for* punishment. His deep conviction was that correctional facilities ought to treat their clients humanely and with compassion. Bob Scott, a lucid thinker and an impassioned advocate, brought a strong moral and ethical perspective to everything he touched. May he rest in peace.

This kind of work could never be accomplished by a single person. Many generously have given of their time and skills to review portions still in preparation and to offer helpful comments and ideas. Two chapters were written by other persons, with only minor editing by this author. Jacqueline Moore, herself a pioneer in private-sector health care for correctional institutions, put her quick mind to work in presenting an important discussion of the many aspects of privatized correctional health care services. Scott Chavez, currently director of the College of Physician Assistants at Midwestern University in Downers Grove, Illinois, graciously volunteered to contribute a chapter on the use of physician assistants and clinical nurse practitioners in correctional facilities.

Three physicians—all close and highly respected friends—took the time to read and comment on a number of the chapters. I relied not only on their medical expertise, but also drew from their vast experience in correctional health care. Dr. Robert S. Ort has been my friend and teacher for many years—while he served as Director of Psychiatry for the Michigan Department of Corrections and during numerous consulting projects on which we continue to collaborate since his retirement. Bob coauthored the chapter on therapeutic environments and offered comments on drafts of several others, in particular, the chapter on "Special Mental Health Issues."

Dr. Craig Hutchinson always has been a person on whom I could rely for sane, considered, and wise advice. Until May 1997, he served as Regional Medical Director for the Michigan Department of Corrections and Medical Director of the State Prison of Southern Michigan. His generous and critical comments were extremely helpful on the several draft chapters he reviewed, and I am grateful in particular for his help with the chapter on "Preventing Contagion." Best wishes to Craig as he interrupts a seventeen-year correctional career to commence a two-year fellowship in infectious disease at the University of Tampa.

Dr. Dean P. Rieger, Medical Director at the Huron Valley Women's Facility and at the State Prison of Southern Michigan, presently serves as Medical Director of the Indiana Department of Corrections. Dean's quick and incisive mind, after spotting every misplaced comma in the manuscript, also found clearer, simpler ways to describe many of the complex clinical concepts. He coauthored the chapter on Women's Health Issues, and gave numerous insightful comments for the draft of Preventing Contagion and other chapters.

Robert Kopek, clinical psychologist at the Wayne County Jail in Detroit, Michigan, thoughtfully reviewed the chapters dealing with mental health issues and ethical considerations. Dr. Glenn Johnson, former Medical Director of the Texas Department of Criminal Justice, was pressed into service during a recent accreditation survey in Nevada to review two chapters. His helpful comments are very much appreciated.

William R. Rold, a New York attorney and nationally recognized expert on correctional health care law, reviewed the chapter on ethical considerations as well as excerpts from several other chapters where legal issues are discussed. His job, according to my instructions, was to see that I did not say anything legally "stupid." Bill also assisted in preparing a current description of the impact of the Prison Litigation Reform Act of 1996.

Thanks also to the Honorable Richard Alan Enslen, Chief Judge, United States District Court, Western District of Michigan for his comments on the pages describing the Prison Litigation Reform Act of 1996.

The writings of B. Jaye Anno, who completed the monumental *Prison Health Care: Guidelines for the Management of an Adequate Delivery System* in 1992, and now edits the *Journal of Correctional Health Care*, have been a rich source of information.

And then there is Alice Fins, Publications Managing Editor, of the American Correctional Association. It was she who proposed the idea of this book and persuaded me to write it. Much cheerful enthusiasm and many encouraging words came along with her always helpful advice during these two years.

I cannot overlook mention of my wife, Rosemary Therese Faiver, who was so warmly supportive throughout this lengthy process, and who also contributed many valuable insights for the text.

Finally, this work is dedicated to my father, Kenneth E. Faiver, EE, D.Eng., who passed away before this book was published. However, he was around during the formative stages. Though his eyesight was gone, at age ninety-six he rarely failed to ask me how the book was coming. At his request, I read some of the chapters in draft form to him and to Mom and welcomed their supportive comments. Dad has been for me a model of integrity and high principle during all of my life.

I said earlier that it has been fun to "have my say" about these things that matter so much to me. I also said that I had no regrets. But there is one. I am well aware that I have not done full justice to the important subjects addressed in this book. I accept the responsibility for these shortcomings and encourage the thoughtful reader to kindly send comments and suggestions, which may be useful for any revised edition. This book is only a beginning in the quest to resolve the many and complex issues surrounding correctional health care. If it in any way spurs some others to engage in dialog, research, and writing on these subjects, all the effort will have been worthwhile.

I have been privileged to attend a number of the American Correctional Association national conferences in recent years and am deeply impressed by the professionalism of this organization and its striving for excellence. I sincerely trust that this work in some small way will enhance and assist its members in their work.

INTRODUCTION

This book is about correctional health care. It addresses many practical issues related to the structure and delivery of health care services to inmates of prisons, jails, juvenile correctional facilities, and detention centers. Its contents range from quality of care to ethical principles to cost-saving strategies. It speaks to practical details of interest to correctional administrators and seeks to explain in nonclinical terms the reasons that health care practitioners and proponents of standards for health care insist on certain principles.

While some of its content may be helpful to clinicians, this book is not a technical or clinical treatise.[1] It does not tell how to practice medicine, dentistry, psychiatry, or nursing. Other sources are available to offer guidance on clinical aspects of correctional health care.[2]

Correctional administrators apply their professional expertise to the business of planning, managing, and evaluating programs for incarceration of men and women in secure facilities, large and small, short- and long-term, across the country. They are not, nor need they be, experts also in health care. Yet, they ultimately may be held accountable for the process and outcomes of health care programs in their

---

[1] Some clinical detail is provided in certain sections of the book, such as in discussing of communicable diseases or in determining what health care services are necessary. This, however, is not intended as a primary or comprehensive source of information for clinicians, but rather its aim is to assist the correctional administrator in understanding the rationale for related polices and strategies.

[2] Standard medical reference texts, of course, are applicable, as are specialized sources of clinical information, such as guidelines from the Centers for Disease Control and Prevention concerning treatment and prevention of tuberculosis and HIV infection in a correctional population. Another excellent resource for both correctional health care staff and correctional administrators is B. J. Anno's *Prison Health Care: Guidelines for the Management of an Adequate Delivery System.*

jurisdictions. Furthermore, the decisions made by health care professionals [3] profoundly can affect the operation of their facility. These correctional administrators also may be sued. And the dollars spent on medical services in their facilities are dollars which they cannot spend on other priorities.

The purpose of this book is to provide an up-to-date and comprehensive reference manual to assist correctional officials in making decisions or in evaluating and understanding issues which will arise in connection with their health services programs. It can serve as a guide for those who are charged with the design, management, and operation of correctional systems and institutions. Its primary audience includes wardens, jail administrators, juvenile detention facility directors, commissioners, directors of corrections, correctional administrators, and other key personnel working with them or under their supervision. It also may be of interest to individuals serving on legislative appropriations committees for corrections, to students of criminal justice programs, and to contractual suppliers of correctional health care services.

This book is neither definitive nor exhaustive. It does not pretend to offer the final word or "the only solution." When examining current issues and describing the pros and cons of various approaches, it tries to share the wisdom of experience gathered from many experts and many correctional systems. The author is well aware that few problems have a unique solution. Generally, there are several, if not many, reasonable approaches to resolving any problem. Some approaches are likely to work better under certain circumstances and not so well in a different setting. Some solutions may attain the desired end more readily than others. Usually, however, it is the people who are involved, and their expertise, their determination, their motivation, and their leadership, which ultimately contribute more to success or failure than the actual method chosen.

There is an old story about the ancient, broken violin which, in the hand of the master, made rich and beautiful music, far surpassing the sound of the new and expensive instrument played by a mediocre musician. We hope this book will shed some light and provide a useful perspective to assist in making sound and effective decisions. But we realize, like the violinist, that it is less the approach that one takes than how well the approach is employed that counts.

This text touches on many topics related to the provision of health services in correctional settings. Beginning with *What is Happening in Health?*, Chapter 1 looks at the "real world" and briefly examines the rapidly changing face of health care in the community. Managed care and cost-containment strategies are in evidence everywhere. There are new technologies for treatment and prevention of disease. But there are also new forms of illness, modern threats to health, and increased numbers of the aging and chronically ill in society. Correctional agencies reflect community trends. Persons comprising the burgeoning prison, jail, and juvenile facility populations are, on the average, as sick as or sicker than their counterparts in the free community.

---

[3] These decisions include both individual clinical matters as well as larger issues, such as planning and implementing sick call procedures, housing of mentally ill inmates, intake or arrival health screening, employing disease-prevention strategies, and locating specialty and inpatient care.

Only a few years ago, medical and mental health services available to prisoners were primitive, woefully inadequate, and even abusive. The courts have played a significant role over the past two and one-half decades to remedy this problem and today, with some exceptions, correctional health care begins to meet the appropriate contemporary professional standards.

Correctional institutions are places of punishment, while medical facilities are places of healing. Those choosing a correctional profession or a health profession start out with immensely divergent philosophies, policies, and methods. Yet, a major responsibility of correctional officials is the "care and safe custody of the confined"—a concern clearly shared by the health care profession. Chapter 2 discusses *Organizational Issues* and points out that recognition of the differences and the similarities of these two disciplines is crucial for their effective cooperation and collaboration. Some organizational models may be more suitable than others to help bring about and promote effective programs.

Chapter 3 provides an overview of the advantages and disadvantages of privatization of health care services. This recent trend toward contract services continues apace, despite the absence of evaluative research. Useful information and suggestions are offered for those who are *Considering the Private Sector*.

How much health care an inmate is entitled to receive is a perplexing concern for many persons in corrections. This is a highly complex issue with many variables. Chapter 4 attempts to provide a useful framework for analysis. The principles which inform and guide these decisions are examined and explored in *Defining Appropriate and Necessary Health Care*.

Strategies for *Preventing Contagion* from diseases—such as AIDS and tuberculosis (including multiple drug-resistant TB)—are considered in Chapter 5. While treatment of these diseases is left to the clinicians, correctional officials must be aware of their characteristics and become familiar with strategies to prevent their spread among inmates, employees, and visitors in prisons, jails, and juvenile facilities.

If just one word were used to say what is most important about caring for the confined, that word probably would be "access." *Ensuring Access to Care* is the first and indispensable component of any correctional health care program. Chapter 6 points out that not only must the correctional agency remove obstacles and impediments to access, it also has an affirmative obligation to screen and observe inmates for indications of undisclosed need for health services.

Within the mass of prisoners are several subsets which merit special attention because of their growing numbers and because of their unique health problems. Chapter 7 discusses the *Special Issues of Aging*, and recognizes the recent and ongoing phenomenon of a rapid increase in the number of old and very old inmates in the nation's prisons. Special housing units and specialized programming are among the strategies to provide humane living conditions and to contain extraordinary expenditures for elder care.

In *Women's Health Issues*, Chapter 8, the unique health problems of women prisoners are described. Though women constitute a small minority of inmates, their representation behind bars continues to increase.

Chapter 9 addresses a variety of *Special Mental Health Issues*. As community resources for care of mentally disordered persons continue to dwindle, society finds it increasingly necessary to incarcerate large numbers of mentally ill and mentally impaired persons. Consequently, those who manage correctional institutions face an enormously difficult task. They, in effect, have become the directors of the nation's newest and largest mental institutions. This chapter addresses many important aspects of managing the mentally ill prisoner.

When numbers of mentally ill prisoners in a given facility (or correctional system) become large enough, it makes sense to separate out those who do not require a psychiatric hospital setting but who also do not cope well in the general population of the institution. These persons can be managed appropriately in a sheltered, therapeutic living unit with special programming adapted to their condition. The concept of *Creating Therapeutic Environments for Mentally Ill Prisoners* is developed in Chapter 10.

The Role of Physician Assistants and Advanced Practice Nurses in correctional medical systems is explored in Chapter 11. Over the past twenty years, prisons and jails have made increasing use of midlevel practitioners. They ably and legally can perform many of the tasks traditionally reserved for physicians.

Chapter 12 recognizes that *Quality Is Also Important*. Once access to care is ensured, the focus of the correctional official must turn to verification that health services which are provided meet the level of care which is rightly expected of health care professionals in the community. This generally is referred to as "the professional standard of contemporary care." The role of accreditation, quality improvement activities, risk management, and the courts are considered.

In Chapter 13, a variety of *Issues in Health Professional Ethics* are presented, particularly as they manifest themselves in correctional situations. Determining whether an action or a policy is ethical and right or unethical and wrong is not always the same as finding out whether it is legal or illegal. Many circumstances can affect whether a particular action is ethical. Practical and common case examples are used to illustrate the reasoning and decision process.

Not every reader will agree with all of the positions expressed in this book. These are the opinions and beliefs held by the author, and they are shared by many of the nation's experts in the correctional care field. A sincere effort has been made to append, as clearly as possible, the reasoning which supports these positions and to indicate also the degree of firmness or certitude with which the various opinions are held, fully acknowledging that this is an uncertain world and that we are at times traversing difficult or uncharted seas. The author readily concedes that others are equally entitled to their own opinions and that those who disagree are not necessarily wrong.

Comments of readers are welcomed, including those which espouse a different point of view. Please, however, add your suggestions and supporting rationale. These ideas will be thoroughly considered during the preparation of subsequent editions.

1 WHAT IS HAPPENING IN HEALTH?

Community Trends in Health Care

Correctional health care never is practiced in a vacuum. It occurs in the context of a larger world. Consequently, this first chapter begins with a brief look at what is happening in free-world health care. Trends and changes there shed light on the more specialized subject of this book.

Containing Rising Costs of Health Care

For many years, costs of medical care in the United States have been increasing annually at a rate higher than the general consumer price index. For example, the consumer price index for medical care in the United States increased by 178.2 points from 1970 to 1994, whereas the price index for all goods and services rose by only 115.8 points.[1]

One reason for this increase has been the constant stream of newly introduced expensive technology—new and costly medications, laser procedures, imaging techniques, reconstructive and microsurgery, organ transplants—so that the "market basket" of health care services now available is much richer, more complex, and more abundant than ever before. Much, though not all, of this progress has been accompanied by an improvement in quality, affording greater likelihood of favorable outcomes from treatment.

Insurance and third-party payment systems have tended to insulate both providers and consumers from feeling the cost of health care services, so that there was little incentive to economize. Physician training has emphasized clinical effectiveness rather than cost containment.

Some of the rise in costs is due to higher earnings on the part of skilled health care professionals, including physicians, nurses, and technicians. Another factor

---

[1] Bureau of Labor Statistics, cited in *The World Almanac and Book of Facts 1995*: 109.

which drives costs upwards is the subsidizing of uncompensated care. Hospitals charge paying patients (self-payers and insurance companies) more than the actual cost of their treatment to cover the care given to uninsured and medically indigent patients. This added cost is a factor motivating an interest in having more people covered by health insurance in our country. If all Americans had access to health care, regardless of their ability to pay, an unfair and disproportionate burden would not fall upon certain providers of care. The road to achieving this goal, however, has proved to be difficult and uncertain.

The average cost in 1993 for a conventional single-coverage health insurance plan in the U.S. was $2,040, and the cost of a family plan was $5,064, up 8 percent from the previous year (the lowest rate of increase in six years, but still twice the rate of inflation).[2] Small wonder, then, that the overall cost of providing health services in correctional systems also has climbed, especially in view of the greatly increased number of inmates.

Diagnostic Related Groups

There is a great deal of interest in stemming the extraordinary growth in cost of health care in the free world. An important step was taken a few years ago with the introduction of diagnostic related groups (DRGs)—which permitted the assignment of an expected length of stay and a specific cost factor to each medical procedure for which persons are hospitalized. Medicare, Medicaid, and insurance companies often reimburse hospitals according to this method, paying a fixed amount for the episode of care, based on the diagnosis at discharge, regardless of how long the patient actually stays or how much it may have cost the hospital. When hospitals were paid for each day of care, there was a tendency to prolong the stay. Now, the incentives have been reversed, and hospitals work very hard to discharge patients as soon as possible to reduce their costs.

Managed Care

Managed care is another approach which increasingly is being used. Essentially, it means that each patient has access to a "gatekeeper" in the health care system (typically a primary care physician, clinical nurse practitioner, or physician assistant) who then determines whether the patient needs to have surgery or other costly services, such as a Magnetic Resonance Imagery (MRI), CAT scan, or consultation with a specialist. In other words, in a managed care system, the patient does not choose to see an orthopedic surgeon, to have a bone scan, or to receive physical therapy. The patient will be reimbursed for the cost of these services only if the "gatekeeper" so authorizes.

Note the similarity of this system to what has been the practice in prisons and jails for a long time. The prisoner generally has unimpeded access to the health care system—for example, to a nurse—but it is the nurse who regulates access to the physician, and it is the physician who controls or rations access to more specialized and expensive levels of care.

---

[2] Tony Munroe, "Health Insurance Cost Rise Slower, but Still Twice Inflation" (*Washington* [DC] *Times*, October 26, 1993).

Utilization Review

Utilization review is a mechanism now widely employed in the community, especially in managed care programs, to achieve greater cost effectiveness. Only recently is it being used in a technically sophisticated way in a few correctional systems. This approach involves close monitoring of trends in frequently used and high-cost and high-risk services.

Utilization review sometimes is accomplished prospectively, when prior authorization is required before very expensive services will be approved. Much of utilization review is retrospective, comparing trends in per capita use of certain services with trends or averages for persons of the same gender, age, and race in other settings. Greater scrutiny is called for when major discrepancies in rates of use are found.

Likewise, provider practice profiles can be compared. Two primary care physicians, with similar patient populations, would be expected to prescribe similar proportions of certain types of medications, laboratory tests, or procedures. When patterns of usage differ widely, closer review is indicated to see if there is significant overuse or underuse.

Other Cost-containment Strategies

Many hospitals and other health providers are negotiating reimbursement arrangements which involve risk sharing. These frequently take the form of a capitation payment. In other words, the provider is paid a fixed amount for each person enrolled, regardless of the amount of health services actually consumed. A claimed advantage of this method of payment is that it radically shifts the incentive structure. The physician and hospital no longer are paid for each service provided, thus not encouraging higher utilization. Instead, their net income rises when they succeed in keeping the patient population healthy so that fewer health services are required. This is the intended result. It also is possible that the incentives under managed care promote denial of costly but needed services to patients. Consequently, economic forces alone ought not to control the outcome. Constant vigilance is required to ensure that both access to needed care and quality of service are not undermined by cost-containment strategies.

The number of hospital beds in the United States is rapidly dropping, as are the number of hospital days of care. People are not staying in hospitals as long as they used to do. There is also a significant increase in the number of nursing home beds and long-term care beds. Coupled with greater emphasis on home health care and various programs for assistance with activities of daily living, this has enabled people to avoid costly hospital care. Hospice programs also are growing, as an alternative and less costly approach for the care of the terminally ill.

Many hospitals are merging and forming partnerships to reduce costs and increase market share. Hospitals also are integrating with physicians and with insurers to form networks of care. Medicare and Medicaid funds are being cut back, and even greater reductions loom on the horizon, resulting in less earnings for hospitals and physicians. There is greater competition and reliance on market forces, with less government regulation of the health care sector.

There is also a greater emphasis today in the medical profession on health and wellness—in other words, on preventing illness and improving health—rather than an almost exclusive focus on curing illness. One manifestation of this is the growing interest in healthy lifestyles, good nutrition, safety, exercise, and abstinence from drugs, alcohol, and tobacco. When correctional administrators become aware of these trends in the marketplace, they are better able to adopt important cost-saving strategies for their systems.

Accreditation

The "seal of good housekeeping" or a "four-diamond" endorsement tells the public what to expect in restaurants or hotels in terms of cleanliness, quality, comfort, luxury, prestige, and cost. These are forms of accreditation. An objective, disinterested organization visits and evaluates restaurants, hotels, and resorts and applies a predetermined set of standards. Being accredited is good for business.

The American Correctional Association (ACA) offers a program of accreditation for adult and juvenile correctional facilities, one important component of which is an evaluation of the health care service. Similarly, the National Commission on Correctional Health Care (NCCHC), a nonprofit agency representing thirty-six nationally recognized professional associations, offers a service of accrediting the health care programs in prisons, jails, and youth correctional facilities.

Hospitals are accredited by the Joint Commission on Accreditation of Health Care Organizations (JCAHO). Nearly all hospitals seek this accreditation, even though they legally may operate without it as long as they have valid state licenses. Patients and physicians who practice at these hospitals have come to expect that the hospitals will maintain their JCAHO accreditation as a testimonial to the quality of services. The Joint Commission also offers its program of accreditation to nursing homes and organizations that deliver outpatient care, including jails and prison health care services.

Generally, the American Correctional Association recognizes current accreditation by NCCHC or JCAHO as evidence of compliance with the health care portion of the American Correctional Association standards. Accreditation by ACA, JCAHO, or NCCHC requires an active quality improvement program—the mark of a professional and a professionally managed program. Institutions which have gone through accreditation know that it requires a good deal of work to prepare for the visit by a survey team. The process is entirely voluntary, and the facility is charged a fee which varies according to its census, primarily to defray the costs of the survey. No law or regulation requires a prison or jail to be accredited.[3] Correctional administrators certainly do not need accreditation for the purpose of attracting clients away from competitor's facilities. But accreditation is a matter of justifiable pride and accomplishment—a sign of a job well done. Moreover, when the facility finds itself in court for any reason as a defendant, the fact of accreditation does not go unnoticed.

---

[3] A few court orders or court-sanctioned agreements require the facility to seek and maintain accreditation. Likewise, some contracts with private vendors require continued accreditation as an indicator of quality.

Communicable Diseases

Advances continue to be made in the prevention, control, and treatment of infectious disease. Some feared diseases, like smallpox, have been eradicated. Others, like measles, mumps, and rubella, are much less common than they were a few decades ago. However, newer diseases have surfaced and these, including AIDS and antibiotic-resistant infections, are particularly troublesome. Tuberculosis, which was on the decline in the United States for decades, began to appear more frequently in the late 1980s, especially among persons with impaired immunity caused by HIV, the infection that leads to AIDS.

Acquired Immune Deficiency Syndrome, Hepatitis B, and Hepatitis C

Acquired Immune Deficiency Syndrome (AIDS), hepatitis B, and hepatitis C are viruses that are spread through blood and other body fluids. Transmission can occur when the skin is pierced with a needle or other instrument that has been used by an infected person, or through exchange of infectious bodily fluids, for example, by sexual intercourse [4] with an infected partner.

Tuberculosis

Tuberculosis (TB) is spread primarily by breathing infected airborne particles or droplets which are sprayed into the air by an infected person when coughing, sneezing, or talking. Tuberculosis usually responds to prolonged treatment with antibiotics. But, when a person takes the antibiotic medication only intermittently, or for less than the required period of time, the surviving TB bacteria may have been selected for immunity to the antibiotic. This leads to new strains of drug-resistant TB, some of which have been discovered among inmates in several U.S. prisons. These represent a serious concern since they are very difficult to treat effectively and may be fatal.

Other Infectious Diseases

Syphilis, gonorrhea, herpes genitalis, hepatitis A, measles, and rubella are among other diseases of concern. The first three usually are transmitted by sexual contact with an infected person. Hepatitis A is spread by the fecal-oral route. Measles and rubella are spread by contact or by airborne droplets. Most state health departments require, by law, that each new case of specified infections be reported promptly to the local health department so that the public health can be protected.

Aging of the Population

A decided shift is occurring in the age distribution of society. People are living longer than ever. Previously, only a very few lived into their sixties—a "ripe old age."

---

[4] Hepatitis C virus can be transmitted through sexual intercourse, but much less efficiently than the hepatitis B virus or HIV.

Fewer still reached their seventies or eighties. It was a rare exception when a person lived beyond ninety. Now, it is no longer so rare. And many people not in their sixties or seventies are not "old." They remain healthy and active.

A significant factor has been the tremendous advances in medicine and in public health. What were common and fatal infectious diseases have been all but eliminated—smallpox, polio, scarlet fever, to name only a few. Infant mortality has been reduced drastically. So have deaths from childbirth and nearly every other cause. The miraculous diagnostic methods and treatments available have revolutionized the way we think of illness. We expect that the doctor and hospital can cure our illness—and often they can, sometimes using organ transplants, skin grafts, mechanical hearts and kidneys, magnetic resonance imaging, radiation therapy, and much more.

As people live longer, the elderly become more numerous and more evident among us. Much advertising now caters to the senior citizens' market. And the business of retirement villages, nursing homes, assisted living centers, and home health aides has proliferated to fill a need.

The aggregate cost of life saving, life prolongation, and rehabilitative medicine is staggering. In fact, a huge percentage of health care expenditures nowadays is incurred during the final three months of life.

Continued Deinstitutionalization of the Mentally Ill

Closing of the majority of mental hospitals across the country during the past thirty years, along with the discharge of marginal patients to the community, has created a situation in which many persons with mental disorders are homeless or without adequate care. These individuals often become public nuisances. Without daily encouragement to take their medications, they soon decompensate. Large numbers of mentally ill and mentally retarded persons are arrested. The nation's prisons and jails now house far more mentally ill and mentally retarded persons than do the few remaining mental institutions.

This situation poses a new and exceedingly difficult challenge for correctional administrators. Mentally ill and developmentally disabled inmates are problematic because they do not adapt easily to the programs and living conditions established for other inmates. In correctional institutions, which regiment most aspects of behavior and insist on close adherence to a set of rules, individuals with diminished ability to comprehend or comply do not fit. In addition, these inmates are exceptionally vulnerable to the predatory behavior of other prisoners who abuse or take advantage of them. Consequently, they require constant vigilance and protection. Mentally ill persons who are prone to violent or aggressive outbursts, or who inflict harm on themselves, also need constant, close supervision.

Renewed Focus on Health Promotion Strategies

Society's renewed interest in healthy behaviors—nutrition, diet, smoking cessation, and aerobics—are apparent, even within the walls of correctional facilities. Weight lifting and exercise activities are popular among many inmates. [5] Those institutions which offer alternative healthy diets have found that a significant percentage of inmates elect this option. Some inmates now request smoke-free living environments. Many correctional facilities have thoughtfully and carefully introduced a completely "smoke-free" environment (at least inside of buildings) without experiencing the predicted dire consequences of constant riots and disturbances.

From a purely economic perspective, encouraging healthy behaviors is a sensible thing to do. It is often far less costly to prevent illness than to try to treat it later. Inmates of correctional facilities, by and large, have not taken good care of their health. They have consumed junk food, are heavy smokers, have abused alcohol and drugs, often have not exercised regularly, are often overweight, have been physically injured, and generally have received inadequate health care. For some, better nutrition, smoking cessation, and proper exercise—coupled with the mandatory abstinence from alcohol and drugs—can retard the disease processes already begun and can prevent at least the early onset of severe and costly chronic illness like chronic obstructive pulmonary disease and coronary heart disease. These are areas in which relatively minor cost outlays can yield major cost savings, especially in long-term prison facilities.

Trends and Issues in Corrections

Population Growth

Between 1980 and 1995, state and federal prison populations have more than tripled. Over this fifteen-year period, the average annual increase was 8.4 percent.[6] In addition, approximately 60,000 youths are currently housed in public juvenile facilities and another 5,000 youths under age eighteen are housed in jails. The staggering impact of these statistics are well known to correctional administrators who must cope with crowding, expansion, and exploding costs.

Looking back just over the past ten years, the census of correctional facilities has more than doubled, from 744,208 in 1985 to 1,585,401 in 1995. Two-thirds are in federal or state prisons, and one-third reside in jails. Figures 1-1 and 1-2, on the following pages, reflect the growth of the correctional populations.

---

[5] Weight lifting and other exercise equipment recently have been banned from some correctional facilities. Bobby L. Huskey, past president of the American Correctional Association, is sharply critical of this approach and comments in "Think Twice Before Abolishing Inmate Privileges," *Corrections Today* (June, 1995): 6.

> Often, we are left with inmates who are lying in their cells doing nothing or are doing unproductive work. Idleness and mindless work many times lead to trouble. But exercise equipment, education and training programs, and drug treatment services are important for more reasons that just making prisons and jails safe for inmates and staff. In an era when health care costs are skyrocketing and the average age of the inmate population is increasing, banning exercise equipment doesn't make sense. If exercise is good for the American public, why shouldn't it be required for inmates, too?

[6] "Prisoners in 1994," *Bureau of Justice Statistics Bulletin* (August, 1995): 5.

FIGURE 1-1. ADULT CORRECTIONAL TRENDS: PRISONS AND JAILS

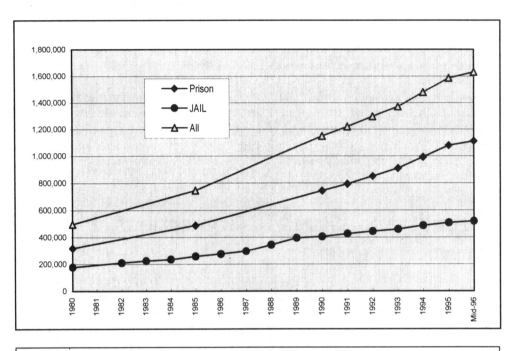

Year	Total Prison	Total Jail	Total All
1980	319,598		
1981			
1982		209,582	
1983		223,551	
1984		234,500	
1985	487,593	256,615	744,208
1986		274,444	
1987		295,873	
1988		343,569	
1989		395,553	
1990	743,382	405,320	1,148,702
1991	792,535	426,479	1,219,014
1992	850,566	444,584	1,295,150
1993	909,186	459,804	1,368,990
1994	991,612	486,474	1,478,086
1995	1,078,357	507,044	1,585,401
Mid-1996	1,112,448	518,492	1,630,940

Source: Bureau of Justice Statistics, *Bulletins*: May 1991, April 1995, August 1996, January 1997.

FIGURE 1-2. ADULT CORRECTIONAL POPULATION INCREASE OVER TEN YEARS

	Prison	Jail	All
Census 1985	487,593	256,615	744,208
Census 1995	1,078,357	507,044	1,585,401
Percent Increase	121.2%	97.6%	113.0%
Average Yearly Increase	8.3%	7.0%	7.9%

Source: Prison and Jail Inmates, 1995, Bureau of Justice Statistics Bulletin, *August 1996*

Female Prisoners

The percentage of female inmates also is growing. In 1974, 3.6 percent of prisoners under the jurisdiction of state and federal correctional authorities were women.[7] In 1980, the percentage was 4.1 and in 1994 it was 6.2.[8] Since 1980, the number of female inmates in the nation's prisons has increased at a faster rate (from 12,331 to 59,878, an average of 11.9 percent per year) than the number of male inmates (from 303,643 to 952,585, an annual average increase of 8.5 percent).[9] In 1995, 10.3 percent of adult jail inmates were women.[10]

Providing care to women presents a distinct set of issues. Women have complex health service needs beyond their need to receive treatment for health conditions shared with men. This includes management of menstruation, pregnancy, and menopause, and treatment of associated disturbances. Additionally, in most of this country, women are more frequent consumers of health care services than men. This generally increased demand for care without a corresponding decrement in quality of health tends to carry over into correctional settings.

---

[7] "Prisoners 1925-81," *Bureau of Justice Statistics Bulletin* (U.S. Department of Justice, December, 1982): 2f.

[8] "Prisoners in 1994," *op. cit.*: 5.

[9] "Prisoners in 1994," *op. cit.*: 5 and 8.

[10] "Prison and Jail Inmates, 1995," *Bureau of Justice Statistics Bulletin* (U.S. Department of Justice, August, 1996): 10.

Minorities

The people who fill our prisons and jails continue to come primarily from the socioeconomically depressed strata of society. They come from major urban centers. They are poor and lack marketable job skills. The majority have been involved in drug use and other hazardous health practices, and, for the most part, seriously have abused and neglected their own health.

A disproportionate number of incarcerated persons are minorities, particularly black and Hispanic.[11] In 1995, only 40.1 percent of the inmates in jails were non-Hispanic whites; black non-Hispanic inmates constituted 43.5 percent; and Hispanics were 14.7 percent.[12] Similarly, for state and federal prisons in 1994, only 35.8 percent were white non-Hispanics, while 44.1 percent were black non-Hispanics, and 17.6 percent were Hispanics.[13]

Aging Prisoners

An unprecedented proportion of our citizen population is elderly. Naturally, this is reflected in the populations of adult correctional institutions, as well. In 1991, 26 percent of jail inmates were more than thirty-five years of age.

The increased number of "senior" criminals is not merely a reflection of the growing number of elderly citizens. Sentences have become longer as well, and fewer inmates are being granted parole. This is a response to the clamor for "law and order" in the face of real and perceived rising crime rates. The obvious consequence is that more and more persons are growing older behind bars. With their frailties, disabilities, infirmities, and history of neglected or abused health, these older prisoners are contributing to the skyrocketing costs of correctional health care—and bringing, as well, whole new sets of challenging and difficult dilemmas and problems. For example, how much is society willing to spend to keep an elderly or infirm prisoner alive? What social amenities, environmental modifications, and procedural adjustments and compromises must be made to accommodate aged and disabled prisoners?

Juvenile Corrections

The number of juveniles in public and private correctional facilities also has grown. An increasing number of juveniles now are being sentenced as adults and are sentenced to adult correctional facilities. Though sentenced as adults, their bodies are still those of juveniles, and the medical treatment of children and adults differ in many respects, but some administrators are not aware of these differences. Whether sentenced as juveniles or adults, these youths present special problems and have great emotional needs. They are at the onset of adolescence, separated from family,

---

[11] An estimated 1,471 blacks per 100,000 black residents and 207 whites per 100,000 white residents were incarcerated in the nation's prisons at the end of 1993. "Prisoners in 1994," *op. cit.:* 9.

[12] "Prison and Jail Inmates, 1995," *op. cit.:* 10.

[13] "Prisoners in 1994," *op. cit.:* 9.

and frequently have no responsible role models. Teenage pregnancies are high-risk pregnancies, especially when compounded with stress and drug use. Some inmates of juvenile correctional facilities have a treatable mental illness. Many have conduct disorders which are less responsive to treatment. Lack of an adequate link between the correctional system and the mental health system is responsible for the "dumping" of many adolescents into juvenile correctional facilities when their needs would be served better in a substance-abuse rehabilitation facility or mental health treatment program. Police and the courts often find that the juvenile correctional facility is the only option available for placement of youngsters brought in for unacceptable behaviors. [14]

Correctional Health Care Costs and Strategies for Cost Containment

From data collected in successive surveys of the state prison systems, Anno [15] estimated that the average increase in health care costs for state prison systems more than doubled from 1982 to 1989 (103.1 percent increase, or an average of 10.7 percent per annum), and increased by 54.3 percent from 1985 to 1989 (an average of 11.5 percent each year). The average reported cost per inmate in 1989 was $1,906.

When of the cost of health care in the community is compared with the cost of providing health services to prisoners, some relevant information often is omitted, resulting in misleading, misinformed, or incorrect conclusions or inferences. Prisoners are sicker than their age-race-gender counterparts in free society. Also, certain security-related inefficiencies in many facilities must be accepted by health care staff as a way of doing business. Moreover, data available from the various state correctional agencies are not comparable directly. For example, some include mental health services and dental services, and others do not. Only a few include transportation costs or capital depreciation.

Working with the Legislature

Without question, the tremendous growth in the number of correctional inmates has placed an immense financial burden on county, state, and federal budgets to house, guard, feed, and care for the prisoners. Consequently, legislative fiscal agencies and appropriation committees are more watchful than ever about the need to eliminate waste and inefficient practices.

Working with legislative committees is (or should be) an important part of the job for many top correctional health care administrators. Elected officials have a responsibility to taxpayers to ensure that public funds are spent appropriately and that programs are managed effectively. Legislators who sit on the correctional appropriations committee (or its counterpart in a county structure) have a legitimate

---

[14] This topic, applicable to adults as well as juveniles, is treated more extensively in the Chapter 9 on Special Mental Health Issues.

[15] B. Jaye Anno, *Prison Health Care: Guidelines for the Management of an Adequate Delivery System* (Chicago: National Commission on Correctional Health Care, 1991): 248.

interest in the details of the budget and in the way the department deploys these funds. They often depend on staff to study budget proposals, expenditure reports, and other data to present the committee members with facts and recommendations. The correctional health care program is a complex and costly undertaking. Fiscal decision makers require a clear understanding of the program needs. Insufficient, inaccurate, or distorted information may lead to disapproval of portions of the program, which the health care administrator knows to be essential.

It is generally a good idea to permit the responsible health care authority to have an active role in the funding process. The administrative services bureau chief, the deputy director, or a fiscal agent of the department should assist, but not substitute for, the responsible health authority in presenting the details and rationale for health care budget items or in providing direct answers to questions posed by the appropriations committee or its staff about the budget request or the expenditure patterns and projections.

Of course, the responsible health authority will need to prepare for this interaction with the funding agency and will need access to accurate and timely utilization and expenditure data for the health care system. The fiscal or appropriations committee staff usually can provide advance notice of the kind of information in which it is interested. It is well to heed these clues and be prepared.

There are no strong public support groups for prisoners. Lawmakers know that they will not improve their ratings with voters by presenting themselves as champions of improved health services for prisoners. But they can show their constituents that they have insisted on cutting waste out of government programs. The legislative decision makers are more likely to support a funding increase if they are satisfied that the program is being managed efficiently and if they find the rationale for the increase to be sound.

Health Management Information Systems

Information is the key to good, cost-effective management. Today, information has to be timely. And it must be in usable format. Not so very long ago, information was laborious and time-consuming to collect and equally costly and time-consuming to organize and analyze. Currently, depending on the methods used, data still may be costly to collect, but processing and analysis almost can be instantaneous with the aid of a computer. Some well-designed systems also can simplify data gathering through use of a computerized health record, a by-product of which is the tally of utilization statistics in any desired format.

Every correctional health program needs a health management information system. Manual systems are adequate in very small programs. Larger jails and prisons will benefit from a computerized approach. Ideally, a comprehensive health management information system will record data on each inmate health-care encounter with a physician, physician assistant, nurse practitioner, nurse, psychologist, social worker, pharmacist, dietitian, or other health care provider. It will register the date and time of the encounter, name and discipline of the provider, diagnostic impression, prescribed therapy, treatment rendered, results of laboratory tests, and dates of scheduled appointments. In effect, all or a part of the patient's medical record can be computerized.

The computer also may calculate an estimated cost (in terms of dollars or minutes) of each component of care. It can combine this data and provide reports on dental services, mental health services, optical services, and other medical and surgical services. It also can indicate the number of patients seen for each type of service as well as the number of patients known to be awaiting these same services. It can calculate the "no show" and refusal rates. It can show the cost of care per patient for each type of service. Within a system, these reports can be compared over time or across facilities to observe trends or variances. Similarly, data from one system can be compared with another.

Cost-conscious managers find this type of information invaluable, not only for day-to-day management, but also when it is time to prepare and defend a budget request. Quality improvement interests, too, are served by these same data.

Centralization, Regionalization, or Clustering of Sophisticated, Low-volume Services

Many large systems consolidate certain high-cost/low-volume services at one or a few locations. In this case, most facilities will provide on-site all of the basic, relatively low-cost/high-volume primary care services. These likely will include nurse sick call and on-site primary care physician visits, and also may include on-site dentistry and limited mental health counseling and crisis intervention. One or a few facilities will offer more specialized care. For example, infirmary or hospital care, orthopedic clinics, dermatology clinics, oral surgery, dietitian services, psychiatric inpatient care, and intermediate level mental health care, can be provided with better quality and in a more cost-effective manner if limited to one or two sites.

This approach will require several companion strategies, each of which places some burden and cost on the correctional system. These are a mechanism for medical classification, an efficient transportation program, and a system for medical clearance prior to transfer. Thus, some trade-off is necessary, and the exact balance point will depend on how great are the potential health care cost savings and how much are the additional costs to the correctional agency.

The medical classification system involves a sorting of prisoners as to type (or degree) of health need. Some systems use a five-point scale, where "one" means no known health needs or restrictions and "five" means major health problems and restrictions. Levels "two" to "four" indicate increasing health problems and restrictions. Thus, a "one" could be housed anywhere. A "two" or a "three" can be housed in one of several facilities, while a "four" or a "five" might require special programming available only at a few locations.

Supplementing this sorting or health-based classification, the system also must be prepared to transport inmates to specified facilities to receive care. Those receiving dental and vision care and many forms of ambulatory care can be returned on the same day or shortly thereafter, whereas others may need to be transferred permanently or for an extended period of time. Finally, there needs to be an efficient mechanism of medical clearance, to ensure that prisoners are not moved inappropriately to locations which are unable to meet their care needs.

Many variations are possible. Sophisticated levels of care can be regionalized rather than centralized, for very large systems.

Cooperation between Prisons and Jails

Many dollars are spent needlessly in duplicating the rituals of arrival screening by jails and prisons. Typically, a county jail conducts a health screening for all new bookings, including taking a complete medical history, performing a mental health assessment, doing TB and syphilis testing, and providing a hands-on physical exam. Considerable time, effort, and money are devoted to gathering this information. The results of these important screening tests and assessments are documented dutifully in the inmate health record at the jail.

Then, once a sentence is handed down by the court, the inmate is transferred to the state prison reception processing center where this same battery of tests is repeated—often only a few weeks or months later—at an additional cost to the taxpayers. It also may be that the inmate had been diagnosed and treated for a chronic illness while at the jail, such as diabetes or seizures or hypertension. After several weeks of repeated blood sugar or blood pressure tests, the doctors carefully determined the proper medication dosage to keep the patient stable. All of this information is written clearly in the jail health record, yet, typically it is not made available to the prison health care staff.

Moreover, if the inmate should be sent from a prison to the county jail on a writ for trial on a new case, for appeal, or as a witness in another case, it is possible that the jail will conduct the routine intake processing all over again because it does not receive a copy of the relevant health information from the prison.

It would be a simple solution and a minimum cost effort for the jail health care staff to prepare a brief summary of the findings of intake screening and the current diagnosis and treatment regimen for each inmate being transferred to the state prison system. Likewise, prison inmates being transferred to a jail should be accompanied by similar documentation. If this were done, costly and time-consuming tests, exams, and treatment attempts could be avoided.

Very few systems, unfortunately, have adopted this kind of reporting. Yet, it is in the inmates' best interest to help bring about this continuity of care, and it would avoid unnecessary health care expenditures and an extra burden for staff. The benefits for the prison and the jail would be mutual. Perhaps the best way to initiate this activity would be for representatives of the state prison reception center to meet with staff of the several largest county jails in the state. Once they have agreed on a plan, other jails could be encouraged to follow suit.

One additional concern remains. Laws may vary from state to state, and competent legal advice should be sought. It may be necessary to obtain inmate consent for transfer of this information from heath care staff at the jail to health care staff of the prison, or vice versa. This easily could be accomplished by including a consent form among the paperwork presented to all new arrivals at the county jail. Some states have enacted statutes to permit transfer of this information without a requirement for individual consent.

Telemedicine

Efforts should be made to provide health services on-site whenever the number of prisoners requiring access to a specific type of care is sufficiently large. Doing so not only avoids costly transport of the prisoners, but also eliminates needless risk of escape or other problems during transport. A medical specialist, for example, might hold a weekly or monthly clinic at the institution so that only a small percentage of the patients will need to be taken off-site for more sophisticated diagnostic procedures or treatment requiring a setting or equipment not available in the correctional clinic.

An extension of this principle is finding rapid acceptance, not only in correctional institutions but also in remote and rural areas of the country. Medical expertise can "come" to the remote area (or correctional facility) by telecommunication, rather than in person. The specialist may be located at a distant university medical center, with all of the vast resources of that center available. When the inmate is brought into the prison clinic and placed before a television camera, the doctor and patient can see and speak directly to each other. In the room with the patient may be a physician or physician assistant who follows the directions of the specialist in performing various diagnostic procedures. If a special stethoscope is placed on the patient's chest, the distant medical specialist can hear the heart beat and listen to the lung sounds. X-ray films can be transmitted electronically, as can many other kinds of medical data. Often, the institutional physician can obtain a consultation with a specialist in this manner without all of the time, expense, and risk of transporting the prisoner.

Those facilities which have tried telemedicine generally have found it to be very helpful and continue to discover new applications.[16] For instance, instead of communicating with a specialist, it is also possible for a large, but widely dispersed, correctional system to interconnect its remote locations to the central prison. Making use of this technology, the physician can speak with and examine a patient and provide advice to a physician assistant or nurse at the remote facility or camp. The Michigan Department of Corrections has adopted this approach and currently has a telemedicine network linking four locations.[17]

In its basic form, telemedicine is "teleconferencing"—communicating by voice and television over a distance. With high resolution cameras and a variety of telemetry sensors and probes, some very sophisticated diagnostic work may be accomplished. It can incorporate use of telephone, fax, electronic mail, data files, and video. The phrase "A picture is worth a thousand words" was really written for telemedicine. Combining a visual presentation with verbal interaction creates a powerful tool for the practice of medicine from a distance.[18]

Trend Toward Privatization

Especially in view of the rising costs of health care, but also out of concern for improving the quality and availability of health services, an increasing number of jurisdictions have turned to the private sector for assistance. These arrangements

---

[16] For additional examples and commentary on telemedicine applications, see the section on Emerging Technologies in: American Correctional Association, *Public Policy on Correctional Health Care,* Lanham, Md. (June, 1996) pp.19-21.

[17] Personal communication with Lynette Holloway, Telemedicine Coordinator and Assistant to the Medical Director, Duane Waters Hospital, State Prison of Southern Michigan (June 10, 1997).

[18] Steve Levens, "Telemedicine as Dial-an-expert Tool Misses Point of Technology," *Telemedicine and Telehealth Networks* (December, 1995): 12

with for-profit and not-for-profit companies take many forms and have met with varying degrees of success. Without question, the private sector often can afford some real advantages: shorter response time due to the elimination of the large bureaucracy of state and county governments; greater flexibility in wages and benefit packages; the profit incentive to reduce costs; and the benefit of economy in the replication or centralization of near identical components (policies, practices, recruitment resources, bulk purchasing, and know-how) in similar systems across the country.

The trend toward privatization has given even greater impetus to the concern for continuous quality improvement methods and for accreditation according to national standards, to maintain and ensure a basic minimum quality of service.

Some Other Cost-containment Strategies

In these days, spiraling health care costs coupled with ever-increasing correctional populations take an enormous toll on correctional budgets for medical, dental, and mental health care. Careful attention and skill are required to improve efficiency and reduce waste. Unnecessary care, duplicative efforts, inappropriate or ineffectual therapies, nonproductive use of staff time, and inefficient purchasing need to be eliminated or at least minimized. Only then can necessary care be provided while maintaining adequate levels of quality.

Health care staff should be deployed efficiently. Doctors are paid high salaries and should not routinely be expected to perform duties which administrators, nurses, or clerks who earn lower salaries can perform as well or, perhaps, even better. Nurses, for example, can handle a good number of the cases which present at sick call. A clinical nurse practitioner or physician assistant can handle even more. Many facilities assign a nurse to work along with the physician at sick call to take vital signs, obtain a brief history, and carry out some of the patient education or treatment. In this way, the physician is able to see a greater number of patients in the same span of time. Except in very small facilities, the use of record clerks and other clerical staff permits nurses, who are more difficult to recruit, to work more efficiently.

Public health agencies (at the state or county level) need to recognize their legitimate role in disease prevention and health promotion among inmates, both during their incarceration and prior to their release to the community. There is a unique opportunity for health-related education during the relatively brief stay in county jails. The state or local public health department should be able to provide free or at little cost an abundance of excellent and up-to-date educational materials, brochures, posters, and videos, both for inmate health education and for continuing education of staff. They also can provide technical advice and consultation, not only on how to curb the spread of disease outbreaks, but also on how to prevent or reduce the likelihood of their occurrence.

Appropriate materials for staff and inmate health education also may be obtained—often without cost—from health organizations like the American Diabetes Association, American Heart Association, American Lung Association, American Red Cross, and from pharmaceutical companies, medical schools, and similar sources.

What the Courts Have Done[19]

One need not look back very far in history to discover almost unbelievably inadequate health care services abounding in correctional facilities throughout this country. In fact, few readers of this book are too young to remember the period in which this was true.

Hands-off Policy

Surprising though it may seem, the courts took no interest[20] in the plight of prisoners. Even though the Civil Rights Act, under which so many prisoner lawsuits are filed in recent years, was enacted in 1871, the courts for nearly a century consistently declared that conditions inside of correctional institutions were outside their scope of interest.

When prisoners on occasion would attempt to file lawsuits, these sometimes were intercepted by prison officials and discarded by wardens before they ever could reach a court or attorney.[21] Occasionally, a prisoner's pleadings would reach the attention of a judge. Typical responses were that the court does not interfere in the internal affairs of prisons, or that the court relies on the expertise of prison officials and correctional experts in these matters. This approach came to be known as the "hands-off" doctrine, and prevailed in this country until the 1970s.

Widespread social unrest during the 1960s played a direct role in bringing this "hands-off" policy to an end. Several events, in particular, deserve mention. In the civil rights movement of the 1960s, many white, middle-class citizens came into conflict with the law for the first time, largely through deliberate acts of civil disobedience.[22] Liberal groups and foundations sponsored legal aid societies, staffed with competent attorneys, to defend persons arrested in connection with civil rights demonstrations. Heretofore, prisons and jails were filled only with society's outcasts and rejects—mostly blacks and other minorities, poor people with little education or

---

[19] The author is greatly indebted to William J. Rold, Esq., for his critical review of this section of the chapter.

[20] There were exceptions. In a 1926 opinion, the judge explained the public's responsibility to provide medical care for prisoners. "(I)t is but just that the public be required to care for the prisoner, who cannot by reason of the deprivation of his liberty, care for himself." *Spicer v. Williamson*, 191 N.C. 487, 490, 132 S.E. 291, 293 (1926).

[21] "Justice, Texas Style," *Newsweek* (October 6, 1986): 50.

[22] Referring to this period, Dubler writes "(F)or the first time since the American Revolution, political activism brought large numbers of well-connected, middle-class people to jail. This atypical prison population contributed to a growing awareness of prison conditions, legislative committee reports, and exposés in the national media." Margaret D. Wishart and Nancy N. Dubler, *Health Care in Prisons, Jails and Detention Centers: Some Legal and Ethical Dilemmas* (Bronx, N.Y.: Montefiore Medical Center, 1983): 9.

influence. Prisons were located far from population centers; the inmates were locked up and quite forgotten. At this juncture, the composition of the inmate population was changing. With the influx of white, middle-class, and affluent persons who had influential connections on the outside, a growing number of effective, articulate, and credible persons reported intolerable, shocking, and inhumane conditions of incarceration. The news media began to report the plight of inmates and courts no longer were able to reject allegations of inmates out of hand.

Secondly, the 1960s and early 1970s was the time of widespread civil unrest and protest against the war in Vietnam. Civil rights activists, having achieved major gains in the mid-1960s, began to turn their attention to the struggle for peace. Dr. Martin Luther King and the Southern Christian Leadership Conference are examples. Influential and well-educated professionals and religious leaders championed the cause of draft resisters, organized boycotts of the draft, invaded federal draft centers and destroyed files, publicly burned draft cards, and conducted protests at munitions factories. Again, correctional facilities encountered articulate, influential, credible, and compassionate inmates who eloquently told their tales of injustice and inhumane conditions to the courts and to the press.

Thirdly, in 1972, the conscience of the nation was awakened by riots occurring at the prison in Attica, New York. [23] Millions of Americans watched their television sets each evening as the media vividly portrayed the atrocities and violence of the Attica uprising and the equally violent retaking of control by the authorities. The plight of inmates, so long successfully hidden, had come suddenly and dramatically to public view and attention.

A fourth phenomenon of the 1960s and early 1970s which facilitated an active role for the courts in prison reform arose from the War on Poverty. This federally funded program of the Johnson administration directed attention to weak, defenseless, and powerless groups in the country and promoted an awareness of their rights and entitlements. Simultaneously, the Supreme Court of the 1960s under Chief Justice Earl Warren also gave attention to the least powerful and the voiceless persons— resulting in the now famous Miranda warning and the civil rights decisions on behalf of various minority and defenseless groups.

Newman v. Alabama

One of the earliest cases involving the plight of prisoners which reached national attention was that of *Newman v. Alabama,*[24] tried in the Alabama federal court of Judge Frank M. Johnson. Plaintiffs alleged inhumane conditions and deprivation of health care throughout the Alabama state correctional system. The court found, for instance, that "unsupervised prisoners without formal training regularly pull teeth, screen sick-call patients, dispense as well as administer medication, including dangerous drugs, give injections, take x-rays, suture, and perform minor surgery."

---

[23] A study of this uprising noted that "medical care was one of the primary inmates' grievances." *Attica: The Official Report of the New York State Special Commission on Attica* (New York: Bantam Books, 1972): 63.

[24] 349 F. Supp. 278 aff'd. 503 F. 2d 1320 (5th Cir. 1974), cert. denied 421 U.S. 948.

Among examples of abuse cited were the case of a quadriplegic whose bedsores had become infested with maggots because his bandage had not been changed in the four weeks before his death, and the case of a patient whose prescribed intravenous feeding had not been administered during the three days prior to his death.

In 1974, Judge Frank Johnson declared that the overall health care delivery system in Alabama prisons was constitutionally impermissible. The court also held that "disorganized lines of therapeutic responsibility" contributed to an Eighth Amendment violation.

Estelle v. Gamble

Not long after the Newman decision, the now famous *Estelle v. Gamble* [25] case was decided in the United States Supreme Court in 1976. Gamble, a state prisoner in Texas, was assigned the job of unloading bales of cotton from boxcars. He injured his back and received treatment from prison medical staff. He later filed suit in federal court, alleging inadequate medical care and treatment and complaining that he had been punished for his inability to work. The case eventually went to the Supreme Court. Indeed, Gamble had been seen seventeen times by prison health care staff and had been treated for his injury. Therefore, the court declared that no constitutional right had been violated, but it acknowledged that Gamble might have a valid claim of tort liability (medical malpractice) in a state court. The criterion proclaimed by the Supreme court in *Estelle v. Gamble* to determine whether a case involved a constitutional issue was whether "there was deliberate indifference to the serious medical needs of inmates." It went on to say that the constitution is violated if care is intentionally denied, if access to care is prevented, or if physicians' orders and prescriptions for care are not followed. [26] The celebrated passage reads as follows:

> We therefore conclude that deliberate indifference to serious medical needs of prisoners constitutes the "unnecessary and wanton infliction of pain," proscribed by the Eighth Amendment. This is true whether the indifference is manifested by prison doctors in their response to the prisoner's needs or by prison guards in intentionally denying or delaying access to medical care or intentionally interfering with the treatment once prescribed. Regardless of how evidenced, deliberate indifference to a prisoner's serious illness or injury states a cause of action under §1983. [27]

The floodgates were now open. Prisoner-initiated lawsuits were filed in great numbers. Many lawyers and legal aid societies were eager and willing to bring these pleadings to court. Time radically had changed during the decade from the late 1960s to the late 1970s. Before that time, the walls of correctional institutions were as effective in keeping the public from seeing what occurred behind the gates as they were in

---

[25] 429 U.S. 97, 59 L. Ed. 2d 251, 97 S.Ct. 285 (1976).

[26] *Ibid.*

[27] *Ibid.*

preventing prisoners from escaping. But ten years later, much of the secrecy was gone. The courts emphatically and with determination had stepped in and made a difference.

Change never comes easily, and there was stubborn and prolonged resistance. States' rights issues were raised. For a time, most state and local jurisdictions stonewalled the courts, tried all manner of delaying tactics, and steadfastly refused to acknowledge or fix the problems. Little by little, however, the courts gained ground. In some cases, wide-ranging consent decrees were wrested from the correctional systems, in which compromise agreements were reached, often promising to improve conditions beyond what the constitution itself guaranteed.

Today, most correctional jurisdictions have been sued successfully by one or more inmates who alleged improper care or conditions of confinement. The majority of suits continue to be brought in federal court, although some are filed in state courts. Many are class action suits, and often are filed under Title 42 USC Section 1983 [28] alleging violation of civil rights.

Civil Rights of Institutionalized Persons Act

With passage of the Civil Rights of Institutionalized Persons Act (CRIPA) [29] in 1980, a new mechanism became available for redressing wrongs in penal institutions. The Attorney General of the United States became empowered to initiate a suit in federal court, acting on behalf of institutionalized persons who are presumed, because of mental illness, mental retardation, prisoner status, or orphan status, to be incapable, or at least to have an impaired ability, to file a suit on their own behalf. The office of the Attorney General must make a determination, so as to have standing to file suit under CRIPA, that under color of state law, the jurisdiction is depriving institutionalized persons of their constitutionally guaranteed civil rights.

Cases thus were filed by the office of Attorney General and were pursued vigorously for several years by competent plaintiff attorneys employed by the federal government. The enthusiasm and aggressive prosecution of these cases waned significantly during the Reagan and Bush administrations, but did not completely vanish.

Pulling in the Reins

A recent National Institute of Justice report [30] gave eloquent voice to the concern that the courts have established a floor under health care for prisoners, but have failed to define an appropriate ceiling. While courts have ordered many services to be provided, they have not placed or defined limits on what must be provided. As a

---

[28] "Every person who, under color of any statute, ordinance, regulation, custom, or usage, of any State or Territory, subjects, or causes to be subjected, any citizen of the United States or other person within the jurisdiction thereof to the deprivation of any rights, privileges, or immunities, secured by the Constitution and laws, shall be liable to the party injured in an action at law, suit in equity, or other proper proceeding for redress."

[29] Pub.L. 96-247, §4, May 23, 1980, 94 Stat. 350.

[30] Douglas C. McDonald, *Managing Prison Health Care and Costs* (Washington, D.C.: National Institute of Justice, 1995): 42.

result, an inexorable and unrestrained pressure to raise costs and quality of health care services for prisoners is alleged.[31]

On the other hand, intervention by the courts has been and remains necessary to ensure that inmates are guaranteed care which is not "cruel or unusual punishment" and which is consistent with the contemporary standards of professional practice in the community. Little political advantage comes to elected officials who increase expenditures for prisoners, but the desire to avoid lawsuits can provide a necessary measure of motivation.

Correctional health care administrators can and should develop a reasonable and fair strategy, consistent with community standards and practice, to ration or limit access to unnecessary health care services. The difficult and somewhat daunting task of defining appropriate and necessary health care is both timely and legitimate. Courts have not implied any prohibition of such efforts.

Incidentally, the last word has not been heard on this subject. Recent decisions have signaled a much more conservative interpretation than that pronounced by the Supreme Court in *Estelle v. Gamble*. In *Wilson v. Seiter et al.* (1991), the Supreme Court made it more difficult to hold correctional institutions and their officials liable for bad confinement conditions.[32] The "deliberate indifference" standard of *Estelle v. Gamble* recently has been challenged by Justice Clarence Thomas, though his views were not shared by the other Justices.[33] It is likely that the Supreme Court will reexamine the subject of Eighth Amendment applicability to correctional conditions during the next several years.

Prison Litigation Reform Act of 1996 [34]

On April 26, 1996, the Prison Litigation Reform Act (PLRA) was signed into law, radically affecting both individual suits brought by prisoners and class actions. It provides new procedural requirements and restrictions on bringing actions, and it limits the ability of courts to order relief. This law extends only to prison and jail cases. Lawsuits brought by inmates of mental institutions, for example, are not covered. It also

---

[31] Rising health care costs in corrections undoubtedly will remain a major issue during the coming decade. One important aspect, the definition of appropriate and necessary health care, is discussed in detail in a subsequent chapter.

[32] 501 U.S. 294, 111 S.Ct. 232 (1991); "U.S. Supreme Court Redefines 'Deliberate Indifference,'" 5:3, *CorrectCare* (July, 1991): 1, 14.

[33] Justice Thomas argued in *Helling v. McKinney* (1113 S.Ct. 2475 [1993]) that there are "substantial doubts" whether prison conditions are within the scope of the Cruel and Unusual Punishments Clause at all, and stated that he "might vote to overrule *Estelle*" if the issue were squarely presented. John Boston, "Court Rules on Smoking Case," 8:2, *CorrectCare* (May, 1994): 7, 14.

[34] The author is greatly indebted to the following persons who reviewed this section of the chapter and provided helpful comments: Richard Alan Enslen, Chief Judge, United States District Court, Western District of Michigan; and Paul R. Belazis, Esq., court monitor for *Inmates of Wayne County Jail v. County Commissioner.*

applies only to the federal courts and not to actions in state courts unless it is a civil rights case brought under Title 42 USC Section 1983.

Administrative remedies now must be exhausted in any federal action involving prison conditions, including civil rights actions under Section 1983. The law also amends Section 7 of the Civil Rights of Institutionalized Persons Act [35] to provide that "[n]o action shall be brought with respect to prison conditions under Section [1983] or any other Federal law by a prisoner confined in any jail, prison, or other correctional facility until such administrative remedies as are available are exhausted."

The same act also provides that defendants need not reply to any action by a prisoner under Section 1983 or any other federal law and that failure to reply will not constitute an admission of the allegation of the complaint. Further, no relief can be granted by the court to the plaintiff until the defendant responds. A judge can order the defendant to reply only if the court finds that the plaintiff has a reasonable opportunity to prevail on the merits of the case.

In addition, the PLRA terminates settlements and consent decrees in cases that are final, and requires all actions to be dismissed where there has been no finding by the court that the relief "extends no further than necessary to correct the violation of the Federal Right, and is the least restrictive means necessary to correct the violation of the Federal Right." [36] If prospective relief is ordered by a court with respect to prison conditions, such relief automatically will be terminable upon the motion of any party or intervenor two years after it was granted or one year after the court has entered an order denying termination. All presently existing court-approved prisoner relief will terminate in April 1998 upon the motion of any party or intervenor.

Until now, many prisoner suits were settled between the parties without any finding or admission of liability. Such settlements, according to the PLRA, also are subject to dismissal.

The PLRA also places limits on the ability of the federal court to appoint special masters, and allows them to be appointed only during the remedial phase of the action. Their involvement is restricted to conducting hearings and preparing proposed findings of fact. Moreover, the special masters are prohibited from any ex parte communications. Consequently, since all contact with any party must take place in a formal hearing, on the record and with all parties represented, the special masters no longer can attempt, through individual negotiation and persuasion, to facilitate settlement or cooperative working among the parties to the case.

The PLRA also severely limits the monetary compensation which may be paid to attorneys and to special masters. Further, compensation of the special master no longer is to be paid by the defendants, but now must be paid out of judicial funds.

Since receiverships are not prohibited by the PLRA, it may be that receivers will be appointed in situations where a special master may have been used in the past. Likewise, the court still may appoint experts, who may be able to perform some of the functions that masters typically have done.

---

[35] 42 U.S.C. § 1997 *et. seq.*

[36] P.L.R.A. § 802, amending 18 U.S.C. § 3626.

These and other provisions of the PLRA already have had a chilling effect on prisoner litigation. Essentially, initial liability will be harder to demonstrate and broad relief will be more difficult to obtain. It is too early to tell what the ultimate impact will be. All of the consent decrees affecting New York City's Rikers Island facilities, for example, were vacated and are now under appeal. Several courts have declared portions of the PLRA to be unconstitutional. The legality of the PLRA remains still very much in flux as of this writing.

As indicated earlier in this chapter, many of the needed reforms of correctional health care have come about through prisoners' access to the courts for relief. In the 1996 PLRA attempt to correct some perceived abuses in prisoner litigation, a major support for good correctional medicine appears to have been lost.

On the other hand, great strides have been made in recent years to professionalize correctional health care. Accreditation programs through the American Correctional Association, the National Commission on Correctional Health Care, and the Joint Commission on Accreditation of Health Organizations will continue to lead the way in signaling the characteristics of an acceptable correctional health care program. Additionally, there are professional associations like the American Correctional Health Services Association. There are professional codes of ethics. The quality of physicians, nurses, health care administrators, and other health care staff serving many prisons, jails, and juvenile correctional facilities has improved notably. But only time will tell whether and to what extent the substantial and needed improvements made during the last quarter of a century will survive. Leadership by correctional officials outside of the health field—especially commissioners and directors of corrections, wardens and jail administrators—is absolutely critical in this regard. Their strong and unwavering commitment to ensure that inmates have prompt access to necessary health care services, and their uncompromising insistence on quality of care which meets community standards of professional practice, will go far to safeguard the progress that already has been achieved.

2 ORGANIZATIONAL ISSUES

Corrections and Health Care— Working Together

The often articulated purpose of corrections, after public protection, is care and custody of inmates. This formulation makes it clear that correctional officials are entrusted also with the care of inmates, and not merely with their custody or confinement. Meeting their health needs is an important aspect of that care.

It follows that good correctional policies and practices ought to be consistent with the principles and requirements of good health care. An adequate correctional system, like an adequate health care program, will place a high priority on all of the following attributes:

- a safe and secure environment

- good order

- good hygienic practices and sanitation

- emergency preparedness

- confidentiality of private and sensitive information

- respect for dignity and basic human needs of inmates

- ethical and professional standards [1]

---

[1] The American Correctional Association published its Code of Ethics in 1974 to promote professionalism and proper practice among its members. Anthony P. Travisono and Mary Q. Hawkes, *Building a Voice: The American Correctional Association, 125 Years of History* (Lanham, Md.: American Correctional Association, 1995): 136. The Code of Ethics was revised in 1994.

Each of these is clearly important to the success of a correctional program as well as any health care program. Neither can accomplish its mission successfully, for example, in an unsafe or disorderly environment. Good hygienic practices and sanitation protect staff, inmates, and visitors. To achieve these goals, both disciplines require clear and consistent policies, ongoing staff training and development, accurate record keeping and documentation, a quality control program, and a focus on prevention.

Recognizing Differences

Even with all of this in common, some important and fundamental differences must be recognized. Correctional and health care programs differ in their purpose, primary client served, means employed to achieve their purpose, use of force, type of employee training, and system of beliefs. Likewise, merely because they focus on or want the same set of priorities does not mean that they will (or should) choose to carry them out in exactly the same manner.

Purpose

Corrections, in addition to societal protection and the care and custody of inmates, also is expected to carry out society's desire to punish wrongdoers. Besides monetary fines, the principal form of punishment ordered by courts is deprivation of personal liberty through incarceration under correctional authority. Lesser restrictions, such as parole, probation, and electronic tether, also are viewed as correctional functions.

Within the correctional institution itself, discipline commonly is enforced through the threat of punitive sanctions. There is due process. A sentence is given and carried out—typically consisting of restriction of privileges or confinement in segregation.

On the other hand, the health care profession is a healing profession. Its avowed purpose is to promote the health and well-being of the patient, never to inflict harm or punishment. This is a profound and abiding difference.

Primary Client

Correction's principal client is society itself, which it serves by humanely confining wrongdoers away from the community and, to the extent possible, by facilitating and promoting rehabilitation of the criminal before the term of incarceration is completed. It is logical, then, that correctional authorities will resort even to the use of lethal force, where necessary, to prevent escape by a dangerous criminal.

A health care service, on the other hand, primarily serves the individual patient, whose well-being holds a preeminent place for the care provider. As a consequence, for example, medications may not be used for controlling the dangerous behavior of a healthy inmate.

Means

The principal means employed by correctional agencies to fulfill their mission are confinement, restraint, and deprivation of privileges. Confinement occurs in the prison itself, and with even greater restrictions, in segregation and lock-down. Another means toward this end is the firm and consistent application of rules. Variances and exceptions are instinctively resisted by correctional managers, who often see such "individualization" as an invitation to disorder.

Health care, in contrast, uses therapeutic measures—medication, surgical intervention, treatment, therapeutic milieu, and counseling, to achieve its purpose. It does not punish. Even when therapeutic seclusion or restraint are ordered, as may be the case for an agitated psychotic patient, it is because this has been determined to be the least-restrictive means available to prevent harm to self or others, and it, therefore, may be employed only for as long as is needed to accomplish this purpose. Outside of the classification and disciplinary processes, health care staff are the primary source of individual accommodations (special diet, lower bunk, prosthetic devices, and work restrictions), a role that is important in providing necessary health care. But recommendations of these practices sometimes place health care staff in conflict with the "rules" and expectations of the correctional system.

Coercion

Many correctional practices negate or diminish individual responsibility. For example, the lives and behavior of inmates are regimented closely. They are afforded few opportunities to exercise free choice, and, then, only within very narrow limits.

Good health care practice, on the other hand, respects and encourages the free, informed choice of each patient. Only in the most exceptional circumstances as when the patient is not mentally competent can health care be administered without consent.

Training

Paramilitary-style training is commonly used for correctional employees. They are expected to obey orders and adhere strictly to laws and agency policies. Quick and dependable response by these employees is necessary for their own safety, the safety of coworkers, and of the public at large. Moreover, the agency is liable for the consequences of employees' actions when they are on duty.

Most training for health care professionals is academically or clinically based. Independent-study and guided self-study approaches are common. Doctors are expected to use their knowledge and skills to diagnose and treat a patient's condition based on their best professional judgment. Of course, doctors also must follow certain laws and rules, just as correctional officers are required to do, and both must exercise good judgment at all times.

Beliefs

Certain "beliefs" pervade every discipline. For example, some security training classes teach that one should never give credence to anything that an inmate says. Many believe, too, that once a direct order is given to an inmate, the officer must never back down.

Health care professionals, in contrast, are trained to listen attentively to their patients to elicit clues about the nature and origin of the illness, and to discover the effect of various remedies. Particularly in mental health settings, treatment staff believe that it is usually better to wait for the patient to comply rather than to achieve compliance through the use of force.

Working Together

With basic differences like these, one well might ask whether correctional staff and health care staff ever can work cooperatively together. Fundamental differences in purpose, means, approach, policy, and procedure exist even in a well-run system. Under less than ideal circumstances, they can become problematic. Following are some strategies which have proved effective in promoting a sound and productive working relationship between security staff and health care staff.

First, both parties need to recognize the important similarities of mission and purpose. Each discipline has a regard and responsibility for the care and the safety of inmates, and each profession places emphasis on personal dignity and on humane treatment. This common ground provides a basis for reaching decisions together.

Second, it is equally important to recognize and respect the differences. Parties which begin with fundamental differences in philosophy, purpose, and policy are not always going to agree. Nor is total agreement necessary or even desirable.

Third, all staff should respect and acknowledge the professionalism and good intentions of the other point of view. Only in a context of mutual respect does a working relationship become possible.

Fourth, so that the parties can work harmoniously together, it is neither required nor helpful that one group dominate the other. [2] To dominate—in other words to impose one's point of view over the other—is to act on the belief that "might makes right." When a domineering structure acts to crush the weaker party, even when it is right, inevitably everyone loses.

Instead, each agency has its own expertise, its own professional ethics, and its own goals to achieve. These approaches, on a practical level, are not irreconcilable or incompatible. When reasonable persons come together in shared respect, it usually is possible to reach decisions which meet the highest and best purposes of each, and which satisfy the fundamental requirements of each. Neither side uniquely possesses the complete truth. A deliberated solution, reached cooperatively, is often better than any choice that either side alone could have made. This fundamental belief of the author is an undergirding principle of all that is said in this book. Were it not so, the book would have no purpose other than to advise on how, in given situations, one or another side should dominate.

Some of the best solutions arise from dialog. In one correctional agency, the topic of discussion was the excessive time spent by physicians in prescribing bed boards. Even the carpentry shop complained. But the officers argued that they could not decide who had a legitimate back complaint and insisted that the physician make the determination. Finally, the director of corrections, after listening to the discussion

---

[2] There is, of course, real danger that the perspective of corrections will tend to dominate, both because it regards itself as the "landlord" (to the "tenant" health care program) and because it typically controls 85 to 90 percent of the resources and staff of the agency.

among both wardens and representatives of health care, said: "It sounds like the real reason the doctors are having to prescribe bed boards is because the bed spring supports are defective. So, let's fix or replace the defective beds." No more bed boards were required after that.

Reasoned and respectful deliberations lead to the best solutions. Each party should view itself as providing a service to the other (who ought to be regarded as a client or customer). How can its services (such as health care, transportation, escort, security and safety, infection control, environmental health and safety, maintenance, personnel, or accounting) best meet the needs of the other? This is the approach of Total Quality Management or Continuous Quality Improvement programs. It is also essential for working together as a team.

Examples abound. When health care staff are not consulted in the planning and design of the clinic for a new or remodeled facility, the space is usually inadequate or ill-proportioned with resulting inefficiencies for staff. Similarly, when a new computerized management information system or scheduling program is obtained for the facility, health care staff should be involved early in the planning and specifications for the system so that the product suitably will serve health care needs, as well. Likewise, a change in schedule of health care events may have unsatisfactory consequences if appropriate dialog with custody has not taken place.

It would alleviate the burden on officers if patients were seen by clinicians at the correctional facility instead of at an off-site location, whenever this is feasible. Downtime for the dentist is reduced if two or three inmates can arrive at the waiting room prior to count time and remain there until the count has been cleared. The optometrist or orthopedic surgeon should be scheduled to hold on-site clinic at a time of day which does not conflict with regular institutional count.

Many such solutions are presented in this book and have proved satisfactory in some settings. Whether they are equally appropriate for a particular location or circumstance will be determined best through study and discussion by an interactive team of persons from that facility who have responsibility for these areas. While the principles and reasoning presented in this reference manual should apply to most situations, collaborative discussion of specific needs and applications will suggest appropriate variations.

Training Concerns

The policy of each correctional system or facility should specify the minimum required training for initial orientation, specific job assignments, and annual inservice training. This book does not address security training requirements for correctional officers nor the clinical training requirements for various health professions. It will focus only on health-related training for correctional officers and security-related training for health care staff.

Officer Training

Officers, deputies, youth counselors, and careworkers, in addition to their required initial and annual training requirements relating to various aspects of security, inmate management, report writing, supervision, and communication, also should be trained in specific health-related topics. Some of this training is provided best by qualified health care staff. All of the training materials at least should be reviewed and approved by the health care authority.

Topics for training should include the following:

- knowing universal precautions for bloodborne pathogens

- preventing infectious diseases

- recognizing the signs and symptoms of mental illness and retardation

- recognizing the signs and symptoms of acute and chronic physical illness

- using nonviolent/nonconfrontational approaches to the management of the mentally ill

- recognizing the signs and symptoms of suicidal tendencies

- knowing how to prevent suicide

- administering first aid

- administering cardiopulmonary resuscitation, leading to current certification in CPR

- recognizing the need for emergency care in life-threatening situations

- being prepared for disaster

- recognizing the signs and symptoms of alcohol or barbiturate withdrawal, particularly in jails and receiving facilities

- knowing how to perform point-of-entry screening, if so assigned, including procedures for appropriate disposition and referral

- knowing how to distribute medications, if so assigned

- knowing how to manage mentally ill patients, if applicable

- understanding ectoparasite control

- understanding relevant health care policies

The amount of time required for this training will vary, but generally, twenty-four to forty hours will be appropriate for the initial training, and sixteen to twenty-four hours will be appropriate for the annual or biannual update.

Health Care Staff Training

Health care staff, including part-time and contractual employees, require training in institutional policies and in security-related matters. This training is more authoritatively, more credibly, and more accurately provided by experts in security than by health care staff. Appropriate topics include:

- familiarity with the institution; how to get from place to place safely

- relevant institutional and departmental policies

- "do's" and "don't's" of safe and proper behavior in a correctional setting

- games inmates play

- contraband

- rules of behavior for inmates

- misconduct reporting

- key control

Other training topics which are required for health care staff, and which must be provided by qualified instructors, include:

- using nonviolent/nonconfrontational intervention techniques

- recognizing signs and symptoms of suicidal tendencies

- administering first aid

- administering cardiopulmonary resuscitation (current CPR certification)

- understanding health care policies and procedures

- responding to disaster

- understanding specific job duties

Some cross-training is helpful towards a better understanding of each others' areas and responsibilities and also to improve cooperation and communication. It even may be feasible to offer some sessions to a blend of participants representing both health care staff and security staff.

As mentioned earlier, there are notable differences in the methodology of training typically employed for correctional officers and health care professionals. Few correctional systems have taken advantage of this fact, and, instead, subject their health care professionals to the same classroom didactic methods which are used with officers. At best, this is inefficient. Instead of requiring health care professionals to attend a two- to four-week new employee orientation, a few days of classroom exposure, plus guided self-instruction using a set of carefully chosen readings, followed by a written or oral examination may be more effective. Given the salary paid to physicians while attending these courses, there are potential monetary savings, as well.

Responsible Health Authority

Who is the responsible health authority for a prison or county jail or youth correctional facility? In one sense, it is the governor of the state, director of corrections, and warden (or sheriff, county commissioner, or jail administrator) because the public responsibility and legal liability for what happens in their systems cannot be delegated. If a suit is brought alleging medical malpractice or violation of civil rights by a doctor or nurse, typically the first-named defendant is the governor or sheriff— the elected officials bearing ultimate executive responsibility. This is true when, through several layers of supervision, the doctors and nurses as state or county employees ultimately are supervised by the governor, sheriff or warden, but it is equally true when the agency has contracted the provision of health services to a private for-profit or nonprofit vendor. The governmental agency does not and cannot delegate or contract away its ultimate responsibility and liability.

As used here, the responsible health authority is the person who makes decisions about the deployment of health resources and directs the day-to-day operation of the health services program.[3] This individual's duties include "arranging for all levels of health care and providing quality, accessible health services to inmates."[4] When the responsible health authority is not a physician, a licensed physician must be given the authority to supervise all medical judgments regarding the care of inmates at a specific facility.

Medical Autonomy

In simplest terms, the essence of medical autonomy was referenced by the Supreme Court in *Estelle v. Gamble*. The court stated that deliberate indifference to the serious medical needs of prisoners can be manifested "by prison guards in intentionally denying or delaying access to medical care or intentionally interfering with the treatment once prescribed."[5] In other words, medical autonomy requires that there be no interference from nonmedical personnel in strictly medical decisions.

Correctional authorities, however, legitimately may determine working conditions and schedules, such as the place or time at which sick call will be held. As the experts and authorities responsible for custody and security, they may impose reasonable restrictions, including preventing health care staff access to a given area until it is properly secured, delaying transport of a high-risk inmate until adequate security provisions are made, or preventing the introduction of a particularly dangerous prosthetic device. Likewise, any third-party payer in the community may ask for clarification or the rationale for a particular procedure which the doctor has ordered, and

---

[3] The ACA *1996 Standards Supplement* defines the health authority as the physical health administrator or agency responsible for the provision of health care services at an institution or system of institutions; the responsible physician may be the health authority. The *1996 Supplement* defines responsible physician as an individual licensed to practice medicine and provide health services to the inmate population of the facility and/or the physician at an institution with final responsibility for decisions related to medical judgments.

[4] National Commission on Correctional Health Care, *Standards for Health Services in Jails*. (Chicago, 1996) Standard J-01.

[5] 429 U.S. at 104-105, 97 S.Ct. at 291.

inquire whether a more conservative, less costly, or safer alternative is available. For example, when transportation officers are busy with court-scheduled movement, it is not inappropriate to ask the doctor to set priorities for the day's medical off-site appointments and to indicate whether there is urgent need to transport a particular patient off-site. On the other hand, it is not acceptable for the correctional officer to determine these priorities or simply to leave transportation schedules unmet.

Rationale for Responsible Health Authority

Several reasons support designation of a responsible health authority for each facility. Their duties should be clearly specified in a job description, policy, or contract.

- *Credibility.* The facility will fare better in court if health care decisions are made only by properly trained and licensed persons whose job descriptions assign this responsibility.

- *Professionalism.* It is prudent to let the health professionals manage the health arena. They are the experts.

- *Recruitment.* It is easier to recruit good health care staff when their line of supervision and reporting is to an appropriate health care professional rather than to a correctional official.

- *Accreditation.* Accreditation standards require it. [6]

- *Legal liability.* Only licensed health professionals legally may exercise medical judgment on behalf of a patient, within the scope of practice authorized by their license. It would be illegal for anyone without an appropriate credential or license to interfere with or countermand the medical judgment of a licensed health care provider. Consequently, if the responsible health authority is not a physician, a responsible physician must be designated.

Role of Responsible Health Authority

The responsible health authority (and responsible physician) must be on-site regularly and frequently. In a very small facility, this may require only a few hours a

---

[6] "Written policy, procedure, and practice provide that the institution has a designated health authority with responsibility for health care pursuant to a written agreement, contract, or job description. The health authority may be a physician, health administrator, or health agency. When this authority is other than a physician, final medical judgments rest with a single designated physician." American Correctional Association, *Standards for Adult Correctional Institutions*, Third Edition (Lanham, Md.: American Correctional Association, 1990), Standard 3-4326. NCCHC words the standard in virtually identical language, and adds: "The health authority's responsibilities include arranging for all levels of health care and providing quality, accessible health services to inmates." NCCHC, *Standards for Health Services in Jails, loc. cit.*

week. Even though a large correctional system may have a central health authority, there is still a need for a local responsible health authority/responsible physician for each individual facility (or small cluster of facilities) who is on-site frequently. This local person is the one who interfaces directly with the facility administrator whenever the occasion requires, who knows the health care staff and their assignments, capabilities, and circumstances, and who is familiar with the setting and circumstances of the inmates.

The responsible health authority has immediate access to any health record, log, or other relevant documentation. This is the person who directs arrangements for care; who interprets to the warden the concerns of health care staff; who relates to health care staff the concerns of the warden; who makes certain that equipment is working and properly maintained, that supplies are ordered and delivered, and that staff are hired, trained, present, and ready for duty.

It is important for the responsible health authority (and, indeed, all health care staff who see inmate patients) to become well acquainted with the facility, its inmates, and the circumstances in which they are confined. For this reason, regular visitation by the health authority and responsible physician to the various housing units; recreation, work, and dining areas; and especially, the segregation units are recommended. These tours can help identify potential barriers to access, problems with environmental sanitation and safety, and other factors relevant to the inmates' health and well being, and provide opportunities for improving efficiency and the quality of health care service delivery.

Role of the Medical Director

Because many duties of the responsible health authority are administrative in nature, it is often desirable to designate a separate responsible physician, leaving most of the administrative functions to a person with special training and qualifications in budgeting, supervising, and managing. This may be more economical. Some physicians, of course, are well qualified in the administrative areas, as well.

The responsible physician, or medical director, must be viewed as much more than one who writes medication prescriptions. Some systems, in the interest of economy and efficiency, have relegated the physician to the role of seeing patients who are referred by nurses, and prescribing for their care. In much the same way, psychiatrists sometimes are placed in a role of only seeing those patients for whom the psychologists determine a need to be evaluated for treatment with psychotropic medication. Thereafter, they might see these patients every thirty to sixty days briefly for medication renewal. This is a false economy, and does not satisfy the proper role of a responsible physician.

The responsible physician should serve as the public health officer for the facility, someone who is concerned and knowledgeable about sanitation, safety, infection control, nutrition, environmental hazards, medication distribution, and stress factors for the inmates. Moreover, the responsible physician, with some regularity, should meet with the health care staff and with the institution head, and also should be involved in quality improvement and peer review activities. Similarly, the psychiatrist must be involved in treatment-planning decisions, and not just the medication review of mentally ill patients.

Organizational Models

Diverse organizational models exist in jails, prisons, and youth facilities across the country. Whatever the historical, philosophical or legal rationale for these arrangements, they may work well or poorly, or they may achieve some purposes rather well and fail miserably by other standards. What is abundantly clear is that there is no single best or correct way to do things. It is probably true that virtually any arrangement can work satisfactorily, given the right players, good leadership, and the will or incentive to succeed. However, experience shows that some forms of organization are more likely to succeed than others, all else being equal. Here we shall examine a few general types or models of organization, and offer some comments on each.

No Central Health Authority

Though it is common practice today, it was exceedingly rare in the past to find a state correctional system that had a central health authority.[7] Typically, health professionals were hired by and responsible to the wardens of individual prisons. The health care service was viewed as just one more of the programs offered by a prison, such as, education, religious services, barbershop, law library, recreation, hobby craft, and work assignments.

It was under this type of system that some of the most serious deficiencies in medical and mental health services developed. They involved widespread employment of inmates in the delivery of health services, use of impaired and unlicensed physicians, and blatant denial of access to care for serious medical needs. When these appalling conditions were brought to the attention of the courts, the revolution in correctional health care practices of the 1970s and 1980s took place.

Without outside scrutiny, the medical services program in a large prison system that does not have a central health authority generally lacks the stature and leverage necessary to insist on conditions essential to good medical practice. There also will be little consistency in practice across institutions, if each facility is essentially autonomous. Efficient management practices and cost-effective bulk purchasing strategies are difficult to implement without a centralized structure. Faced with other pressing monetary needs, health care issues may not rate very high among the warden's priorities.

Brecher and Della Penna[8] described the situation as one in which the health care personnel, on the one hand, are not involved in planning or budgeting and have no real authority to implement improvements, while, on the other hand, they are simultaneously free to let things slide because they receive no effective professional supervision from the warden.

---

[7] A study by NCCHC found only ten states that were still without a central health authority in 1989. B. Jaye Anno, *Prison Health Care: Guidelines for the Management of an Adequate Delivery System* (Chicago: National Commission on Correctional Health Care, 1991): 72.

[8] Edward M. Brecher and Richard D. Della Penna, *Health Care in Correctional Institutions* (Washington, D.C.: U.S. Government Printing Office, 1975): 45.

Health care personnel in such an organizational structure are at the same time impotent to foster improvement and free to tolerate deterioration. This is a recipe for chaos. A change in this organizational structure is the most important initial step which any state can take toward improving correctional health care—more important even than increasing appropriations.

Based on a more recent study of the organizational structure in all fifty state prison systems, Anno [9] commented on this same traditional model as follows:

> For now, it is enough to note that the traditional organizational model of correctional health services does not serve anyone well—not the warden who wants to provide good health care, not the health professional who wants to serve the patients' needs, not the director of the department of corrections who wants to avoid lawsuits, not the taxpayer who wants the most efficient utilization of public funds, and not the inmate who is less likely to have his/her health needs adequately served under this model.

Outside Public Health Authority

In some county jails and juvenile facilities, responsibility for medical services has been given to the county health department and responsibility for mental health services has been assigned to the community mental health services agency. Similarly, some state prison systems have arranged for the state mental health department to provide some or all of the mental health services. The rationale offered for these approaches is that the health agency has specific expertise as well as a public responsibility, and may be able to achieve certain efficiencies. A close working relationship with correctional authorities is required. Usually, the funding is separately appropriated by the county commission or state legislature to each agency. Less often, the correctional agency contracts with and purchases the services from the health agency.

Success of this arrangement requires a genuine commitment by the health agency, so that the correctional activities are not viewed as lowest in priority and, also, to ensure that the correctional program does not become a source of revenue for subsidizing other agency functions.

Sometimes the health services program is divided into distinct and autonomous programs: medical, mental health, and dental. This fragmentation does not promote a holistic approach, since no one provider is looking at the entire individual. Communication is rendered more difficult because each program typically maintains its own separate medical record for the patient.[10] It is also less efficient, to the extent that bulk purchasing and coordination of similar functions such as data and record keeping, purchasing, supervision, and budgeting cannot be accomplished.

To minimize these deficiencies, Anno recommends that the responsible health authority for the department of corrections be responsible for coordinating mental health services and dental services with medical services and work with representatives of the outside agency(-ies) to ensure that services are not duplicated and that pertinent information regarding patients is shared. Similarly, where one or more

---

[9] Anno, *loc. cit.*

services are contracted out to vendors while the department of corrections operates the remaining services, a health services director needs to be designated. This individual would oversee the contract services and supervise services provided by the department of corrections.[11]

Coordination by a Central Health Care Authority

Probably, the most common arrangement today for multi-institutional correctional systems is the appointment of a central coordinating health authority (a position that reports to the director or deputy director). This person exercises oversight, planning, and monitoring of health care operations at the institutions. In this model, health care staff may be hired by and under the supervision of the warden or head of each institution, although the central health authority often plays some role in recruitment and selection.

While this approach can and sometimes does work well, success is highly variable from institution to institution and from system to system and depends in large part on the chemistry and style of the individual institution head and the medical staff at each location. Sometimes an outwardly "compatible" match may be less than satisfactory, such as an overly authoritarian warden and an overly compliant health services administrator. Similarly, a mediocre physician and a mediocre warden may get along quite well socially, but provide inadequate services.

Line Authority from a Central Office of Health Care

In some state systems, the role of the central health authority is stronger. The responsible health authority at the central level even may be a deputy director or a bureau chief—and exercise line authority to hire, fire, and supervise the institutional health care staff. These systems tend to achieve greater uniformity across institutions and more consistency in the application of criteria for treatment or for the medical transfer of inmates. They also more readily can take advantage of significant efficiencies in bulk purchasing, contracting for services, and regionalizing more costly services. An analog of this arrangement is typical in the county jail. Here, the sheriff or jail administrator employs a medical director or health administrator to supervise the remaining health care staff.

---

[10] While fragmentation of this sort is typical in the free world, the critical difference is that we, as free citizens, choose our own doctors, dentists, psychologists, and hospitals. If we do not like them, we are free to choose someone else. Coordination thus becomes our own primary responsibility. In the correctional setting, the inmate does not have these choices. Thus, if the physician prescribes a medication which conflicts with medication ordered by the dentist or psychiatrist, a judge may determine that the correctional system selected these providers and, therefore, ought to have known that this particular combination of medications was contraindicated. Unless providers are sharing a single medical chart, this is difficult to accomplish.

[11] Anno. *op. cit.*: 80.

Many of the administrative aspects of a large correctional health care program more closely resemble a hospital operation than a prison or jail system. This is true of the types of personnel employed, methods of recruitment and credential verification, kinds and sources of supplies and equipment (and their maintenance requirements), and formats used for expenditure reporting. In view of this fact, even greater efficiencies are possible when the central health authority is given a dedicated personnel officer and business officer to ensure that transactions such as hiring, purchasing, and cost reporting are performed appropriately for the highly specialized requirements of a health care system. Given their other priorities, it is often very difficult for the personnel or business offices of individual institutions to meet the legitimate requirements of a large health program in a consistent and timely manner.

With a strong central health authority, on the other hand, continuing efforts must be made to include the institutional wardens as important players who have a significant investment in the successful outcome of the program. Not only is the warden's cooperation essential to the successful implementation of health services, the way in which health services are managed can affect the operation and the efficient accomplishment of the mission of the institution.

It is simplistic to conclude that the only way to enlist the warden's investment and cooperation and to ensure that the health care program will fit smoothly into the institutional operation is to give the warden ownership, in other words, direct supervision and control over the health care program—perhaps even over its budget. It is equally counterproductive to ignore or bypass the warden and attempt to direct, from the central office, a program of the magnitude and significance of health care within the facility. At worst, this can invite active noncooperation. At best, it fails to enlist an important ally and partner. Either way, the efforts will be more costly and less effective. Partnership and teamwork are important.

In practice, the institution head should ratify and cosign every health care policy and procedure which in any way involves administrative, security, or safety issues. This ensures consistency and avoids any reasonable claim by an employee that the policy was not binding. It is not essential that the warden cosign strictly clinical policies and procedures, such as nursing protocols, practice guidelines, chronic disease treatment protocols, and pharmacy formularies. The responsible health authority similarly should cosign institutional policies and procedures, which are related directly to health care, including the health care aspects of the disaster plan, the training curriculum, as well as the food service, and the environmental safety and sanitation policies. This approach encourages a high-quality and efficiently managed health care system.

Enlisting Support from the Private Sector

In recent years, a number of correctional systems have turned to the private sector for all or a portion of their health services. This is not surprising. Dissatisfaction with "big government" and rising costs have prompted a move toward privatizing a wide variety of services and functions traditionally performed by government. Even large industries—such as automobile manufacturers—are purchasing many components from contractors, which they previously had designed and built themselves.

Private vendors offer some advantages. They can move in quickly and shortcut or sidestep some of the obstacles and impediments that often hobble and slow the progress of state or county agencies. They bring with them a ready-made set of policies and procedures, and they apply the know-how they have developed and perfected elsewhere. A qualified administrator and a physician, employed by the contractor, usually serve as the responsible health authority and the responsible physician for the facility. Contractual vendors employ managed care practices and other cost-saving technology, avoid the overhead involved in expensive civil service salary and fringe-benefit packages, and purchase supplies and equipment without the cumbersome and paralyzing slowness of large governmental agency purchasing divisions. They can recruit and hire staff quickly and also can readily divest themselves of unproductive and marginal employees. They may guarantee accreditation within a year or so of acquiring the contract. They also can indemnify the state or county for costs incurred as a result of a lawsuit. And the private vendors claim to do all of this at significant cost savings, offering a per-inmate-day price, which is competitively bid and guaranteed for the duration of the contract.

While this may seem the best of all possible worlds, there are important concerns and cautions, as well. Managed care is by no means winning unanimous acclaim in the free-world community. Critics point out that the potential cost savings from managed care tend to go to top corporate executives, while patients are being denied the care that their physicians believe to be in their best interest. Patients in most managed care systems experience limited choice among providers. Some corporate-owned hospitals allegedly go to such lengths to curtail costs that the health and safety of their patients are unduly compromised. Excellence sometimes gives way to expediency. And with all this, the overall cost of health care in the United States continues to rise.

The savings which private vendors of correctional health care services achieve are due in part to reduced personnel expenditures (typically the major segment of any system's costs), in part from avoiding unnecessarily expensive types of care, partly from skilled management, and partly through efficient purchasing and other economies of scale. It is to be hoped that only fully qualified personnel are employed, that employees receive a fair and just wage, that necessary care is not denied to any inmate, and that the quality of care is not diminished. These parameters are not easy to measure and require ongoing vigilance and careful monitoring by the correctional agency.

It is certainly possible for many state or county correctional agencies to provide a well-managed, efficient, and high-quality health care program through their own resources. Some do so, combining good management expertise with aggressive quality improvement activities and effective cost-containment strategies. In the past, many state and county systems lacked the motivation which drives contractual providers to curtail costs through utilization review and careful management, since the correctional agency simply could request a supplemental appropriation if expenditures exceeded budget. Today, with shrinking tax-based resources in comparison to growing correctional populations, this option usually is not available.

Some systems, on the other hand, have found it best to arrange for the provision of health services through a university medical center. Private for-profit companies also can provide excellent services and may be ideal in some situations. Correctional agencies that are considering the contract approach are well advised to look careful-ly at the potential advantages, as well as the disadvantages. Bid specifications must thoroughly describe what is expected of the vendor, and should provide potential ven-dors with all relevant information. Criteria for selection of the vendor explicitly should include more than lowest price. [12] Quality and dependability are of utmost importance. Creative approaches to resolving unique problems also are important.

An agency does itself a great disservice if, through promoting cutthroat compe-tition, the final price is so low that the company must compromise quality to avoid los-ing money. In the end, no one benefits if the company cannot earn a reasonable return on its investment.

Finally, careful and ongoing monitoring of the practices of the vendors, the qual-ity of care provided, and compliance with terms of the contract is essential. Accredi-tation, while a helpful strategy for encouraging quality, cannot substitute for watchful supervision by the state or county agency.

The following chapter contains much useful information about the nature and history of privatization and offers helpful suggestions on how to go about it—if such a course is in the best interest of the institution or the system.

---

[12] One useful approach for evaluating bid proposals is to adopt a formula which allo-cates a quality multiplier to the price bid. This is an improvement over the simple two-step process which requires the choice of the lowest bidder meeting minimum-quality criteria.

3 CONSIDERING THE PRIVATE SECTOR

This chapter was written especially for this book by Jacqueline Moore, Ph.D., R.N. Dr. Moore was cofounder of Prison Health Services. After leaving this company in 1988, she assisted two other companies to enter the correctional health care arena. She also has served as Director of Operations for the National Commission on Correctional Health Care.

Privatization of Inmate Medical Care
Emergence of Privatization

Over the past several decades, prison populations across the nation have increased dramatically. Since 1980, the incarceration rate has risen by 188 percent and continues to grow at an annual rate of 8.5 percent.[1] At year end 1995, the U.S. Bureau of Justice reported that 1,078,357 men and women were incarcerated in state and federal prisons.[2]

Since the early 1970s, poor medical care has become a major prisoners' rights issue. The alleged absence of adequate health care has led to countless lawsuits filed by dissatisfied inmates. Court decisions resulting from these suits have declared that the unreasonable deprivation of medical and dental care is unconstitutional, and some states and counties—including some using privatized health care services—have been ordered to take remedial action.

---

[1] Bureau of Justice Statistics, "Correctional Populations in the United States, 1993," (Washington, D.C.: U.S. Department of Justice, 1994).

[2] Bureau of Justice Statistics, "Prison and Jail Inmates, 1995," *Bulletin* (Washington, D.C.: U.S. Department of Justice, August, 1996).

Limited Financial Resources

Any discussion of the basic features of inmate medical care must include a discussion of the all-pervasive factor of inadequate resources. The soaring costs of health care services have affected the middle class as well as the indigent, the free world as well as those incarcerated. Between 1980 and 1989, national health expenditures for personal health care increased by 142 percent or 10.3 percent a year on the average.[3] The average cost of health care per inmate in state prisons rose by an average of 10.7 percent per year from 1982-1989.[4] Although inmate health care budgets are attempting to maintain costs with general increases related to confinement costs, continued growth in the inmate population, and an increased need for specialized care threaten to increase health care budgets.[5] Florida provides an exception.[6] Its Department of Corrections' per diem health care costs have not risen since 1991 despite a major increase in the inmate population.

The October 1996 *Corrections Compendium* reported that health care spending in state and federal prison systems exceeded $2.3 billion for 1995.[7] It is not surprising that the jurisdictions reporting the greatest spending for inmate health care were systems containing the largest populations. The greatest expenditures were reported by California, which spent $368,370,000 for health care services, an increase of 5.3 percent over the previous year. The Federal Bureau of Prisons reported the next highest figure at $300,800,965, a 12.6 percent increase over last year; and Texas spent $254,583,960 representing an increase of over 78 percent compared to its previous budget. The substantial increase in Texas' budget may be explained partially by a concurrent increase in the number of prisoners statewide and the number of new inmates processed for 1995. Texas' average correctional population increased over 34 percent between 1994 and 1995, and the number of new inmates processed rose from 16,017 in 1994 to 54,966 in 1995, an increase of 243 percent.[8] Together, these three systems accounted for 40 percent of the total increase in state inmate health care expenditures in the United States[9]

While it is difficult to determine the extent to which the cost data among various states are comparable, the report does provide a basis for some comparisons. The portion of the total budget devoted to health care averaged 10.45 percent for all

---

[3] "U.S. Health Expenditures, 1960-91," *The World Almanac and Book of Facts 1995*: 968.

[4] Derived from data provided by B. Jaye Anno, "Appendix L: Cost Comparison Tables," *Prison Health Care Guidelines for the Management of an Adequate Delivery System* (Chicago: National Commission on Correctional Health Care, 1991): 248.

[5] G. Wess, "Inmate Health Care, Part 1: As New Commitments Climb, Health Care Budgets Follow," 10:2, *Corrections Compendium* (1996).

[6] Personal communication from Charles Mathews, M.D., Assistant Secretary for Health Services, Florida Department of Corrections, May 14, 1997.

[7] G. Wess, *Ibid.*

[8] *Ibid.*

[9] *Ibid.*

respondents, and varied considerably across jurisdictions—ranging from 4 percent in Iowa to 20 percent in Arkansas. The average cost per inmate per year was $2,308, an increase of 5.6 percent over the average reported in 1994. [10]

In many localities, inadequate financial support has been identified as a major block in the development of adequate and humane services for prisons. Officials of state governments claim that their treasuries have been caught in a crunch between limited revenues, increased prisoner populations, and a greater demand for all services, including health care. Consequently, funding for correctional health care often is given a low priority when it must compete with funding for security, which is the primary goal of the correctional system.

In the last two decades, courts have taken the position that cost should not be a factor in determining what is "adequate" health care for prisoners. The principle that a limited budget will not justify insufficient care has been clearly acknowledged by numerous courts. The position of Judge Blackman in *Jackson v. Bishop* is representative: "Humane considerations and constitutional requirements are not to be measured or limited by dollar considerations." [11] Thus, it appears that where health care is needed, the court would require that it be provided—regardless of cost.

As a result of severe crowding, limited financial resources, and judicial decisions that have mandated higher levels of health care, many states have sought "privatization" as an alternative way to provide inmate medical care. While total privatization of prisons has been received with both deep reservations and high expectations, the private sector has been involved for the past twenty years in the contracting for food services, halfway house operations, commissary, and inmate medical services. Virtually every state system has at least some professional service contracts with individuals, hospitals, or ancillary providers.

State of the Industry

The first jail system to contract for a wholly provided inmate health system by a private vendor was Rikers Island in June of 1973. [12] Under contract, Montefiore Hospital agreed to provide all health care services except psychiatric services to approximately 7,000 inmates at Rikers Island in New York City. By 1976, other systems were following suit. Sacred Heart Hospital of Chester, Pennsylvania contracted to provide management and services to the 400 inmates of the Delaware County Prison in 1976. In 1978, the Baltimore City Jail contracted out for physician staffing and medical services to Chesapeake Physicians Professional Association. Broward County Jail in Fort Lauderdale, Florida and Clark County Jail in Las Vegas initiated contracts in 1979 and 1980, respectively, with a new contract health care firm, Prison Health. Since that time, private sector involvement in inmate health systems has grown steadily. Today, there are at least thirteen private sector firms that provide inmate health care on a

---

[10] *Ibid.*

[11] *Jackson v. Bishop*, 404 F2D 572 (CA 1968).

[12] B. Cotton, "Privatization of Jail Health Care Services," *American Jails* (January-February, 1995).

national or regional basis, and twenty-nine states have privatized all or part of their inmate health care services.[13]

Scope of Health Care Service Delivery

The principal design characteristics employed by contractual health care firms closely resemble those employed in a health maintenance organization (HMO). In this model, access is provided to a complete health care system, with the correctional institution's cost being fixed and prepaid. The companies provide complete staffing, pharmaceutical services, equipment, supplies, x-ray, and administrative services inside the correctional facility and arrange with local providers for outside services and with hospitals for specialty services and inpatient hospitalization. There are basically three methods of contractual health care delivery used to provide health care services to penal institutions. The services may be provided by a public health agency, a local hospital, or a contractual firm.

A number of county jails rely on public health departments to provide care for their detainees. While these arrangements have assisted the local jail in obtaining the needed services, they have not developed a good track record in their ability to control costs. The combination of political, civil service, union, and bureaucratic constraints can make the government an extremely cumbersome vehicle for delivering quality and cost-effective care.

Early arrangements with hospitals were not effective in controlling costs. This is because there was frequently an overutilization of inpatient services, laboratory, and radiological services, and a conflict of interest on the part of the hospital about limiting diagnostic studies or controlling costs. An open-ended system of financing invites uncontrolled expenditures.

In 1993, the Texas Department of Criminal Justice established contracts with two university medical centers to provide inmate health care: Texas Tech University Health Sciences Center in Lubbock and the University of Texas Medical School at Galveston. The University of Texas Medical School provides health care at two-thirds of the state's correctional institutions and Texas Tech provides care at the remaining one-third. Both universities have been able to curtail costs by establishing utilization review programs, providing on-site primary care, and capping expenditures with specialists.

Texas was the first state to use the university-based managed care model for providing health care to its inmate population. More recently, the State of Georgia has announced plans to use the services of the Medical College of Georgia in 1997, and the State of Connecticut is currently in negotiations with the University of Connecticut to provide their inmate health care.

---

[13] Telephone interview with states that have private health care contractors, including Alabama, Massachusetts, Idaho, Illinois, Maine, Missouri, Nevada, Virginia, New Mexico, and Ohio (October, 1996).

Options Regarding Services to be Contracted

Some or All Clinical Services

The scope of services performed by contractors varies along several dimensions. Contractors can obligate themselves to provide specific clinical services or all of the health care services. For example, contractors may provide only pharmaceutical services, physician services, or specialized services such as hemodialysis. Some contracts exclude dental services or mental health services, since the state or county may choose to provide these directly. Often, mental health services are provided through the state department of mental health or through a community mental health agency. When only a portion of the health services are contracted to a private vendor, careful thought must be given to coordination. For example, will a single integrated medical record be used? If not, how will providers share information? Other considerations include whether the shared services will use the same clerical and other support staff or equipment. If not, how will administrative support be provided? Who will be the responsible health authority? Alternatively, contractors may be engaged to provide all of the prison's health care services and personnel staffing, and to assume management responsibilities as well.

States or counties that have issued personnel service contracts generally have done so in response to staffing shortages or to overcome restraints imposed by bureaucratic personnel regulations. Medical staff recruitment is frequently problematic for correctional institutions. Prisons often are located in isolated rural areas where professionals choose not to live. Salaries tend to be low and inadequate to attract young and competent professionals. Correctional administrators, unfamiliar with credentialing procedures, unknowingly can employ impaired or incompetent providers.

Most jurisdictions that have issued personnel service contracts usually include physician services. Examples of this type of contractual arrangement can be found in state systems in North Carolina, Pennsylvania, Montana, New York, and Michigan.

A few state systems, such as Illinois and Pennsylvania, have both civil service and contracted health care employees. Often, states decide to maintain the service of long-term employees who have accumulated years of seniority and have a vested interest in the state or county retirement system. This also may be the result of a compromise reached with a labor union to protect salary and benefits of its members. Thus, some or all of the nurses, record clerks, or other health care staff may be retained as civil servants while other staff are employed by the contractor.

Difficulties with this arrangement can arise when issues of accountability and employee discipline have not been well addressed in the contract. Early contracts in Pennsylvania excluded the nurses from the management contract. Tim Ringler, chief financial analyst for the state, reported that difficulties in personal relationships ensued between the civil service staff and the vendor. State nurses were concerned about their job security, and vendors reported issues of contract sabotage. Additionally, there was a duplication of services. The state was paying for two health administrators at each institution, which increased time spent in meetings and other functions involving communication or coordination of care.[14] In a 1997 request for

---

[14] Tim Ringler, "Monitoring Compliance," Presentation at NCCHC Conference (November, 1995).

proposal issued by the Commonwealth of Pennsylvania, nursing services were listed as an optional bid. Mr. Ringler reported that most vendors offering proposals decreased their price to the state for overall services, provided nursing was included in the contract. Wexford Health Services, one of the current state vendors, lowered its costs over $100,000 per year if the provision of nursing services were included in the total contract.[15]

One or Many Prisons

Firms also may be contracted to provide services to one, several, or all prisons in a state's system. Sometimes states opt to undertake a pilot project to test comprehensive contracting. For example, in 1988 the Georgia Department of Corrections entered into a comprehensive contract for medical care at a single location, the Lowden Correctional Institution in Valdosta, Georgia.[16] Subsequently in 1994, a statewide contract was awarded for the provision of health care services at all of the Georgia Prisons.[17] In 1986, South Carolina contracted for medical care at three facilities. Today, the contractor provides services at nine of their correctional institutions.[18]

Other states have chosen to privatize the medical care of facilities where they have experienced cost overruns, had difficulty managing the institutions, or experienced rapid construction of new facilities. For example, the Greensville Correctional Center in Virginia had a history of experiencing cost overruns and recruitment problems. In 1992, the State of Virginia privatized the inmate medical care of this institution. This was the only facility that was privatized in the state.[19] Recently, Virginia has privatized the medical care at two additional correctional institutions.

The Ohio Department of Rehabilitation and Correction contracted the medical care for the Trumbull Correctional Institution in 1992. The facility was located in a remote area of the state and was geographically distant from the other Ohio correctional institutions. The institution had been built recently, and union antagonism was prevalent.[20] The geographical distance of this facility from the central office staff hindered the state's ability to manage the institution's medical services. Thus, privatization of inmate health care became a viable option.

---

[15] Telephone interview with Tim Ringler, Director of Finance for the State of Pennsylvania (March, 1997).

[16] D. McDonald, *Managing Prison Health Care and Costs* (Washington, D.C.: National Institute of Justice, May, 1995).

[17] Review of RFP document, State of Georgia Proposal #467-019-9534 27 (March, 1995).

[18] Telephone interview with Gary McWilliams, Vice President of Marketing for Correctional Medical Services (October, 1996).

[19] *Ibid.*

[20] Telephone interview with Larry Mendel, Medical Director for the Ohio Department of Corrections (November, 1996).

Rapid construction of new facilities and inherent lags in recruitment of staff have provided the impetus for other states to contract their medical services. In 1995, North Carolina contracted the medical services for two of its new facilities.[21]

Both states and contractual firms generally feel that the opportunity to achieve greater cost savings increases with the scope of services provided and the number of institutions at which they provide care. Consequently, the more institutions that are included in the contract and the more services that a contractor is able to provide, the greater will be the ability to organize a state's health care resources, achieve economies of scale in its staffing patterns, and spread financial risks over a larger population pool. The Georgia Department of Corrections concluded, from its demonstration effort, that the comprehensive contract for medical care at a single facility with a relatively small population was not cost effective and that the state could operate such a program as cheaply as a vendor. The department felt, however, that contracting would be more advantageous if it encompassed a larger population of inmates and a larger number of institutions.

Many of the states that have privatized their health care services have opted to establish comprehensive contracts at all of their institutions. States that have developed comprehensive contracts include: Alabama, Arkansas, Delaware, Georgia, Indiana, Kansas, Maine, Maryland, Massachusetts, Missouri, New Jersey, New Mexico, South Carolina, South Dakota, Vermont, West Virginia, and Wyoming.

Some states have followed another pattern in the development of their contracts with vendors. For example, Illinois and Pennsylvania have issued regional requests for proposals, clustering several institutions under a single contract. The institutions generally are grouped according to geographical location or type of institution, such as all female, sex offender, mental health, and so forth. These states contract with several different vendors to provide medical services in various regions of their state; they claim that competition among the vendors enhances the state's ability to obtain quality services at competitive prices and avoids the creation of contractor monopolies, and any diminution of benefits which flow from open-market competition.

Benefits of Privatization

Lower Costs/Better Cost Containment

Excessive cost or lack of financial budgetary control is a strong motivation for many clients seeking health services from the private sector. In a contractual arrangement, a specified group of services is provided for a fixed guaranteed fee.

Financing for the correctional health care program is done on a capitated or per inmate population basis. The total annual charge to an individual prison or jail is based on the inmate population of the facility. The contractor is responsible for all costs associated with the provision of health care services, enabling the department of corrections or county to establish an annual budget and be assured that budgeted expenses will not be exceeded. The result is that the government agency is able to

---

[21] Telephone interview with Bert Rosefield, Director of Health Services for the State of North Carolina.

plan and budget for health care costs with a defined limit of expenditures which require no governmental regulations, additional legislative appropriations, or need for emergency funding to provide health care to prisoners.[22]

In a telephone survey conducted by Abt Associates of ten states [23] that have privatized their medical services, cost overruns were frequently mentioned as a reason for contracting.[24] Steve Stedtfeld, contract monitor for the State of Idaho, stated that

> . . . saving money was one of the main goals of contracting. Prior to contracting, every year the DOC would have to make requests for additional funding for recurring catastrophic costs because they could not budget for the unexpected. Since they've established a comprehensive contract with a national vendor, they have no hidden surprises to worry about.[25]

However, most contracts include a catastrophic ceiling that limits financial exposure for an individual requiring major medical attention. The contract also may specify limitations and exceptions for catastrophic events, such as riots or acts of nature.

While there are no definitive studies that compare the cost of contract medical care with a self-managed system, many advocates claim substantial savings. A recent award in New Jersey was $20 million under what the state was currently spending.[26] In Massachusetts, the deputy director estimated that contractual health care has saved the state from $5 to $8 million dollars, and the Missouri Department of Corrections estimates savings of over $3 million.[27]

Capitation financing provides obvious incentives to the managers of these contracts to deliver health care as economically and efficiently as possible. The result is frequently lower hospitalization rates, decreased use of emergency rooms, and more care provided on-site or on an outpatient basis. However, a reduction in services does not necessarily correlate with a lower quality of care. For example, when Texas contracted with the University of Texas Medical School and Texas Tech to provide a managed inmate health care program, an emphasis was placed on primary care. Institutional physicians were expected to treat conditions on-site that they previously had

---

[22] Jacqueline Moore, "Privatization of Prison Health Services," 2:4, *The Privatization Review* (1986).

[23] Abt Associates, telephone interview conducted with ten states that have privatized (October, 1996).

[24] Generally, such cost overruns in the 1980s were due largely to litigation, but this is not the case today, according to Charles Mathews, M.D., Assistant Secretary for Health Services, Florida Department of Corrections, personal communication (May 14, 1997).

[25] Telephone interview with Steve Stedtfeld, Contract Monitor for State of Idaho (October, 1996).

[26] Telephone interview with the Deputy Commissioner for New Jersey Department of Corrections (March, 1996).

[27] Abt Associates, *loc. cit.*

referred out for off-site specialty care. Additionally, the stabilization of emergency patients on-site avoided unnecessary trips to the hospital emergency room. The result has been a larger number of inmates treated for nonemergency complaints at the inmate's institution with a subsequent reduction in off-site care.

Most contractual firms operate a centralized companywide utilization review program, which is responsible for monitoring hospitalization activities at each of its contracted sites. The components of these programs include preadmission review, concurrent review, ambulatory surgery, discharge planning, claims review, and on-site specialty clinics. The programs are designed to assure that medical services are rendered in an efficient manner and that unnecessary services, lengthy stays in the hospital, and overcharges are avoided. The provision of on-site care has the added advantage of not only decreasing medical costs but of reducing security and transportation costs, as well.

Sharing Financial Risk

Contractual arrangements most likely to encourage effective cost control are those that establish a fixed price for delivering all health care and place the contractor at financial risk of losing money if costs exceed budgetary constraints. Cost plus or cost-reimbursement contracts create few incentives to restrain spending. Incentives to contain costs are probably greater if the contractor is required to cover primary as well as secondary and tertiary health care.

Requiring the contractor to provide comprehensive coverage poses difficulties given the prospects of a catastrophic illness or injury. Cost proposals for comprehensive coverage likely will be higher for the state since the vendor must either self-insure or purchase catastrophic insurance, which ultimately will be billed back to the state.

States have considered various options regarding catastrophic illness or injury. At one end of the spectrum, contractors have been responsible for covering all potential costs, thereby relieving the state of any financial exposure. Other options include a specified catastrophic limit such as the first $25,000 or $50,000 of financial liability per inmate. Costs exceeding the catastrophic limits are paid by the state or county.

Still another variation on this theme is a graduated cost-sharing arrangement whereby the department of corrections or county and the contractor will share costs which exceed a catastrophic limit. Georgia has a provision for a graduated cost-sharing arrangement whereby the department will assume a larger share of the costs that exceed a $25,000 limit.[28] Other states have opted to exclude high catastrophic cases. For example, in Illinois the contractor is not financially responsible for the treatment or hospitalization of patients with AIDS.[29]

In establishing catastrophic limits and exclusions, the contracting agency should examine its own inpatient utilization data and perform a cost analysis of all outside services. The catastrophic limits set should be able to encompass the majority of the

---

[28] Review of RFP Document, State of Georgia Proposal, *op. cit.*

[29] Review of RFP Document, State of Illinois (1994).

inmate expenditures. Likewise, the agency should perform a case analysis prior to excluding any illnesses. For example, the State of New Jersey has had a high number of inmates who were receiving AIDS medication and treatment. If the state had excluded this illness from their health care contract, the state still would have maintained a large financial exposure.

Improved Quality and Service Delivery

An unacceptable level of quality or the impetus of a court order or consent decree has been another motivating factor for privatization. The alleged absence of adequate health care has been cited in lawsuits affecting 32 percent of the prisons in America. [30] More than two-thirds of the states were under court-ordered consent decrees to correct conditions that violate the U.S. Constitution's prohibition against cruel and unusual punishment. [31]

Both Kansas and Delaware developed contractual relationships in response to court orders. In these cases, the state turned to the private sector to implement the court's demands. Since then, health care has improved dramatically in both systems, and both state systems have achieved accreditation by the National Commission on Correctional Health Care. However, at the same time, some private vendor contracts have been cancelled because of problems with the quality of inmate health care. [32]

Provision of Adequate Equipment

Limited budgets or cumbersome purchasing laws or procedures can result in an institution not being able to purchase necessary medical supplies or equipment. Frequently, the bureaucratic process of approval for purchasing requests may result in excessive delays. As a consequence, sophisticated electronic or computerized equipment may be obsolete by the time it is purchased. Moreover, lengthy delays in repairing or replacing defective equipment sometimes can necessitate the use of very costly off-site services.

A private contractor is not obligated to any particular supplier or purchasing guideline, and, therefore, quickly can select the equipment best suited for the application and can expedite purchase and installation. Additionally, contractors can institute strategic operational planning from the corporate as well as the institutional viewpoint. They are able to take advantage of economies of scale when purchasing equipment, medical supplies, and laboratory and pharmaceutical services. Thus, they may purchase for a group of contracts as opposed to an individual prison or jail, possibly resulting in a lower cost per item. Often, this proves to be a significant advantage to both large and small correctional systems.

---

[30] J. Moore, "Prison Health Care: Problems and Alternatives in the Delivery of Health Care to the Incarcerated," (Part I and Part II). 73: 8, *Florida Medical Association* (July, 1986): 531-35, and 73: 9 (August, 1986): 615-20.

[31] *Ibid.*

[32] Charles Mathews, M.D., Assistant Secretary for Health Services, Florida Department of Corrections, personal correspondence, May 14, 1997.

Recruitment of Health Care Staff

A problem frequently encountered by those responsible for providing health care services is the recruitment and retention of professional health care workers. Due to such factors as a poor workplace environment, low wages, and rural settings, it is often difficult for correctional facilities to attract qualified health care professionals. Staff ratios also may be poorly managed. There may be few medical staff in a system, and they may consist primarily of paramedics or licensed practical nurses.

The most common reason for contracting health services has been to obtain needed health care staff. Nursing shortages coupled with below-market wage rates have made it difficult for correctional institutions to recruit qualified staff. Many correctional institutions that fill their nursing positions with temporary-staffing agency nurses have experienced major cost overruns.

For example, in the State of New Jersey a hiring freeze was initiated in 1988, which severely inhibited prisons from replacing anyone retiring, resigning, or going on medical leave. As a result of the hiring freezes and noncompetitive wage rates, the prison used agency nurses. In November 1994, the Office of Institutional Services reported that the New Jersey Department of Corrections had contracts with forty-six temporary staffing agencies. A study of salary expenditures conducted by the New Jersey Department of Corrections' Central Office in 1995 concluded that if all of the RN positions had been filled with state employees rather than agency RN's, there would have been an estimated savings of $1.8 million.[33]

In addition to the obvious savings associated with salaries and the cost of medical care, there may be indirect savings to the department of corrections, as well. Malpractice insurance, legal fees, pension plans, and security costs associated with outside medical care often are reduced under contract care.

Conversely, it also is possible to find a professional who has manipulated the system to his or her advantage. For example, a physician may be paid an annual salary of $95,000 for less than twenty hours of clinical work per week. In a northeast state department of corrections, the full-time medical director for the state system had a full-time practice in addition to his responsibilities in the correctional system.[34]

A private contractor generally is able to demonstrate more success in staffing as a result of a larger personnel pool, established recruitment networks, better pay and health benefits, as well as other advantages which may prove attractive to potential employees. The company's resources and national reputation as a professional health care manager gives it a distinct recruitment advantage over the state's or county's past efforts. Most contractors offer an orientation and ongoing professional development program, established career programs, geographical mobility, and financial incentives based on performance versus seniority. Because of these advantages,

---

[33] J. Moore, "New Jersey Department of Corrections Master Plan Medical Services," presented October 25, 1995.

[34] University of Connecticut review of Department of Corrections inmate health care budget, (November, 1996), University of Connecticut Health Systems, Managed Care (untitled working papers).

many of which may not be available to a corrections administrator or government due to budgetary restraints or inflexible civil service or personnel policies, a private contractual arrangement is often a viable solution to staffing problems.

In the event of a crisis or new system start-up, most contractors draw upon the expertise of staff within their own organization, using per diem employees or established traveling nurse programs for temporary assignments. Contractors also may be more skilled at negotiating professional salaries and professional discounts.

Control and Accountability

In some correctional health care systems that function under the supervision of a warden or superintendent, the care is extremely fragmented, uncoordinated, and expensive. Each service component, hospital, physician, nurse, and laboratory is purchased separately from different providers. In this type of arrangement, all providers have a financial incentive to maximize the use of their services and to increase their revenue regardless of correctional budgeting constraints or the health needs of the population. The warden or jail administrator, unfamiliar with health care administration, often is unable to find ample time to address the organization or delivery of a complex health care system.

Frequently, the results are a patchwork of services with little medical communication or coordination among the providers. Thus, when problems arise, the warden or administrator may not be able to determine accountability or rely on any one person to solve the problem.

By contrast, in most contractual arrangements, the contractor assigns a health administrator to the institution who has the responsibility, authority, and accountability for managing health care delivery systems on a day-to-day basis. The administrators generally are experienced in providing health care management in correctional institutions.

Under a contractual system, health care decisions no longer are made by lay people, such as correctional administrators and officers, but by people with medical expertise. Under a contractual system, administrative authority can be retained by the warden, but the professional responsibility for health care is in the hands of the provider. An important ramification is that the contractual firm becomes responsible for indemnifying the governmental agency for legal costs and any damages which may be awarded in a lawsuit over the quality, accessibility, or continuity of the health care program. Yet, as shown later on, contracting out for health care does not relieve the administrator of responsibility or legal liability.

However, the transfer of this responsibility from the correctional administrator to the private contractor has significant appeal to a warden who reluctantly has been responsible for managing a critical inmate service over which he or she has little real control or understanding. It is the candid admission of many correctional administrators that the provision of inmate health care services is one of the most time-consuming and problem-producing day-to-day responsibilities that they experience. By privatizing health care, the administrator creates a buffer zone in the person of the health administrator. Moreover, the health and corrections staff have a professional expert with recognized qualifications in inmate health care to assist them in the resolution of problems.

Generally, the contractual firms are client-oriented and strive to develop open and collaborative relationships with their clients. Usually, they are responsive to changing system needs and try to maintain a high performance.

Another perceived benefit of contracting is the development of a management information system. Most firms have developed computerized programs capable of providing statistical data necessary for the evaluation and monitoring of each facility's health service.

Risks of Privatization of Health Services

Cost versus Efficiency

Concerns about the quality of service probably are heightened when the services are to be delivered by for-profit firms whose profits are at financial risk. The fear of most prison officials is that the private contractor will reduce services to inmates to reduce their costs and increase their profits. Generally, most contractors contend that the potential risk of underservice frequently is offset by threats of liability and the likelihood that the correctional institution or department of corrections can and will opt not to renew their contract.

In theory, it would not be in the contractor's best interest to cut corners or decrease quality. The ability of a contractor to secure new business or to retain existing business is dependent upon its reputation as a service provider. Poor performance not only would create unfavorable media coverage and liability issues, but it also would jeopardize the contractor in the marketplace.

Financial Risks

Contracting for health care also has financial risks for the department of corrections or county. Early contractors in Arkansas and Alabama went bankrupt and left many providers with unpaid invoices. Similar experiences were reported in Pennsylvania, where a few of the early contractors experienced poor cash flow and providers waited over 120 days for payments.[35] One way of minimizing this risk is for the department of corrections to pay bills for off-site services directly as is the current procedure in the State of Tennessee.[36]

Certain types of compensation arrangements also may expose the government to unanticipated risks. For example, high per diem rates for increases in population, low catastrophic limits, or above average prices for subsequent years all impose financial risks on the department of corrections or county.

Resistance to Privatization

Legal and ethical issues have been the most persistent argument against privatization. Opposition to private management runs highest in jurisdictions where the

---

[35] *Ibid.*

[36] *Ibid.*

power of organized labor is strong. Certainly, that would explain why early contracts were more acceptable in the South and Southwest, such as in Georgia, Arkansas, and Alabama, and only recently have penetrated the labor-strong Northeast.

Public employee resentment may lead to difficulties in implementing private-sector programs. To avoid union problems, consider contracting for private health care services for new facilities. At the very least, if a takeover is planned, careful planning is required for the transition. Anticipated benefits of privatization must be communicated clearly to current staff, and active internal lobbying must be instituted to diffuse their opposition.

There is consensus in the general literature that the privatization of public services increases the political power of the private sector. Unlike government personnel who are prohibited from lobbying, private organizations have developed considerable lobbying skills. Attorneys, political lobbyists, or consultants have been used to solicit inmate health care contracts for a commission, a percentage, or a contingency fee. It is imperative that standards prohibiting conflicts of interest be delineated clearly in any request for proposals and subsequent contracts. [37]

Another risk associated with contracting is the potential of a work stoppage. If professional staff choose to strike, the contracting agency would be in a weak position to assume provision of care. Due to bureaucratic policies regarding advertising and recruiting for positions, very likely there would be a long lag time before new personnel could be recruited and trained. Moreover, the more a governmental agency relies on private-sector firms for the provision of inmate health care, the greater the threat becomes of disruption by potential strikes or bankruptcy. When considering privatization, it is important for the agency to develop contingency plans such as the requirement of posting performance bonds and obtaining financial references to diminish or avoid potential financial risks.

Liability

One of the primary reasons for the use of contractual medical firms has been the result of inmate lawsuits and the body of evolving case law that guarantees inmates the right to health care. The courts see health care as a basic human right, and the health care provided to the incarcerated population is judged against current community standards.

One of the most significant selling points of private contractors is that they will assume responsibility for any liability arising from the administration of or delivery of health services. The private contractor claims to eliminate the prison's or jail's involvement by indemnifying the state or county, defending all lawsuits, and paying all associated legal costs and settlements. While it is true that the contract provider assumes responsibility for malpractice tort liability, contracting does not abrogate the

---

[37] "Generous campaign donations and even putting sitting legislators on the payroll of the vendor are common practice, and standards prohibiting conflict of interest are insufficient to stop these practices," according to Charles L. Mathews, M.D., Assistant Secretary for Health Services, Florida Department of Corrections, personal communication, May 14, 1997.

jurisdiction's or the contractor's potential liability for violation of the Civil Rights Act, 42 USC Section 1983.

In a 1988 judicial decision, the U.S. Supreme Court affirmed that a government is responsible for its health services—whether they are supplied by government employees or by consultants under contract. The Court concluded:

> Contracting out for prison medical care does not relieve the state of its constitutional duty to provide adequate medical care to those in its custody and does not deprive the state's prisoners of the means to vindicate their Eighth Amendment Rights.[38]

Regardless of whether the provider is a government agency or a contractual health care firm, inmate health services are and always will be a shared responsibility of the health services and administrative staff of the institution. Because governments cannot shield themselves from civil rights liability claims, it behooves the contracting agency to establish clear contract parameters, high standards of care, and a rigorous system of monitoring designed to identify potential incidents prior to their becoming liability threats.

Change in Health Care Providers

Once a state or county chooses to contract for health services, agrees to a provider, and services are implemented, then these health care services continue uninterrupted over a period of time. Most purchasing guidelines require that the contract be rebid periodically. Generally, there are three reasons that may prompt a client to change providers: (1) the agency is dissatisfied with service delivery, (2) the contractor discontinues provision of service, or (3) the contractor is underbid by a competitor.

Dissatisfaction with Service Delivery

When a client perceives that services provided do not meet his or her expectations and the lack of an established relationship with the contractor contributes to continued dissatisfaction, there is sufficient motivation to change providers. It may be that the vendor was never fully staffed, as promised in the proposal, or that the client has difficulty working with the contractor's health administrator or other employees. When communication between a county or state and the vendor either breaks down or is never well established, very likely the contract will be rebid.

Contractor Chooses to Discontinue the Provision of Service

While there may be legitimate reasons to discontinue service for the selected contract site locations, such as poor cooperation of security staff with the medical program or an unrealistic fine schedule, a repeated history of a contractor leaving

---

[38] *West v. Adkins*, 108 S.Ct. 2250 (1988).

prior to completion of a contract term will significantly reduce the client's confidence in the provider.[39]

The Current Contractor is Underbid by a New or Competing Company

The reason cited most often as to why states and counties change vendors is because the current provider was underbid by a competitor. The price differential may be because the current vendor is charging too much for the service, or it also could be because the new vendor is inexperienced in the industry with an inadequate knowledge of costs or is attempting to gain new business or gain entry into the industry. In a review of contracts, some competitive companies unknowingly have bid too low for a contract. In Illinois, one of the health care vendors lost three state facilities because it failed to realize that one of the institutions was a female intake center and priced its contracts too low.[40] Because the state remains liable if the contractor is unable to deliver services, the state (in this case) allowed the vendor to renegotiate the contract.

Companies have been known to bid low on new contracts to gain entry into the market. In Mesa County, California the price that a vendor submitted was well below cost proposals submitted by other vendors. The vendor was new to the correctional health care industry and freely admitted that its goal was to gain entry into the market.[41] While taking the low price initially may seem appealing, selection of new firms that are "low-balling" prices is risky business for a state or county government. The inexperienced vendor may deliver an inferior service, in which case the government agency still retains liability, or the vendor may experience excessive cost overruns and be unable to complete the contract because of insufficient funds.

Companies also have been known to "low-ball" the first-year's contract price and to increase the price of the contract substantially through subsequent year negotiations or by the provision of additional staff.[42] If the cost of additional staff is negotiated in the initial contract, governments are provided with some protection from these "high-jacker" scenarios.

A major difficulty with contracts when they are rebid is the disruption of staff. An incumbent contract company has greater personnel salary and benefit costs than a company proposing to begin new services at a site. This poses a cost disadvantage

---

[39] This most often occurs because a contractor has underbid and is losing money. It also may occur because of negative media coverage, according to Charles L. Mathews, M.D., Assistant Secretary for Health Services, Florida Department of Corrections, personal correspondence, May 14, 1997.

[40] Telephone interview with Harry Schuman, Medical Director for Illinois, concerning contracts with the Pontiac, Dwight, and Kankakee correctional institutions (January, 1997).

[41] Telephone interview with Doug Flood, Marketing Director, United Health Care (April, 1992).

[42] J. Moore, Review of multiple county and state contracts for correctional health care with private firms (March, 1997).

for the incumbent because the competing companies base hiring their staff at entry-level wages and with restricted benefits. While costs to the state or county are initially reduced, employee turnover and dissatisfaction are increased, which ultimately has a negative impact on the health care program.

Sometimes, especially when the private vendor contracts are rebid every few years and new vendors take over, the employees who have chosen to remain on the job are repaid poorly for their loyalty and experience. They may have to accept a lower wage. They may not have had the opportunity to vest fully in a pension plan. Other fringe benefits, such as health insurance or educational reimbursement, also may be different. To alleviate this, government agencies might consider incorporating appropriate safeguards into their bid specifications, such as pension plans that are quickly vested or portable. Requiring the contractor to provide a synopsis of its employee wage and benefit program is a strategy that also can help to address legitimate concerns of current employees.

Besides personnel issues, turnover of vendors is also costly to the state or county, and this cost ought to be factored in the total cost—whether the switch is from government to private contractor, or between contractors, or back to the government. The incumbent vendor has considerable information regarding the facility and its medical programs. The vendor may have solved individual facility deficiencies regarding space or equipment problems, whereas the new vendor could waste time and money in formulating new solutions and transitioning into a new program.

In summary, the effect of contracting on costs and savings has not been evaluated. Such comparisons of costs between the public and private sector are exceedingly difficult, not only because of different accounting procedures used by each domain, but also because states and counties cannot always identify their complete health care costs. Inmate health care expenditures may be included in one budget while personnel services, subcontractors, and retirement benefits may be derived from another budget. Lacking such comparative studies, some correctional administrators believe that contracting for health care is more costly than direct provision because of the overhead and profit earned by the contractor. It is felt that the government agency could eliminate these fees by providing the services directly.

These arguments must be regarded cautiously because, all things being equal, if the state or county were able to provide these services, they would not have sought the assistance of contractual firms. Incompetent staff, poor management, and bureaucratic rigidity probably all contribute to the agency's inefficient health care delivery system. Thus, the real comparison should be between the cost and value of the contractor's service and what the government agency would pay to deliver the same service in the absence of contracting.

Managing Risks and Monitoring Quality

It appears that the contractual approach for inmate health care has distinct advantages in the provision of medical care. Recruitment of staff, formulation of a medical program, and creation of appropriate conditions for the delivery of medical care are facilitated by this type of arrangement. However, too often, the existence of appropriate policies on paper may not translate into quality health care. As so often happens with traditional health care, the only criterion for filling positions may be that the candidate is licensed and breathing. No matter how good a program appears on paper, it must be evaluated in practice, particularly as it responds to complicated medical cases, burgeoning inmate populations, and resistant infectious diseases.

The key elements to maintaining quality are relatively simple. They start with a well-thought-out contract that clearly specifies all expectations regarding service delivery; it incorporates payment provisions that create incentives for efficiency; and it implements monitoring procedures designed to identify and resolve problems quickly.

The American Bar Association (ABA)[43] issued guidelines regarding the privatization of corrections, which were adopted by the ABA's House of Delegates in February of 1990. These guidelines included some provisions for contract health care which are summarized below:

    a.   There should be a clear statement that the contract is to be cost effective and provide for proper care.

    b.   The contract term should be fair to both parties; three years seems to be a good balance.

    c.   The agreement should require the contractor to achieve accreditation by the National Commission on Correctional Health Care (NCCHC).

    d.   Contract employees should receive the same level of training as required for public employees.

    e.   The state should appoint a contract monitor who has access to "any and all" information from the contractor . . . that is determined to be necessary to carry out monitoring provisions. The monitor should issue reports on the contractor's performance at least annually.

    f.   The contractor should be required to assume all liability arising under the contract and should not be prohibited from using immunity defenses (which are available to governments to limit liability).

    g.   The contractor should be required to provide adequate insurance coverage.

    h.   The state should have a transition plan in the event the contract is cancelled or not renewed.

To ensure that these recommendations are incorporated into the agreement between the state and the winning contract firm, they should be incorporated into the request for proposal (RFP) or bid specification. Of course, the better the RFP document, the better the understanding that will ensue between the firm and the agency.

---

[43] American Bar Association, "Guidelines Concerning Privatization of Prisons and Jails," Washington, D.C.: Prison and Jail Problem Committee, Criminal Justice Section (1990).

Developing a Request for a Proposal

In developing a request for proposal, the effort should be coordinated by a single individual with input from budget, legal, purchasing, correctional administration, and medical personnel. The first step is to review your current health care unit. Look at your previous year's budget report. The following cost categories should be identified and reviewed.

Identify Your Current Health Care Costs

The first and generally easiest line item to identify is the cost of personnel. Personnel costs include salaries, professional fees, fringe benefits, and overtime for each position or subcontracted position which provides staff at the institutions that you will be privatizing. Also, you may want to include advertising costs for recruiting and the cost of orientation of new personnel. If your facility provides inservice training for your security and medical staff, identify the manpower costs associated with this service. Also, include overtime, replacement personnel, and costs to maintain adequate security and medical personnel.

Next, collect budgetary information on your on-site operating expenses. Costs in this category include office equipment and supplies, as well as pharmaceutical and medical supplies. Included in this category also should be your annual expenditures for equipment repair or maintenance. The next item should include your costs for on-site dental, mental health, and ancillary services. Included in ancillary services should be expenses for lab, x-ray, plus cost for any off-site diagnostic procedure such as CT scans, ultrasound, EKGs, and EEGs. Identify your annual hospitalization, emergency room, and ambulance costs, and off-site specialty consult costs. Calculate the number of days spent in the hospital for both inpatient and outpatient procedures, such as same day surgery or other diagnostic procedures.

Lastly, look at your administrative cost. This category includes costs of recruiting, hiring, and relocating personnel, paying invoices, performing utilization management reviews, paying attorneys' fees, providing malpractice insurance, and any other administrative functions or fees associated with judgments and settlements.

After you determine the total cost of maintaining your health care unit, examine any additional expenses that you might incur to achieve accreditation; compliance with Occupational Safety and Heath Administration (OSHA) standards; as well as preemployment and annual physicals for correctional officers; or the costs of additional new programs, for example, telemedicine or computerized medical records.

Organizing the Project

Once you have reviewed and tabulated your health care program's cost, you will have essential information that will enable you to generate a set of bid specifications for qualified vendors. Proper planning and organization will help you accomplish this task.

First, establish a schedule to allow you a reasonable amount of time to accomplish each step. The following timetable will guide you with specific tasks involved.

Figure 3-1. Timetable for Privatization

Task	Expected Duration
Reviewing your health care costs	2—3 weeks
Selecting bid specifications committee	1 week
Definition of program needs	1 week
Preparing bid specifications	2 weeks
Receipt and review by vendors	3 weeks
Pre-bid conference and survey of facility(s)	1 week
Submission of written proposal by vendors	4 weeks
Evaluation of proposals by selection committee	3 weeks
Oral presentation by selected vendors	1 week
Final evaluation of proposals	1 week
Development of a written contract	1 week
Contract approval	1 week
Transition for new contract	8 weeks
Approximate total time	29—30 weeks

Describe Your Facility

Describe your correctional facility and its geographical location. Include information regarding the existing medical unit, floor plan, characteristics of the inmate population, and space and equipment allocated to the medical unit. Identify any equipment that may need to be purchased or repaired. State whether the agency or the vendor will assume responsibility for maintenance of the equipment. You also may want to consider how to handle your existing inventory of medical supplies and what will happen to medical supplies that have been purchased by the vendor if the contract is not renewed.

If you are planning an expansion or change in your institution to help relieve crowded housing conditions, remember to include the cost of adding personnel, equipment, and space to your health care unit. Likewise, if the mission of your facility changes, for example, to house maximum-security inmates or is converted to a reception center, hospice unit, or mental health unit, remember to mention this in the bid specifications as it will alter the cost of the proposed health care program. You also may want to include provisions for renegotiation in the event of a new or costly treatment, new statute, court order, legislative action, or standard which is adopted after the contract's inception.

Required Scope of Work

In the RFP document, provide detailed instructions on the services that you want the vendor to provide. Services to consider are dental and mental health services, sick call (how often held and where), emergency services, infirmary care, hospital and specialty consults, medical records, communicable diseases, prenatal care, and so forth. If there is a new program that you are considering, for example, telemedicine or computerized medical records, list it as an optional program and request that it be priced separately. Identify any areas that you would like to see improved or modified.

Describe the current health care staffing patterns. If you feel that additional staff are required to provide the services or to meet accreditation standards, be sure to state this in the RFP. It also is helpful if you can provide the vendors with a list of names, addresses, and telephone numbers of the current physicians or health care services your facility uses, such as laboratory or x-ray vendors and so forth, and a salary schedule or range.

Describe any security-clearance procedures or orientation programs in which the vendor is expected to participate. Also, identify the fiscal responsibility for the cost of urine drug screens and orientation programs.

In the RFP, you may want to require that the prospective vendor identify the salary to be paid for each staff position or subcontracted position. This information will help you when you evaluate your proposals and also will assist you with future negotiations in the event that you decide to add additional staff. You also may want to request a synopsis of the vendor's employee-benefit program or information on employee turnover at its other contracted sites.

Include information requiring quality improvement and utilization review programs that you want the vendor to accomplish. If the vendor will be required to obtain accreditation in a specific period of time, be clear regarding the timetable. Often, the request for proposal allows one or two years for the vendor to achieve accreditation, and may levy a monetary fine for each month beyond this date that accreditation is delayed. Instead of a fine, some jurisdictions make continuation of the contract contingent on obtaining and maintaining accreditation. Language in the contract should be clear, however, so that the vendor is not penalized for delays occasioned by the accrediting agency in conducting a requested survey or in announcing a decision on accreditation. Moreover, the vendor should not be penalized if failure to be accredited is due to violation of standards that are within the control of the correctional agency itself, such as insufficient training of correctional officers.

Provide Sufficient Information on Current Costs

Include information regarding the use of off-site services that will assist the vendor in pricing your contract. Provide information on the number of hospital admissions, average length of stay, number of emergency room and ambulance trips, number of on-site and off-site specialty consults, number of inmates on medication—including psychotropic or AIDS medications. If there is an inmate copayment program for medical services, be sure to describe it and how you expect the vendor to participate in it. If possible, allow prospective vendors to review current contracts that you have in place for hospital or physician services. Be sure that you know when these contracts will expire so that you can provide sufficient cancellation notice to current providers.

Define Pricing-reimbursement Requirements

Define catastrophic limits and any items or services to be excluded from the proposal. For example, some states have excluded the cost of care of inmates on dialysis or of inmates diagnosed with AIDS. Define any performance guarantees, fines, or liquidated damages that will be imposed for nonperformance. Define insurance and performance bond requirements. Check with your legal department for language relating to indemnification and affirmative action.

Define Organizational Capability

List mandatory requirements for vendors, such as corporate stability, experience in the field of correctional health care, amount of professional liability insurance, adequate financial resources, satisfactory client references, experience with similar-sized systems, programs that demonstrate ability to manage health care services, and experience with accreditation standards. Develop a contractor evaluation sheet to tally the results of each vendor's proposal. After the selection committee has evaluated each proposal and tallied the results, it should be clear which vendor will deliver the best health care program to fit the needs of the institution(s).

Factors to Consider in Selection of a Vendor

In selecting a vendor, many jurisdictions consider the lowest bid. The low bid may not always be the wisest selection, as the contractor may have had a previous history of poor performance, be inexperienced in the marketplace, or have hidden costs associated with the proposal.

In evaluating contractors, several areas should be considered: corporate experience, innovativeness of the program, staffing plan and personnel issues, references of prior clients, history of lawsuits, fines incurred, adequacy of the company's finances and insurance, bid price, and, of course, the quality of the technical proposal.

Corporate Experience

The provision of health services is a service industry. Generally, a company is only as good as its management. Therefore, the leadership and qualifications of the corporate as well as regional staff are probably the most important considerations in selecting a vendor. Other evaluation criteria include prior experience in the industry and experience with correctional systems of similar size, experience in obtaining accreditation, corporate stability, and adequacy of the company's financial statements and malpractice insurance.

One should be cautioned not to place too much emphasis on size or longevity in the industry. The argument can be made that while Ford may have started the auto industry, look what GM did with it; or that while Pan-Am might have been flying for sixty years, the airline went bankrupt several years ago. Does it really matter if a firm was the first or the largest in the industry if they are financially unstable today or provide poor service?

It is not uncommon for established firms in this industry to argue that vendors must have five years of corporate experience to qualify to bid on certain RFPs. They even have sent sample RFPs to counties and states on their company diskettes listing such requirements. The only purpose served by a mandatory-experience requirement is to create an artificial barrier to entry for new firms wishing to enter the marketplace and thereby to reduce competition. Thus, for new ideas and competitive bids, the RFP process should be open to all interested firms.

Technical Proposal

The technical proposal should show innovative approaches to solve the agency's problems and not be a "rehash" of the RFP document. It should provide a clear description of the services provided as well as support programs, for example, continuous quality improvement, utilization review, and special needs. The proposal should be compliant with the terms of the RFP with no unnecessary exceptions or exclusions.

Staffing Plan

The staffing plan should be adequate in terms of the number and mix to meet the needs of the correctional system. It should discuss the integration of current staff, recruitment plan for new staff, benefit package, and hourly wages.

References

Both written and telephone references of current and prior contracts should be contacted. Areas to be considered may include the satisfaction of current clients, number of renewals, and reasons for contracts lost. Ask clients to identify the strengths and weaknesses of their current providers, if they would consider extending their current contract, if they have saved money by privatizing their medical care, if the incidence of litigation has been reduced, and if and how they have benefitted from privatizing.

Risk Management

Be sure to evaluate a contractor's litigation history. It is important to know the number of lawsuits or settlements that a contractor has been involved with for a defined (two-to-five-year) period of time. Other information used to evaluate risk management would include whether the vendor has prematurely terminated contracted services, the number of fines or penalties incurred over $10,000 for issues relating to service delivery or staffing vacancies, and instances where liquidated damages or performance bonds were invoked.

Price

Price is certainly a factor in the purchasing of medical services. In addition to total price, consider future year costs, catastrophic limits, per diem costs for increases in inmate populations, and exclusions.

Contract Monitoring

The vendor needs to be held accountable for the effectiveness and quality of a health care delivery system. Determining quality of care in a correctional environment is beset with many problems because routine indicators of quality are difficult to evaluate. The self-limiting nature of illness in an ambulatory setting and difficulties in defining an episode of illness have hindered comparable methods for review. Additionally, the provision of appropriate patient care relies on the judgments of an array of professionals whose decisions are difficult to codify and regulate. Monitoring patient care requires well-trained and experienced professionals and the development and establishment of relevant criteria to be used to monitor the contract.

Effective contract monitoring requires balance in the procedures and reports that are established. Jurisdictions should not exert so much control that they inhibit autonomy of the contractor's providers to make sound medical decisions in a cost-efficient and effective manner. Overly stringent penalties and monitoring criteria can be self-defeating. Contractors can spend so much time responding to reports that their programs never are developed fully. Conversely, a jurisdiction cannot afford to be so lax in supervision that services decline, staffing is never at the specified level, and costs accrue.

Create Effective Monitoring Procedures

Single Monitor versus Regional Monitor

Both Pennsylvania and Illinois use a partial contractual model.[44] These may be regional contracts, or the state department of corrections may retain some services such as dental, medical records, and so forth. In each of these state systems, the contract-compliance monitor is a correctional health care administrator who is also the chief health care administrative employee in the institution. This individual is employed by the state and maintains a dual responsibility as contract monitor and institutional health administrator.

In New Jersey, a different regional approach is used. Sixteen contract monitors were selected to monitor various prisons throughout the state. The monitors report to a central office medical department and have no responsibility for health care administration.

Other states have chosen to select a single contract monitor. Examples of this approach occur in Delaware, Idaho, and Wyoming, where there are only a few facilities contracted and the inmate population is small.

It is essential that whatever approach, few or many monitors, is taken, the monitor(s) be familiar with the contract and all vendor documentation. Reports that routinely should be submitted to a monitor include employee and subcontractor time sheets; credentials of all employees and subcontractors; a monthly log delineating inmate health care grievances and the contractor's response; program information regarding new programs or existing programs, for example, substance abuse, telemedicine, or annual testing for tuberculosis; meeting minutes of the CQI committee, staff and administrative meetings; documents relating to all critical incidents and mortality; and utilization data regarding service usage, such as the number of inmates hospitalized, number of sick call visits, emergency room trips, or outpatient or on-site appointments for specialty services. The monitor also should have access to all legal documents, subpoenas, lawsuits, and so forth, and all inmate medical records.

---

[44] Harry Schuman, *loc. cit.*; and Tim Ringler, *loc. cit.*

Performance Guarantees

Performance Bond

To encourage compliance with specified performance standards, contractors frequently are required to post a performance bond. The performance bond can be posted from a surety company, or can be a certified check or letter of credit. The performance bond is used as a means to guarantee service delivery. It usually is estimated based on the bid for the first year of services.

Jurisdictions have varied in the amount of the bond required. Some require no performance bond; others insist on 100 percent bonding. It is recommended that a 20-25 percent bond be required of all contractors proposing full-service contracts for total state systems or large jails over 1,000 bed capacities. In the event that the contractor defaults, this would allow the agency three to four months of funding either to return to self-operation or to select another vendor.

Penalty Provisions

Other municipalities have instituted penalty or fine provisions for contractual deficiencies. Pennsylvania contracts have penalty provisions for staffing deficiencies, missed sick call, failure to produce records in a certain amount of time, and slow referrals to a specialist. Massachusetts has a $50,000 penalty for failing to achieve NCCHC accreditation for each state institution within a certain time frame. Maryland has a several-page fine schedule incorporated into its contract. Fines range from $100 for failing to file documents in a timely manner to $1,000 for default on certain service delivery issues.[45]

While it is necessary that the agency be able to exert some control over a vendor's performance, and certainly a financial incentive is a very strong one, if the contractor spends so much time writing exception reports or correcting or disputing fine schedules, the health care program surely will suffer. Pinellas County Jail has had contract medical care since the early 1980s. In January 1997, the jail reissued an RFP for inmate health care and only three vendors responded. Several vendors stated that the monitoring tactics used by the county were so severe and intrusive that they did not want to do business with the county.[46]

Liquidated Damages

Other states, such as Delaware,[47] include provisions for liquidated damages. If staffing specified in the contract falls below a certain level, or if the contractor terminates a service without sufficient notice, the contractor is given thirty days from the

---

[45] Review of RFP Document, State of Maryland (1997).

[46] Telephone interview with several private sector firms, and Janice Hill (February, 1997). The firms requested that their identities not be disclosed.

[47] Telephone interview with Larry Sussman, Delaware Department of Corrections, Department of Administration (March, 1997) and review of Delaware RFP.

date of notification to rectify the deficiency. If after thirty days, the department is not satisfied that the contractor has resolved the deficiency, the contractor agrees to pay the department a sum of $2,000 per calendar day for each day that the contractor provides services that are unacceptable to the department. Broad-based fine schedules such as this can lead to trouble because the contract has not defined what an unacceptable level of service is. The criteria used for penalties must be clear and objective, not arbitrary or political. Ideally, the agency and the vendor might develop a collaborative, problem-solving approach prior to a threshold at which penalty options become operative, and if they are unable to reach this point, some provision for arbitration could be established.

Accreditation

In the last two years, the majority of requests for proposals that have been issued have had a requirement that the contractor achieve accreditation. There are four sets of national standards that are used to evaluate correctional health care in the United States: those of the American Correctional Association (ACA), the American Public Health Association (APHA), the Joint Commission on Accreditation of Health Care Organizations (JCAHO), and the National Commission on Correctional Health Care (NCCHC). Of these, the ACA, NCCHC, and JCAHO offer accreditation programs. Other professional associations such as the American Nurses Association and the American Psychiatric Association also have developed standards for their areas of expertise, but the four sets noted previously are more comprehensive in covering a broader range of health services to be provided.

The standards of ACA and of NCCHC are designed for specific use in jails, prisons, or juvenile facilities. The standards have been developed for use in various correctional facilities, and size differences and types of facility are factors taken into account.

Regardless of what standards are followed, accreditation promotes an efficient and well-managed health care delivery system, deters lawsuits, and assures incarcerated individuals that appropriate health care is being provided. Accreditation also has had the added benefit of providing the agency with a sense of achievement and the satisfaction of knowing that it is rated among the best in the nation. In a contractual health care system, accreditation serves as an outside monitor for reviewing the quality of inmate health care. It provides a peer review for the facility—rating the care against nationally accepted standards.[48]

Staffing; Outside Trips

Other performance guarantees that are occasionally found in RFPs relate to vacancy rates or outside trips to specialists. The State of New Jersey required that the contractor would not use more than 10 percent of agency nurses to fill budgeted positions and that the vacancy rate not exceed 25 percent for more than thirty days. If either of these conditions occurred, penalty provisions were invoked.[49]

---

[48] R. Scott Chavez, "Achieving Risk Management Through Accreditation of Health Services," *American Jails* (September-October, 1991).

Other RFPs have requested that contractors decrease the use of outside services by reducing consults and emergency room trips. The State of Pennsylvania required that if six or more inmates required the services of a specialist in a given month and if space and equipment were available, the contractor would make arrangements to bring the specialty service on-site. [50]

[49] Review of RFP document for the State of New Jersey, 95X22764 (1995).

[50] Review of RFP document for the State of Pennsylvania (1993).

DEFINING
APPROPRIATE AND
4 NECESSARY HEALTH
CARE

This chapter is adapted with permission from an article published in the Journal
of Correctional Health Care, *3:1 (Spring 1996), "A Preliminary Model for Determining Limits for Health Care Services," by B. Jaye Anno, Ph.D., CCHP-A; Kenneth L.
Faiver, M.L.I.R., M.P.H.; and Jay K. Harness, M.D., FACS. An earlier version of this
material, "Setting the Standard for Correctional Health Care Services," by Kenneth L.
Faiver, M.L.I.R., M.P.H., in collaboration with B. Jaye Anno, Ph.D. and Jay K. Harness, M.D., FACS, was first delivered by Dr. Harness at the Fourth World Congress
on Prison Health Care in London, England, August, 1988.*

Occasionally, someone asks, "How much health care is an inmate entitled to
receive?" This is not an easy question to answer. Established standards for correctional health care primarily emphasize structural issues involved in the delivery of
care, but do not specifically address the quality of care that must be provided nor the
extent of care that is required. Although courts have given a few hints, they have not
dealt directly with the problem nor are they likely to do so.

The issue is complex because so many variables are involved. How badly is the
care needed? How quickly is it needed? What will happen if it is not provided? How
much does it cost? How long has the inmate had this condition? How did it happen?
How long will the inmate remain in the correctional system? What other treatments
are available, and how effective are they? How much does the patient want the care?
What evidence has the patient shown that he or she will cooperate in the treatment
process? Will the intervention bring significant improvement? How old is the inmate?
Is it a prison or a jail?

Each of these kinds of issues merits serious consideration. Jails, for example, are
short-term facilities and, therefore, usually are not held responsible for more than the
maintenance of patients at their present level of health, stabilization and treatment of
emergencies, relief of pain, avoidance of loss of limb or function, and prevention of
contagion. Prison systems, on the other hand, must do more. They must invest in the
restoration of preexisting conditions when this can be expected to lengthen life,
improve (or prevent loss of) function, or significantly affect the quality of life.

Because resources are limited, priorities must be set. In a sense, the first priority service for any correctional system is intake health screening. Actually, this is a

prerequisite for service. By knowing what health problems enter through the front door, a system can know what services will be required and who will need them.

This chapter will not provide precise or definitive answers, but will approach the issues by discussing criteria for decision makers to consider in determining whether a particular health service should be provided in a specific case.

Universal Issues

Adequate health care services are essential for all elements of society in all parts of the world. These services are equally important to inmates of jails, prisons, and juvenile facilities. Receiving health care is as fundamental as obtaining food, clothing and shelter. Health care, or its absence, never must be used as part of the inmate's punishment.

Given the universal requirement for health care, certain basic standards and norms related to those services must apply equally in and out of correctional facilities. These primarily have to do with the fundamental ethical principles of beneficence[1] and autonomy.

The norm of *beneficence* requires the medical system to intervene to do some good for the patient and does not allow it to cause intentional harm. Thus, it will provide those specific services which correspond to the contemporary[2] standard of professional practice, consistent with the wishes and condition of the patient. It will do so in a manner (quality) which is also in keeping with the contemporary standard of practice. Because it will do no harm to the patient, the medical intervention will respect the patient's *dignity* (in other words, causing no unnecessary embarrassment), protect the patient's *privacy* (including, safeguarding the confidentiality of the patient's medical record), honor the patient's *liberty* (choosing the least-restrictive mode of management), and ensure the patient's *safety* (achieving a safe and sanitary treatment setting to avoid undue risk of infection or other harm).

The norm of *autonomy* respects the decision-making capabilities of the patient. The medical procedure will be performed only if the patient has given informed consent. Therefore, the patient is entitled to truthful information about the condition, diagnosis, and treatment plan, and has a right to participate in determining treatment

---

[1] The term *beneficence*, as used here, includes both its positive aspect (the norm of providing a benefit) and its double-negative aspect, sometimes called *nonmaleficence* (the norm of avoiding causation of harm).

[2] *Contemporary*, for the standards of professional practice evolve over time and, to some extent, from place to place. The standards depend on scientific and technological advances; on the ability to process, disseminate, and use information; and on the availability of skilled practitioners. Some aspects of the professional standards of practice are influenced by culture. Economic factors also can shape the standards, a process much in evidence today as third-party payers apply the principles of managed care and as incentive shifting occurs in the medical marketplace. The amount which a society can afford to pay is relevant.

decisions. It likewise recognizes the right of a competent person to refuse any unwanted and unlawful touching of his or her person.

Inmates are entitled to the same contemporary standard of medical, dental, surgical, psychiatric, nursing, and other professional practices of care as are noninmates. For example, management of diabetes would be essentially the same, whether or not the patient were incarcerated. In the United States and in most industrialized countries, a "contemporary standard" for the management of diabetes and its known complications has evolved. This is true of most medical, dental, and psychiatric maladies. In many countries, the failure of care professionals to meet an acceptable contemporary standard constitutes negligence and malpractice. No convincing ethical or legal argument can be made that would justify denying to correctional inmates a level of health care that is equivalent to the contemporary community standard.

The inmate also must be considered to have the same fundamental rights as any noninmate patient. This includes, for example, respect for the inmate's dignity as a human being, as well as the right to receive care in a safe and clean environment with an adequate amount of space and in an area that is sufficiently equipped to allow the delivery of a contemporary quality of care. The qualifications and credentials of the providers must meet the same licensing and certification standards as are required in the community. Contemporary health care cannot be provided in a substandard setting with inadequate space or equipment or by unqualified providers.

The entitlement to receive health care is basic, just as is the right to receive adequate information about one's health condition, diagnosis, and treatment plan. Adequate informed consent is essential prior to granting permission for an invasive or operative procedure. Inmates must be allowed to participate actively in the informed consent process just like any private patient in the free world. Further, any competent patient has the right to refuse a procedure or treatment. This is challenged in the noncorrectional setting only if there is any question about the patient's ability to make a competent decision, and not merely because someone in authority may not happen to agree with that decision. Inmates must have this same right. A reaffirmation of the universal health care issues just discussed is essential to ensuring that inmates receive adequate and dignified care.

Conceptual Framework for Decision Analysis

Resources available for providing health care in correctional settings are limited. In a free market economy, scarce resources are allocated according to the price consumers are willing to pay. An insurance mechanism, affording benefits to enrollees, may be available to offset the out-of-pocket costs to the consumer. Some governments provide health care to all their citizens on an entitlement basis through a national health service. In the United States, many who cannot afford private health services and do not have insurance are aided through a system of welfare or other social assistance.

Prisoners, generally, are recognized as having a right to receive health care, their entitlement resting on a common law theory that the warder is responsible for the life, safety, and well-being of the ward. In the United States, there is a constitutional obligation to provide health care to prisoners who are deprived of the opportunity to seek care on their own. To be "deliberately indifferent" to their serious medical needs is a violation of the Eighth and Fourteenth Amendments to the Constitution.[3]

Not every request that a prisoner makes for a health service must be granted. How much care should be provided, as a matter of good public policy, is the subject of this chapter. The guidelines described here are not founded, in every case, in law or enforceable by a court. They do represent, however, what is becoming recognized as the proper level of care by many qualified expert groups, agencies, and individuals; namely, care which generally is recognized as being important or necessary in the free community. Of course, the quality of whatever care is provided must be in keeping with contemporary standards of professional practice.

One could attempt to construct an exhaustive list of procedures and treatments to which prisoners are entitled under any conceivable circumstances. It may be more helpful, however, to develop a conceptual framework to consider factors that influence the selection of services that will be provided. This framework begins by describing a spectrum of services, ranging from those that ought to be provided to those that appropriately may be denied. In between these extremes are diagnostic and therapeutic procedures that arguably should be provided to prisoners or whose acceptability depends on one or more relevant circumstances. For example, almost no one would withhold emergency first aid, but few would believe that prisoners are entitled to cosmetic hair transplants or face lifts at public expense.[4] There may be disagreement, however, on whether a prisoner should be afforded open-heart surgery or a kidney transplant.

After describing characteristics of the spectrum of care and providing a few illustrations, a model is presented for the decision-making process. The model attempts to cope with the multiple factors that can or should influence the outcome, sometimes independently and sometimes in combination.

A Spectrum of Care

Imagine a spectrum or range of health care interventions. At one end are those to which an inmate is *always* entitled. An example would be emergency treatment to save a life or limb or to alleviate severe pain. Giving first aid to a burn victim, setting a broken limb, cleaning and dressing a wound also illustrate interventions of this type. Other examples might be treatment of acute and severe psychiatric illness; an emergency appendectomy; gall bladder surgery; medication for chronic conditions like hypertension, diabetes, or epilepsy; and emergency dental care to relieve pain. These are represented in the zone labeled "always" in Figure 4-1.

Those items *usually* recognized as services to which prisoners are entitled are psychological counseling, group therapy, prosthetic limbs and orthotic devices, dental fillings, hernia repair, orthopedic surgery, physical therapy, renal dialysis, a CAT scan

---

[3] *Estelle v. Gamble*, 429 U.S. 97 (1976).

[4] Thus, it is clear that not every medical procedure which is technologically possible or which is commonly performed in free society is obligatory for prisoners.

or magnetic resonance imaging (MRI) for certain symptoms, and preventive interventions and immunizations. When these services safely can be deferred for a time,[5] the expected length of incarceration becomes particularly relevant to the decision process. For these, a somewhat greater need is required, relative to cost, to justify the intervention. These services are depicted in Figure 4-1 in the area labeled "usually."

A third group of procedures *rarely* is approved for prisoners, or at least is subjected to greater scrutiny and review. These include very expensive procedures as well as those of doubtful necessity. Examples are bone-marrow and other major organ transplants, certain plastic and reconstructive surgeries, and completion of transsexual surgery. Here the need (and expected benefit) must be recognized as very great to justify the procedure, as illustrated in Figure 4-1.

FIGURE 4-1. LIKELIHOOD OF APPROVAL FOR MEDICAL CARE DECISIONS: EFFECT OF *COST* VERSUS *NECESSITY* OF CARE

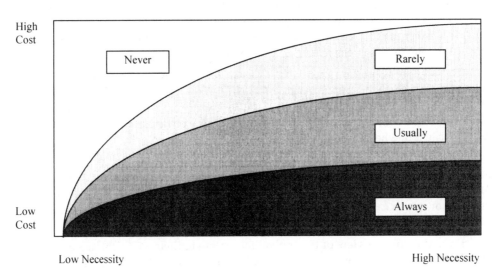

Finally, there is close to universal consensus that prisoners are *never* entitled to certain procedures at public expense. Examples include purely cosmetic or luxury treatments, initiation of transsexual surgery,[6] or expensive alternatives to conventional treatment—such as gold crowns.

---

[5] Medical procedures that safely can be deferred for a time often are called "elective procedures." Another common, but very different, meaning of "elective" signifies "of doubtful necessity." Since this chapter is about the determination of medical *necessity* rather than *urgency*, the term "elective" will not be used. Should the term arise in deliberations regarding what services to provide, its meaning should be clarified to avoid miscommunication.

[6] Though this is regarded by many lay persons as frivolous, the justifying medical rationale for excluding this service from the benefit package usually has more to do with its lack of urgency and the great difficulty of assessing the success of the initial procedures.

Undoubtedly, there is some level of need that is so trivial as not to be required, no matter how low the cost. Likewise, there is perhaps some intervention whose cost is so high that it would not be provided, however great the need. Hence, the idealized curves in Figure 4-1 begin somewhat to the right of the origin and gradually decrease in slope over their relevant range.

Cost usually is measured in dollars or can be translated into dollars. For example, the cost of guarding a patient at an outside hospital is as real an expenditure as the hospital bill or the doctor's bill. Other less tangible costs also can be incorporated into this model, at least conceptually, such as the cost of the potential harm to society from the escape of a violent prisoner during a hospital stay.

Some may object to a model that allows a tradeoff between cost and need on grounds that human life cannot be valued in dollars, or that the courts have ruled that a state is not excused from providing required care simply because it would be too costly. The response to the first objection is that the cost versus need tradeoff is made every day by all of us, often implicitly. A smoker decides to risk cancer for the present enjoyment of tobacco. An insurance company covers certain benefits and not others. A society quickly would go bankrupt if it were bound to spend any amount whatever—even millions of dollars per death averted—on behalf of each of its citizens. In answer to the second objection, the court rulings in these instances were far down the scale of costliness from the level envisioned here as an outer boundary.

The argument can be phrased in different terms. How much should be paid at the margin to achieve various levels of benefit? For example, while one willingly might pay a million dollars to extend a life by twenty years, how much would the same person be willing to pay if the expected benefit were an additional year? Or one week? Or just one hour?

Where costs are high, a greater benefit must be expected to justify the proposed intervention. But from whose perspective should costs and benefits be considered? Among the possibilities are the perspectives of the individual patient, of the attending provider or health care delivery system, and of society in general (whose representative is the government agency charged with incarceration).

From the point of view of the individual inmate patient, often the desired benefit will be a cure or improvement as far as is technically achievable, no matter what the cost. In contrast, in free society, there comes a point at which most people reach a balance between the marginal benefit to be gained from additional units of treatment and the marginal cost (or price) of that treatment. At some point, the patient who must bear all or a portion of the cost of the treatment finds that the additional care "is simply not worth it."[7]

From the perspective of the provider or the correctional health care agency, the objective may be to accomplish maximum good for the patient and also to protect oneself from liability (if sued for deprivation of necessary care). Thus, whether out of benevolence or as a defensive practice of medicine, there may be a tendency to overtreat. On the other hand, the health care providers in a jail or prison usually are given a limited budget and, therefore, have an incentive to be cost conscious. In attempting to use available dollars to provide essential services to the greatest number of prisoners, they necessarily engage in some rationing of care.[8]

Finally, there is the societal perspective. In part, it comprises the summed perspective of all of its members, even if these are not always consciously expressed. But more, it calculates the overarching good of the society, even though this might be in conflict with the summed good of individuals, a point well illustrated by the paradox of the commons: what is best for all in general may be less than what each would want individually.[9] Society necessarily considers tradeoffs involving tax increases or foregone social improvements in this context.

The decision-making process is considered here primarily from the point of view of society, which recognizes the importance of strategies that foster good public policy. Fundamental to this approach is the belief that society is not well served if the rights and the basic needs of prisoners are ignored. In fact, as previously indicated, it is sound public policy to accord prisoners the quantity and quality of care that is consistent with contemporary standards of professional practice in the free community.

Factors That Should *Not* Influence the Decision on Medical Care

Certain factors should be regarded as irrelevant to the decision process. These are shown in Table 4-2 and include such matters as gender, race, ethnic origin, nature of the crime, behavior in prison, contributory behavior, and celebrity status. It should be obvious that gender, race, and ethnic origin ought not be considered at all in determining whether to treat a prisoner. To do so would be unjust discrimination and a violation of the individual's civil rights.

---

[7] This certainly can be said of inmates as well, since nonmonetary costs also temper the demand for health services. For prisoners, just as for free-world patients with full health benefit coverage through an insurance plan, the time spent and the inconvenience incurred in seeking and receiving care are real "costs." Sometimes, treatment brings its own discomforts or hazards. One can acquire an infection from another patient in the hospital, or one could die from a reaction to the anesthetic during surgery. There are times when people object to the "probing" or the "guessing" of doctors and choose more conservative or "natural" remedies or even no treatment at all. People can resent the assault on their privacy that certain types of health care involve. These disincentives to seek care are operative among inmates as well, serving effectively to curb a theoretically limitless desire to avail themselves of every possible treatment option. There may be, in correctional settings, a countervailing secondary gain from the receipt of health services because of the opportunity for social contact with other inmates, nurses, and so forth. This perceived "nonhealth care" benefit is greatest in those institutions which severely curtail prisoner movement.

[8] The budgetary limitations need not be regarded as absolute. In meritorious cases of extraordinary need, the health care provider may seek a supplemental appropriation or other adjustment from the funding authority.

[9] The reference is to the practice in times past for farmers to graze their cattle in the commons, a publicly owned plot of land in the center of the village. While each farmer would desire to bring additional animals to graze on this free land, each also knew that overgrazing soon would render the land worthless to anyone. Consequently, a form of rationing had to occur, whereby each one would choose to bring a limited number of cows, thus ensuring the perpetuity of this benefit.

There may be some disagreement concerning the other factors. In keeping with the norm of beneficence, denial of medical care never should be used, nor even appear to be used, as a punishment. Incarceration, itself, is the punishment imposed by law. The patient's behavior in prison—even hostile, reprehensible, or threatening behavior—should not be considered in making a decision to approve or deny a needed therapeutic procedure. The correctional agency ought not to withhold, or threaten to withhold, health care services as a punishment for rule violations or as a deterrent to such behavior by prisoners. Accordingly, the model prisoner and the prisoner in disciplinary segregation should be assessed equally as candidates for a needed medical intervention. In fact, it is perhaps best when the decision maker is unaware of the criminal history or the prison behavior of the patient.

FIGURE 4-2. FACTORS THAT SHOULD NOT INFLUENCE THE DECISION

• Gender	• Behavior in prison
• Race or ethnic origin	• Contributory behavior
• Nature of crime	• Celebrity status

Some suggest that the correctional system appropriately may withhold treatment to persons who have brought upon themselves the seeds of their own illness or injury. Thus, the ravages of alcohol or substance abuse, of sexual promiscuity, of tobacco, or of self-mutilating behavior might be given a lower priority for treatment than would an illness for which the patient is without blame. This moralistic and self-righteous line of reasoning is deficient on at least two counts. First, since it is not generally the practice in the community to determine whether the patient is at fault before providing or paying for treatment, it has no place in the prison. Second, true culpability is not easily determined in many cases, since all of the relevant and possibly mitigating circumstances cannot be known.[10] In fact, self-injurious behavior may be a consequence of mental illness. Self-inflicted injuries sometimes are managed with a conservative therapy until the propensity for repetition of the injury is reduced. This is a narrow, but appropriate, exception to the position proposed here. For example, an inmate who frequently swallows foreign objects may be examined and then closely observed for any signs of an impending problem, rather than be rushed each time to the emergency room for an endoscopic or surgical procedure.

The issue of celebrity status or notoriety poses a somewhat thorny problem because the decision maker knows that the eye of the world—magnified and perhaps distorted through the media—will be watching closely. There will be political

---

[10] On the other hand, a current heavy smoker appropriately might be very low on the priority list for receiving a lung transplant because, as will be shown, the probability of successful outcome of treatment is a relevant factor in the decision.

ramifications. If costly care is given, it will be labeled an "extravagance." If it is denied, it will be called "inhumane." The press will scurry to discover how many other inmates have received this type of care. From both an ethical and a pragmatic standpoint, the facility should try to be as neutral as possible about the identity of the recipient.

Factors Influencing the Decision to Intervene

A variety of factors can affect the decision to provide or deny a particular health benefit. Figure 4-3 shows the factors that should be taken into consideration. They include the following: urgency of the procedure; necessity of the procedure; expected remaining duration of incarceration; probability of successful outcome of treatment, including the risk of adverse side effects; expected functional improvement as a result of the intervention; patient's desire (expressed or implied) for the intervention; whether the intervention is for a preexisting condition; whether the intervention is a continuation of previous treatment for a chronic condition or is the initiation of a new course of long-term treatment; and cost. The decision maker must determine how much weight or value to assign to each factor.

Urgency. An emergency or urgent procedure, in contrast to a deferrable procedure, is one that cannot be delayed without risk of incurring additional harm to the patient or reducing the likelihood of a successful outcome later. Of itself, it does not address the necessity or importance of the procedure. For example, a patient may experience moderate pain (for example, from a thrombosed hemorrhoid) which could be alleviated quickly through treatment or which would spontaneously remit after some days. In such a case, the treatment would be described as urgent, though low in terms of necessity, since life, limb, or function is not at risk and severe pain is not involved.

Necessity of Procedure. Necessity can be viewed on an ordinal scale. At one extreme, the intervention may be a life or death matter that assumes the highest importance. At the next level, the intervention may be intended to save a major limb or organ (such as an arm, a leg, or an eye) or to alleviate severe pain and distress.

Farther down the scale is the situation in which a minor limb or organ (such as a finger or toe) is at risk or the intervention is intended to alleviate moderate pain or distress. Examples might include corneal transplant or cataract surgery for a patient with another sighted eye, surgical repair of a hernia that also could be relieved by use of a truss, knee surgery to relieve moderate pain and improve ambulation, or provision of a hearing aid or an artificial limb. Finally, at the lowest end of the scale are situations where the intervention is of trivial therapeutic benefit or is purely cosmetic in nature, such as surgical removal of a tattoo.

A reasonable reference point for determining generally whether a procedure is unnecessary or experimental may be whether Medicaid and/or Medicare covers the procedure for its beneficiaries in the state.

Expected Length of Incarceration. The urgency factor is particularly relevant for jails, since many prisoners are incarcerated for only a few hours or days. If the expected length of stay is short, a procedure of low necessity and/or of low urgency legitimately may be deferred until the prisoner is able to obtain care in the free world at no cost to the correctional system.

Probability of a Successful Outcome. A correctional agency, like a third-party payer,[11] usually is more willing to cover a treatment that has a high likelihood of achieving the desired successful outcome than one that will probably not succeed or one that, even though successful, will leave the patient with other serious adverse consequences. To recognize this factor, the expectation of an overall successful outcome, considering all of the risks and potential adverse side effects, might be rated as excellent, good, guarded, or poor. As an example, a bone marrow transplant assessed as having a 50 percent probability of a five-year survival is much more defensible than the same costly procedure for a person whose likelihood of even a one-year survival is between 5 and 10 percent.

The patient's history of compliance with prescribed treatment in the past sometimes can serve as a predictor of future noncompliance, and may be considered in evaluating the probability of a successful outcome. The potential effects of the delay of treatment on the eventual outcome are also important, but these are considered in the context of urgency.

FIGURE 4-3. FACTORS INFLUENCING THE DECISION TO PROVIDE MEDICAL CARE

1. Urgency of procedure

2. Necessity of procedure

3. Expected remaining duration of incarceration

4. Probability of successful outcome of treatment, including the risk of adverse side effects

5. Expected functional improvement as a result of the intervention

6. Patient's desire (expressed or implicit) for the intervention

7. Whether the intervention is for a pre-existing condition

8. Whether the intervention is a continuation of previous treatment for a chronic condition, or is the initiation of a new course of long-term treatment

9. Cost

Expected Functional Improvement. If the proposed intervention is expected to restore substantial or complete function to the patient, there is added reason to support the procedure. For example, a total hip replacement may enable an elderly prisoner to ambulate and avoid confinement to a wheelchair. On the other hand,

---

[11] Such as a health insurance carrier or a health maintenance organization (HMO).

extensive measures to avoid amputation of a permanently paralyzed limb may be less justifiable. Care should be taken to ensure that this variable is measuring something more than what already is incorporated in the probability of a successful outcome or in the necessity of the procedure.

Patient's Desire for Treatment. Just as the right of a competent patient to refuse treatment should be respected, so also the intensity of desire of the competent patient to receive treatment can be a relevant factor for the decision maker. A patient making an informed decision, considering the advantages and risks of a given intervention, eagerly may desire to receive the treatment. Another patient may give consent to the treatment, but remain substantially indifferent.

The likelihood of successful outcome may be influenced by the patient's desire for the treatment. Cooperation and compliance with the prescribed treatment plan can affect the outcome significantly.

Preexisting Condition. Some persons have advanced as a general premise that the correctional system has an obligation to maintain the prisoner in as healthy a state as when he or she entered prison, after adjustment for aging and natural deterioration, but that it has no obligation to improve health or to restore health that was lost before incarceration. It is proposed that this position be modified by taking into consideration whether the condition, if preexisting, was known by the patient and had been long neglected. A condition that previously existed only in subclinical or mild form and, after the patient is in prison, is discovered or progresses to the point of causing significant pain or disability, should not be regarded as preexisting. In using this criterion, consideration also should be given to cases that were untreated in the community because of inability to obtain effective access to health care, whether owing to ignorance, lack of resources, or other reasons.

Preexisting conditions also should be considered for treatment when the anticipated benefit is the alleviation of severe pain or the restoration of ability to perform activities of daily living, such as walking, feeding, bathing, and toileting.

If the condition did commence in the institution, a further question arises about liability for the condition. As an employer is responsible for treatment associated with a job-related injury, there should be no question about treating an injury sustained through no fault of the patient while in the facility. This may be due to willful or careless action by another inmate or an officer, or may be accidental. Contributory negligence by the patient may be a mitigating factor.

Chronicity of Care. The intervention may be a single, one-time episode for an acute condition, after which the patient is expected to resume normal good health. At the other extreme, the condition may be chronic, and life-long care may be required. This factor can become important in one of two ways. First, if the prisoner arrives with a chronic illness currently under treatment, it would be difficult for the prison to deny continuation of the treatment except when medically contraindicated. An example might be an HIV-seropositive patient receiving antiretroviral therapy or a cancer patient undergoing radiation therapy. Second, the decision maker may be considering whether to initiate a long and costly course of treatment.

It often happens that the whole cost and course of treatment cannot reasonably be anticipated at the beginning. Decisions are made one stage at a time. Complications and relapses lead to more expenditures and new decisions. These must be made on the basis of altered prognosis and future costs, without looking retrospectively to the costs already incurred.

Cost. The cost of the intervention is appropriately taken into consideration when approving or disapproving a procedure. Given that the intervention is desirable on medical or therapeutic grounds, the overall benefits must be commensurate with the cost incurred, as a matter of good public policy. It is possible to describe costs in a variety of ways. Here, seven ranges of cost are suggested: (1) exceedingly high, (2) very high, (3) high, (4) moderate, (5) low, (6) very low, and (7) trivial. The administrator also should consider whether the cost of the intervention will be offset by direct savings (for example, if hepatitis B vaccination were determined to be cost effective considering direct medical care and legal costs which eventually may be avoided thereby, or if a renal transplant were deemed less costly in the long run for a lifer than many years of hemodialysis).

Other Factors

Several other factors are not explicitly included in the model because they tend to duplicate matters already incorporated in one or more of the factors discussed. These include:

Expected Duration of Treatment. If the intervention is seen as a single episode of care, rather than as the beginning of a long and involved sequence of treatments, the decision maker is more apt to approve. This factor is, to an extent, a combination of three others that were identified: cost, chronicity, and functional improvement. Therefore, it probably should not be considered separately.

Age and General Health of Patient. All else being equal, it is reasonable to predict more favorable outcomes for a younger patient than for an elderly one. Similarly, expected outcome and useful functioning are more likely to be improved in the case of a patient who is otherwise generally healthy than for one who suffers from multiple serious maladies. Therefore, while the age and general health of the patient are relevant to the decision maker, the calculus should carefully identify the correct variable of interest to avoid double counting.

Quality of Life. Whether the intervention will appreciably improve or possibly detract from the quality of life for the patient is a most important consideration. This, too, however, may be redundant with other factors explicitly included in the model, such as functional improvement, the patient's desire for the intervention, and the probability of successful outcome. Therefore, it is not appropriately employed as a separate factor in the analysis.

Conclusions

This preliminary model of criteria for decision makers is presented to assist in weighing the appropriate criteria for determining whether to provide a particular type of health care in a specific case. Ultimately, it may be possible to assign numerical values to the salient factors to improve the usefulness of the model. The input of correctional health colleagues and others is needed to refine the model and improve its utility. In the same way that national standards for correctional health care evolved through a deliberative and inclusive process, so, too, consensus is needed in deciding how much health care is enough.

There is already a growing recognition in the correctional health care community of the importance of striving toward a consensus policy on medical necessity. [12] Although each jurisdiction could attempt to reach its own definition, it may be difficult to defend and explain the differences. Why, for example, does one jurisdiction "always" treat a deviated septum or an elective hernia while in a nearby state this is "never" done?

Armond Start[13] has proposed a structured process for gathering and organizing information prior to reaching a decision. At some point it would involve the completion of a form in the presence of the patient. This questionnaire, illustrated in Figure 4-4, comprises a set of questions to assist the decision maker in approving very significant expensive technical diagnostic studies or ordering expensive but nonurgent procedures.

FIGURE 4-4. EVALUATION FOR APPROVAL OF A MAJOR MEDICAL PROCEDURE

1. What medical evaluation has been done previously to solve or define this problem?

2. How long has the problem existed?

3. Did the problem exist prior to incarceration?

4. What was done about the problem?[†]

5. Did the problem begin or occur during incarceration?

6. How long before the inmate's release?

7. What is the degree of disability?

8. Can housing or work supervisors validate the degree of disability?

9. How long has the inmate cooperated in the primary management of the problem?

10. Why do you believe the inmate will cooperate in a therapeutic alliance if this problem is addressed?[††]

11. What are the chances for long-term therapeutic success if the problem is treated?

† The question refers to previous efforts made by the patient to take care of the problem.

†† This question seeks to establish whether the patient can be expected to cooperate in the treatment.

---

[12] Roderic Gottula, "The Importance of Defining Medical Necessity," *CorrectCare* (Fall, 1996): 4.

[13] Armond H. Start, "Physician Recommends Format for Determining Necessity," *CorrectCare* (Fall, 1996): 4, 7.

Once completed, the form is to be sent by the primary physician to the medical director of the health care system or to the utilization review committee. If the medical director or utilization review committee renders a negative decision, the patient should have an opportunity to express in writing to the decision maker why the "no" decision is perceived to be wrong. Many issues covered in the form are related directly to the factors proposed in the model, so that it can be a complementary and useful instrument.

The health care provider who must decide whether or not to employ a specific treatment modality is, in reality, making an ethical as well as an administrative decision. Dr. Robert Jones, Medical Director of the Utah Department of Corrections, suggests that the correctional health care provider should consider the following series of questions (See Figure 4-5).

FIGURE 4-5. ROLE OF PROVIDER IN THE DECISION PROCESS

- What factors have I considered in making my judgment?
- Am I acting as an advocate for my patient?
- What are my responsibilities to society at large?
- Would a panel of my peers, faced with the same situation, come to the same conclusion?
- Does the patient have the right to appeal?
- When we meet as citizens on the street, will we both respect and accept the decision that was made?
- Would I accept the decision if the situation were reversed?

While indicating that there is no "good" legal definition of medical necessity, Dr. Jones offers the following components of such a definition. Care is medically necessary when:

(a) it is absolutely essential and indispensable for assuring the health and safety of the patient

(b) it treats a disease or injury or improves a bodily function where a true or meaningful functional impairment exists

(c) it is in accordance with accepted standards of medical practice for diagnosis and treatment

(d) it is not rendered solely for the convenience of the patient or the provider. [14]

_____

[14] *Ibid.*

5 PREVENTING CONTAGION

The author is deeply indebted to Dean P. Rieger, M.D., M.P.H. and Craig Hutchinson, M.D., who suggested many additions and revisions to this chapter, based not only on their medical knowledge, but especially on their considerable experience with correctional health care programs.

Preventing the spread of contagious disease is an important component of the correctional facility's obligation to safeguard the health and welfare of its inmates. It also is a matter of risk management since the correctional institution thereby avoids the potentially large costs of treating preventable illness. In addition, the agency has an obligation to protect its employees, insofar as possible, from disease transmission. There are Occupational Safety and Health Administration (OSHA) regulations on tuberculosis and bloodborne pathogens which must be followed in the workplace. Finally, there is a responsibility to shield the public from infectious diseases.

Basic Principles

Preventing transmission of communicable diseases in correctional settings requires constant vigilance. Conditions typically found in prisons and jails—close or crowded living arrangements, poor hygiene practices, inadequate ventilation, old or faulty plumbing, high-risk behaviors and practices, and the frequent introduction of persons from population groups with high disease prevalence—are factors which, singly and in combination, encourage the spread of infection.

Injection drug users, because of their high-risk behaviors and physical susceptibility, are particularly vulnerable to AIDS and other diseases, most notably tuberculosis and sexually transmitted diseases.[1] There has been a steady increase in the

---

[1] Andrea G. Barthwell and Cynthia L. Gibert, *Screening for Infectious Diseases Among Substance Abusers* (Rockville, Md.: U.S. Department of Health and Human Services, 1993): xiii.

incidence of hepatitis B in the United States, despite the availability of a vaccine since 1982, primarily because of intravenous drug use.[2]

Infectious diseases are commonly transmitted in one of several ways:

- by fecal-oral route (typhoid, amoebic dysentery, hepatitis A)—for example, through faulty plumbing, sewerage problems, and poor hygiene

- by breathing infected air—in other words, airborne contaminated nuclei and droplets (especially tuberculosis, but also many types of meningitis and pneumonia, pharyngeal diphtheria, pertussis, mumps, influenza, rubella, and so forth)

- by animal vector (dengue or malaria)—for example, a mosquito bites an infected person, then this same mosquito bites another person, leaving the disease organism in the blood

- by direct contact with an infected person or by contact with fomites [3] from an infected person (herpes, chicken pox, mumps, measles, and many forms of gastrointestinal, respiratory, skin or wound infections)

- by direct contact with an infected animal or animal droppings (rabies or psittacosis)

- by blood or body fluid transmission or sexual contact, such as human immunodeficiency virus (HIV), hepatitis B, hepatitis C, gonorrhea, or other sexually transmitted diseases

The correctional official need not know all of this in detail, but must have ready access to the basic information. The responsible physician for the facility should be conversant with modes of disease transmission and strategies for prevention. In particular, the physician must know where to obtain quickly the most up-to-date and authoritative information on prevention, identification, and treatment of each specific disease. At times, the answer will not be evident immediately, and it may be necessary to invite outside experts in infectious disease and epidemiology, including the local or state health department, or the Centers for Disease Control and Prevention. Their help may be needed to (1) identify the disease, (2) locate the index case (the infected person who passed the disease to the person in custody who now has the illness), (3) advise how to treat the patient, and (4) recommend strategies to prevent (or minimize) transmission to others (inmates, staff, and the public).

To the trained health professional, the answers to these questions about contagious diseases may be relatively simple, and established means of treatment and prevention may be well known and understood. Other cases can prove more difficult. As

---

[2] Centers for Disease Control and Prevention, "Changing Patterns of Groups at High Risk for Hepatitis B in the United States," *Morbidity and Mortality Weekly Report* (Atlanta, Ga.: U.S. Department of Health and Human Services, July 22, 1988): 429-437.

[3] Saliva, skin fragments, or articles freshly soiled with saliva or mucous discharges.

is to be expected, the earlier the intervention, the more likely the discovered cases can be treated successfully and further transmission prevented.

Most state health departments require, by law, that each new case of certain types of infection be reported promptly so that the health of the public can be protected. Correctional facilities should forge close ties with local or state health departments to ensure that their communicable disease programs are adequate and up-to-date.

Inmates who refuse to be tested for infectious diseases should not be subjected to disciplinary action based solely on that refusal. Where there is a genuine public health threat to other patients or staff, appropriate steps to protect others, which may include involuntary separation (segregation), may be employed.

All inmates should be educated about the benefits to themselves and others from proper and early diagnosis and treatment of infectious diseases. Pre- and post-test counseling services assist inmates in preparing for and completing infectious disease screening and treatment, especially with reference to HIV. Infected patients also should be encouraged to provide information for contact tracing and partner notification.

Tuberculosis

Tuberculosis (TB) is much more contagious than either HIV or hepatitis. While a person may choose to avoid high-risk behaviors to prevent HIV infection, one only has to breathe infected air to contract tuberculosis. The longer the exposure and the closer the quarters, the greater the risk.

After thirty years of declining incidence of tuberculosis, in 1985 the number of new cases began to increase in the United States. There was an 18 percent increase in the number of new cases from 1985 to 1991.[4] This increase occurred primarily in areas with high rates of HIV/AIDS, such as urban areas with a large, poor, minority population, many of whom are injection drug users.

The recent resurgence of tuberculosis in the United States has been particularly noticeable in inmate populations. At least eleven TB outbreaks in prisons were reported between 1985 and 1989. During the 1990s, there were at least three outbreaks of multidrug-resistant tuberculosis in correctional facilities.[5] TB case rates in correctional facilities are six to eleven times the rates in the general community.[6]

A 1994 survey[7] of all state and federal correctional systems and a sample of large city and county jail systems showed that TB infection frequently continues to be

---

[4] Barthwell and Gibert, *Screening for Infectious Diseases*: 35.

[5] Theodore M. Hammett and Lynne Harrold, *Tuberculosis in Correctional Facilities* (Washington, D.C.: National Institute of Justice, 1994): 3f.

[6] "Inmate Screening Process Helps Identify Active Cases," *TB Monitor* (Atlanta, Ga.: American Health Consultants, July, 1994): 103.

[7] Karen Wilcock, Theodore M. Hammett, Rebecca Widom, and Joel Epstein, "Tuberculosis in Correctional Facilities 1994-95," *Research in Brief* (Washington, D.C.: National Institute of Justice, July, 1996): 3, 8.

observed among inmates in correctional facilities, although relatively few of the infected persons developed an active disease. The survey also found that a significant minority of facilities admittedly are not following recommended TB control procedures—despite their own systems' policies calling for such measures.

Tuberculosis is spread primarily by breathing infected airborne particles or droplets which are so small that they remain suspended in the air for long periods of time. An infectious person can spray these particles into the air by coughing, sneezing, or talking. These tiny particles are not screened out by ordinary facial masks. Some high efficiency particulate air (HEPA) masks, however, have filters fine enough to be effective in protecting uninfected individuals from inhaling infectious particles. These masks are not designed to filter exhaled air.

A person can be infected with TB, yet not have an active case of the disease, because bacteria are present but inactive. At a later time in life, however, the bacteria can awaken and cause the active disease. At this point, the patient becomes infectious to others, especially if it is the lungs which are infected (as most frequently is the case).[8] Symptoms of active disease usually include one or more of the following: chronic coughing, night sweats, fever, loss of appetite, or unexplained weight loss.

Screening for Tuberculosis

Presence of the disease usually can be confirmed by a sputum culture or by a chest x-ray. Infection (with or without disease) usually will cause a cellular reaction to a skin test (Mantoux or PPD test) which is placed between layers of skin in the forearm. The size of the induration (hard swelling) around the point of injection, depending on the patient's condition, indicates whether infection has occurred. Health care staff need to recheck an inmate within forty-eight to seventy-two hours after application of this test to measure the peak reaction, or the results may be misleading. To effectively prevent the spread of this potentially fatal disease among inmates and staff, institutional authorities must cooperate by ensuring that this test can be applied as soon as possible after booking or arrival of an inmate, that the inmate is made available for reading the test result between forty-eight and seventy-two hours later, and that opportunity for close contact with other inmates is minimized until the test results are known.

Particularly in large jails, with a large volume rapid turnover of inmates at high-risk for TB, a chest x-ray of each newly admitted person is proving to be a highly effective strategy for rapid identification of persons suspicious for TB. With its new technology, the "mini" chest x-ray unit has only one-tenth of the normal radiation exposure while producing high-resolution pictures.[9]

The U.S. Centers for Disease Control and Prevention (CDC)[10] issued new guidelines for preventing TB in correctional facilities which emphasize the role of screening by symptoms rather than by skin tests alone, and distinguish between short-term correctional facilities in high-risk and low-risk areas of the country.

---

8 Other but rarer sites of infection are the kidneys, bones, and so forth.

9 "Inmate Screening Process Helps Identify Active Cases," *op. cit.*: 103-104.

Symptom screening can be performed quickly by a nurse (or, in small jails, by an officer) and should be incorporated into the checklist documenting the intake health screening that is accomplished within an hour or two after arrival. If symptoms are present, the inmate immediately should be isolated until evaluated. For short-term inmates in high-risk areas, it is well to obtain a chest x-ray even if they are without symptoms. For longer-term inmates in jails serving high-risk populations and in all prisons, a detailed medical history should be obtained for nonsymptomatic inmates, to determine whether a skin test and/or x-ray needs to be performed. While somewhat more complex than previous guidelines, this process provides a much greater likelihood of identifying contagious persons immediately before they can infect others, either in the facility or in the community.

Skin testing provides an early signal to let a system know that transmission is occurring, even if an index case has not been identified. A chest x-ray does not provide this signal and cannot substitute for skin testing. While the chest x-ray serves to identify the active disease, it does not recognize a recently infected person without the disease. Most infected persons do not develop active disease, and thus would not be found by the chest x-ray alone.

Isolation

Key to prevention of further contagion is the prompt and effective isolation of persons suspected or known to have active tuberculosis. This is accomplished in a private room ventilated to the outside and kept at an air pressure less than that of the rest of the facility (so that air does not recirculate from the isolation room into other parts of the facility). Small facilities probably will choose to send such persons to a hospital, but it may be cost effective for larger facilities or systems to provide their own negative-pressure isolation rooms. Pressure of these rooms should be checked at least daily to ensure their proper operation.[11]

Prevention and Treatment

When a person has recently become infected, a preventive antibiotic treatment given regularly over a course of six to twelve months usually can kill the organism and render subsequent active disease unlikely. The commonly used antibiotic is INH,[12] though in some cases a different medication or combination of medications is prescribed. The antibiotic must be taken faithfully for a period of six to twelve months at the frequency and dosage prescribed if it is to be effective. The concern here goes

---

[10] "Prevention and Control of Tuberculosis in Correctional Facilities: Recommendations of the Advisory Committee for the Elimination of Tuberculosis," *Morbidity and Mortality Weekly Report, 45:RR-8* (Atlanta, Ga.: Centers for Disease Control and Prevention, June 7, 1996): 1-27.

[11] "Maintaining Negative Air Pressure Requires Vigilance," *TB Monitor* (Atlanta, Ga.: American Health Consultants, August, 1994): 113-114.

[12] Isoniazid Hydrochloride.

beyond safeguarding the health of the individual patient, and extends to protecting the health of others, as well.

For a second and very cogent reason, strict adherence to the prophylactic (preventive) regimen as prescribed is necessary. When the antibiotics are taken only intermittently or for less than the required period of time, it is possible that not all of the TB bacteria will be killed and that those which remain will be resistant to the antibiotics.

Many patients who have been started on appropriate therapy have failed to complete treatment. Some of these unsuccessfully treated people have become sources of new strains of drug-resistant TB bacteria which are very difficult or impossible to treat. Multidrug-resistant TB has been discovered among inmates in several prisons and is a cause of great concern because it raises the threat of a treatment-resistant disease spreading among a closely confined population of inmates and staff. It strongly is recommended that each administration of TB medications be directly observed by staff to ensure compliance.[13] Inmates who do not take their TB medications regularly should be medically counseled and, if appropriate, the medication should be discontinued.[14]

A thorough investigation should be undertaken promptly to identify all persons who may have come into contact with (or who have been housed near) any person with a suspected or confirmed case of TB. The purpose of this "contact tracing" is to curb further spread of infection within the facility among inmates or staff. The health department should be notified as well, and it becomes the responsibility of that agency to investigate possible contacts the person may have had in the community. Contact tracing generally is conducted in "expanding circles." In other words, those persons who have had the closest contact with the known case are screened first. If none of these are found to have become infected recently, there is no need to investigate further. On the other hand, if some of these are recently infected, a wider "circle" is drawn to include those persons who had been somewhat less exposed to the known case. The scope of the investigation is progressively widened until no further cases are found.

TB control is an essential element in health care in correctional facilities. All correctional facilities, including those in which few TB cases are expected to occur, should designate a person or group of persons who have experience in infection control, occupational health, and engineering to be responsible for the TB infection-control program in the facility. These persons should have the authority to develop, implement, enforce, and evaluate TB infection-control policies.[15]

---

[13] "New TB Guidelines Could Save Prisons Money," *TB Monitor* (Atlanta, Ga.: American Health Consultants, November, 1996): 129.

[14] This prophylactic treatment is elective and, therefore, may not be coerced.

[15] "Prevention and Control of Tuberculosis in Correctional Facilities: Recommendations of the Advisory Council for the Elimination of Tuberculosis," *op. cit.*: 5.

Screening of Staff

TB testing for health care and custody staff of correctional institutions is also a high priority, except perhaps in those areas where there is very low incidence of tuberculosis. Mandatory new employee testing and subsequent annual screening are recommended. There has been some debate over who should pay for the testing of employees: the employee or the department, and if the department, whether the cost should be paid out of institutional or medical appropriations. It can be argued that medical staff and resources of a correctional agency are intended exclusively for care of inmates. Regardless, the occupational exposure of employees to airborne disease is a very real concern. The agency should consider making periodic screening available at no cost to employees, while allowing them an alternative of seeking the care at their own expense from a private source with the obligation of providing timely documentation of the test results to the agency.

A cooperative effort between the Missouri Department of Health and the Missouri Department of Corrections resulted in TB testing of 84 percent of the nearly 6,000 Missouri Department of Corrections' employees within two months' time. Special funding was obtained for this project from the legislature, at no cost to employees. Employees are required to have TB testing as a condition of employment and annually, thereafter.[16]

Human Immunodeficiency Virus and Hepatitis B, C, and D

Human immunodeficiency virus (HIV) suppresses a person's immune system, rendering the patient more likely to contract tuberculosis and other diseases. Infection with the virus often leads to the disease called AIDS (acquired immunodeficiency syndrome). In 1994, AIDS was the leading cause of death among all Americans twenty-five to forty-four years old, outstripping homicide, suicide, heart disease, and cancer.[17]

From 1981 through 1996, a total of 573,800 persons aged thirteen and over with AIDS were reported by state and local health departments.[18] As of December 1995, at least 4,588 cumulative AIDS-related deaths had occurred in prisons and jails, and at least 5,279 AIDS cases had been reported. HIV-positive rates ranged from less than 1 percent to more than 20 percent.[19] There were 923 deaths for AIDS-related conditions

---

[16] "Multi-agency Effort Results in Testing of Correctional Workers," *TB Monitor* (Atlanta, Ga.: American Health Consultants, August, 1994): 1, 11f.

[17] Theodore M. Hammett, Rebecca Widom, et al., 1994 *Update: HIV/AIDS and STDs in Correctional Facilities* (Washington, D.C.: National Institute of Justice, December, 1995): 1.

[18] "Update: Trends in AIDS Incidence, Deaths, and Prevalence—United States, 1996," *Morbidity and Mortality Weekly Report. 46:8* (February 28, 1997): 165.

[19] Anne S. DeGroot, Theodore M. Hammett, and Rochelle Scheib, "Barriers to Care of HIV-Infected Inmates: A Public Health Concern," *The AIDS Reader* (May/June, 1996): 78-79.

among sentenced prisoners under the jurisdiction of state and federal correctional institutions during 1994,[20] representing 30.7 percent of all deaths. In general, the HIV-seropositivity rate among inmates is 1 to 100 times higher than the rate in the general population. Moreover, the rate among women inmates is higher than among men. It is estimated that at least 2 percent of current prison and jail inmates are HIV-infected. In some states, such as, Florida[21] and Michigan,[22] AIDS has become the leading cause of death among prison inmates, ranking ahead of heart disease and cancer.[23]

There have been some very promising recent medical advances in the treatment of this disease, and this has contributed to a noticeable decrease in the AIDS-related death rate nationally.[24] However, management of HIV-positive patients, including those with AIDS, those suffering from various complications related to AIDS, and those who have TB as well as HIV, is extremely complex. In light of ongoing research and new discoveries, the clinical guidelines are being revised constantly. Few practicing physicians are able to remain current in this area unless management of patients with this disease has become a substantial part of their practice or a special area of interest to them. Consequently, correctional administrators should not be surprised to find that their medical director does not always have immediate answers or that the guidelines for management and treatment of these patients frequently are revised. The cost of these newer treatments is also very expensive, and budgets may have to be adjusted to recognize this cost in systems with many HIV-positive inmates.

Because the costs of treatment are so high, some experts[25] have raised a concern that the growing trend toward use of for-profit, managed health care may result in cost-containment strategies which reduce case-finding efforts and which fail to provide treatment consistent with community standards. It is true that the long-term benefits of early intervention with costly medications, in terms of reduced mortality and morbidity, may not be directly felt by correctional officials or by managed care companies which provide health care in prisons and jails, because many of the individuals in their charge are released from custody before they reach the final stages of AIDS. As a result, budgetary pressures, unfortunately, may lead managed care systems as well as correctional agencies to adopt a short-term view, with adverse public and personal health consequences.

To avoid this possibility, some states have included a provision in their contracts with health care providers to exclude costs relating to treatment of HIV and AIDS,

---

[20] Bureau of Justice Statistics, *Sourcebook of Criminal Justice Statistics 1995* (Washington, D.C.: U.S. Department of Justice, 1996): 602.

[21] Donna O'Neal, "Prison to House Inmates with AIDS," *Orlando* (Florida) *Sentinel* (August 24, 1993).

[22] Personal correspondence with Craig Hutchinson, M.D.

[23] Donna O'Neal, *Ibid.*

[24] "Update: Trends in AIDS Incidence, Deaths, and Prevalence—United States, 1996," *Ibid.*

[25] Such as DeGroot, Hammett, and Scheib, *op. cit.*: 78-79, 86.

making these costs a direct pass-through to the state. Alternatively, if managed care systems are to achieve public health objectives, they must be held responsible, through adequate oversight mechanisms, both for access to care and for the quality of service.

Route of Transmission

Unlike tuberculosis, human immunodeficiency virus (HIV)—the infection that leads to acquired immunodeficiency syndrome (AIDS)—and hepatitis B virus (HBV) are not spread by breathing airborne particles or by touching an infectious person. Thus, they cannot be contracted through casual contact or by exposure to coughing or sneezing. Instead, they are transmitted by exposure to body fluids, particularly blood and semen. Because it is impossible to know the identity of all persons who are infected, no matter how thoroughly inmates and staff might have been screened, where blood and body fluids are concerned, everyone should be regarded as infected. In other words, fluids from a known case should be treated no differently than fluids from a person not suspected of having the infection. This principle is called "universal precautions." Emphasis should be placed on avoiding (or minimizing) the exposure to any blood or body fluids. Use of universal precautions is required by the Occupational Safety and Health Administration.

Other disease entities have been identified recently, including hepatitis C virus (HCV) and hepatitis D virus (HDV or delta-hepatitis), which, in most respects, are similar to hepatitis B and often coexist in the same person. In fact, hepatitis D is an "incomplete" virus that requires coinfection with the hepatitis B virus. Because the means of transmission and prevention are nearly identical,[26] what is stated here about HBV applies as well to HCV and HDV, and they will not be discussed in further detail. Note, however, that hepatitis A (HAV), also a viral infection which affects the liver, usually is not fatal and is transmitted by the fecal-oral route rather than by blood and body fluids.

The most common ways of transmitting HIV, HBV and HCV are through sharing contaminated needles and sharps (as is sometimes done by intravenous drug users, or accidentally through skin puncture by a needle used to inject medication or to draw blood from another person, or by being cut with a knife or sharp instrument which has recently cut or pierced another person), and through unprotected sexual intercourse (most especially anal intercourse).

Prevention

If one does not engage in these high-risk behaviors and effectively avoids accidental exposure to blood or body fluids of other persons, there is practically no chance of contracting HIV, HBV, or HCV. But certain high-risk practices must be recognized as occurring among inmates, despite the fact that they represent behaviors already prohibited by regulation or law, namely intravenous drug abuse, homosexual activity, and tattooing. Every facility should employ the following measures to minimize the risk of contagion from these activities:

---

[26] There is some debate about how readily hepatitis C virus is transmitted sexually.

- Thorough training of every security and health care employee in the practice of universal precautions

- Employment of appropriate engineering solutions and protective barriers, whenever applicable, such as gowns, masks, and face shields whenever blood or tissue is likely to be sprayed or spattered, as in some surgical, dental, or emergency room procedures; wearing of gloves while drawing blood, giving injections, or cleaning up blood spills; use of masks [27] with one-way valves for cardiopulmonary resuscitation (CPR)

- Training of staff and inmates in how to avoid HIV and other bloodborne viral disease

- Careful instruction in methods of searching inmates and cells—to avoid being cut on sharp concealed objects ("Look before you feel.")

Other strategies, including politically sensitive approaches, also should be seriously considered as part of a comprehensive strategy to prevent contagion with bloodborne pathogens. The discussion should include both correctional and health care authorities. Support for such extraordinary measures was recently expressed in a position statement of the National Commission on Correctional Health Care. [28]

Some correctional facilities are making condoms available to inmates because they recognize that, even though homosexual behavior is prohibited, the rules sometimes may be broken. This practice also teaches inmates the importance of avoiding unprotected sexual activity when they return to the free community. Infection is much less likely to result if a condom is worn, but still may occur.

The Mississippi and Vermont departments of corrections, for several years, have made condoms available to inmates. Several large jails, including San Francisco, Philadelphia, New York City, and Washington, D.C. also do so. Condom availability also has been instituted in all Canadian federal prisons and in some provincial prisons. In all of these systems, few if any problems have occurred with condoms being used as weapons or for smuggling contraband, as had been predicted. [29] In some cases, the inmates are allowed to purchase unlimited supplies of condoms at the

---

[27] While use of these masks does afford protection from bloodborne pathogens, their primary value is avoidance of exposure to tuberculosis.

[28] "Massive educational efforts should be undertaken to inform all inmates and all staff (correctional and medical) about HIV disease and the steps to be taken to prevent its spread. Further, while the Commission clearly does not condone illegal activity by inmates, the terminal absoluteness of this disease, coupled with the potential for catastrophic epidemic, require (consistent with security) the unorthodox conduct of making available to inmates whatever appropriate protective devices [that] can reduce the risk of contagion." (Adopted by the NCCHC Board of Directors and last amended September 25, 1994).

[29] Hammett, Widom, et al., *op. cit.*: 36.

canteen. Other systems will provide one or two condoms to those receiving health services or attending HIV education sessions. In one case, a physician has a fishbowl filled with condoms on his desk, accessible to his patients during clinic visits.

Some correctional institutions also make bleach available, along with instructions on how to use it. With creative ingenuity, inmates occasionally succeed in gaining access to needles. Note that if any needles are available, their very scarcity increases the likelihood of needle sharing in the correctional institution. The effectiveness of bleach, of course, depends on the care and thoroughness with which it is used. Even though there is evidence that proper cleaning with bleach will reduce the risk of HIV transmission, the only way to be sure is to use new sterile equipment each time. Thus, the CDC recommends use of bleach only when no other safer options are available.[30]

In the United States, the San Francisco and the Harris County (Houston, Texas) jail systems officially make bleach available to inmates for cleaning drug-injection apparatus. A pilot program is being implemented in Canada to make small quantities of full-strength bleach "easily and discretely accessible" to inmates.[31]

To repeat, the provision of condoms or bleach does not condone or approve the prohibited behaviors. Instead, it strongly teaches that those who choose to violate the rule and engage in these activities at least should reduce the risk of infection to themselves or others.

Vaccination for Hepatitis B

A vaccine has been available since 1981 for preventing hepatitis B infection.[32] It is very effective, typically conferring long-term immunity. Risk of adverse side effects is low. In 1997, the cost for the three-dose course of vaccination was about $100.

Some have proposed vaccinating all inmates and correctional officers. Applicable state or federal Occupational Safety and Health Administration regulations may require that the vaccine be offered to correctional officers who are at increased risk of body fluid exposures, and to health care staff. When a sufficient number of persons in the group are believed to be already immune to the disease, it may be less costly to screen for immunity first, reserving the vaccine for those who are not immune.

In keeping with a 1993 state law, the Michigan Department of Corrections now offers hepatitis B vaccine to all inmates. A study was conducted in 1995, with the help of Centers for Disease Control and the state health department, which demonstrated that, for this population, vaccination of all male inmates age thirty and younger, coupled with testing of males over thirty years of age followed by vaccination if not

---

[30] Centers for Disease Control and Prevention, *HIV/AIDS Prevention Bulletin* (April 19, 1993).

[31] Hammett, Widom, et al. *op. cit.*: 39.

[32] This vaccine is specific to HBV and does not immunize against HCV. It indirectly does protect against HDV for those not already infected, since infection with HBV must be present for HDV to be established.

immune, would be the least-costly strategy ($3,140,000 each year, compared to $3,460,000 if everyone were vaccinated with no testing).[33] For females, the same study showed that it was most cost effective to screen those over twenty. However, the Michigan study did not address whether vaccination itself is cost effective in terms of the number of cases of serious illness it might be expected to prevent, nor did it estimate the average cost per expected case prevented.[34] Funding for the vaccination did not come from the correctional health care budget, but rather from a special appropriation for this public health initiative.

Should HIV Positive Inmates Be Housed Separately from Other Inmates?

Once the initial panic subsided after the early public awareness about AIDS, it generally was advised that HIV-positive inmates should not be segregated from other inmates. Transmission occurs only through behaviors which already are prohibited in correctional institutions. One does not get AIDS from an infected individual by breathing the same air, sitting at the same table, or touching the same objects. Establishment of "AIDS wards" and special housing units for HIV-positive inmates out of fear of contagion is reminiscent of the leper colonies of old.

However, there can be advantages in separating persons requiring special treatment and accommodation. There is nothing wrong with housing persons with similar health conditions together in a centralized location to achieve better access to care and more efficient use of scarce resources. Alabama, for instance, has successfully implemented a centralization of all HIV-infected persons at one institution. This facilitates the making of skilled diagnosis, monitoring, and treating of persons during early as well as advanced stages of the disease. Because state law also requires HIV testing of all prisoners upon arrival and discharge from the system, it has been possible to conclude that no transmission thus far has occurred during incarceration, at least among those who have been released, since no person who entered the Alabama system HIV-negative has left HIV-positive.[35]

Florida is planning to set up a facility to serve as a halfway house and hospice for up to 100 AIDS patients and inmates with complex subacute AIDS-related illnesses. It is expected that up to one-fifth of the Florida inmates with AIDS will qualify to

---

[33] Subsequently, the Department abandoned the screening altogether because of logistical problems which it posed, not the least of which was that many inmates whose screening indicated that they were not at high risk, nevertheless, objected to being denied the vaccine. Consequently, now the vaccine is being offered to all inmates upon intake. Rochelle Daneluk and Daniel T. Welihan, "The Management of Hepatitis in the Correctional Environment" (Indianapolis, Ind.: American Correctional Association Winter Conference, January 28, 1997).

[34] Lawrence J. Elliott, "Presentation of a Pilot Study of Hepatitis B Vaccinations in Michigan Correctional Facilities," Michigan Department of Public Health (August, 1995).

[35] Samuel Eichold, "HIV Care in Correctional Facilities," 2:2, *Journal of Correctional Health Care* (Fall, 1995): 111.

be housed at this unit. According to the Florida Department of Corrections, the facility will have volunteer group access, flexible visiting hours, mental health care, recreation, and other programs for AIDS patients, as well as a full range of medical specialty services required by this population. In support of this approach, the department cites the difficulty of attempting to provide this same high quality of care in forty-seven separate institutions.[36]

A decision to establish a specialized hospice facility in Illinois for inmates with AIDS and other terminal illness was prompted in part by the discovery that some HIV transmission appeared to be occurring behind bars.[37]

These approaches are reasonable when they are based on the premise that it is more feasible and economical to concentrate the delivery of specialized medical services in one or a few locations. Also, as discussed elsewhere, the medical management of ill HIV-positive persons, and especially those who also have tuberculosis, is becoming too complex for the typical physician in general practice. Moreover, there may be substantial cost savings for a large correctional agency which has the capability of managing most AIDS patients on-site, instead of sending them to a hospital where the costs, including custody, easily can reach thousands of dollars each day.

Safeguards in Screening for HIV

It is well to encourage inmates to be screened voluntarily for HIV if they manifest clinical indications of HIV disease, or if they have engaged in high-risk behaviors. There are forms of treatment available that at least can retard the progression of the disease. Some states have laws that require all inmates to be screened. Unless there is such a law, inmates should not be coerced to submit to screening.

No one should be screened for HIV without prescreening counseling, intended to answer any questions that the inmate may have. If the screening is voluntary, a written informed consent also should be obtained. In the prescreening counseling, the inmate should be advised of the confidentiality of test results, and told that they will be informed of the results as soon as they are available.

Post-test counseling is essential for anyone who has tested positive. The inmate now will have many more questions, because of the personal involvement. The counselor should attend to the fears, anxiety, and depression which may be present. Care must be taken lest anyone be able to conclude from the appointment with a post-test counselor that this is an inmate who has tested positive.

Some large systems appoint full-time HIV counselors. Many systems contract with a local health department or other appropriate agency for counselors to come to the institution at regular intervals. In small facilities, the physician or nursing staff often perform the counseling.

---

[36] "Facility for Inmates with AIDS Aims to Lower Costs, Improve Care," *Correctional Health Care Management* (March, 1994): 37-39.

[37] Ray Long, "Increase in AIDS Burdens Prisons," *Chicago Sun Times* (December 6, 1993).

Other Sexually Transmitted Diseases

Syphilis

Syphilis is a systemic infection that has been known since the fifteenth century. It almost always is spread by direct contact with infectious lesions during sexual intercourse.[38] Symptoms of primary syphilis usually occur within three weeks of the initial infection. Secondary syphilis occurs within four to ten weeks following exposure. Tertiary syphilis typically appears two to twenty years after the initial infection. Sexual contact with a person with early (primary or secondary phase) syphilis carries the greatest risk of infection. About one-third of those having sexual contact with persons in these early phases will become infected.

The number of reported cases of syphilis in the United States declined steadily from the 1940s to the 1970s. In the late 1970s, the incidence of syphilis increased, especially among homosexual men. From 1985 to 1990, with the beginning of the AIDS epidemic, the incidence of syphilis rose by 75 percent. The greatest increase in this disease has been among young African-American men and women in the inner cities and is related to use of illegal drugs, especially crack cocaine.[39]

Most correctional systems screen all new arrivals with a blood test for syphilis. The best advice on whether screening should be done for this or other infectious diseases usually can be obtained from the state or county health department or by examination of screening results. Syphilis can be treated effectively with antibiotics, but may require an extensive diagnostic work-up.

Gonorrhea

Gonorrhea is a bacterial infection, usually transmitted by sexual intercourse with an infected person. Persons at highest risk are those with multiple sexual partners, especially when coupled with unsafe sexual practices such as failure to use a condom. In men, gonorrhea takes only a few days for symptom presentation, while in women extended asymptomatic periods (months, perhaps years) may occur. In men, typical symptoms include a penile discharge, and in women, a spreading and very aggressive pelvic infection eventually develops. Prompt detection and treatment of gonorrhea in its early stages is medically important to avoid complications and continued transmission of the disease.

Chlamydia

Chlamydia is a bacterial infection, also transmitted mainly through sexual intercourse with an infected person, and is one of the most common of the sexually transmitted diseases in the United States. The rate of infection is highest in adolescents,

---

[38] Barthwell and Gibert, *op. cit.*: 73.

[39] Barthwell and Gibert, *op. cit.*: 73. Use of cocaine is associated with increased sexual activity with multiple partners, facilitating the spread of syphilis.

young adults, and among drug users. Chlamydia in women can lead to pelvic inflammatory disease (PID) with subsequent infertility or risk of ectopic pregnancy.[40] In men, chlamydial infection is often without symptoms, although a mild discharge may exist.

Screening for chlamydial infection is strongly recommended, particularly for high-risk pregnant women, adolescents, and patients with multiple sexual partners. Chlamydia can be treated with antibiotics.

Herpes

Herpes Simplex, whether genital, rectal, or oral, is an acute inflammatory viral infection. It usually is transmitted by genital-genital or oral-genital contact. The incubation period is from two to seven days, with subsequent recurrent episodes. Treatment with one of several antiviral antibiotics will decrease the symptoms of herpes or the frequency of outbreaks, but will not cure the infection.

Other Contagious Diseases

From time to time, other diseases may be of concern in correctional faciltiies. Among these are chicken pox, measles, mumps, rubella, and legionella. The best immediate sources of information and advice will be the responsible physician and the local or state health department.

Chicken Pox

Chicken pox (varicella) and shingles (herpes zoster) both are caused by the same virus. They are of concern in a correctional facility primarily because persons who are immunosuppresed (such as patients with HIV or leukemia) and women early or late in pregnancy and their fetuses are at increased risk of complications if they are not immune. Visitors, staff, and female prisoners thus may be at risk. Consultation with the local health department is advised to guide the facility's response.[41]

Measles, Mumps, and Rubella

Measles, mumps, and rubella are viral diseases, that prior to the development of vaccines, typically were acquired in childhood. Lapses in vaccination of children with the "MMR" vaccine can result in cases of these diseases occurring in juvenile and adult correctional facilities. Rubella is of particular concern, since infection of the mother before the fifth month of pregnancy can lead to congenital malformations. As with chicken pox, the facility's response to identification of an inmate with any of these diseases should be guided by consultation with the local health department with respect to isolation of cases, notification and reassignment of staff, restriction of

---

[40] Barthwell and Gibert, *op. cit.*:109f.

[41] Abram S. Benenson (ed.), *Control of Communicable Diseases Manual*, Sixteenth Edition (Washington, D.C.: American Public Health Association, 1995): 87-89.

movement, transfer of prisoners, vaccination programs, or other activities. State systems with cases in more than one facility may benefit from early consultation with the state health department to ensure consistency of responses and to help allay fears of concerned staff, inmates, and the public.

Legionnaire Disease

Legionnaire disease (legionella) is not transmitted from person to person, but is a highly lethal (as high as 39 percent fatality rate) bacterial pneumonia, which can occur sporadically as well as in outbreaks. Outbreaks can be caused by legionella "blooms" in poorly maintained evaporative cooling towers. Facility administrators must ensure that evaporative cooling towers on facility grounds are maintained professionally in strict accordance with accepted standards for descaling, use of appropriate biocides, and draining when not in use. [42]

Public Health Function of Jails

Jails, in particular, have a unique opportunity to serve a very important public health function. The vast majority of persons leave the jail within a few days after booking. Many of them come from (and return to) settings with high exposure to contagious disease, and where altered behavior and correct information could have very great benefit in education, treatment, and prevention of diseases—such as in situations in which prostitution, homosexual promiscuity, TB-infested housing, intravenous drug abuse, overcrowded and unsanitary housing, homeless shelters, and abusive families are common. Where else will it be possible to bring significant numbers of these high-risk persons together long enough for exposure to some education on disease prevention? Video presentations, classroom lectures, printed material, supervised group discussions—all can be useful ways to impart correct and timely information. The focus of these educational sessions must be realistic in terms of practical strategies to interrupt the cycle of disease.

Jails and prisons can assist in this public health function by treating and reducing community prevalence, testing, and identifying diseases of concern, and advocating behavioral changes to reduce community risk. It is not unreasonable to expect the cost of these educational efforts to be borne by the public health agency, since the primary objective is to reduce the risk of disease transmission in the community.

Discharge Planning

The correctional agency should make an effort to assist in arranging continued care in the free world for the medical needs of any chronically ill inmate facing release to the community. But for those with communicable disease, there should be special concern. Persons receiving treatment or preventive (prophylactic) therapy for tuberculosis, for example, should continue that therapy without interruption, not only

---

[42] Benenson, *op cit.*: 256-257.

for its effectiveness, but also to prevent the development of drug-resistant strains of the disease. At a minimum, the agency should refer such persons to the local public health department at discharge. These inmates also may require assistance in finding a suitable place to live and adequate nutrition to remain healthy and minimize the risk of infecting others.

A number of states, including Rhode Island, Maryland, and Connecticut have sponsored model programs of discharge planning and post-release assistance for HIV infected inmates.[43] These efforts should focus not only on arranging adequate food and shelter and finding access to needed medical care, but also in assisting with finding employment, obtaining substance abuse treatment, and helping inmates get reintegrated with their family.

A Few Legal Considerations

Courts attempt to achieve a balance among competing claims and entitlements, and their decisions reflect the specific findings of the case before them. Often, these decisions appear to be contradictory. Not every decision, particularly of the lower courts, serves as a precedent for other situations. Consequently, each agency is advised to consult with its own attorney on important policy decisions in light of statutes and judicial decisions applicable in their jurisdiction. The following cases reflect some recent legal developments.

DeGidio v. Pung[44] is a clear judicial declaration that delivery of medical care to hundreds or thousands of people housed in correctional institutions is a problem requiring systemic solutions. An inmate admitted in 1982 with active tuberculosis infected several hundred other inmates, at least eight of whom developed TB disease. The Federal District Court in Minnesota emphasized the importance of coordination, follow-up, and supervision in correctional medical care systems, especially with cases of tuberculosis.

The Appeals Court of Massachusetts ruled in *Langton v. Commissioner of Correction*[45] that, although an inmate's incarceration does not divest him of the right of privacy and interest in preserving his bodily integrity, it does limit those constitutional rights when the state's interests in prison security and inmate health are at issue. Thus, the court found in this case that the disciplinary procedures implemented by prison officials to compel inmates to submit to mandatory TB testing were lawful.

On the other hand, a Federal District Court judge in New York ruled that the state corrections department must return to the general population a person who had been held in "medical keeplock" (solitary confinement) for three and a half years because he refused a skin test for tuberculosis. The inmate claimed that "accepting artificial substances into the body constitutes a sin and shows profound disrespect to our creator."[46]

---

[43] Theodore M. Hammett, Rebecca Widom, et ai., *op. cit.*: 55-57.

[44] 704 F.Supp. 922 (D. Minn. 1989). Cited in Hammett and Harold, *op. cit.*: 46-49.

[45] 614 N.E. 2d 1002 (Mass. App. Ct. 1993). (Cited in Wilcock, et al., *op cit.*: 11).

Inmates have a constitutional right to privacy in their medical diagnoses and other medical information. The "[c]asual, unjustified dissemination of confidential medical information to non-medical staff and other prisoners" is unconstitutional,"[47] as are actions or policies by prison administrators that indirectly disclose medical information without justification.[48]

A 1995 decision by the Seventh Circuit Court of Appeals[49] ruled that prisoners have no constitutional protection against unwanted disclosure of their HIV status by officers, even if the breach of privacy was motivated by spite. The court in *Anderson v. Romero and Douglas* held that state prison officials are entitled to qualified immunity because they were obliged to warn other prisoners from engaging in sexual intercourse with HIV-positive inmates. The court further stated: "We cannot find any appellate holding that prisoners have a constitutional right to the confidentiality of their medical records" and that the uninfected prisoners' protection under the Eighth Amendment takes precedence over the infected inmate's statutory privacy interests. This decision, however, is clearly in the minority.

In *Doe v. City of New York*,[50] the Federal Appeals Court held that "individuals who are infected with the HIV virus clearly possess a constitutional right to privacy regarding their condition." The court said that the right to confidentiality includes the right to protection regarding information about the state of one's health. While this case did not involve an inmate, it raises important issues regarding disclosure of HIV status.

---

[46] James C. McKinley, Jr. ,"Isolation Ends for Prisoner Who Refused Testing for TB," *New York Times* (August 22, 1995), p. B5. Cited in Wilcock, et al., *op. cit.*: 11.

[47] *Woods v. White*, 689 F.Supp. at 877.

[48] *Casey v. Lewis*, 834 F.Supp. 1477, 1546 (D. Ariz. 1993).

[49] Seventh Cir., No. 94-1251. Decided December 15, 1995. (Cited in "Inmates Have No Privacy Claim Against HIV Disclosure," *The Corrections Professional* (February 2, 1996: 11).

[50] 15 F. 3d 265 (2d Cir. 1994). (Cited in Hammett, Widom, et al., *op. cit.*:69.)

6 ENSURING ACCESS TO CARE

Unimpeded Access

For inmates of jails, prisons, or juvenile detention facilities, access to the health care system and to needed care essentially must be unimpeded. This means that the inmate, without risk of interference by anyone and without fear of reprisal, must be able to alert health care staff of a health need, to receive a timely professional evaluation of that need, and to receive treatment in the manner prescribed by a competent provider.

Note that the requisite unimpeded access is to the *health care system*, not to a specific provider or type of treatment. What must be assured is that the inmate, without fail, can inform health care staff that he or she has a need for care. Thereafter, it is the responsibility of the qualified health care staff to decide in a timely manner, based on appropriate professional evaluation and clinical skill, what the next step in the treatment process will be.

A jail, for example, need not comply with the insistent request of an inmate who is demanding to be taken to the hospital, while at the same time the inmate refuses to see the nurse who has been sent to evaluate the complaint. Except in a situation in which the need for immediate hospitalization would be obvious and apparent to any reasonable person, the facility is well within its rights to establish the nurse as "gatekeeper."

The inmate simply does not have the right to go to the hospital upon demand. This is not inconsistent with the practice of many third-party payers (such as health insurance companies and health maintenance organizations) in the community which require prior authorization before certain costly treatments or hospitalization can be provided (outside of emergencies), and will simply refuse to pay for the care if, in fact, it is obtained without proper authorization. This basic practice of managed care is becoming increasingly prevalent in free society.

Simply stated, no correctional officer ever should prevent, impede, or inhibit an inmate from alerting a health care provider of a need for health services, even when the officer believes the request to be trivial, fictitious, or undeserved. This is not the kind of judgment that the officer is charged to make.[1] The nurse, physician assistant, social worker, or other appropriate clinician, after evaluating the request, properly will determine what happens next. The nurse may review the sick-call request slips, briefly speak with the inmate during cell rounds, or speak to the officer (or, when possible, the inmate) by telephone. This is often called a "triage" of the request for health care.

Triage involves a sorting of requests by health care staff, whether these requests have been made orally or in writing, directly to a nurse or through an officer. The requests are first sorted according to priority for attention by the health care system, so that the more urgent cases are seen first. They also are sorted by type of service in order to schedule dental cases, for example, to see the dentist and patients with mental health concerns to see the mental health staff. Some situations require urgent response; others easily can wait a few days. In some cases, the nurse (or other health professional) should consult the medical record to ascertain the patient's health history, previously documented condition, and response to treatment. In other cases, the nurse also may need to examine the inmate before a reasonable determination can be made.

Sick Call Requests

It is good policy from a risk-management standpoint to establish a method whereby each inmate, on a daily basis, may transmit a request for care to the health care staff with no possible opportunity for interference by any other staff. Such a policy in no way presumes that officers will intentionally interfere with access to health care. But it does recognize the inherent difficulty of proving that an officer did not interfere. It is much easier to demonstrate that the inmate had readily available a daily means of direct contact with health care staff without needing to rely on any officer as an intermediary.

Specifically to be discouraged is a system in which inmates write their sick-call request slip and give it to an officer who holds the slips until they are delivered to a nurse. Theoretically, the officer could destroy or lose a request slip which then never would be delivered to the nurse. Confidentiality of the contents of the request is also an issue here.

Likewise to be discouraged is the use of a sick call sign-up sheet which is posted in each housing unit, kept at the officers' station in the housing unit, or passed from cell to cell by an officer or inmate. Potential problems with this system include lack of confidentiality both with officers and with other inmates, all of whom can read whether an inmate has requested to see the psychologist, nurse, or dentist, has a rash on the groin, or wishes to be tested for HIV. These are private matters and ought not be shared. Yet, their inclusion on the request form is extremely helpful for health care staff to determine what type of provider should see a given patient, and with what urgency. A second problem with the sick call sign-up sheet is the possibility that an

---

[1] For their part, health care staff are well advised to disregard such opinions (in other words, that the inmate is manipulating or abusing the health care system) until *after* they have made an objective evaluation of the inmate.

officer or another inmate might cross an inmate's name off the list, thus interfering with timely access.

As with other requirements or regulations whose origin can be traced to past abuses, there have been instances in which officers knowingly and maliciously have interfered with access of certain inmates to health care, just as there have been documented instances of staff brutality and inhumane treatment toward prisoners. It is not assumed that this occurs frequently, but it is prudent to safeguard against its occurrence by structuring a path whereby no officer intermediary is required for the inmate to communicate with a representative of the health care staff.

There are a number of ways to accomplish this, including a telephone access system. Probably the most common means currently employed is the provision of locked boxes at strategic points throughout the correctional facility, into which inmates may place a sick-call request slip. These boxes are opened and the contents are retrieved by a nurse (or other health care employee) on a daily basis. Only the health care staff possess keys to these boxes. In some facilities, where all inmates eat in a common dining area, boxes may be posted at the entrance to the dining hall, and access to health care is thereby virtually assured. Obviously, this will not work in institutions where inmates are fed in their housing units or where their movement is severely limited. In these cases, the boxes will need to be placed in carefully selected areas, and nurses will need to make daily roundings of all locked-down areas to ensure direct access. On the other hand, particularly in a minimum-security facility where considerable freedom of movement is allowed and prior authorization is not required to cross the grounds and approach the health care unit, walk-in visits to the clinic may be allowed and no formal sick-call request system is needed.

Once health care staff are made aware of the inmate's request and have determined the course of action to be taken, there should be no interference with the carrying out of this decision. Specifically, officers should take care that they in no way hinder an inmate from receiving the prescribed care, such as by threat, innuendo, ridicule, or by undue delay, failure to notify, failure to escort, or grossly and unnecessarily inconvenient scheduling. If there is a legitimate concern about the appropriateness or necessity of the prescribed care, or if significant delay will be incurred because of other pressing priorities, there should be a ready channel for the officer, either directly or through a supervisor, to bring the matter to the attention of the health care provider and explain the difficulty. Often, the provider will be able to select an alternative treatment modality without compromising the patient's well-being. The point to be emphasized is that decisions of this nature are beyond the competence of the officer or anyone but a qualified health care provider.

A special note of caution is in order regarding mental illness. Few persons would assert that a person with severe bleeding or a high fever did not require the attention of a physician. But sometimes aberrant or aggressive behavior is perceived as a "bad attitude" or a disciplinary problem, when, in reality, it is the consequence of a mental disorder. Again, such matters require a professional diagnosis.

Whatever method is adopted, it is essential that each inmate at arrival at the facility be given an explanation of how to obtain access to health care. This also must be a part of each officer's training. Many recommend that, in addition, printed notices containing this information (in multiple languages, if indicated) be posted conspicuously in areas used for booking, intake screening, and inmate housing.

Unimpeded Access: The Standard

As a requisite for accreditation, the American Correctional Association insists that a written policy, procedure, and practice provide for unimpeded access to health care.[2] No member of the correctional staff should approve or disapprove requests for attendance at sick call. Moreover, it is required that the policy on access to care be explained orally and in writing to each inmate upon arrival in a language clearly understood by the inmate. The same standard obliges the facility to implement a system for processing inmate complaints regarding health care.

In 1997, the National Commission on Correctional Health Care added a new essential prison standard [3] which specifically addresses access to care. Its purpose is to make explicit a most basic principle. The discussion provides five examples of unreasonable barriers to access:

(1) punishing inmates for seeking care for their serious health needs

(2) assessing excessive copayments that prevent or deter inmates from seeking care for their serious health needs

(3) establishing disincentives that deter inmates from seeking care for their serious health needs, such as holding sick call at 2:00 A.M. when this practice is not reasonably related to the needs of the institution

(4) permitting unreasonable delays before inmates are seen by prescribing providers or outside consultants to obtain necessary diagnostic work or treatment for their serious health needs

(5) interfering with prompt transmittal to health care staff of an inmate's oral or written request for care

Segregation and Lock-down Units

Because segregated inmates may have difficulty making their health needs known, and also because of the potentially adverse impact which conditions of segregation may have on health, it is widely recommended that all inmates on lock-down status be seen and assessed regularly by health care staff. The American Correctional Association standard points out that "because they are restricted from normal movement within their institution, it is imperative that inmates in segregation are

---

[2] American Correctional Association, *Standards for Adult Correctional Institutions* (1990), Standard 3-4331.

[3] The standard itself simply states: "Written policy and defined procedures require, and actual practice evidences, that inmates have access to care to meet their serious medical, dental, and mental health needs." NCCHC, *Standards for Health Services in Prisons* (Chicago, 1997), Standard P-30.

visited regularly by key staff members who can ensure that their health and well-being are maintained." Consequently, the standard requires daily visits from a qualified health care official (unless medical attention is needed more frequently).[4]

Most systems rely on the nurse to make rounds of lock-down units each day, but some do so in a manner which seriously diminishes the efficacy of this procedure. For example, the nurse may not actually enter the unit and round each cell. If only those prisoners are seen who have informed the officer that they want to see the nurse, the officer is placed in a position to determine who, in fact, will be allowed to get to see the nurse and who will not. It is better to arrange for the nurse (psychologist, and so on) to enter the housing area of a lock-down unit and round each cell, observing through the bars or opening in the cell door and speaking briefly with each inmate. Except under very special circumstances, the officer should not accompany the nurse at close enough range to be able to listen to the conversation.

Often the configuration of the door and the basic noise level of the area require that the conversation take place in fairly loud tones, permitting a nearby officer, and possibly inmates in nearby cells to overhear. A nurse who perceives that matters of an especially private nature need to be discussed, or that a proper assessment of need cannot be made under these circumstances, should request that the inmate be brought to the clinic or to another suitable area which will afford the necessary privacy, lighting, and environment for the encounter. A second problem with requiring the inmate to initiate a request to an officer is that the inmate who is too sick, either physically or mentally, to complain or to seek help, may be ignored by the officers and thus not receive needed attention.

If nurses make rounds in housing units each day, without fail, the nurse could pick up the request slips (or receive them orally and make a note) as he or she rounds the unit. It would not be acceptable, however, if the nurse does not "walk the galleries," in other words, walk past each locked-down cell in regular housing units, looking in at each inmate as he or she passes. If the nurse only comes to the door of a housing unit, it is possible that some inmates locked in their cells will not be able to make their needs directly known. "Kites" placed by inmates in segregation on cell doors are used in some places, but the possibility exists that staff or another inmate could remove them. As you consider the best solution for your situation, remember that the aim is to ensure that inmates have unimpeded access to health care, and to minimize your liability which could result from interference with access by any officer. It is not at all acceptable for an inmate "runner" to take a sick call list from cell to cell, or to collect sick-call request slips from each cell.

While daily rounding of segregation units by nursing staff is a fairly routine and well-established practice, it can be somewhat more difficult to accomplish in those facilities where inmates regularly are placed on lock-down status in their own cells. The problem is twofold: (1) knowing where they are, day-to-day, and (2) using excessive time to accomplish this task. Basically, if this is the situation, careful consideration is needed, through dialog among medical and custody staff, on how this

---

[4] American Correctional Association, *Standards for Adult Correctional Institutions* (1990), Standard 3-4246.

can be accomplished best. It may require additional resources to do so in a satisfactory manner.

It is a requirement of the American Correctional Association standards that a qualified mental health professional personally interview and prepare a written report regarding any inmate who remains in segregation for more than thirty days.[5] The standard also recognizes that inmates whose movements are restricted in segregation units may develop symptoms of acute anxiety or other mental problems. In view of the stresses of long-term segregation, the American Correctional Association requires a follow-up mental health assessment at least every ninety days, or more often if so prescribed by the chief medical authority.

Intake Screening
Point-of-entry Health Screening

Access to health care actually begins with arrival and intake screening. Even before a new inmate requests health care services, the agency already has an affirmative obligation to discover whether there are obvious and urgent health needs. This obligation commences as soon as the inmate steps out of the arresting officer's squad car or the inmate transportation bus. Typically, the first representative of the correctional agency who bears the responsibility for arrival health screening is the officer who meets the transporting vehicle. He or she immediately must recognize a medical emergency, such as profuse bleeding, impaired consciousness, significant physical weakness, or an urgent request for help. A seriously ill or injured inmate should not even be accepted at the facility; there should be a standing policy requiring the receiving officer to direct the driver of the vehicle to transport the inmate to an appropriate hospital or emergency room until the inmate is medically cleared to return.

The division of labor for arrival screening can be handled in various ways. The net result must be that a prompt and competent assessment is made and that appropriate response and referral takes place. If a nurse is present during the off-loading of newly arrived inmates, the principal responsibility will belong to the nurse. If, however, the nurse does not see the inmates until an hour or so after arrival, or perhaps not even until the following day, the responsibility of the officers is significantly greater. Commensurate with their increased responsibility comes the requirement that these officers receive more in-depth training in this matter.

In large systems which have a central reception center where intake health assessments have been completed prior to transfer,[6] the responsibility of the officer is limited to:

- Observing any apparent serious medical or mental health disorder as the inmates disembark from the transporting vehicle and enter the facility, paying particular heed to any

---

[5] American Correctional Association, *1996 Standards Supplement*, Standard 3-4244. The Glossary of the *Supplement* does not define a "qualified mental health professional" but provides a definition of "professional staff" as an individual who generally possesses at least a bachelor's degree and advanced training in the social or behavioral sciences.

trauma, accident, or mishap which may have caused injury or illness to the inmate en route. It is appropriate to inquire of the transporting officer whether any such event may have occurred during the trip.

- Promptly referring inmates for any serious health problems

- Promptly referring inmates for any subsequent health complaints they make

- Ensuring that any accompanying[7] inmate health record is confidentially handled and promptly given to designated health care staff

Arrival Health Screening

If, however, the nurse will not be evaluating the inmates shortly after arrival, the officers take on added responsibility, increasing with the length of the time interval before the nurse sees them. As a rough guideline, if the inmates are not to be seen by a nurse for one hour or longer, the officer must also:

- Conduct a formal arrival health screening and use a checklist which has been approved by the responsible health authority

- Ask each inmate whether he or she has any urgent health problems

- Refer any ill inmate so he or she can be seen promptly

- Document the findings and record the disposition of each screening

In addition to what the officer does, the arrival screening nurse[8] has at least the following responsibilities:

- Assess each inmate using an arrival screening form or, if the officer has performed the formal arrival screening, promptly

---

[6] For intrasystem transfers where the health screening has been completed already, the nurse need not visually assess each new arrival, but at least must conduct a chart review of the health record to ensure timely follow-up of any immediate or chronic health needs, including prescribed medications or scheduled specialty visits.

[7] Intrasystem transfers always should be accompanied by health records.

[8] Note, the arrival health screening could be performed as well by a physician assistant, clinical nurse practitioner, or a physician. However, this higher level of skill is not required and nearly all correctional facilities appropriately assign this function to a registered or licensed practical nurse who has been properly instructed in the procedure.

review the findings of the officer and perform such additional screening functions that were not assigned to the officer [9]

- Review the accompanying medical record and provide
  appropriate follow-up, such as place a call to the physician,
  submit a prescription to the pharmacy, administer prescribed
  medications in a timely way, or schedule an appointment
  with a physician, a dentist, or a mental health professional

Intake Health Appraisal

Unless the inmate is accompanied by an established health record for the current incarceration that documents the fact that intake health processing already has
been completed, an intake health appraisal, mental health assessment, and dental
examination must be scheduled. The time intervals required by the American Correctional Association[10] are as follows:

FIGURE 6-1. SUMMARY OF TIME INTERVALS ALLOWED FOR INTAKE HEALTH PROCESSING BY ACA ACCREDITATION STANDARDS[†]

INTAKE FUNCTION	MAXIMUM INTERVAL AFTER ARRIVAL		
	PRISONS	JAILS	JUVENILE FACILITY
Arrival Medical Screening	upon arrival	upon arrival	upon arrival
Transfer Medical Screening[†]	12 hours	—	—
Arrival Mental Health Screening	immediately	immediately	immediately
Arrival Dental Screening	14 days	14 days	7 days
Intake Health Appraisal	14 days	14 days	7 days
Intake Mental Health Assessment	14 days	14 days	7 days[††]
Intake Dental Examination	3 months (unless a problem)	14 days	1 month

† This refers to the health screening of intrasystem transfers, when the inmate arrives with a health record
from the previous institution and has already completed the intake health appraisal process. At a minimum, this screening includes reviewing the incoming inmate's health record or health summary.

†† If problems are identified at intake screening.

9 For example, inquiry about communicable diseases, detailed health history, administration of TB skin test, and so forth.

The intake health appraisal may be a comprehensive physical examination performed by a physician, physician assistant, or clinical nurse practitioner. In smaller correctional systems, the intake health appraisal is often performed by a registered nurse who has had special training in physical assessment, in which case the physician should review and co-sign the findings. Vital signs (pulse, blood pressure, temperature, as well as height and weight) also should be recorded. The American Correctional Association requires early identification and treatment of offenders with alcohol and drug abuse problems through a standardized battery assessment.[11]

Clinic Appointments

Scheduling of Appointments

There is abundant variety across the country in the way in which health care appointments are scheduled. To some extent, this depends on the size and the security level of the facility. No appointment may be required to see the nurse in a small minimum-security camp where walk-in visits are welcomed. Even here, however, the inmate probably will need to make an appointment when the nurse determines that the inmate should be seen by the physician, dentist, or eye doctor. Especially in medium-security institutions, a prior appointment is necessary for the inmate to be issued a pass to go to the clinic. Typically, in maximum-security situations, officer escort is required, again indicating the need for appointments outside of emergencies.

Over-the-counter Remedies

Unnecessary movement of inmates, especially movement which must be escorted or that which requires a pass, should be minimized. Many trips to the clinic are for obtaining medication. If over-the-counter remedies can be provided in the commissary, as is done successfully in many places, an inmate does not need to see the nurse to obtain a small quantity of aspirin, Tylenol, or an antacid.

"Keep on Person" Medications

The pill line is another occasion for high volume traffic to see the nurse. This can be reduced significantly by a policy which allows inmates to keep a quantity (such as a one-week or one-month supply) of certain types of medications on their person. This sometimes is referred to as the "Keep on Person" or "KOP" method. This approach has worked well in facilities of all security levels, but it must be planned thoughtfully and monitored carefully. Any medication that is deemed likely to be abused should be excluded from this program, such as those which might be taken in large quantities to cause an illness, or those which would be used as tender in the prison economy. Inmates who previously have abused medications at the facility also

---

[10] Note that the time intervals required by NCCHC do not differ significantly from those of the the American Correctional Association.

[11] American Correctional Association, *1996 Standards Supplement,* Standard 3-4344-1.

should be excluded from participation in the program. Medications which are recommended for directly observed therapy (DOT) also should not be included in the program, such as those used in treatment or prevention of tuberculosis. Before being allowed to participate in a KOP program, inmates should be instructed, typically by the nurse, in their responsibilities.

Packets of medications which are given to the inmates should be prepared and labeled strictly in accordance with state laws and regulations. In many jurisdictions, it is illegal for a nurse to repackage medications from a stock bottle. Labeling on the package usually is required to include the patient's name, the prescribing physician's name, the dispensing institution, a control or lot number, the date of dispensing, the name of the medication, the quantity dispensed, dosage instructions, and cautionary or advisory information.[12] Consequently, it probably is not legal or proper for a nurse to prepare the medications by counting out pills, placing them into a small envelope, and writing the inmate's name on it. It is becoming increasingly common to have these KOP medications packaged by a pharmacist (or by a pharmacy assistant with the requisite supervision of a pharmacist). While this may be somewhat more costly, it is legal, and it is safer. It avoids the need to store large quantities of bulk medications at the facility, and it relieves nursing staff of a very time-consuming function.

A common variation of this approach employs a "blister pack" which many pharmacies now are equipped to produce. Typically, these contain thirty-one transparent plastic "bubbles" into which medications are placed for each day of the month, then sealed with a foil or paper film through which the pills, tablets, or capsules can be punched. For those taking medications two or three times a day, more than one card is used, each marked with the time of day that it is to be taken. Affixed to the blister packs is a label prepared by the pharmacy, containing all of the legally required information for the patient.[13] This system facilitates regular compliance with the prescribed treatment.

Location and Timing of the Pill Line

Another way to reduce traffic to the clinic is to schedule the pill line at a time and place that is accessible to the majority of inmates without the need for special arrangements for each individual. Some facilities successfully have scheduled the pill line in association with meal time. If inmates do not regularly pass by the clinic on the way from their housing unit to the dining hall, it may be possible to use a portable medication cabinet for this purpose. Other creative possibilities exist. These always should be worked out in collaboration between representatives of security and of health care so that all relevant factors are considered.

---

[12] In pharmacies today, all of this information is very quickly and automatically printed on the label by a computer. It would be tedious and very time consuming for a nurse to attempt this manually.

[13] In fact, these "blister packs" are used in many facilities for nurse-administered medications, as well. They can be stored alphabetically in a file drawer and be readily available for use at the pill line. Since the medication itself has not been handled, unused or partially used cards often can be returned to the pharmacy for credit.

Computers

Computers can be very helpful for scheduling. Some very sophisticated systems are entirely online; they are keyed to the inmate locator system, and automatically print out at the appropriate housing unit location a notice to the inmate and a pass for the officer to permit access to the clinic. Computers also may flag any conflicting schedule for the inmate, such as a family or attorney visit or a court date. Simpler approaches use only a word processor or database on a personal computer, enabling a list to be printed that is sorted alphabetically and by housing unit for each day's appointments. Obviously, the larger and more complex the system, the more sense it makes to use electronic labor saving and error-avoidance devices to the fullest extent.

Agencies which are planning to acquire or upgrade their data management capabilities should seek extensive input during the planning phase from key health care staff of the facility, including representation of those line personnel who will be using the system on a day-to-day basis. It is much less costly to design their needs into the system from the start than to retrofit the program later. Many of the commercial vendors have designed products with the advice and involvement of correctional experts, but have not made their systems equally useful for health care applications. Appointment scheduling is only one of a number of important applications which computers can have for clinical staff.

Callouts for Clinic Appointments

Scheduling can facilitate or hinder access to care. If the method in use consists of a nurse working from a day-old roster of inmates to prepare callout slips which then are routed to the control station of the respective housing units on the day before the appointment, several undesirable things may happen:

- An inmate who has no advance notice of the appointment does not want to get up when roused at 7:00 A.M., and so refuses.

- An inmate is confused[14] about the reason for the appointment and so refuses.

- An inmate does not get the message because he or she was transferred to another housing unit on the preceding day. Moreover, the nurse may interpret the "no show" to be a refusal and, therefore, not reschedule the appointment.[15]

---

[14] This readily can happen if the inmate submitted a medical request slip for a sore throat, but now feels better, not realizing that the appointment had been scheduled for something quite different—such as a periodic physical examination or follow-up for a chronic condition.

[15] This, of course, would be indicative of another problem. A missed appointment should be rescheduled unless it is determined not to be clinically significant or if an adequately informed refusal has been made. Some facilities automatically reschedule any missed provider-initiated appointment. Too often, appointments are missed through no fault of the inmate because notification was not received or no escort was available, or, as in this case, because of confusion over the purpose of the appointment.

Where an online computer is not available to prevent misdirected callouts, additional cooperation of the housing unit officers is required. Upon receipt of the callout list, they immediately should telephone to notify the officer at the inmate's correct location of the appointment. Or, they may call the nurse who is then made aware that the appointment will be missed and can decide either to notify the correct unit or simply to reschedule the visit for the next available opportunity.

Keeping track of chronic patients' appointments requires special attention and diligence. If not done well, the care is without continuity and becomes "episodic," exposing the patient to risk of harm and the facility to increased liability. The treating physician (or other appropriate provider) always should determine the frequency of visits which are best for the patient. This should be stated in the treatment plan, which is documented in the patient's health record. A busy physician, especially with a large number of patients to be seen, sometimes can forget to indicate a return-to-clinic date. The nurse, who is charged with noting the doctor's orders after a clinic visit is completed, should bring such an omission to the doctor's attention if the interval for the next appointment (or an explicit notation that no further follow-up is required) is not indicated. As a failsafe backup, the responsible health authority may determine that, unless the care provider specifies otherwise, the next visit automatically will be scheduled (by the nurse, clerk, or computer) in thirty days.

Some systems attempt to place the burden on the patient, either by giving him or her an appointment notice for the following visit or by requiring that the inmates sign up for sick call just prior to exhausting the KOP medication supply. While the practice of giving notice is excellent, even in the community, most of us also receive a "day prior" phone call (or postcard) from our dentist, physician, or eye doctor reminding us of the appointment. People who live in an institution easily can lose track of days—each seeming much like any other.

There also is extra paperwork involved in handling another kite. Beyond this, there is some risk for the institution when it relies solely on the inmate's initiative to request a follow-up visit for a health condition, which clearly is recognized by the provider as important—though its necessity may be less apparent to the patient—such as the need for periodic blood pressure or blood sugar check.

Prior Authorization for Treatment

Many systems now require that costly health services and perhaps all off-site care except for life-threatening emergencies, receive prior authorization. The institution's medical director, regional medical director, or other designated person reviews documentation supporting the request for the service and determines whether it is warranted. Consideration is given to expected benefits and expected consequences if the treatment were omitted or if an alternative therapy were selected. Cost (including the cost of custody transportation and supervision) also may be a factor. By use of telefax or other rapid means of transmittal, this review should not result in an undue delay.

On-call Arrangements

Only a few facilities have twenty-four hour on-site physician coverage. All others need to make some arrangement for obtaining emergency services when health care staff are not on duty. This is necessary to ensure that inmates have the required access to urgent care whenever it is needed. Several methods are available to accomplish this.

The simplest acceptable method is a policy to transport any inmate claiming an urgent need immediately to the local emergency room or "walk-in" clinic. This, however, quickly can become excessively costly. It also tends to place the officer in the awkward and risky role of exercising medical judgment about the urgency or necessity of these trips.

Another method requires the officer to telephone the nurse or physician who can advise whether the inmate's request can be deferred or if an immediate trip to the emergency room is warranted. Alternatively, a nurse who is on duty and has seen the patient may telephone an on-call physician for treatment orders. The clinician, in either case, must arrange to always be available by telephone or paging device. A local on-call physician (or physician assistant or clinical nurse practitioner) can advise by telephone or can come in to evaluate, treat, or suture, as needed.

Sometimes the on-call physician service is arranged on a statewide or regional basis, and a single physician covers multiple institutions. Though at first blush this approach would appear to be very cost efficient, there are some concerns. Physicians are often uncomfortable about rendering a treatment decision for a patient whom they have never seen and are not likely to see in the near future. This discomfort is enhanced when the physician does not have a clear picture of the on-site capability for managing the patient in terms of equipment, staffing, or other resources. Nor can physicians place a lot of trust in the observations and interpretations of nurses whom they do not know. Consequently, they tend to decide conservatively and order a transfer to the local emergency room much more often than would a local on-call physician who knows the facility, knows how much confidence to repose in the nurse, and perhaps also knows the patient or at least is likely to see the patient on the following day. One method to increase the quality of such phone triage is to have the physician talk directly to the inmate on the telephone. This is not always possible from a custodial point of view, but a portable phone may help.

The on-call method selected depends on the size and health of the population and on the proximity to an emergency room. Managed-care contract firms are leaning toward the use of the local on-call physician. Many large state systems have relied on a central on-call physician, but some find that a few very costly trips to an emergency room make the option of a local on-call physician attractive.

The physician will expect to be paid for on-call time, though this is sometimes "built-in" to the regular compensation of the physician. Being "on-call" generally means that the physician is obliged to remain within telephone (or pager) reach at all times and to remain "work-ready"—in other words, not intoxicated nor otherwise unfit or unable to act in a rational and professional manner. Unless the on-call arrangement is strictly for telephonic advice, the doctor also must remain at all times within a specified distance (usually stated in terms of time, such as thirty minutes or one hour) from the facility. This obviously places a significant burden and responsibility on the physician, and for this he or she should be financially compensated. With this in mind, it also should be clear that an arrangement which requires the full-time (or part-time) doctor for the facility to be on twenty-four-hour, seven-day call may be unrealistic. It would place an unreasonable strain on any doctor to meet all of these requirements all of the time without relief. Thus, there must be a designated backup. An ideal arrangement is for two or more doctors to rotate call coverage for one or more institutions in the vicinity.

The correctional agency is paying for the on-call service, and one important reason is the issue of liability. Therefore, the facility administrator should be very clear (in writing) with the doctor about expectations. It is unfortunately too late to discover in the courtroom, after a tragic occurrence, that the doctor did not realize that he or she was expected to carry a pager whenever away from the home telephone.

Copayment—A Strategy to Limit Access

Charging Inmates for Health Care

Plans to charge inmates for health services have proliferated in recent years.[16] This is not at all surprising, given that the idea of a copayment eloquently speaks to the theme of cost-containment, a pressing concern for most states and counties in the context of the burgeoning number of prisoners and the soaring costs of incarceration. Popularity or receptivity to the approach in some quarters also may be related to the current fascination with "getting tough on criminals."

Most copayment programs have been implemented in jails. As of the end of January 1996, only twelve state correctional systems were imposing a charge for inmate health services.[17] These programs range widely in policy, amount charged, and services covered.

1. Michigan's Macomb County Jail is one of the pioneers [18] in inmate copayment. The basic charge is $10. The cost of operating the Macomb County Jail (average daily census of 960) was $18.3 million in 1992. A program of charging inmates for food, clothing, shelter, medical and dental treatment yielded income of $2.7 million over a seven year period from 1985 to 1992. The law [19] permits the county to charge inmates up to $30 per day for expenses. Inmates are not billed until after their release from jail. Then, they are invoiced at thirty, sixty, and ninety days after release.

    An average of 700 accounts are billed monthly; and more than 15 percent result in payment. Indigent inmates

---

[16] The reader who is seriously interested in this topic is referred to the Fall, 1996 *Journal of Correctional Health Care*, which is dedicated to the subject of inmate copayment for health services. In addition to thoughtful articles on the legal implications of charging inmates for health care, the journal contains excellent reports on two recent nationwide surveys of the use of copayment mechanisms.

[17] Frances T. Gipson and Elizabeth A. Pierce, "Current Trends in State Inmate User Fee Programs for Health Services," 3:2, *Journal of Correctional Health Care* (Fall, 1996): 165.

[18] Of course, charging prisoners for their health care is not really so new. It was not very long ago—a common practice until well into the 1970s—that inmate clerks responsible for scheduling of clinic visits typically, though unofficially, would charge a carton of cigarettes for a visit to the eye doctor.

[19] Inmate Reimbursement to the County Act of 1984 (Macomb County).

receive medical and dental care equal to community standards; and no one is denied medical or dental services because of an inability to pay. The county does not charge for intake physical examinations, but inmates subsequently are charged $10 for each self-referred visit to a physician or dentist. This system is said to have achieved a significant reduction in the number of medical and dental consultations, and the county receives nearly $25,000 annually from offenders to defray the cost of medical and dental services.[20]

2. The State of Nevada was also an early starter in this field. A 1987 statute authorized the Director of Prisons to establish, with the approval of the Prison Board, internal policies which allowed the assignment of reasonable charges against offender accounts to "defray the costs paid by the department for medical care for the offender." [21] Although the policy has been amended frequently, basically there is a $4 charge for each visit to a provider for examination or treatment and a $2 charge for prescriptions. The inmate also is charged for 100 percent of the cost of elective procedures.

    A number of exemptions are provided so that there is no charge for such services as intake physical examinations, pill call, post-operative examinations, prenatal care, visits for mandatory infectious disease consultations, prophylactic treatment for tuberculosis, mental health unit services, approved prosthetics, approved emergency care, follow-up visits, chronic clinic care, ectoparasite treatment, or primary psychiatric/psychological care.[22]

3. The Kansas Department of Corrections began a statewide copayment program in January 1995, assessing a basic fee of $2 for inmate-initiated visits. Mental health clinic contacts are excluded, and a number of other important safeguards have been established.

4. Florida's Pinellas County Jail (1,896 bed) reportedly has reduced inmate medical requests by half, eliminating frivolous requests and allowing staff to spend more time caring

---

[20] Donald J. Amboyer (Jail Administrator of the Macomb County Sheriff's Department), "Michigan County Requires Inmates to Defray Cost of Incarceration," 55:6, *Corrections Today* (October, 1993): 88f.

[21] Nevada Department of Prisons, *Correctional Health Care: A Provider Review* (June, 1966): 25.

[22] Nevada Department of Prisons, *op. cit.*: 29f.

for legitimate illness.[23] Its program of charging inmates for care was begun in January 1995. Only a small amount of revenue is generated from the copayment. The policy permits a negative balance to accrue in inmate accounts, so that requested care is never denied. Fees are $8 for a self-initiated visit to a doctor or dentist, $4 to a nurse or dental hygienist, $2 for prescriptions, $4 for x-rays, and $2 for laboratory tests. No charge is assessed for follow-up visits requested by the physician, for the intake health appraisal, or for pre- and postnatal care. Initiation of the program was preceded by a facilitywide education effort.

5.   The State of Florida charges between $1 and $5 for each nonemergency visit initiated by a prisoner.[24]

There are programs which charge for any health service, including prescription and over-the-counter medications, hospital stays, emergency room visits, follow-up care, and even transportation to off-site care. Though the express purpose of most copayment plans is to provide a disincentive to frivolous abuse of sick call and health services, there are other reasons as well, as is evident from programs in which charges also are imposed for receipt of clearly necessary health services. Reasons given include: "to teach inmates responsibility" and "because in the community free citizens also pay a portion of the cost of health care." Of course, in the free community, one also pays for food, clothing, and shelter, which, like health care, are considered necessities of life. In one jail, the physician claimed that a tangible benefit of the copayment program was that it greatly reduced the requests for "special shoes." One might wonder whether a program as costly and burdensome to administer as a copayment program is really necessary to discourage what never should have been allowed to become a "medical issue" in the first place.[25] Very few jurisdictions have found that the copayment actually defrays any significant portion of costs.

Some have asserted that, while an inmate is entitled to receive necessary medical care, the obligation of the state (or county) does not necessarily extend to paying for the care.[26] This has not yet been adequately tested in the courts. It eventually may be held to be tenable so long as adequate safeguards are in place to ensure that the cost of care does not impede timely receipt of needed health services.

---

[23] *Corrections Cost Control and Revenue Report*, Aspen Publishers, Inc. (August, 1995): 6.

[24] Bernard P. Harrison, "In the Matter of Charging Prisoners for Health Services," 3:2, *Journal of Correctional Health Care* (Fall, 1996): 114.

[25] As is pointed out elsewhere in this book, ill-fitting shoes, which are caused by careless dispensing of clothing to inmates, are best corrected at the source, not with an evaluation by physicians for unneeded, but very costly, orthopedic shoes.

[26] Harrison, *op cit.*: 112.

Establishing Safeguards

A major concern about copayment plans is that they could impede access to necessary care. This, of course, never would be an intended result, and with adequate safeguards and careful monitoring, this risk may be reduced. Appropriate safeguards include reasonable charges, an allowable negative account balance, a protected minimum balance, an exemption for provider-initiated care, an exemption for mental health care, a clear explanation about how the copayment program works, an appeal mechanism, and a system for monitoring.

FIGURE 6-2. APPROPRIATE SAFEGUARDS IN A COPAYMENT PROGRAM

- Reasonable charges

- Allowable negative account balance

- Protected minimum balance

- Exemption for provider-initiated care

- Exemption for mental health care

- Exemption for prenatal and postnatal care

- Clear explanation to inmates

- Appeal mechanism

- Monitoring

- *Reasonable charges.* The prevailing inmate economy must be taken into consideration. For example, if the typical wage earned by an institutional job is 50 cents a day, a $10 copayment for a sick-call visit is equivalent to one month's pay—clearly excessive by any community standards. Copayment charges in correctional facilities around the country generally range from $2 to $15, with most being in the lower third of this span.

- *Allowable negative account balance.* If there are insufficient funds in the inmate's account to cover the copayment, it is possible that some necessary care will be denied unless adequate safeguards are taken. Many systems are allowing the inmate to seek care regardless of the status of the inmate's account. In this way, requested care never is denied because of the inmate's inability to pay. When the account is charged, a negative balance remains if there were insufficient funds. At some future time that funds are deposited into the account, they first are applied to the amount owed by the inmate.[27]

- *Protected minimum balance.* Some systems establish a protected minimum balance for each inmate's account, below which a charge for health services will not draw. The concept is that copayment should be made by those who have adequate resources, but ought not to require expenditure of the last farthing. This, at least, reduces the likelihood that a prisoner would have to choose between making a sick-call visit for a sore throat and buying toothpaste or postage stamps.

- *Exemption for provider-initiated care.* Another safeguard commonly employed is not to charge for provider-initiated care. This would apply to routine screening and physical exams, communicable disease testing and treatment, and follow-up care for acute or chronic conditions. Similar reasoning would imply that there should be no charge for prescribed medications or other treatments ordered by the doctor, precisely because they have been prescribed.

The reasoning here is twofold. For chronic conditions, the cost of regular follow-up care quickly could become prohibitive for most inmates and thus necessary (and prescribed) care effectively would be discouraged. Preventable catastrophic illnesses could cost the agency much more than any savings achieved through the program. The second reason has to do with the objective of the copayment mechanism. Its usual stated purpose is to discourage frivolous and trivial use or abuse of sick call. But provider-initiated care and follow-up care for chronic and acute conditions are clearly not frivolous or abusive. If the dentist has examined an inmate's mouth and determines that certain fillings or other restorative procedures are needed, access to that care is surely not trivial, and, therefore, should not be discouraged.

- *Exemption for mental health care.* It is also reasonable to exempt mental health care from the copayment. Untreated mental illness is a source of major problems for the custody and management of inmates. Some mentally ill inmates will not make the rational choice to seek needed treatment if any obstacle at all is placed in their way. Finally, compliance with the prescribed therapeutic regimen—in particular, taking psychotropic medication—consistently should be encouraged, and a copayment either for the visit to the mental health professional or for the medication would seem counterproductive.

---

[27] In jurisdictions where this would not be allowed (because a negative balance would be interpreted as an illegal loan by the warden to the inmate), other creative solutions would have to be found so as not to deny necessary care to an inmate without funds. In this situation, it may be necessary to refrain from charging an account without funds at all, so as not to leave a negative balance.

- *Exemption for prenatal and postnatal care.* Most pregnancies in the correctional system are high risk. It is important that pregnant and postpartum women receive medical care. This is discussed more fully in Chapter 8.

- *Clear explanation to inmates.* Without adequate information dissemination to inmates, considerable confusion can arise. The greatest risk is that inmates may be reluctant to seek needed care out of a mistaken fear that they will be charged, even though the program appropriately has excluded, for example, care for chronic conditions. Clear and concise explanations must be given both orally and in writing. Clinic staff also must expect to devote some of their time during sick call, pill line, clinic visits, or segregation rounding to explain the process and clear up misunderstandings.

- *Appeal mechanism.* Inmates are entitled to due process before money is taken from them.[28] Thus, the rules must be applied fairly and administrative review of grievances and complaints must be assured. Terms like "indigent" or "necessary" or "emergency" are subject to interpretation and may be challenged, and should, therefore, be defined as precisely as possible in policy. As Rold [29] points out, the *Delverne v. Klevenhagen* decision makes it clear that an inmate, under the Due Process Clause, must have a fair opportunity to contest any decision regarding his or her indigence, and the *Johnson v. Department of Public Safety and Correctional Services* decision held that inmates also must be able to contest the applicability of exceptions to a copayment system.

- *Monitoring.* Charging inmates for health care, though initiated out of legitimate concerns, can have unintended effects, either due to misunderstandings by inmates or overzealous implementation by staff.[30]

---

[28] William J. Rold, "Charging Inmates for Medical Care: A Legal, Practical, and Ethical Critique," 3:3, *Journal of Correctional Health Care* (Fall, 1996): 134.

[29] Rold, op. cit.: 134f. The referenced cases are *Delverne v. Klevenhagen*, 888 F.Supp. 64 (S.D. Tex. 1995) and *Johnson v. Department of Public Safety and Correctional Services*, 885 F.Supp. 817 (D. Md. 1995).

[30] In one large urban jail where a copayment system was implemented, medical staff adhered to the established policy and accordingly did not charge for provider-initiated visits. The dentist, however, was circumventing this safeguard and charging a fee to inmates for subsequently scheduled treatments, which he had determined through the dental examination to be necessary. He did this, he told the author, because he "did not feel that inmates should get free health care."

Indeed, it appears that most states are adopting safeguards of this nature. In a 1966 study [31] of the prison systems in fifty states, the District of Columbia, and the Federal Bureau of Prisons, all twelve states which have implemented a copayment program have exempted the following from the user fees:

- inmates in diagnostic centers who are just entering the system

- pregnant inmates

- inmates diagnosed with clinical mental illness

- chronically ill inmates

- physically disabled inmates

The Impact of Charging for Care

Few correctional systems realistically would view the user fees as a meaningful source of revenue to offset the cost of health care. As a matter of fact, the administering and monitoring of the program is likely to cost more than the money received, unless exorbitant rates are assessed and collected.

When the stated purpose of charging inmates for health care is to reduce the volume of clinic visits, it is reasonable to interpret this as an effort to eliminate trivial visits, as noted previously. The experience in many places has been that, after noting a steep decline in clinic visits during the first month or two of initiation of a copayment, the volume then begins to increase up to a new plateau—not far below the original level. The reason for this may be that the shock effect soon wears off and because inmates find new ways to get the care they feel they need. One such device is the multiple purpose visit—actually not an entirely bad idea in terms of efficient use of a clinician's time.[32]

An inmate may delay seeking care in the early stages of an illness because the discomfort does not seem bad enough to warrant the cost. By the time that the pain or symptoms become severe enough, the illness may have progressed to a point

---

[31] Gipson and Pierce, *op. cit.*: 176f.

[32] At one institution, the nurse informed the author that it was their practice that, if an inmate attempted during a sick-call visit to discuss a health problem other than the one for which the visit had been scheduled, he immediately would be told to submit a kite for a separate appointment regarding the new complaint. How wasteful of resources! Presuming that the health complaint was one which appropriately could be addressed by the current provider, it potentially would have saved significant time and effort for the physician, health record, and clerical staff, nurses, and correctional officers if both issues could have been disposed of at once.

Most of us, when visiting our physician for a specific complaint, will take advantage of the opportunity to discuss other, nonrelated health concerns, which either are viewed as not important enough in and of themselves to require a visit to the doctor, or which, if dealt with together, might save us the cost and bother of a second visit. Why should an inmate look at it any differently?

where irreversible damage has occurred, costly treatment is required, or an epidemic of infectious disease has begun. Early diagnosis and treatment might have avoided these serious and costly consequences. Caution is advised lest copayment serve as a deterrent to necessary care.

Two distressing examples are cited by Rold.[33] Self-appraisals of copayment programs claimed, in one jail, "a decrease in the number of outside clinic visits by nearly 300" and another jail reported that "the cost for prescriptions had declined significantly because fewer inmates were seeing the doctor." If the facts as presented are true, these findings would indicate that either the jails previously had been very lax about approving off-site clinic visits (presumably to specialists) and that perhaps the physicians had been writing prescriptions merely to appease the patient even when medication was not medically needed, or else one is led to the inescapable conclusion that, under copay, necessary care effectively was being discouraged.

Is There a Better Way?

Faiver and Anno[34] point out that in the community, as well as in correctional institutions, only a small minority of persons consume the vast majority of health services—generally persons with bona fide acute, chronic, or terminal illness. They state:

> There is a better solution [to the concern about trivial overuse of sick call] than copayment. It begins with ensuring full and unimpeded access to the primary level of the prison's health care delivery system. Here, the prisoner typically encounters a nurse, or possibly a psychologist, social worker or other clinically trained person who listens to the complaint and evaluates the extent of need. Once the prisoner has "entered" the delivery system, all referrals to more specialized and more costly levels of care should be the decision of professional staff based on an objective assessment. In this way, the relatively few persons who choose to abuse sick call regularly will not impose significant monetary costs on the system, while legitimate users will have ready access to all appropriate levels of care.

Some thoughtful persons[35] are suggesting that it may not be in the best interest of correctional agencies to institute programs which discourage access to health

---

[33] Rold, *op. cit.*: 139.

[34] Kenneth L. Faiver and B. Jaye Anno, "Cost Considerations: Financing, Budgeting and Fiscal Management," in B. J. Anno, *Prison Health Care: Guidelines for the Management of an Adequate Delivery System* (Chicago: National Commission on Correctional Health Care, 1991): 234.

[35] Among them, M. Lopez and K. Chayriques, "Billing Prisoners for Medical Care Blocks Access," 9:2, *National Prison Project Journal*: 1-2, 17. Cited in William J. Rold, "Charging Inmates for Medical Care: A Legal, Practical, and Ethical Critique," 3:2, *Journal of Correctional Health Care* (Fall, 1996): 137.

services, even when all due safeguards are in place to ensure access to necessary care. One reason is that, at least for long-term facilities, good health care now may reduce future expenditures by helping to keep inmates healthy. As expressed earlier, it is clearly in the interest of the institution to avoid placing any obstacles which would tend to dissuade mentally ill persons from complying with their recommended treatment or from seeking counseling early as they begin to feel that the pressures and stresses of life are becoming unbearable. In much the same way, inmates who seek care early after they perceive symptoms sometimes may be treated at lesser cost than if the condition goes untreated for a long period. Early interception and treatment of infectious conditions may prevent contagion to others. Ignoring an injured ankle or knee while continuing active exercise may cause permanent damage and necessitate expensive surgery or physical therapy. Hence, perhaps we should be developing creative ways to encourage inmates to become active partners in taking good care of their health.

Careful Research Is Required

Though many systems are experimenting with copayment arrangements, few if any have conducted careful evaluation of the results. Some have reported an immediate sharp reduction in use of sick call, followed by a gradual return to nearly the initial level of usage. Others have found a continuing reduction in usage, but are unable to describe with any certainty what types of usage has dropped off. Has the reduction primarily been due to deterrence of the frivolous use of services, or are chronic patients now receiving episodic rather than regular care? Are provider-initiated visits being refused because of cost, or at least because of fear of being charged? Without such data, it is impossible to evaluate outcomes accurately. It may be easy to count a reduction in clinic visits, but it is appreciably more difficult to discover whether it is only the frivolous and trivial services, which are avoided or whether needed care is being discouraged. Unless a system is willing and able to carry out this type of research, it is perhaps unwise to initiate a program which charges inmates for health care.

The concerns raised in this chapter about charging inmates for health services are serious. The burden of proof should rest on those wishing to break new ground. Without careful and objective research, one cannot say confidently that there are no unintended consequences. Without in any way denying that abuses do occur and that frivolous use of costly health services should be discouraged, there probably are more effective and less costly means of achieving the desired result. The consequences of error are great, in terms of irreparable harm to the health of a patient as well as the potentially high costs of treating those who have waited too long for care.

7 SPECIAL ISSUES OF AGING

Portions of this chapter were adapted from "Perspective from the Field: Golden Years and Iron Gates," by Kenneth L. Faiver in Correctional Assessment, Casework, and Counseling, *Second Edition, edited by Anthony Walsh (Lanham, Md: American Correctional Association, 1997): 351-354.*

Much of what is discussed about the frail elderly in this chapter applies to disabled and physically handicapped inmates. In fact, for those persons who do not cope well in the general population, it may be feasible to provide special housing arrangements which accommodate both handicapped as well as elderly persons.

Aging of the Population

Everyone is familiar with the term "baby boomer." In the euphoria and economic growth following World War II, many more babies were born in the United States than in any comparable period of history. This caused a "demographic bulge"—a distortion from the stylized "Christmas-tree" pattern of age distribution in a typical population, in which the gradual effects of mortality steadily reduce the number of living persons in each older age group until, at the top, remain just those few who reach the highest ages.

As the "bulge" of persons born between 1946 and 1964 [1] has moved progressively upward, we have witnessed the greatly increased demand for goods and services associated with specific ages, for example, childhood toys, grade schools, high schools, colleges and universities, automobiles, houses, and recently, retirement homes and nursing homes. These growth spurts in the various industries often were followed by a dip, or decrease in demand, for the same goods and services. Then, an "echo" boom followed twenty to thirty years later, a result of the offspring of the baby

---

[1] Cf. *Modern Maturity* (January/February, 1996): 32 ff.

boomers themselves. Over the next few decades, the original baby boomer bulge will be entering the senior-citizen category.

The shape of a population distribution is not determined solely by birth rates. The other major factor is the death rate. The most important contributor to the present increase in number (and proportion) of elderly citizens is the decrease in mortality. People are living longer than ever before. Infant mortality has been reduced. Impaired, weakened, or worn-out tissues and organs can be repaired or even replaced. Improved diagnostic and treatment modalities continue to work their miracles. Modern communication and transportation enable fast life-saving responses to medical emergencies.

Fewer people die from raging epidemics and infections than a generation ago, chiefly because of better sanitary practices and the introduction of powerful antibiotics and vaccines. Poliomyelitis, a dreaded crippling disease, has all but been eliminated in the U.S. within our own lifetime. Deaths from heart disease and stroke have been reduced significantly and, with proper diet and exercise and lifestyle adjustments, can be reduced still further. Surgical, radiation, and chemical treatments now are available for many forms of cancer. Organ transplants and treatments, like hemodialysis, dramatically can extend life. Significant breakthroughs in the treatment of AIDS, such as protease inhibitors, are offering new hope for those who had believed there would be no cure.

An important consequence of the baby boomer phenomenon and the reduced death rate is the greatly increased number of the old, older, and very old. Nursing homes, retirement villages, and senior citizen discounts are proliferating as evidence of this trend. Of relevance also is the high cost of medical services consumed by this group.

Geriatric and Frail Elderly Prisoners

Naturally, this increase in the proportion of elderly in the free world population is reflected also in the nation's adult correctional institutions. The Federal Bureau of Prisons estimated that by 2005, 16 percent of its prisoner population will be fifty years or older compared with 11.7 percent in 1988.[2] In 1989, the nation's prisons held 30,500 inmates fifty years of age or older. By 1994, that number had risen to more than 55,000.[3]

Additionally, longer sentences are being imposed and fewer inmates are being granted parole. Thus, more and more persons are growing older behind bars. With their frailties, illness, and disabilities, they require large amounts of care and services. As their numbers increase, these older prisoners are on their way to becoming a major factor in the skyrocketing costs of correctional health care. They bring new and challenging problems for the correctional facilities. For example, how much is society willing to spend to keep an elderly or infirm prisoner alive? What social amenities, environmental modifications, and procedural adjustments/compromises must be made to accommodate aged and disabled prisoners?

---

[2] Douglas C. McDonald, *Managing Prison Health Care and Costs* (Washington, D.C.: National Institute of Justice, 1995): 2.

[3] Larry Linton, "Alabama's Solution to an Old Dilemma," *Corrections Forum* (November/December, 1996): 82.

Elderly inmates, like the chronically ill and often the handicapped, also tend to be housed in facilities which offer the greatest amount of medical services—typically in maximum-security institutions. The cost per bed to construct and operate these high-security facilities is far greater than is the cost for minimum-security facilities. Thus, many of these persons, whose criminal record and institutional behavior otherwise would classify them as minimum security, are being housed in much more costly beds.

The geriatric population of prisons often is defined to include inmates who are fifty years of age or older. A primary reason for selecting such a relatively young age is that, due to socioeconomic status, lack of access to medical care, their lifestyle, and other factors common to this population before entering prison, many inmates have aged more rapidly than their contemporaries in the free world.

A Profile of Elderly Offenders in Michigan [4]

The median age of inmates in Michigan climbed to 32.4 years in 1995, the oldest in state history, as shown in Figure 7-1. For the past ten years, the median age has been rising by six months each year and shows no tendency of slowing down. In 1989, Michigan prisons held 400 men and women in their sixties or above; this number reached 706 in 1996.[5] Some older persons suffering from mental illness used to live out their days in state mental institutions. But now that most mental hospitals are closed, many find themselves in jail or prison as a result of socially unacceptable behavior.

FIGURE 7-1. ELDERLY STATE PRISONERS IN MICHIGAN AS A PERCENTAGE OF TOTAL PRISON POPULATION*

	Number and Percent at Each Age, 1986 to 1996					
	1986		1991		1996	
Age 55-59	223	1.1%	392	1.1%	737	1.7%
Age 60-64	132	0.6%	237	0.7%	368	0.9%
Age 65+	82	0.4%	217	0.6%	364	0.9%
Total Age 55+	437	2.1%	846	2.4%	1,469	3.5%
Mean Age	30.8		32.0		33.8	
Median Age	29.2		30.5		32.8	

*All prisoners, including correctional camps and community corrections centers. Data for 1996 are preliminary. Personal communication with William W. Lovett, Research Division, Michigan Department of Corrections (March 25, 1997).

---

[4] Much of the material in this section was published in Faiver, *op. cit.*: 352-353.

[5] William W. Lovett, Research Division, Michigan Department of Corrections, personal communication (March 25, 1997).

The number of older state and federal prisoners in the United States has risen from 10,232 in 1985 to more than 24,641 in 1996,[6] an average annual increase of 141 percent. In Michigan, the number of elderly prisoners has nearly doubled in six years from 622 in 1988 to 1,171 in 1994, for an average annual increase of 11.1 percent.

The 469 offenders in the Michigan Department of Corrections who were in their sixties or older in April of 1992 exhibited the characteristics shown in Figure 7-2.

FIGURE 7-2. ELDERLY MICHIGAN PRISONERS (AGE 60+) BY TYPE OF CRIME AND NUMBER OF OFFENSES [7]

	Assaultive Crime		Property Offense		Total
	Criminal Sexual Conduct	Other	Drug Sale or Possession	Other	
First Time Offenders	141	91	27	19	278
Repeat Offenders	55	86	16	34	191
Total	196	177	43	53	469
Percent	41.8	37.7	9.2	11.3	100.0

Note that 42 percent of elderly prisoners are serving time for criminal sexual-conduct charges. Nearly three-fourths of these had no prior criminal record in Michigan. Another 38 percent are guilty of other assaultive crimes. Almost half of these have multiple convictions. Many have been incarcerated since youth, and are serving one or more life sentences. The remaining 20 percent are in prison for drug or property-related offenses (See Figure 7-3 on page 127).

These elderly inmates can be categorized into three groups, as shown in Figure 7-4 (page 127), according to the length of their sentence and whether the crime is related to sexual misconduct. Thus, 72 percent of inmates aged sixty or over are serving sentences of six months to fifteen years. Half of these are incarcerated for sexual misconduct and will require special counseling and rehabilitation before returning to society. Most of the remaining 28 percent are unlikely to be released to the free world, and will die in prison.

---

[6] American Correctional Association, *Directory of Juvenile and Adult Correctional Departments, Institutions, Agencies and Paroling Authorities* (Lanham., Md: American Correctional Association, 1997): xxxii.

[7] Lovett, W. W., et al., *Report on Michigan's Elderly Prison Population* (Lansing, Mich.: Michigan Department of Corrections, April, 1992): 20.

FIGURE 7-3. ELDERLY MICHIGAN PRISONERS (AGE 60+) BY TYPE OF CRIME AND DURATION OF SENTENCE[8]

Minimum Sentence	Assaultive Crime		Property Offense		Total	Percent
	Criminal Sexual Conduct	Other	Drug Sale or Possession	Other		
6 Months to 5 Years	105	39	21	40	205	43.7
5 to 15 Years	62	47	13	11	133	28.4
16+ Years	16	9	3	1	29	6.2
Life Sentence	13	82	6	1	102	21.7
TOTAL	196	177	43	53	469	100.0

FIGURE 7-4. ELDERLY INMATES IN MICHIGAN, BY LENGTH OF SENTENCE AND CRIME [9]

Length of Sentence	Number	Percent
Relatively short sentences for sexual misconduct	167	35.6
Relatively short sentences for other crimes	171	36.4
Long sentences, including life sentence	131	27.9

Some Practical Considerations

Data such as these in Figures 7-1 through 7-4 are helpful for those planning to meet the needs of this population. There are significant implications for discharge planning, sexual-offender counseling, long-term housing, medical care costs, and hospice care. These trends, which reflect a greater percentage of elderly prisoners as well as increased numbers of inmates serving longer sentences,[10] have some important practical implications (See Figure 7-5).

---

[8] Lovett, et al., *loc. cit.*

[9] Lovett, et al., *loc. cit.*

[10] Tracy L. Snell, *Correctional Populations in the United States, 1991* (Washington, D.C.: Bureau of Justice Statistics, August, 1993):26f.

Figure 7-5. Important Practical Considerations

- Significant cost of medical care for the elderly

- Consideration for compassionate release

- Hospice care

- "Do not resuscitate" orders

- Extended care facilities, nursing homes

- American with Disabilities Act

- Health screening tests

Cost of medical care for the elderly is significant. Not all elderly inmates, of course, are ill. Some fifty, sixty, and seventy-year-old inmates are in excellent health. But overall, both the frequency and the seriousness of illness tends to increase with age. Unfortunately, many jurisdictions currently are not able to track costs by age, but data from several sources suggest that the cost of medical care for elderly prisoners approaches three times the average cost. California,[11] for example, recently reported that the average annual cost of a thirty-year-old inmate was $21,000, while the state was spending an average of $69,000 for each prisoner over age sixty. Similarly, the state of Washington [12] indicated that its average cost per prisoner in 1994 was $27,000, whereas the cost for an elderly inmate was $77,000, most of which resulted from a higher demand for health care. A report of the National Criminal Justice Commission indicates that the annual cost of an elderly state inmate is $69,000, or more than three times the $22,000 a year it costs to imprison the typical adult inmate.[13]

Compassionate release. More persons will complete their lives while under sentence. Some of these may not need to die in prison. Especially as they become disabled or terminally ill, and depending on a number of factors, many will no longer represent a real threat or danger to society. Under such circumstances, consideration should be given to seeking approval from the parole board or the governor for release in a time-sensitive manner. Special laws may be necessary in some states to enable or facilitate compassionate release.

Hospice Care. In 1994, 3,011 sentenced prisoners under the jurisdiction of state and federal correctional institutions died. [14] For those who cannot be released, humane environments should be prepared for the terminally ill. Hospices in the free

---

[11] *Detroit Free Press* (March 31, 1996): 10A.

[12] "Elderly: Regular Inmates or Nursing Home Residents?" *Correctional Health Care Management* (April, 1994).

[13] *The Real War on Crime*, (Harper Perennial, 1996), cited in "Prison Care," *Modern Maturity*, (March/April, 1997): 33.

[14] Bureau of Justice Statistics, *Sourcebook of Criminal Justice Statistics 1995* (Washington, D.C.: Bureau of Justice Statistics, 1996): 602.

world can serve as a model. People associated with the hospice movement are often happy to provide advice and valuable assistance for replication of features of this program in the prisons. [15]

"Do not resuscitate" orders. Facility policy needs to be specific about "do not resuscitate" orders, advance directives, and durable power of attorney. It is appropriate to respect the inmate's wishes and to permit death with dignity. Legal advice should be sought in preparing the policy, and due care must be observed to ensure that the terminal patient (or this person's properly constituted representative) provides witnessed informed consent and does so without coercion. Where feasible, family members should be consulted. The chaplain also may be helpful. Clearly unacceptable is the statement made recently by one correctional facility administrator: "We don't bother with DNR orders here. We just run a slow code."

Secure extended-care facilities, or nursing homes, may need to be developed. A number of systems already have done this. However, if these were planned at a time when the number of elderly and chronically disabled inmates was far less, most likely they no longer will be adequate. Besides in-house units, nursing home beds also can be contracted in the community. The number of inmates who are frail and disabled and who require assistance with activities of daily living (dressing, feeding, bathing, toileting, walking) will continue to increase. Some of these will need nursing home care. Those who are incontinent must be diapered and bathed frequently. These are costly, highly labor-intensive services. Disorders such as Alzheimer's disease and organic brain syndrome resulting from the aging process also place major burdens on caregivers.

Specialized housing for the elderly, perhaps in a low-security unit constructed near a prison medical complex, may be a cost-effective solution to some difficult management problems. It even may be possible to parole some prisoners to a community long-term care facility, enabling support from Medicaid and Medicare programs.

Americans with Disabilities Act. Compliance with the requirements of the Americans with Disabilities Act (ADA) will place greater burdens on correctional systems as the number of elderly and disabled inmates increases.[16] Concerns include many items, such as steps and barriers, width of doorways, handrailings and grab bars, and height of lavatories. Most older correctional facilities have deficiencies in these areas.

Health screening tests. Given the more rapid aging of prisoners, some health screening tests should be offered to inmates perhaps ten years earlier than generally is recommended for the citizenry at large. The physiological age of many prisoners tends to be greater than their chronological age. [17]

---

[15] Donald Fiske, "Pennsylvania Department of Corrections Joins with Local Hospice to Meet Needs of Dying Inmates," 8:3, *CorrectCare* (August, 1994): 4.

[16] *Correctional Health Care Management* (July, 1993): 92.

[17] Some experts, including John Clark, M.D., M.P.H., medical director of the Los Angeles County Jail, and Dean P. Rieger, M.D., M.P.H., medical director of the Indiana Department of Corrections, estimate a ten-year differential, in other words, that a typical inmate population exhibits physiological characteristics ten years older than does a free-world group of the same chronological age. (John Clark, *Correctional Health Care Management* (April, 1994): 52. Dean P. Rieger, personal correspondence).

Special Housing Units

When there were only a handful of elderly inmates, the younger offenders typically protected and assisted them. Officers could make some allowances for special needs of the old timer. With the increasing number of elderly, this is often not the case anymore. The younger inmates take advantage of and abuse the old and the weak. Officers cannot make exceptions for some inmates. As a result, some systems have found it helpful to arrange suitable living units, with special programming that is separate from younger inmates, such as in, Alabama.[18] A study by Joann B. Morton in 1991 found fourteen special units for the elderly in prison systems. [19] These included units in the following systems: Florida, Georgia, Illinois, Indiana, Kentucky, Minnesota, North Carolina, Ohio, South Carolina, Virginia, West Virginia, Wisconsin, Wyoming, and the Federal Bureau of Prisons.

Older inmates who wish to live in special housing units should be given this option, but available space and security considerations should be taken into account. Mainstreaming should remain an option for those older inmates who are physically able and who express a preference to live this way. This practice recognizes the cultural and behavioral differences among disparate age groups and seeks a healthy accommodation to lifestyle preferences and requirements. The mainstream approach is appropriate for healthy, agile, and alert persons, regardless of their age. But as physical limitations and confusion begin to appear, it probably is cost effective to create separate living areas. The physical plants commonly found in correctional facilities were designed for young and physically active inmates. Living units and support-service buildings frequently are scattered over wide areas, and inmates must walk long distances for meals, medical services, and other activities. Architectural barriers, such as steps, narrow doorways, and lack of handrails or grab bars, present additional problems which older inmates encounter. Poor ventilation and inadequate climate control can be extremely hard on the elderly as well as on persons with chronic lung conditions.

There is nothing wrong with enlisting the assistance of other prisoners for the disabled. Other, healthy elderly inmates may excel as "wheelchair pushers" and be able to assist in feeding, helping an inmate ambulate, or writing letters and medical request slips. Carefully selected younger prisoners also may be assigned to this task. Such a programs is in place at the Federal Medical Center in Rochester, Minnesota. The inmate workers in the hospice program are volunteers, recommended by the unit team and medically approved. They demonstrate maturity and are willing to participate in initial and regular ongoing training. Duties include assisting the terminal patient by providing companionship, reading, talking, feeding, letter writing, and assisting with recreational, and institutional activity. [20]

---

[18] Larry Linton, "Alabama's Solution to an Old Dilemma," *Corrections Forum* (November/December, 1996): 82 f.

[19] Joann B. Morton, *An Administrative Overview of the Older Inmate* (Washington, D.C.: National Institute of Corrections, 1992): 21-24.

[20] "Hospice Program Procedures," (Rochester, Minn.: Federal Medical Center, July, 1995).

At the Lakeland Correctional Facility in Coldwater, Michigan, prisoner assistants help elderly prisoners with correspondence, assist nonambulatory prisoners in getting from one place to another, aid in cleaning the room and changing bed linen, assist in pick-up and delivery of laundry, and perform other duties individualized to a particular prisoner with approval of both health care and housing unit staff. They do not cook food, remove soiled linen, assist with personal hygiene and toileting, clean urinals or health care appliances, give medication, or transfer the prisoner in and out of bed.[21]

FIGURE 7-6. MANAGEMENT PROBLEMS WITH ELDERLY INMATES

- They are vulnerable to predatory abuse

- They need accommodation for their individual disabilities

- They have difficulty mixing with younger, more aggressive inmates

- They may require special types of programming

- They consume a disproportionate share of health care services

Such units bring about reduced management problems within the remaining prisons operated by the system. Elderly and disabled inmates require special accommodations for their deteriorating physical and mental condition, increased supervision and protection, and more frequent escort to health care services. They also frequently are annoyed by or become a source of irritation to younger, more active prisoners who share the same housing and activity space.

Geriatric prisoners who have chronic or debilitating illness require a significantly greater expenditure of financial resources than other prisoners. For example, health care costs for Medicaid patients over sixty years of age in the community are approximately three times greater than for younger patients. Older persons are disproportionately heavy consumers of health care services. "Approximately 31 percent of all personal health care expenditures nationwide were for persons sixty-five years of age or older."[22]

Specialized Programming

A specialized program for elderly and handicapped can include preventive health activities to decrease medical costs; provide a diet appropriate to elderly

---

[21] "Job Duties: Prisoner Assistants for for Disabled Prisoners," (Coldwater, Mich.: Lakeland Correctional Facility, 1996).

[22] U.S. Senate Special Committee on Aging, American Association of Retired Persons, Federal Council on Aging and Administration on Aging, *Aging America: Trends and Projections* (Rockville, Md.: U.S. Department of Health and Human Services, 1986).

persons; develop enhanced creative therapy programs; offer self-help programming; community service and work opportunities; sex-offender counseling and therapy; life-coping skills for maturing adults; assistance with activities of daily living and personal care needs related to Alzheimer's disease, arthritis, diabetes, cardiovascular and respiratory problems, loss of eyesight and hearing, and other chronic or acute debilitating conditions; opportunity for worship and religious counseling; a hospice program for terminally ill residents; nursing care; and discharge and reentry planning, as shown in Figure 7-7.

FIGURE 7-7. A SPECIALIZED PROGRAM FOR ELDERLY AND HANDICAPPED CAN INCLUDE:

- Preventive health activities
- Diet appropriate to elderly persons
- Enhanced creative therapy programs
- Self-help programming
- Community service opportunities
- Sex-offender counseling and therapy

- Life-coping skills for maturing adults
- Help with activities of daily living
- Worship and religious counseling
- Hospice program for terminally ill
- Nursing care
- Discharge and reentry planning

A social work component is essential for a facility specializing in the elderly. Discharge planning is important for those who have any likelihood of being returned to the community. The focus would include Medicare and Medicaid enrollment, Veterans' benefits, community mental health, housing, employment, public assistance, and renewal of family ties.[23]

Douglass et al. pointed out the importance of considering the plight of long-term prisoners who return to a world that rejected them and that they rejected. The older, discharged prisoner usually faces substantial difficulties upon reentry to the community, as highlighted by a 1988 study of elderly homeless persons in Detroit. It showed that the probability of homelessness for the elderly was as strongly associated with prior prison experience as with mental hospitalization (about 30 percent). The authors concluded that discharge planning for older prisoners was indicated.[24]

---

[23] Kenneth L. Faiver, "Perspective from the Field: Golden Years and Iron Gates," *op cit.*: 354.

[24] Richard L. Douglass, Mary Lindemann, and William Lovett, *Oldtimers: Michigan's Elderly Prisoners* (Lansing, Mich.: Michigan Office of Services to the Aging and the Gerontological Society of America, 1991).

8 WOMEN'S HEALTH ISSUES

This chapter was co-authored by Dean P. Rieger M.D., M.P.H., currently Medical Director of the Indiana Department of Corrections and former Medical Director of Huron Valley Women's Facility in Michigan.

Incarcerated women are overwhelmingly poor. Their crimes often were committed for economic reasons. According to statistics from the National Women's Law Center, 8 to 10 percent of women are pregnant when they enter prisons while 15 percent are postpartum. [1]

Kaminer [2] found that the first time some pregnant women receive prenatal care is when they are incarcerated. The support network within the prison often is better than the women experienced on the outside. In the institution, they may receive counseling and prenatal classes on how to care for their babies.

A recent study of pregnant inmates conducted at a major correctional facility for females in a southern state provides evidence that pregnant inmates tend to have high-risk lifestyle behaviors, inadequate prenatal care and follow-up, increased general stress, poor psychological health, and inadequate social support. [3] More than half of the women in this study had received inadequate prenatal care, and about 5 percent had received no prenatal care whatever.

The proportion of women in prisons and jails is increasing steadily, and their number has tripled in the past decade. Women continue to comprise a small minority of the total prisoners in most jail and prison systems, but their health care needs tend

---

[1] Renee Pitre, "Jail Introduces Healthy Start Project," 8:1, *CorrectCare* (February, 1994):1.

[2] Anita Kaminer, "Women in Prison: Study Looks at Life, Maternal Feelings," 6:3, *CorrectCare* (Summer, 1992): 14.

[3] Catherine Ingram Fogel, "Pregnant Prisoners: Impact of Incarceration on Health and Health Care," 2:2, *Journal of Correctional Health Care* (Fall, 1995): 169-190.

to exceed those of incarcerated men. The reasons for this are myriad. Incarcerated women tend to carry all the health risks that accompany extreme poverty. In addition, they are usually of childbearing age, and many are pregnant at the time of incarceration. As a group, women, in general, require more health care services than do men. Serious mental illness, especially major depressive disorders, are diagnosed more frequently in women than in men—incarcerated women also reflect this gender disparity.

The American Correctional Association's Public Policy on Correctional Health Care eloquently makes this point:

> Correctional facilities are generally designed for male detainees and do not reflect women's stronger need for physical privacy and sustained group interactions. Little or no attention has been paid to the physical reproductive issues and special needs for services and treatment of mental disorders. Some of the gender-specific needs of women that require special and differential focus revolve around pre- and postpartum problems and complications of pregnancy, primary responsibility for minor children, a history of domestic violence, early childhood physical and sexual abuse, adult rape, and a high probability of a dual diagnosis of mental disorder and substance abuse. In addition, the prescription of psychotropic medications that may be necessary to treat these disorders may carry untold side effects that, in turn, further affect physical and emotional functioning.[4]

Female prisoners have tended to be managed as the system's stepchildren, being placed in out-of-the-way places in larger, mostly male facilities, or in older facilities noted to be inadequate even before they were emptied of male prisoners to become female units. Correctional systems often have to recognize the increased demands and needs for health care services for female populations. Providing only the same per prisoner resources as were provided to male prisoners, or even providing less is an inadequate response. Thus, a secondary role for female prisoners is reflective of society itself.

During the past twenty-five years, prison systems have undergone great changes as the numbers of female prisoners grew faster than did the numbers of male prisoners. Court-ordered requirements for equalized distribution of resources by gender (both inside and outside of correctional settings), enhancement of the role and visibility of female staff members, and successful lawsuits have combined to increase the likelihood that services provided to female prisoners will be adequate. The legal basis for delivery of health care services to women is indistinguishable from that for the delivery of such services to men, with the added necessity of maintaining gender equity. Women have a right to access to care, the right to care that is ordered, and the right to a professional medical judgment—they must be free from deliberate indifference to their serious medical needs.

---

[4] American Correctional Association, *Public Policy on Correctional Health Care* (Lanham, Md.: American Correctional Association, June, 1996): 15.

Intake and Screening Activities

The obligation of the correctional agency to deliver health care services begins at the moment of incarceration. (This is true both for short-term and long-term facilities. Where significant differences in management of these types of facilities exist, the differences will be noted.) Screening at the point of entry must identify serious medical needs requiring immediate treatment and must protect the existing facility population and staff from the introduction of serious communicable diseases. During the early period of incarceration, more thorough screening is required (depending upon the length of stay) to identify serious but less obvious conditions needing treatment. In addition to the content of the screening procedure for men, women need to be screened for pregnancy and certain sexually transmitted diseases. Inquiry regarding care for children left behind also should be made. Depending upon age and duration of incarceration, women also need to be screened for menstrual difficulties, breast cancer, cancer of the cervix, and additional sexually transmitted diseases.[5]

Most of the women in jails and prisons are of childbearing age. A significant percentage are pregnant (some unknowingly) and will require prenatal services while incarcerated. It is important to identify pregnant prisoners and plan for their care during incarceration. It is also important to recognize that the majority of pregnant prisoners are definable as "high-risk pregnancies" because of drug use or other concurrent health conditions. This concern is supported by the American Correctional Association standard which requires specific pregnancy management considerations with respect to pregnancy testing, routine prenatal care, high-risk prenatal care, management of the chemically addicted pregnant inmate, and postpartum follow-up.[6]

Some sexually transmitted diseases, such as pelvic inflammatory disease, may be immediately and acutely obvious and require immediate care, possibly even hospitalization. Others, such as syphillis, may run a more indolent course. Still others, such as gonorrhea or chlamydia, sometimes may be present acutely and at other times be completely asymptomatic. The receiving facility should be prepared to identify and initiate treatment for acute sexually transmitted diseases such as chlamydia and gonorrhea. Nonacute conditions should be identified during the early portion of incarceration but not necessarily at the point of entry. Some jurisdictions may have additional sexually transmitted diseases of concern, and the local and state departments of health can be very helpful in advising on what screening is necessary.

A large number of incarcerated women are single heads of households. Short-stay facilities, in particular, should inquire about the care of a female prisoner's children[7]

---

[5] An important point is raised in the *Public Policy on Correctional Health Care* of the American Correctional Association: "Regarding women's issues in prisons, the Task Force recommends developing a diagnostic process that is sensitive to the differences between men and women. The instruments currently used are not appropriate for women." Lanham, Md. (June, 1996): 18.

[6] American Correctional Association, *1996 Standards Supplement,* Standard 3-4343-1.

[7] See Cynthia Blinn, ed., *Maternal Ties: A Selection of Programs for Female Offenders* (Lanham, Md.: American Correctional Association, 1997) for a description of programs.

and make necessary referrals to child protection agencies. This is not necessarily a health care responsibility, but in some settings may be assigned to a social worker or psychologist.

Menstrual irregularities are common among inmates of female facilities. In part, this is because of the poverty and accompanying poor nutrition and medical care prior to incarceration, in part because of prior drug use, and in part because of the stress of incarceration itself. Menstrual irregularities should be identified and, if serious, treated. Menstrual cramps and premenstrual syndromes almost universally can be managed with over-the-counter or prescription nonsteroidal anti-inflammatory medication, but in severe or persistent cases the physician may wish to prescribe other therapy.[8] Provision of personal sanitary supplies—napkins and/or tampons—should be an obvious responsibility. Douches have no value in managing menstrual flow, although some cultures prefer their use. Providing access to douches is not a health care responsibility.

Routine breast care should be provided in longer-stay facilities. Identification of breast cancer is part of the provision of necessary medical services, and should include both physical examination by a health care professional and mammographic examination. The facility's health authority should review the various guidelines for these services and determine at what ages and frequency they will be offered. There are several different and conflicting recommendations by expert bodies, and there is no one "right" way to carry out this service. The facility should choose the least expensive but acceptable schedule for these services. It is possible to bring a mobile mammogram unit to a prison or jail and, thereby, reduce the logistical difficulties associated with off-site services.

Female prisoners are more likely than women in the general population to have had multiple sexual partners and thus are more likely to be infected with the human papilloma virus. Because of this, female prisoners have a higher than otherwise would be expected frequency of abnormal Pap smears suggestive of cancer of the cervix. All but short-stay facilities should screen for the presence of cervical cancer with Pap smears. As with screening for breast cancer, there are many different recommendations regarding the appropriate intervals for screening. Generally, but not universally, accepted practice is that two negative Pap smears, one year apart, should be followed by smears every third year, unless a high-risk condition (such as HIV positivity) is present. The National Commission on Correctional Health Care standards require a pelvic examination and a Papanicolaou (Pap) smear within seven days of arrival into a prison system,[9] and further require a gynecological assessment within seven days of arrival at a juvenile correctional facility.[10]

Women, and particularly women in the socioeconomic groups primarily represented in correctional settings, are at high risk for HIV infection. Women comprise

---

[8] See also Anthony Walsh, *Correctional Assessment Casework and Counseling*, Second Edition (Lanham, Md.: American Correctional Association, 1997): 326-330.

[9] NCCHC, Standards for Prisons, op. cit., Standard P-34.

[10] NCCHC, Standards for Juvenile Facilities, op. cit., Standard Y-33.

the fastest growing component of HIV-infected individuals in this country, and the incidence of HIV infection among female prisoners long has exceeded that of male prisoners, reversing the picture in the general society. Screening for HIV infection, while generally desirable, must conform to local regulations and laws. Certainly voluntary screening should be offered, with counseling prior to and following the testing. In some jurisdictions, mandatory screening is legislatively supported. The safeguards necessary for carrying out HIV screening for men are equally applicable to women.

General Outpatient Considerations

Female prisoners, like females in the general society, demand health care services at a frequency higher than males. In many correctional settings, this female demand is two to three times as high as in male facilities. Health care resources in correctional settings (in terms of physical plant, equipment, staff, and budget) need to reflect this expectation. Actual recommendations regarding staff-to-patient ratios cannot be provided because of variability in programs that make any such recommendations unreliable and misleading. The three rights established by federal case law (right to access, right to ordered treatment, and right to a professional judgment) must be respected, and resources adequate to address these issues must be made available.

Correctional facilities should arrange, if at all possible, for office gynecological care (including prenatal services) to be provided on-site. On-site services are much more cost effective than continued off-site trips. Moreover, on-site providers come to understand the correctional setting as well as the games that prisoners play much better than do off-site providers.

Examination areas should be equipped in a manner appropriate to the care that will be provided in them. If Pap smears and pelvic exams are to be performed, adequate lighting, a table with stirrups, supplies, and equipment must be available.

Examination of genitalia and breasts requires a chaperone, no matter the gender of the examiner. This chaperone should be of the same sex as the patient, but when this is not possible, the chaperone should be a health care employee. This is more consistent with a professional and clinical atmosphere, and is likely to reduce complaints.

Some conditions managed primarily in outpatient settings, while seen in both men and women, are significantly more common in women. These include obesity, diabetes, and depression.

Being overweight, while a significant medical condition often associated with other health problems, is not by itself a serious problem unless body weight reaches at least 50 percent above the ideal weight. Obesity can be addressed in a general fashion by making available information about ideal weight and the calorie content of the facility diet, and by making a scale available to inmates to monitor their own weight gain or loss. It need not be addressed with counseling or specific weight reduction diets. These interventions, while desirable, are not especially effective and carry with them the potential for great expense and a degree of secondary gain.

Morbid obesity (weight greater than 50 percent above ideal body weight) is a serious medical problem and should be addressed during prolonged incarceration. Because of the availability of close supervision, correctional facilities faced with treating this condition may use controls on access to food and need not consider interventions such as stomach stapling. As with other treatments, informed consent is necessary when treating morbid obesity. The close supervision should not be abusive but should be overseen by health care personnel with an understanding of obesity and eating disorders as health issues.

Diabetes management requires a practitioner familiar with the up-to-date management of both insulin- and noninsulin-dependent diabetes. If the facility's primary care provider is not extremely familiar with the issues involved, a specialist also should be involved. Proper management of diabetes requires:

- An understanding of the medications

- Dietary provision

- Nutritional counseling

- Counseling regarding the balancing of food, activity, and medication

- The capability to address hypoglycemia

- The capability to monitor, up to four times a day, finger-stick blood glucose; monitoring (especially in long-stay settings) for the development of retinopathy, nephropathy, cardiac disease, and other long-term diabetes sequelae

Some depression is to be expected when arrest or incarceration occurs. It is not unusual for disturbances in mood usually associated with depression to be noted during these stressful life changes. Facilities, while ever mindful of suicide and serious depressive disorders, should not rush into an early diagnosis of major depression during the period of adjustment to incarceration, absent a history of significant illness. Still, it must be recognized that a significant percentage (up to 25 percent) of incarcerated women may be depressed. It is necessary to have available services to identify and manage major depressive disorders. When feasible, it is cost effective to have these services on-site.

Separation from their children is a significant source of stress for incarcerated women. The great majority of female inmates are mothers of young children. Clinicians should be aware of manifestations of this stress in the women's physical and emotional health. Parenting issues also should be appropriately addressed in the services provided.[11]

Very many of the women in prisons and jails and juvenile correctional facilities have been victims of physical, verbal, and emotional abuse, as well as sexual abuse. Consequently, they may experience lifelong problems of post-traumatic stress disorder, depressive and anxiety disorders, substance abuse, dependence, behavioral disorders, and learning problems. Some of the abuse may have caused serious physical impairment or traumatic brain injury. Appropriate counseling to help resolve issues

---

[11] American Correctional Association, *Public Correctional Policy on Female Offender Services*, originally passed 1984, reviewed and amended 1995, in Cincinnati, Ohio at the Congress of Correction. *NCCHC, Position Statement: Women's Health Care in Correctional Settings,* adopted by the NCCHC Board of Directors (September 25, 1994).

of victimization and perpetration of violence against intimates, such as conflict-resolution skills or parenting skills, should be available.[12] Unfortunately, too few health care professionals have been trained adequately to take the experience of victimization effectively into account when they treat patients.

Additional Reproductive Issues

Contraception[13] usually is made unnecessary during confinement by the absence of heterosexual activity. However, in jurisdictions that permit conjugal visits or furloughs, or in community correctional settings in which sexual intercourse is permitted or possible, provision for contraception should be made. Condoms, useful both for contraception and reduction of transmission of certain diseases, are readily available in the community without a prescription, and certain jurisdictions may determine that they should be available also within the correctional setting. This decision has potential political ramifications, and should be made in association with system administrators. Information on contraception should be made available during incarceration and before release from incarceration. It is not necessary (although it may be desirable) to provide contraceptives of various types upon release from prison or jail.

Abortion, although currently established as a legitimate medical service to which women have a right, is handled variously in different jurisdictions. No system should provide an outright ban on this procedure, as that is likely to result in litigation and a reversal of the ban. However, it is necessary to work within the local political structure and provide greater or lesser access to this procedure in accordance with local ordinances and the current local political climate.

Of the approximately 55,000 female inmates in state and federal prisons in 1993, approximately one quarter were pregnant or newly delivered.[14] Studies repeatedly have shown that pregnancy outcomes of these women are poor and problematic, with a high rate of neonatal deaths. In part, this is due to use of drugs, inadequate prior health care, inadequate prenatal care, and the presence of sexually transmitted diseases.[15] A clear consequence of this is the need for greater attention to providing comprehensive maternity health care services in correctional facilities which house females. This need is likely to be even greater in jails and juvenile detention facilities.

Aging

Women live longer than men—perhaps six to nine years longer. As female prisoners age, additional needs develop. During menopause, hormonal replacement

---

[12] NCCHC, *Position Statement on Women's Health Care in Correctional Settings, op. cit.*

[13] Birth control pills used for menstrual regulation are a standard medical intervention and should be permitted when prescribed by the physican, even in jurisdictions which choose not to authorize the issuance of contraceptives.

[14] Fogel, *op cit.*: 170.

[15] Fogel, *op. cit.*: 175.

therapy usually will be appropriate and should be offered. Screening for endometrial cancer may be appropriate in selected populations. The health authority should review local practices regarding this condition and determine what, if any, screening should be provided. (This is applicable primarily to long-term stay facilities.)

With old age comes frailty. Facilities must plan for the care of elderly women with various disabilities. Depending upon the facility size and population, specialized housing units may be necessary and appropriate. Likewise, organic brain conditions, Alzheimer's disease, forgetfulness, and confusion are common conditions among the aging. Some women will require assistance with the activities of daily living.

Osteoporosis, a loss of bone calcification with subsequent bone weakening, is seen primarily in older women. In longer-stay facilities, measures to reduce or prevent the development of osteoporosis should be considered. Calcium supplementation appears to slow or prevent progression of osteoporosis. However, the regular diet should contain adequate calcium to meet the adult minimum daily requirement for women and supplementation should not be forced upon a facility population. Foods rich in calcium should be available. Physical exercises, such as movement against resistance (not just weight training) will help women avoid osteoporosis. Physical activity of this type should be encouraged in correctional facilities, though it is not suggested here that the current community standard would obligate a facility to structure such activity.

Cosmetic Concerns

Medical staff in correctional institutions often are called upon regarding cosmetic concerns of inmates. Purely cosmetic concerns are rarely, if ever, serious medical conditions and health care staff should not have to address them. Mild to moderate acne, simple dry skin, dandruff, and so on may be addressed through commissary items or may be ignored. A consistent policy on this type of issue will help reduce unnecessary sick-call activity. It will be helpful to prisoner morale if female prisoners are provided some routine access to cosmetics and hair care items, but it is not strictly necessary. On the other hand, surgical correction of severe facial scarring or facial deformity should be considered. Likewise, encouragement and assistance given to a patient of a psychiatric unit with her grooming, make-up, hair care, and personal hygiene is a very therapeutic activity and can promote self-esteem and a healthier outlook for the patient.

Health Education

Health education is an integral part of disease management. Health care services should be capable of providing health education targeted both to specific diseases, to reproductive issues, and to general hygiene issues. As indicated previously, classes and educational materials regarding parenting skills and coping with victimization also should be considered. These programs and materials not only should be available to those who come to the clinic for health care services, but also to those women who are not currently complaining of illness but who, nonetheless, may derive significant health benefit from this information.

Job Assignment

With the exception of pregnancy, assignment of women to work activities need not be any different from the assignment of men. With training, women can handle the same jobs as men, including jobs requiring manual labor. Restrictions based upon frailty, handicap, and illness are, of course, appropriate.

This consideration also applies to boot camp placement. Women, although not as strong (at least on the average and initially), successfully may participate in and complete boot camp programs.[16]

---

[16] American Correctional Association, *Juvenile and Adult Boot Camps* (Lanham, Md.: American Correctional Association, 1996) contains a description of successful programs, including several for women.

9 SPECIAL MENTAL HEALTH ISSUES

The author is greatly indebted to the collaboration of Robert S. Ort, M.D., Ph.D., who during countless and lengthy conversations, generously offered the benefit of his expertise in psychiatry and clinical psychology and extensive correctional health experience to elaborate on topics discussed in this chapter, and who also provided many helpful comments on early drafts.

Growth of the Problem

Most arrests of persons with mental disorders occur because they have been a nuisance, not because they are dangerous. Jails have become major intake centers for all kinds of health, welfare, and social problem cases in disguise. Too frequently, mental patients are passed along to the criminal justice system because community treatment and support programs cannot or will not handle their needs. Arrest has become a method commonly employed by police to manage the mentally ill, and studies have demonstrated that while the mentally ill suspects are no more likely to commit serious crimes than the nonmentally ill, their arrest rate is significantly higher.[1]

Linda A. Teplin,[2] who studied the Cook County Jail for the National Institute for Mental Health, has suggested that the jail is now the poor person's mental health facility. While the mental health system can say "no" to a patient, the criminal justice system may have become the system that cannot do so.[3] The dollars saved through

---

[1] Linda A. Teplin, "Policing the Mentally Ill: Styles, Strategies, and Implications," in Henry J. Steadman (ed.), *Jail Diversion for the Mentally Ill: Breaking through the Barriers* (Washington, D.C.: National Institute of Corrections, 1990): 11-13.

[2] *Ibid.*

[3] Ronald Jemelka, "The Mentally Ill in Local Jails: Issues in Admission and Booking," in Steadman (ed.), *op. cit.*: 39.

mental health program cutbacks may represent no real savings at all if they are off-set by higher expenditures in the criminal justice system.

Studies consistently have demonstrated that about 20 percent of inmates of prisons and jails are seriously mentally ill and in need of psychiatric care, and that up to 5 percent are actively psychotic.[4] A 1991 report from the General Accounting Office estimates that between 6 and 14 percent of the incarcerated population may have a major psychiatric disorder.[5] A large number of inmates also have been victims of closed head injury, with resultant neurological deficits. The chronically mentally ill who enter correctional systems also tend to serve more time than other inmates facing similar charges. One reason may be their limited ability to develop adequate parole plans.[6]

Life in correctional settings can be profoundly stressful. Environmental factors play a part, such as noise, crowded conditions, confined space, and too little sunshine. So also does the fear, real and imagined, of assault or injury from inmates or officers. Taunts and threats from other inmates can be terrifying. This is particularly so for first-time arrestees. Young, weak, and physically attractive persons quickly may discover themselves to be targets of sexual abuse. Prison and jail environments are also particularly hard on those who in their past have been subjected to physical or sexual abuse or to other traumatic stress, because they encounter so many stark reminders of these terrifying events. Particularly vulnerable also are persons with histories of mental illness, such as schizophrenia, depression, and anxiety disorder. Any of these persons may decompensate psychologically much more rapidly when experiencing the powerful stressors of jail and prison.

E. Fuller Torrey described very eloquently the plight of a mentally disordered inmate of a correctional institution:

> Being in jail or prison when your brain is working normally is, at best, an unpleasant experience. Being in jail or prison when your brain is playing tricks on you is often brutal.
>
> One reason for this is that jails and prisons are created for people who have broken laws. These institutions have rigid rules, both explicit and implicit, and a major purpose of incarceration is to teach inmates how to follow such rules. The system assumes that everybody can understand the rules and punishes anyone who breaks or ignores these structures. Because of illogical thinking, delusions, or auditory hallucinations, many of the mentally ill cannot comprehend the rules of jails and prisons and this has predictable, and sometimes tragic, consequences.[7]

---

[4] Henry C. Weinstein, "Psychiatric Services in Jails and Prisons: Who Cares?" 4:1, *CorrectCare* (January/February, 1990): 7.

[5] *Mentally Ill Inmates: Better Data Would Help Determine Protection and Advocacy Needs* (Washington, D.C.: General Accounting Office, April, 1991).

[6] Jane E. Haddad, "Management of the Chronically Mentally Ill within a Correctional Environment," 5:1, *CorrectCare* (January, 1991): 5.

The American Correctional Association, in its public policy statement of June 1996, said that competent treatment for serious mental illness should be provided to inmates and detainees in order

> to reduce the unnecessary extremes of human suffering that can be caused by untreated mental illness. Though inmates (not detainees) are sentenced to prison or jail as punishment, the terror that can accompany hallucinations or delusions, the profound grief that can accompany a suicidal depression, and other symptoms of mental illness go far beyond the expectations of a civilized society and serve no reasonable correctional purpose. Mental health professionals have a duty to provide such treatment in correctional settings. [8]

It is difficult to know how many inmates suffer from developmental disabilities and other forms of retardation. Santamour [9] has suggested between 4 and 9 percent. Most are not profoundly retarded. Many probably go unrecognized. These people have impaired cognitive skills and therefore are subject to being preyed upon and misled. They are not clever enough to assess a situation adequately. Therefore, they can be unduly influenced.

There is no need to perform intelligence testing on all newly arrived inmates. This would be an exceedingly costly process. Some jurisdictions have used a simple, often nonverbal, screening instrument, which can be administered by an officer or a mental health technician to a group of inmates. The validity of such screening may be questionable if it is administered soon after arrest or incarceration or if the inmate is poorly motivated to cooperate. Other, typically long-term, facilities use educational achievement testing to assist in proper program placement; low scores may indicate persons who are developmentally disabled or otherwise impaired and who should be referred for professional evaluation. Through the intake mental health assessment and arrival mental status examination, alert interviewers usually will recognize persons who have some problems in comprehension or function, and these should receive further professional testing and evaluation.[10]

Special housing units for persons with mental retardation offer a more structured environment, with significantly less stress for the inmates and also for the officers who must supervise them. Separated from the jeers of other inmates and from officers who become impatient with their slow comprehension, they begin to feel

---

[7] E. Fuller Torrey, *Out of the Shadows: Confronting America's Mental Illness Crisis* (New York: John Wiley & Sons, 1997): 31.

[8] American Correctional Association, *Public Policy on Correctional Health Care* (Lanham, Md.: American Correctional Association, June, 1996): 8.

[9] Miles B. Santamour, *The Mentally Retarded Offender and Corrections* (Lanham, Md.: American Correctional Association, 1989).

[10] The author is grateful to Thomas Fagan, Ph.D., of the American Psychological Association for his helpful comments of this subject. (Telephone conversation, May 28, 1997).

better about themselves. With increased self-esteem, the retarded become more cooperative. The environment should be simple, consistent, cooperative, and routine. It is a larger issue for prisons than jails, due to long-term stay of inmates in prisons.

Retarded persons become highly frustrated in jails, where they are separated from familiar surroundings and people. They become confused and overwhelmed with the countless variables involved in their court appearances, trial, and sentencing. Under these circumstances, supportive counseling becomes very important.

Mental illness sometimes is complicated by the simultaneous presence of mental retardation. Persons with these problems will experience functional impairment even when their psychosis or depression is adequately treated with medication.

The growing number of mentally disordered persons in penal institutions suggests the importance of addressing some of the significant issues being faced daily by correctional administrators and officials. This chapter discusses a variety of such concerns. The following chapter is devoted to the specific strategy of creating a therapeutic environment for those mentally ill prisoners who do not cope well in the general population setting.

Development of Policies for Management of Mentally Ill Inmates

Every jail, lockup, detention center, or prison, no matter how small, must provide or have access to a range of mental health services. These include arrival mental health screening; intake mental health assessment; professional evaluation of those inmates identified as having mental health problems; crisis intervention; outpatient follow-up services by a mental health specialist and, for those requiring psychotropic medication for mental illness, a psychiatrist; and access to a psychiatric inpatient unit. As indicated previously, there are reasons to develop an intermediate care unit for those who, due to their mental disorder, are not able to cope adequately in the general population. Not all of these services need to be on-site or available on a daily basis. Some correctional systems concentrate their mentally disordered prisoners in selected institutions where necessary services can be arranged more efficiently. In this case, assuming intake health screening is also centralized, all other facilities need only have an adequate crisis intervention and referral program, with readily available transportation for urgent cases.

Arrival Mental Health Screening

Arrival mental health screening may be performed by a correctional officer who has received special training for this purpose. It must occur immediately upon arrival at the facility, and should involve use of a structured questionnaire or checklist with documentation of the findings. It should ask whether the inmate has any current mental health problems, is experiencing suicidal ideation, or is taking any medication, and it should note whether the inmate appears to be disoriented, unconscious, confused, agitated, or depressed.

The screening process must have a low threshold for referral to more extensive evaluation.[11] Any indication of a mental health problem, whether by history or current symptoms, requires referral for a follow-up evaluation. An affirmative answer to questions like the following must be referred: Have you ever been in a mental hospital? Have you been treated for mental illness? Do you take medication for your nerves? Have you ever attempted suicide? Are you thinking about committing suicide now?

Intake Mental Health Assessment

Each inmate [12] should receive a formal mental health assessment within the first two weeks of arrival at the facility.[13] This may be performed by a mental health professional such as a psychologist or social worker, or by a physician, nurse, or physician assistant, who is qualified by education, credentials, and experience to evaluate and care for the mental health needs of patients. It is essential that mental health professionals be involved in developing the screening and assessment methodology, training those who carry it out, and setting up guidelines for referral. If the intelligence screening is performed in a group setting, each complete mental health assessment need not take more than five minutes of staff time for the vast majority of patients. The National Commission on Correctional Health Care recommends that this intake mental health assessment include all of the elements shown in Figure 9-1 (see page 148).

Professional Mental Health Referral Resources

Professional resources for evaluation and follow-up care must be identified in advance and available when a need for this service is identified during arrival screening, intake assessment, or on a subsequent occasion. Small facilities often arrange for these services through a community mental health agency which assigns a psychologist, social worker, or mental health nurse to come periodically, as needed, to assess those who have been identified as having a mental health problem and to provide follow-up and therapeutic support to a caseload of patients. Larger facilities usually employ psychiatrists, psychologists, social workers and others, as needed, to provide these services.

---

[11] Joel A. Dvoskin, "Jail-Based Mental Health Services," in Steadman (ed.), *Jail Diversion*, op. cit.: 68.

[12] The American Correctional Association's nonmandatory standard 3-4345 requires "collection of additional data to complete the medical, dental, mental health, and immunization histories" as part of the fourteen-day full health appraisal for all inmates. This also is required for each inmate by NCCHC standards J-39 (important standard for jails) and P-35 (essential standard for prisons).

[13] In a multifacility correctional system, this function sometimes is performed at a central reception/diagnostic unit. If so, the facility to which the inmate is transferred need only verify and review documentation in the health record of the findings of this assessment and ensure initiation of any indicated follow-up.

FIGURE 9-1. ESSENTIAL CONTENT OF FOURTEEN-DAY (POST ADMISSION) MENTAL HEALTH ASSESSMENT

1. A structured interview which inquires into:

   - history of hospitalization and outpatient treatment
   - current psychotropic medication
   - suicidal ideation
   - history of suicidal behavior
   - drug usage
   - alcohol usage
   - history of sex offenses
   - history of expressively violent behavior
   - history of victimization due to criminal violence
   - special education placement
   - history of cerebral trauma
   - history of seizures
   - emotional response to incarceration

2. Testing of intelligence to screen for mental retardation

Outpatient Follow-up Services by a Mental Health Specialist

Outpatient follow-up services may be provided on-site or at an off-site location. For the most part, there is no urgency, and these services may be scheduled at convenient times for clinicians and transport officers. If volume is high, efforts should be made to have the mental health specialist, typically a psychologist or clinical social worker, come to the facility since transporting the inmates is very costly.

In short-stay jails, psychological services primarily are focused on providing support during the stressful period of incarceration and the difficult process of trial and sentencing. Both time and resources are too short for any realistic attempt to work on more complex problems in this setting. In prisons, however, long-term follow-up of chronically ill patients also should include some focused therapy consistent with the individually developed multidisciplinary treatment plan.

Case Management

Symptoms of mental illness sometimes go into remission—in other words, become less pronounced for a time. This may be the result of specifically prescribed and administered medication or other aspects of treatment. Patients also may improve when stressors are mitigated or for other reasons. Particularly for persons with chronic mental disorders, in recognition of the stressful circumstances of incarceration, staff should take great care lest patients be "lost to follow-up" simply because they have not "acted out" for a while. Many crises, and their costly consequences, could be avoided by regular and proactive follow-up and case-management. Persons should be scheduled for regular follow-up, even though often this may involve no more than "touching base" through a brief exchange to be sure that all is well and that there are no signs of excessive stress or pending "breakdown."

Some facilities establish a 90-day or 180-day interval for follow-up of outpatients. These intervals are in keeping with the practice of many community mental health centers for stable patients. Two factors, however, suggest that follow-up of outpatients in a jail should not occur less frequently than every thirty days. First, the stability of the patient is probably not very well known to staff. Second, the patient is in highly stressful surroundings, and the process of trial and sentencing may provoke great anxiety and subsequent decompensation. In a prison setting, as the stability of patients is evaluated, longer intervals can be appropriate in individual cases.

Crisis Intervention

Crisis intervention is an immediate response to an unforeseen acute episode of severe mental distress. It provides brief assessment and short-term care, including supportive counseling and referral, as necessary, for further follow-up. Crisis intervention workers need not be mental health professionals, but may be specially trained nurses, correctional counselors, and even correctional officers. Initial and ongoing training of such workers by mental health professionals should cover recognition of symptoms of mental illness and basic crisis intervention skills.

Crisis intervention merits a high priority in all correctional settings. A properly designed crisis intervention and supportive counseling program is not costly.[14] Many inmates are unhappy with their lives, depressed, or terrified by their surroundings. When these responses can be alleviated through supportive counseling, inmates can make a better adjustment to prison life and even begin to make plans for their future. Inmates who know that they can talk to someone when they need to do so are much less likely to complain of psychosomatic symptoms or to resort to more dramatic attention seeking—including suicide gestures, self-mutilation, or aggressive behavior. Use of more costly health services is thus avoided, and the frequency of unacceptable behaviors is reduced.

---

[14] Walter Y. Quijano, among others, has pointed out the fallacy of cutting back on supportive counseling service. Cf. B. Jaye Anno (ed.), *Prison Health Care: Guidelines for the Management of an Adequate Delivery System* (Chicago, Ill.: National Commission on Correctional Health Care, March, 1991): 127f.

Often, simply providing information or offering timely support significantly can improve an inmate's response to his or her situation.[15] All it takes is a sympathetic correctional officer, nurse, or other employee who will take the time to listen and be supportive. Sometimes anxiety can be relieved simply by reassuring the inmate (if true) that an appointment has been arranged for Monday morning with the mental health counselor, or that there will be an opportunity to speak to an attorney later in the day, or that a particular rumor is without basis.

Persons with cognitive impairment may require more than one explanation of rules and procedures. They do not process complicated information rapidly. Speaking slowly and clearly, listening to their questions, and repeating the explanation several times may be necessary. If this is not done, the developmentally disabled person may become very confused and anxious and, out of frustration, become disorderly and violate institutional rules, thereby incurring disciplinary sanctions. Under these circumstances, punitive detention may be an almost unbearable torture for someone who really has no understanding as to why it is all happening.

Services of a Psychiatrist

For those requiring psychotropic medication for serious mental illness, services of a psychiatrist are required. Again, this may be scheduled on-site or at other convenient locations and times. Sometimes the psychiatrist does not come to the small jail, but advises the medical doctor by telephone concerning diagnostic impressions and psychotropic medications. Some psychiatrists and physicians are more comfortable with this arrangement than others.

Involvement of a psychiatrist is also important when dealing on a long-term basis with very sick patients. The psychiatrist is an essential member of the treatment team.

Access to a Psychiatric Inpatient Unit

Access to a psychiatric inpatient unit is only necessary for that very small percentage of inmates whose acute mental illness cannot be managed appropriately in another setting. Such units are costly to staff and to operate, and should be provided on-site only in large correctional systems. The primary purpose of these units is to achieve stabilization of psychotic symptoms, and often this can be achieved within a few days. On the other hand, some psychotropic medications do not reach full effectiveness with a patient for up to six weeks, and, consequently, an accurate determination of the proper dosage cannot be made in a shorter period.

Arrangements often are made with a state mental hospital or forensic center, or with a local community hospital, to take care of these patients at least on an emergency basis. As with correctional patients who are hospitalized for medical or surgical reasons, it may be necessary for the facility to supply security coverage.

For those mentally ill inmates who do not require a psychiatric inpatient unit, an intermediate-level therapeutic setting may be appropriate, as described in the

---

[15] Dvoskin, in Steadman, *op. cit.*: 71.

following chapter. Others may be accommodated in the general population of the correctional facility. The American Correctional Association recognizes the need for special attention to the needs of inmates suffering from serious mental illness in its standard [16] which specifies that they be provided with single occupancy cells/rooms when indicated. The determination of suitable housing for persons with serious mental disorders, of course, should be made in each case by the responsible mental health professional.

Increased Sensitivity to Heat among Persons Who Take Psychotropic Medications

Institution heads and correctional officers should be aware of medical warnings concerning prolonged heat exposure of patients receiving psychotropic medications. Excessive exposure to heat can occur, for example, while working in the fields on a hot day or living in a poorly ventilated cell block during warm weather. This is not an issue of "coddling," but a vital necessity. Many of the psychotropic medications significantly reduce the natural ability of the body's cooling system to adjust to high temperatures. The consequence of not heeding this precaution can be fatal.

Medical or psychiatric staff should include such warnings in the treatment plans of susceptible patients and also should communicate this information to the appropriate classification or custody personnel. In some instances, air conditioning or improved ventilation may be required.

Psychological Testing
Appropriate Time for Mental Health Screening

Many prison [17] systems use the Minnesota Multi-phasic Personality Inventory (MMPI) and other testing instruments as a component of intake screening for newly arrived inmates. The MMPI is an excellent instrument and can be very useful. Its use on newly arrived inmates, however, produces results of questionable validity. The upheaval and emotional stress which follow close upon trial, sentencing, and transfer to a state or federal prison may lead to unreliable test findings, which are not at all indicative of the true profile of the individual. It may be wise to postpone complex and expensive psychological test batteries, personality profiles, and aptitude testing until some weeks after arrival, limiting intake testing to a brief mental health screening sufficient to detect persons in need of urgent attention. Some systems would find this

---

[16] American Correctional Association, *1996 Standards Supplement*, Standard 3-4128-2.

[17] In jails, this testing is generally not performed for incoming inmates. Because of the sheer volume, cost would be too high, and most inmates do not remain in jail long enough for the profiles to have useful application.

delay inconvenient if it requires decentralization of the testing functions. Whether the expected improvement in accuracy of findings by a deferral of test administration would offset this disadvantage is a matter for local determination.

Access to Psychological Screening and Testing Information

Raw psychological test results, scoring sheets, graphical displays, and narrative findings of the MMPI or other psychological profiles occasionally are found in the institutional files of inmates. Sometimes this is merely done "because we always did it this way," with no meaningful or functionally useful rationale.

First of all, these are highly technical documents, which can be correctly understood or interpreted only by a mental health specialist, such as a psychologist or psychiatrist. Consequently, they will be of little or no use to correctional staff, and even may lead to incorrect conclusions or misleading inferences.

Secondly, the presence of these documents in the institutional jacket also would represent a breach of confidentiality if the data were collected as part of a mental health screening or evaluation. Any information which is obtained in the course of arrival health screening or intake health appraisals should be filed only in the medical record.

Usually, however, these personality profiles are obtained by educational psychologists or institutional psychologists who are not associated with the delivery of mental health services, and are used for classification and institutional management. In this instance, the documents would not belong to the health record of the inmate. Nevertheless, the raw documents should be retained in a confidential manner with access reserved to those professionally qualified persons in classification or educational departments who are skilled in their use and trained in their interpretation.

Use of Restraints

Sometimes, a mentally ill person needs to be restrained to prevent injury to self or to others. Mental health professionals, under certain circumstances,[18] are permitted by law to order restraint for patients in mental health facilities. Correctional officers, in the exercise of their duties, also are authorized to employ restraining devices on prisoners, when necessary, to prevent them from harming themselves or others or to prevent escape. In dealing with mentally ill inmates within a correctional facility, these jurisdictions sometimes overlap. In an emergency situation, of course, the officer should use whatever measures are deemed necessary to prevent or minimize injury or damage. Facility policy should provide guidance on the steps to be followed once the crisis has passed. In the case of a person with diagnosed or suspected mental illness, the officer should notify mental health personnel as soon as possible and be guided by competent clinical advice as to continuation of any form of restraint.

---

[18] Typically, state laws and/or regulations require as a condition for application of restraints: a diagnosis of mental illness, imminent danger to self or others, and determination that less-restrictive measures would be ineffective.

Policies covering restraints employed by mental health professionals for mentally ill prisoners should be consistent with applicable state mental health codes.[19] The policy should address who may order the restraints, what type of restraints should be used, the length of time for which an order for restraint is valid, alternative measures which must be considered prior to employment of restraints, a requirement for periodic inspection of the restrained patient by qualified mental health and/or medical staff, a requirement for visitation of the restrained patient by a mental health professional who is qualified to order restraint, and adequate documentation. Generally it is unwise to employ medically ordered restraints except in (or on the way to) a unit in which the patient will be managed and observed by qualified medical or mental health staff, such as in an infirmary, nursing unit, or psychiatric hospital. A permanent log should be maintained which documents each application of medically ordered restraint in the facility.

It is customary in some correctional facilities for a mentally ill person who is combative or self-injurious to be restrained in an area supervised by custody personnel—such as an observation cell in a booking area or a segregation area. In these cases, mental health staff should collaborate in preparing the policies which guide correctional officers in their supervision of inmates in these units. Ongoing consultation with mental health staff always should be sought when inmates with diagnosed or suspected mental illness are restrained. The authority for use of restraint in these cases is that delegated by the warden or jail administrator, but it is advisable to employ it only in consultation with mental health staff.

Metal restraints, such as handcuffs and leg irons, may be appropriate in a crisis or for brief use, as immediately following an altercation or in escorting a person from one location to another within the facility, but should not be applied for extended periods. Plastic or leather restraints are more suitable for longer use.[20] Also available are so-called "ambulatory restraints," often used in mental hospitals for persons with poor impulse control. These devices allow the patient to be in a day room and to socialize with others, but limit the range of arm or leg movement to minimize the possibility of causing injury to anyone. The extent of permitted movement is adjustable.

So called "humane restraints" are available, but even soft restraints may be quite inhumane if applied improperly or imposed without adequate reason or for prolonged periods. In all cases, the principle of "least restrictive environment" should be observed. Restraints should be applied only when less restrictive devices are judged to be insufficient, and when applied, the type of restraint itself should be the least restrictive method which is determined to be effective.

---

[19] In the absence of relevant state legislation, a helpful guide would be the restraint policy of a state mental hospital or community psychiatric unit. Following such a policy will serve defendants well in a lawsuit as evidence of adherence to contemporary professional standards.

[20] "When restraints are part of a health-care treatment regimen, the restraints used should be those that would be appropriate for the general public within the jurisdiction. Written policy should identify the authorization needed and when, where, and how restraints may be used and for how long." American Correctional Association, *1996 Standards Supplement*, Standard 3-4362.

Among the many varieties of restraint devices in use, at least two clearly inappropriate applications deserve comment. One large county jail used a device called a "Stokes' Basket"—a long, narrow basket upon which a patient is strapped, face downward, with hands behind the back. Jail officials defended its use as appropriate for persons withdrawing from alcohol intoxication, on grounds that it prevented choking when the inmate became nauseated. [21] On one occasion, the basket was used to restrain a patient who was experiencing severe withdrawal symptoms, including DTs and seizures. Documentation by nurses and psychologists described him as disoriented, confused, at times belligerent and incoherent, hallucinating, shivering, and refusing nourishment. He was kept strapped in this restraining device during the final thirty-six hours of his life. Though he was regularly seen by nursing staff while in this condition, he had no contact with a physician or a psychiatrist during the four days of his incarceration.

Whether there might ever be appropriate indications for the use of a Stokes' Basket (or similar device) in a correctional setting, it is clear that this is not a medically appropriate device for treatment or prevention of choking for a nauseous or seizing patient. Nor should it be used for a mentally ill patient. It is certainly not a suitable or acceptable intervention for a patient experiencing severe withdrawal and detoxification symptoms or who is disoriented and hallucinating. Such a person urgently requires a hospital, probably an intensive care ward.

An increasingly popular device in small jails is the restraining chair. In one facility it was being applied, with reported effectiveness, to calm aggressive, assaultive, or agitated inmates, including persons with a psychiatric disorder. When strapped tightly into the chair, which was then tilted to an uncomfortable position, it was claimed that the inmate rarely remained agitated or combative for more than an hour, after which time he would become docile and could be released from this restraint. Without commenting on whether this could be viewed as an appropriate strategy for restraining and calming a healthy but combative inmate, it is observed that the "tranquilizing chair" is by no means a new idea. This mode of therapy had been used in mental hospitals in the United States for a few years during the early 1900s, but was long ago discarded as an inappropriate and unacceptable treatment for mentally ill persons.

Suicide Prevention

Much has been written about the need for constant vigilance in correctional settings to prevent or reduce the risk of suicide. There are excellent published training manuals and reams of suggestions have been offered. [22] A mandatory standard of the American Correctional Association requires a written suicide prevention and intervention program that is reviewed and approved by a qualified medical or mental health professional, and further requires that all staff with responsibility for inmate

---

[21] The author knows of no community treatment setting where such a device is employed as a safeguard for persons undergoing withdrawal from alcohol or other drugs.

supervision are trained in the implementation of the program.[23] A few important policy considerations are mentioned here.

Not all suicides are humanely preventable. A person who is truly bent on committing suicide probably will find the opportunity to do so and eventually will be successful. There comes a trade-off between imposition of excessive measures to prevent suicide on the one hand, and the cruelty or inhumanity[24] of these measures themselves on the other. For example, all inmates might be subjected to constant four-point restraint except for directly supervised toileting, eating, or bathing. While this might approach 100 percent suicide avoidance, no one would judge it to be a reasonable or appropriate strategy. Yet, to make no effort at all would also be unjustified in a known high-risk situation such as a jail or prison.

One study found that inmates in a prison were 2.1 times as likely to commit suicide as their race-age-sex counterparts in free society.[25] It is recognized that jail inmates are generally at an even higher risk for suicide than are prisoners in long-term correctional facilities, and that the first hours and days after arrest are the highest risk periods. Also, a very high-risk situation occurs for many inmates of jails during stressful points of their trial and sentencing procedure, particularly among young persons facing long sentences. Persons under the influence of alcohol and barbiturates also pose a high risk of suicidal behavior, as do persons suffering from acute or chronic depression. Those who, due to their professional status or prominent social position in the community, have reason to feel extreme shame or disgrace on account of the offense or the fact of incarceration, also may be at risk of suicidal behavior.

---

[22] Examples include Joseph R. Rowan, *Suicide Prevention in Custody: Intensive Study Correspondence Course* (Lanham, Md.: American Correctional Association, 1991); Joseph R. Rowan and Lindsay M. Hayes, *Training Curriculum on Suicide Detection and Prevention in Jails and Lockups* (Mansfield, Mass.: National Center on Institutions and Alternatives, February, 1988); and Lindsay M. Hayes, *Prison Suicide: An Overview and Guide to Prevention* (Mansfield, Mass.: National Center on Institutions and Alternatives, June, 1995).

[23] American Correctional Association, *1996 Standards Supplement,* Standard 3-4364.

[24] The author has witnessed instances in which such cruel extremes were routinely employed. One prisoner lay shivering on the cement floor of his bare cell, attempting to keep warm by wrapping the only available covering, toilet paper, around his nude body. Another facility routinely applied four- or five-point restraints for days at a time to suicidal prisoners. A large urban county jail clothed all persons in its mental health unit with suicide garments. Another inmate of a state prison was placed in four-point restraints, fully unclothed and in plain view of any officer or inmate who passed by the large observation window or who looked at the television monitor. These strategies deprive the patient of all human dignity, inflict considerable discomfort, and are tantamount to punishing persons for their illness.

[25] Kenneth L. Faiver, "Epidemiologic Review of Deaths in a Prison Setting," Conference on Suicide Prevention in Michigan Jails, Lockups and Holding Centers (East Lansing, Mich.: Michigan State University, April, 1984): 5-6. The rate was 2.9 times higher for whites (N=22) and 1.4 times higher for blacks (N-14).

Rates of Suicide

The suicide rate in jails is estimated to be more than nine times greater than in the community.[26] Most suicides in jails occur within the first twenty-four hours of admission. A nationwide study in 1993 found that 158 suicides had occurred out of a population of 889,836 state prisoners.[27] Given a community rate of 12.2 suicides per 100,000 persons, this is 45 percent higher than in the community. The rate of prison suicides has declined since 1984. There were 155 suicides among sentenced prisoners under the jurisdiction of state and federal correctional institutions during 1994, representing 5.2 percent of all deaths.[28]

Manipulation

Some persons are not truly suicidal in the sense that they have no real intent to kill themselves. However, they may feign suicidal behavior to obtain secondary gain—such as a transfer to another location, a change in conditions of confinement, or some special privilege. The danger is that these activities may end in unintended self-inflicted death. Often cited is the scenario in which the officer makes rounds of the cell block at regular intervals. The inmate knows this and times the suicidal gesture—usually a noose around the neck—to coincide with the expected arrival of the officer, hoping to be cut down before any real injury occurs. But should the officer be detained for some reason during rounds, such as by stopping to talk with an inmate a few cells away, the awaited rescue may arrive too late to prevent an accidental self-inflicted death.

The lesson here is that great caution is needed in interpreting the "manipulative" label. Just because a mental health professional determines that an individual does not have a genuine suicidal intent does not mean that he or she is not at risk of suicide. According to the Michigan study,[29] there was documentation by the psychologist or psychiatrist in many of completed suicides, within a few days or even hours prior to the event, that the person was merely "manipulative" and would not actually take his or her own life.

Strategies to Prevent Suicide

Television monitors sometimes are employed in correctional facilities to implement a suicide watch. While this technology can be helpful, it is not as effective as direct observation. The image on the screen is not always clear. The camera may have blind spots. The observer easily can be distracted and not notice an untoward event

---

[26] Lindsay M. Hayes, *Prison Suicide: An Overview and Guide to Prevention* (Mansfield, Mass.: National Center on Institutions and Alternatives, June, 1995): 28-30.

[27] *Ibid.*

[28] Bureau of Justice Statistics, *Sourcebook of Criminal Justice Statistics 1995* (Washington, D.C., 1997): 602.

[29] Faiver, "Epidemiologic Review of Deaths in a Prison Setting," *loc. cit.*

until too late. In a busy control center, there is a limit to how much an officer can monitor simultaneously.

Restraints sometimes are employed to prevent suicidal behavior. Full or partial clothing deprivation and paper gowns also are used. For an inmate under direct observation, however, the need for these measures is rare, and the true motivation is perhaps to punish the "troublemaker" and make it so unpleasant that the inmate will be dissuaded from suicidal intent. Adequate staffing is more costly than restraints or suicide garments, but is much more effective and humane when a person is determined to be at a very high risk for suicide. It is also hard to argue in court that direct monitoring was not available because it was deemed too costly. There is no adequate substitute for direct observation.

Conventional wisdom suggests that a room will be safer if it is without protrusions (like doorknobs, window latches, bars, screens, rigid clothing hooks, towel racks, bolts, and so forth) to which a rope or sheet might be attached; without sharp corners on which one might cause an injury to self; and without platforms from which one could jump headlong onto the floor. But there is no really suicide-proof room. These measures can help, but provide only limited protection, and again are not a substitute for direct observation. While they might serve as some deterrent, they will not absolutely prevent a determined person from engaging in suicidal behavior.

A body does not need to be totally suspended for a person to die from hanging. Death by asphyxiation can occur within minutes from only the weight of the head itself held a few inches above the floor by a ligature fastened around the neck and attached to a doorknob or door hinge, bedpost, or chair rung.

Risk Factors; Warning Signs and Symptoms

Early detection of signs or indicators of high risk is essential, and must be incorporated into the point-of-entry screening procedure for every jail, detention facility, and prison. The checklist should include at least the items shown in Figure 9-2.

FIGURE 9-2. POINT-OF-ENTRY SCREENING FOR SUICIDAL SYMPTOMS

- current suicidal ideation

- an identified plan for carrying out suicide

- recent prior attempt on one's life

- acute depression

- recent consumption of alcohol

- history of mental illness

Probably, the most significant indicator of high risk is that the inmate admits to having a specific plan and an available means of carrying out the suicide. The following excellent checklist of key signs and symptoms of suicidal behavior is provided by Rowan.[30]

- Current depression (depression is the single best indicator of suicide)

- Strong guilt or shame over the offense

- Threats of suicide

- Prior suicide attempts

- Current or prior mental illness, particularly paranoid delusions (having an irrational thought that others are out to harm him or her) or hallucinations (believing that he or she hears, tastes, feels, or smells something that is not there)

- Unusual agitation

- Being under the influence of alcohol/drugs at arrest

- History of alcohol/drug abuse

- Projection of hopelessness or helplessness—no sense of future

- Unusual aggressiveness while sober, particularly in a juvenile

- Unusual concern over what will happen

- Noticeable behavior changes

- Period of calm following agitation

- Increasing difficulty relating to others

- Unrealistic talk about getting out of the facility

- Inability to deal effectively with the present—preoccupied with the past

- Desire to pack up belongings

- Desire to give away possessions

- Attention-getting gestures by self-injury

- Excessive risk-taking

---

[30] Joseph R. Rowan, *Suicide Prevention in Custody: Intensive Study Correspondence Course* (Lanham, Md.: American Correctional Association, 1991): 53.

Following a finding that risk factors are present, contact should be made immediately with a qualified mental health professional. If, for any reason this is not feasible, it is incumbent on the security personnel without delay to implement effective and humane methods to prevent suicidal behavior until the inmate can be evaluated by a qualified mental health professional. This implies constant or frequent direct observation, and perhaps also removal of objects (belts, shoelaces, and so forth) with which the inmate readily could harm himself or herself. Note, however, that the closer the surveillance, the less need for removal of these objects. Generally, it also is preferable to place a suicidal person in a dayroom with others and under direct observation than to isolate and/or restrain such a person and rely on deprivation of potential instruments for committing suicide. Company of others, television, and other distractions, afford some degree of relief from self-pity and depressed thinking, rendering suicidal behavior less likely. Rarely does one carry out a suicide plan in the presence of other people.

Experienced officers, through their close observation of inmates, are often very perceptive in recognizing signs of suicidal tendency. Even after a mental health professional has evaluated the inmate and declared that the person is not suicidal, the officer may continue to have doubt. In such a case, the officer is well advised to use his or her own best judgment and to implement appropriate suicidal precautions even though the mental health professional has determined that they are not necessary.[31]

A mentally ill person who is acutely suicidal probably belongs in a psychiatric inpatient unit. Prolonged management in segregation or an observation room usually should not be attempted.

When a suicide, or for that matter, a near-suicide attempt does occur, a thorough investigation and review should be conducted by both custody officials and health professionals, and their findings should be reviewed jointly to determine the lessons learned from the event and the appropriate corrective actions to be taken.

Levels of Supervision

Hayes[32] outlines two levels of supervision for suicidal inmates:

- Constant, uninterrupted observation by staff for actively suicidal inmates, who are either threatening or engaging in the act of suicide

- Close observation by staff (at staggered intervals not to exceed fifteen minutes) for inmates who are not actively suicidal but who express suicidal ideation and/or who have a recent prior history of self-destructive behavior

---

[31] Joseph R. Rowan, "Suicide Prevention in Adult and Juvenile Institutions, 1997 ACA Winter Conference (Nashville, Tenn., January 27, 1997).

[32] Lindsay M. Hayes, *Prison Suicide: An Overview and Guide to Prevention* (Mansfield, Mass.: National Center on Institutions and Alternatives, June, 1995): 21.

Closed circuit television monitoring or inmate companions may supplement the procedures, but are not acceptable substitutes for direct observation by the staff.

Very many facility policies have adopted the "fifteen minute" standard for persons who are at less than the highest risk for suicide. These policies need to be carefully reconsidered. It is readily possible for an inmate to carry out a suicide plan and to die or cause permanent brain damage in less than fifteen minutes. Consequently, such a policy is not an adequate safeguard.[33] Probably, a five-minute interval is the longest which will ensure reasonable protection, even for those who pose a moderate risk of suicidal behavior. The intervals should not be regular, so that the inmate cannot estimate with precision when the next observation will occur.

The admonition to implement one-on-one or constant observation for actively suicidal persons is certainly appropriate. The "one-on-one" formulation, however, literally would not permit an officer to observe two or more persons simultaneously even though they were in the same room. The "constant observation" wording could prohibit an officer from observing two or three patients who were occupying adjacent rooms. For liability reasons, the facility must insist on strict interpretation of the regulation and, therefore, the wording must precisely express the intent. A requirement to observe at least once each minute, for example, would appear to meet the intent of the "constant observation" or "one-on-one" standard.

Particularly for small facilities, the burden of providing the close observation which suicidal inmates require can be very great. A strategy increasingly being employed is the use of carefully selected and specially trained inmates to become "peer observers." They can be assigned to occupy the same cell or can be posted to sit in the corridor outside of the cell of the potentially suicidal inmate so as to observe constantly. They may engage the watched inmate in conversation or other appropriate activities as a distraction from thoughts about self-harm. However, it would not be prudent to adopt this approach unless the facility is also prepared to afford the peer observers a reasonable degree of supervision.

Considerations for Transport of Mentally Ill Inmates

Adequate Preparation of Patient

Unnecessary or frequent moves of mentally disturbed inmates should be avoided. Housing relocation is disorienting to anyone, especially when unwanted and unplanned. It is much more problematic for a mentally ill person. Relocation requires adjustment to new surroundings, unaccustomed lighting and sound patterns, different furniture, new companions, unfamiliar officers, and sometimes different regulations and rules.

Because any relocation is potentially disorienting and stressful to a mentally disturbed inmate, every reasonable effort should be made to mitigate or assuage these

---

[33] A fact to which expert witnesses will readily attest in court.

disorienting effects whenever such a move is deemed necessary. Of particular importance is that the inmate be adequately prepared. It is not acceptable for the officer to enter the living unit and announce loudly to the mental patient: "All right. Get your things together! You're moving out—now!" Informing the patient several times and allowing an opportunity to reflect on its impact is usually more effective than only letting the inmate know prior to the move. The officer, for example, can engage in some reassuring and nonthreatening conversation. The officer also should carefully avoid any appearance of haste or urgency. Offering some options for self-determination can be helpful—not whether to be moved, but perhaps a choice of where, or what time of day, or how, or even whether assistance in packing is desired. Even what may appear to be a trivial choice may be better than no choice at all, since no one likes to lose all control over one's life and destiny. Preference for the upper or lower bunk, this room or that room, to move in the morning or the afternoon, are examples of choices which could be offered. In devoting some energy and time to making the choice, the patient becomes less preoccupied with the fact of the move itself. It also may be helpful to explain that if it does not work out, he or she may be able to return to the more familiar setting.

Unless clearly contraindicated by security considerations, such as a significant escape risk, the inmate should be informed about the intended destination. It is very disorienting and stressful to be taken involuntarily to an unknown destination.

For an inpatient of a psychiatric unit, the notification of transfer ordinarily should be given by the nurse or therapist rather than by a correctional officer. When possible, a person who gives this message should be someone who already has the trust and confidence of the inmate.

Accompanying the Transfer

Depending on the mental status and condition of the patient at the time, it may be advisable to assign a member of the patient's treatment team to accompany the inmate on the actual transfer. This is likely to be a nurse or a direct care worker. Officers assigned to the function of transporting mentally ill inmates also should be selected carefully, thoroughly trained to be sensitive to the needs of patients in these circumstances, and in appropriate techniques of managing them. When the transport officer is a stranger to the patient, it is helpful for a trusted caregiver to introduce the officer by name and to remain for a brief period to minimize some of the anxiety and fear of the unknown. This is not a complete substitute for assigning a person with whom the inmate already has a trusting relationship. Being escorted by a nurse or other clinically trained person is especially relevant for persons whose mental condition is unstable or whose response to psychotropic medications is unknown.

The vehicle employed in the transfer of mentally ill inmates deserves some consideration. Severely disturbed inmates ought not be transported, for example, on a chain bus or other transport vehicle in which many others simultaneously are being transported. Sitting in handcuffs or chains during a lengthy trip on such a vehicle can be terrifying to a mentally ill person. Sometimes, transportation can be provided in the backseat of a passenger car. In rare instances, an ambulance might be necessary. Often, the presence of a trusted member of the treatment team is sufficient to allay extreme anxiety and to provide the necessary reassurance. Advice of the mental health clinician always should be sought prior to the transfer of an acutely disturbed person.

Providing information to the mental patient en route also is helpful, for example, how much longer the trip will take, how long before lunch, and when the next scheduled bathroom stop will occur. Reminders and orienting information should be provided as often and as clearly as needed, given the inmate's ability to comprehend and retain the information, and the degree of disorientation that is being manifested by questions or behavior.

Of equal importance is what happens upon arrival at the new destination. Usually this is adequately handled if the transfer is to a medical or mental health facility, where the inmate should be met and promptly evaluated upon arrival by a qualified caregiver.

Considering Mental Health Factors in Inmate Discipline

It is a commonly accepted principle of British and American jurisprudence that no one should be punished for behavior for which he or she is not mentally responsible.[34] The Mississippi Supreme Court wrote, "[I]t is certainly shocking and inhuman to punish a person for an act when he does not have the capacity to know the act or to judge of its consequences."[35]

The sheer number of mentally ill and mentally retarded persons in the general population[36] of prisons and jails renders it inevitable that persons with serious mental disorders will face disciplinary proceedings as a consequence of their behavior. If the standard disciplinary process is followed without careful consideration of the pertinent mental health factors in each individual case, a serious injustice may result. The inmate may have acted with greatly diminished capacity to understand or with very limited ability to exercise control of behavior. Indeed, the behavior itself, may be the direct response of a psychotic person to the stimulus of an auditory or visual hallucination. These actions are the direct consequence of an impaired mental state caused by the illness and should not be punished. Because there are gradations of impairment, if punishment is imposed at all, it should be tempered according to the extent of the diminished awareness or control. It is also of concern that some punishments, such as solitary confinement or extended segregation, may cause extreme stress for a mentally ill person and can promote decompensation and exacerbation of the illness.

Rold[37] cites the case of a prisoner who was tried for killing a fellow inmate, but was found not guilty by reason of insanity. Nevertheless, he was charged by the

---

[34] William J. Rold, "Consideration of Mental Health Factors in Inmate Discipline," *CorrectCare* (Spring, 1992): 4f.

[35] *Sinclair v. State*, 132 So. 581, 584 (Miss. 1931).

[36] Of course, for inmates who are inpatients of a special mental health unit, a therapeutic approach is far more appropriate than are disciplinary sanctions as a response to unacceptable behaviors, as will be discussed in the next chapter on creating therapeutic environments.

[37] Rold, *loc. cit.*

prison with assaulting another inmate and was given seven years solitary confinement and four years loss of good time. The court vacated the punishment, ruling that, where an inmate has been found insane with respect to the same acts for which he or she faces discipline, or where a "documented history of serious psychiatric problems" exists, "the prisoner's mental condition is a factor which must be considered in deciding whether the disciplinary determination is supported by substantial evidence." The court directed the hearing officer to "make specific inquiry" concerning the prisoner's "competence to conduct his defense at the hearing" and concerning his "mental state at the time he engaged in the proscribed conduct." This decision was approved by New York's highest court: "[I]n the context of a prison disciplinary proceeding in which the prisoner's mental state is at issue, a Hearing Officer is required to consider evidence regarding the prisoner's mental condition."[38]

A number of jurisdictions have specific regulations addressing this matter. For example, the Texas Department of Criminal Justice has adopted the following policy on the disciplining of mentally disordered inmates[39] (see Figure 9-3). The policy further requires that the disciplinary committee adhere to the evaluation, findings, and recommendations of the patient's psychiatric treatment team, and indicates that no sanction may be imposed which would impair or impede the patient's psychiatric treatment plan.

While it is appropriate for the mental health professional to advise that the inmate's mental status precludes participation in the disciplinary process, contributed to the offending behavior, or contraindicates any particular form of punishment, it would be inappropriate for the treatment team to impose or to recommend imposition of any disciplinary sanction, since this would be inconsistent with the role of the healing professional.[40]

FIGURE 9-3.DISCIPLINING MENTALLY DISORIENTED INMATES

In the event a [mental health] patient is charged with a disciplinary infraction, the psychiatric treatment team must make autonomous judgments as to:

1. whether the patient's current mental status precludes participation in the disciplinary process

2. whether the patient's mental status contributed to the alleged disciplinary offense

3. whether the patient's mental status contraindicates any particular form of punishment, such as confinement in punitive segregation

---

[38] *Huggings v. Coughlin*, 76 N.Y.2d 904, 561 N.Y.S.2d 910 (Ct. App. 1990).

[39] Texas Department of Criminal Justice, *Manual of Policies and Procedures*, No. 3-12D (August, 1987).

[40] This concern is discussed in greater length in Chapter 13 on the ethics of the health professional.

Rold [41] advises following a set of administrative procedures to ensure that the rights of mentally disordered prisoners are protected appropriately. The first seven of these items are discussed elsewhere in this book.

(1) Screen for mental illness and disability at reception

(2) Provide appropriate classification and housing assignment based on mental status

(3) Review classification and housing when mental status changes

(4) Train security staff and hearing officers to recognize mental health issues in misbehavior

(5) Establish intermediate and chronic care capability for mental health services

(6) Review by mental health professionals of mental health status of inmates before placement in segregation and regularly while in segregation

(7) Prohibit the placement or maintenance in solitary confinement of inmates with severe mental disorders or current psychotic disability

(8) Provide opportunity for inmates to submit proof of mental health factors underlying misconduct

(9) Make counsel available for inmates unable to assist themselves

(10) Make it an affirmative duty of hearing officers to inquire into the mental health status of the inmate when the issue is presented fairly, even if the inmate fails to raise it

(11) Inquire into the consequences of mental health treatment of proposed dispositions and use of clinically appropriate sanctions

(12) Make available a variety of disciplinary dispositions that take into account the mental health bases for behavior, including dismissal of charges

(13) Limit the maximum time spent in punitive segregation, as adopted by many states

(14) Review the mental status of inmates discharged from psychiatric hospitalization who "owe" segregation time before returning them to solitary confinement

---

[41] Rold, *loc. cit.*

Ongoing Staff Education

Accepted and effective means of safely managing mentally ill persons are not the same as those commonly employed in management of correctional inmates.[42] A courteous verbal request followed by patiently waiting for the person to process the information and decide to comply is a more effective strategy than loudly barking out direct orders, physically confronting the inmate, and initiating a show of force—all of which may cause a mentally disturbed person to become combative or resistant. Without attempting to pass judgment on the merits of these correctional techniques, it is important to recognize that they are less effective with mentally disturbed persons and even may have an opposite effect than what is intended. Most mentally ill patients can be "talked down" to calmness if one is willing and able to take the time.

Important inservice training topics for every correctional officer include recognizing the signs and symptoms of mental illness, preventing suicide, and effectively managing mentally ill inmates. These topics need to be covered in considerable depth for officers who are regularly assigned to work on mental health units.

It is good practice to designate fixed posts in mental health units, so that these officers do not continuously rotate through other institutional assignments. Stability and constancy are important characteristics of the patients' environment. It is disquieting to have to get acquainted with new authority figures every day. And it does take a special kind of officer to work effectively in these units over a prolonged period. Careful selection of personnel, specialized training and qualifications, as well as a personal interest in working on these units are essential.

Credentials of Clinical Staff

Every facility needs to have carefully developed job descriptions for the mental health staff, whether they are employees or contracted individuals. These should be reviewed and approved biannually by the responsible health authority and by the head of the institution.

Outside consultants can be helpful in recruiting and interviewing key clinical staff. For example, upon request, a medical school might assign a faculty member to assist in preparing a position description and an announcement of the opening for a mental health director. A faculty member also might serve on the interview panel.

Subtle distinctions often are overlooked. For example, not every psychologist or social worker has the same qualifications. There are clinical psychologists, educational psychologists, industrial psychologists, and child psychologists. Some social workers are very familiar with public assistance and welfare programs and entitlements, but have not had clinical experience with mental patients. Also, state licensing requirements differ in the supervision requirements for a psychologist. A health professional who is well-versed in applicable provisions of the local jurisdiction should be consulted to avoid costly errors and delays.

---

[42] See Chapter 2 for further discussion of this point.

Transition Back to the Community

Diversion Programs

If there are no alternatives, there can be no diversion.[43] In most jurisdictions, diversion alternatives for mentally ill persons are severely limited or nonexistent. Moreover, once a mentally ill person is arrested, attitudes towards that person change. They are feared by the public, and are not viewed sympathetically by care providers, policy makers, or legislators.[44]

While the jail administrators must accept those who are arrested, it is in administrators' own interest to encourage the development of alternatives to arrest for mentally ill persons who are not accused of committing a crime. Agreements with community mental health and social service agencies, for example, might contain a "no decline" clause so that these agencies clearly are committed to accepting mentally ill and retarded persons whose behavior has become problematic.

Continuity of Care after Release

When chronic mentally disordered offenders are returned to the free world, rearrest rates can be significantly reduced when the stress of readjustment is minimized and when appropriate psychiatric intervention and adequate social support are made available.[45] Unless these persons are quickly incorporated into an ongoing program of follow-up care, they will not be taking their medications, they will have no one to turn to when anxious, and they again will engage in the kinds of behavior which previously got them into trouble. Unfortunately, the majority of inmates identified in the jail as mentally ill are being released to the community with no formal discharge plan or arrangements for community mental health services.[46]

The task of arranging postrelease mental health care is easier for those working in prisons than for those working in jails, because more time is available for discharge planning and because the release date is much more predictable. Although the average length of stay in jails is only a few days, it is somewhat longer for mentally disordered arrestees because they are less able to cooperate in their bail process, and because of delays incurred when issues of competency are raised and an evaluation must be scheduled.[47] Moreover, release from jail occurs for legal reasons, such as arranging bail, posting bond, dismissing the case, or imposing the sentence. There is no reason to suppose that the timing of these events will coincide with the clinically opportune moment. Release must occur, even though the patient may be highly unstable.

---

[43] Ronald Jemelka, "The Mentally Ill in Local Jails: Issues in Admission and Booking." In Steadman (ed.) *op. cit.* p. 36.

[44] Eliot Hartstone, "The Mentally Ill and the Local Jail: Policy and Action." In Steadman (ed.), *op. cit.*: 115.

[45] James H. Carter, "The Chronic Mentally Ill in the Criminal Justice System," 2:1, *CorrectCare* (January, 1988): 10.

[46] Hartstone. *op. cit.*: 120.

Planning for discharge should begin as soon as the mentally ill inmate arrives at the jail. This is particularly essential in view of the expected short stay and the unknown date of release. Linkage with the community referral source should be made upon admission of the offender whenever the initial assessment indicates a history of mental illness and/or suicide attempts, or evidence of current mental health impairments.[48]

It is advisable that the initial mental health contact routinely occur within a week or ten days postrelease. Frequency should be greater in the beginning, and tapered as the patient's readjustment becomes evident. Those jails which make regular use of community mental health agencies for ongoing services have an advantage in that, theoretically, linkage to the patient already has been established. Continuity and successful intervention are improved when the same therapist who had been seeing the patient in the jail can continue to see him or her on the outside, at least for the first visit or two.

It is not sufficient to hand the inmate who is about to be released a list of community mental health resources, with addresses and phone numbers. This information probably will not be used. It is far better to actually arrange an appointment and to ensure that transportation is available or can be provided.

Jails (and prisons) unfortunately, but understandably, devote their attention and resources to the issue of managing the mentally ill inmate while in the facility, but place little priority on ensuring continuity of care upon release. Yet, without this effort, recidivism is much more probable. It is, in part, at least, an issue of perceived responsibility. Even though the jail cannot be charged with provision of aftercare, it surely has a primary responsibility to take the initiative in giving notice to the community agency. It is really a shared responsibility, and both the community mental health agency and the jail need to develop an agreed upon set of protocols whereby notification will be given and follow-up will occur. Liaison persons should be appointed from each agency to coordinate these efforts. The courts also need to be involved. A clearly articulated goal of the jail mental health treatment program must be arrangement of referrals for aftercare upon release.[49]

---

[47] G. L. Axelson, *Psychotic vs. Non-psychotic Misdemeanants in a Large County Jail: An Analysis of Pre-trial Treatment by the Legal System.* (Doctoral Dissertation) George Mason University (1987). Cited in Patricia A. Griffin, "The Back Door of the Jail: Linking Mentally Ill Offenders to Community Mental Health Services." In Steadman (ed.), *op. cit.*: 92.

[48] Hartstone, *op. cit.*: 121.

[49] Griffin, *op. cit.*: 94.

CREATING THERAPEUTIC ENVIRONMENTS FOR MENTALLY ILL PRISONERS

10

This chapter was written by Kenneth L. Faiver, M.P.H., M.L.I.R., and Robert S. Ort, M.D., Ph.D. It is adapted from two papers delivered by them entitled "Managing the Mentally Ill in Correctional Settings: Creating Therapeutic Environments" (Eighteenth National Conference on Correctional Health Care, San Diego, California, September 27, 1994) and "Strategies to Manage the Mentally Ill in Jails" (Twentieth National Conference on Correctional Health Care, Nashville, Tennessee, October 29, 1996).

Coping with the Mentally Ill in Corrections

Veteran employees of correctional facilities are keenly aware of a greatly increased number of mentally ill inmates in their institutions. The free world has witnessed a steady closing of state psychiatric hospitals over the past three decades as emphasis has shifted toward community mental health services. These two phenomena are not unrelated. For many persons, deinstitutionalization of the mentally ill really means reinstitutionalization into a prison or jail.

Some mentally disordered persons cannot cope very well with life's complexities unless they have a structured environment, regular therapeutic interventions, and daily encouragement to take their medications. Their bizarre and unacceptable behaviors soon bring them into conflict with the law. But courts no longer can commit mentally ill persons for long-term treatment and now must remove them from society by way of the criminal justice system. Behaviors which result from illness thus become criminalized. Indeed, many of the persons housed in prisons and jails today are the very same people who used to populate the mental hospitals.

We know from experience that some mentally ill prisoners are able to function quite adequately in a general correctional population, given access to periodic outpatient treatment and occasional crisis intervention. There are a few others with severe psychosis who need to be in an acute psychiatric hospital. But the majority of the mentally ill in our institutions simply do not do well in the general population and need some level of care in between outpatient treatment and an acute psychiatric hospital—such as, "intermediate care," as illustrated in Figure 10-1 (see page 170).

FIGURE 10-1. THEORETICAL DISTRIBUTION OF MENTALLY ILL POPULATION IN A PRISON OR JAIL

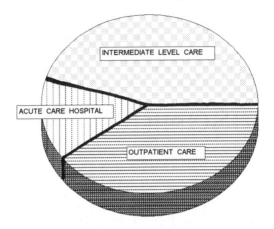

INTERMEDIATE LEVEL CARE

ACUTE CARE HOSPITAL

OUTPATIENT CARE

Inmates who belong in this intermediate group are, by definition, misfits in the general population of a jail or prison. Without structured programming and frequent monitoring, they tend to discontinue taking their medications and begin to act inappropriately. They annoy others, cope poorly with stress, and do not follow rules. They exhibit limited skills to deal with incarceration. And they easily become victims of predatory behavior. Even when not in an acute phase of their mental illness, these chronic patients pose very difficult management problems for correctional administrators.[1] Too often, they are found in administrative or even punitive segregation.

Many correctional systems are choosing to create special living units, variously called: "mental health units," "protective environments," "treatment units," "transitional living units," or "intermediate care units." Whatever the name, they are "intermediate" between the two extremes of outpatient status in the general population and hospitalization in an acute psychiatric facility.[2]

---

[1] "Individuals with more serious psychiatric disorders often do not function well when placed in a general population." B. Jaye Anno, *Prison Health Care: Guidelines for the Management of an Adequate Delivery System* (Chicago: NCCHC, 1991): 127.

[2] "For better or worse, correctional facilities are communities, with stressors and assets that affect each person who lives and works there. This is especially true in prisons, where inmates may live for long periods of time, and predictable cultures develop within the institution. The most effective and efficient service delivery model is an adaptation of the community mental health model to prisons and jails. This model requires the availability of an array of services at varying levels of intensity within the community (in other words, the prison or jail) in addition to the need for occasional transfers to inpatient hospital settings."

American Correctional Association, *Public Policy on Correctional Health Care* (Lanham, Md.: June, 1996): 9.

When the State of Kansas established such a program in its "extended care unit," it found that the inmates derived important therapeutic benefits. Their hygiene, social skills, treatment compliance, and rapport with staff significantly improved. Reduction in behavioral disturbances and in incidents involving self-harm or harm to others is reported to have more than justified the reasonable expenses incurred in developing and implementing this program. [3]

Merely gathering the mentally ill together into one living area, however, does not constitute an intermediate care unit. This chapter describes the essential ingredients of a therapeutic environment and discusses some strategies for implementation.

Contemporary Professional Standards of Care

A general consensus has emerged among mental health professionals since the 1970s regarding the nature and mix of disciplines necessary to create and maintain an appropriate therapeutic context for each phase of the mental health care delivery system. Through a combination of professional experience and rigorous research, optimal levels of team staffing were established for each aspect of the spectrum of care. Even the physical structure and the general nature of the buildings in which mental health services are provided were found to be important for effective treatment.

Through a similar process, certain basic principles regarding mental health care have evolved. These represent contemporary professional standards of care. They include, as Figure 10-2 shows: adequate access, a therapeutic environment, therapeutic programming, continuity of care, the least restrictive environment, competent staff in adequate numbers, informed consent, due process for involuntary treatment, confidentiality, and quality assurance.

FIGURE 10-2. CONTEMPORARY PROFESSIONAL STANDARDS APPLICABLE TO MENTAL HEALTH PROGRAMS

• adequate access	• competent staff in adequate numbers
• therapeutic environment	• informed consent
• therapeutic programming	• due process for involuntary treatment
• continuity of care	• confidentiality
• least restrictive environment	• quality assurance

---

[3] Jane E. Haddad, "Management of the Chronically Mentally Ill within a Correctional Environment," 5:1, *CorrectCare* (January, 1991): 5, 7.

Through judicial decisions, state legislative actions, state mental health codes, and other mechanisms, these standards, for the most part, have become the accepted norm for the care of mentally disordered persons in America.

Adequate access to care must be available when needed without interference or undue delay. This begins with case-finding—a diligent effort to identify persons in need of mental health care, both at the time of incarceration and subsequently, leading to timely referral for psychiatric evaluation and treatment. Periodic inquiries should be made into the needs and condition of each identified patient. Twenty-four-hour emergency response capability is required.

A *therapeutic environment* provides asylum from the many counter-therapeutic features of a regular jail or prison setting. It gives the patient a sense of safety and security by offering refuge, shelter, and protection. Staff members demonstrate their understanding and tolerance of patients' aberrant behaviors and develop a therapeutic alliance with them. Staff function as a team, providing ongoing care based on an individual treatment plan. In such an environment, punitive measures such as ticketing and lockdown are inconsistent with contemporary standards of care and only serve to increase the patients' sense of isolation and abandonment. In addition, the physical locale and characteristics of the therapeutic environment must be conducive to mental health treatment, similar to the structural standards for community facilities.

Therapeutic programming enables patients to participate in treatment activities appropriate to their clinical condition. Based on formal assessments by members of various disciplines represented on the treatment team, an individual treatment plan is developed for each patient. At least thirty hours of out-of-cell structured or planned therapeutic activity routinely are available each week for the vast majority of patients. Regular contact with the same care providers fosters a therapeutic alliance and helps to elicit compliance with the prescribed treatment regimen. A patient education program also may encourage compliance.

Continuity of care means reliance on a single, comprehensive medical record for each patient. Psychiatric staff must have a voice in the criteria and decisions for placement and treatment of mentally disordered prisoners as well as for the transfer of select patients to the general population.[4] A patient transportation system capable of twenty-four-hour response is required.

The principle of *least restrictive environment* dictates that patients will be housed and treated in settings which are suited to their current clinical status and which impose no more restriction than is deemed necessary. This is more easily accomplished if the treatment program affords multiple levels of care settings. A full spectrum of care ranges from a hospital bed to various levels of subacute, chronic, transitional, and outpatient care.

An *adequate number of competent staff* must be provided. Staff must practice within the boundaries of their professional credentials and qualifications. Further, there needs to be adequate and competent supervision to ensure accountability. Staff must participate in professional and inservice education programs. All correctional

---

[4] For large correctional systems, a computerized tracking and scheduling system is recommended to help ensure timely follow-up care.

personnel who work with mentally disordered inmates also need basic psychiatric training. Proper staffing for each level of care is required for an effective therapeutic program and for the safety of patients and employees.

Informed consent requires a method to ensure that the patient's knowledgeable consent is obtained for admission to acute psychiatric units and for treatment. The potentially harmful side effects of medication should be explained to patients and a formal consent procedure is recommended. A "generic" or universal consent for "any and all treatment prescribed," such as some correctional facilities give to the inmate to sign upon admission, is not adequate. It is reasonable to obtain a specific consent for psychotropic medications.

Due process for involuntary treatment is required. For patients who refuse, or are not competent to give, informed consent for necessary treatment, there should be an acceptable procedure to ensure due process. Obtaining an order from the probate court for involuntary admission and treatment is one approach. In most jurisdictions, however, it is accepted practice [5] to administer psychotropic medication for up to forty-eight hours without a court order if the following considerations are observed: a physician (typically a psychiatrist) has examined the patient and determined that an emergency exists, that the patient has a diagnosis of serious mental illness, that in consequence of the mental illness the patient is in imminent danger of injuring self or others, and that less invasive measures would not be satisfactory.

Confidentiality of the medical record and of information derived from provision of care must be safeguarded in keeping with the law and contemporary professional standards. Information may be shared with custody officials when this is necessary for safety and security or for the appropriate management of patients.

Fully consistent with these contemporary professional standards of care are the principles [6] set forth by the American Psychiatric Association Task Force on Psychiatric Services in Jails and Prisons in its 1990 position statement shown in Figure 10-3 (see page 174).

Advantages of Intermediate Care Units

As Figure 10-4 shows, intermediate care units provide safe and humane accommodations for mentally ill patients, afford relief to the remainder of the institution from burdensome and difficult inmates, and reduce the cost, frequency, and length of psychiatric hospitalization (see page 174).

---

[5] The American Correctional Association Standard 3-43422-1 requires written policy and procedure to govern the administration of involuntary psychotropic drugs in compliance with applicable laws of the jurisdiction. American Correctional Association, *1996 Standards Supplement* (Lanham, Md.: American Correctional Association, 1996).

[6] Henry C. Weinstein, "Psychiatric Services in Jails and Prisons: Who Cares?" 4:1, *CorrectCare* (January/February, 1990): 7.

Figure 10-3. Principles for Mental Health Services*

1. The fundamental goal of a mental health service should be to provide the same level of care to patients in the criminal justice process that is available in the community.

2. The effective delivery of mental health services in correctional settings requires that there be a balance between security and treatment needs. There is no inherent conflict between security and treatment.

3. A therapeutic environment can be created in a jail or a prison setting if there is clinical leadership, with authority to create such an environment.

4. Timely and effective access to mental health treatment is a hallmark of adequate mental health care. Necessary staffing levels should be determined by what is essential to ensure that success.

5. Psychiatrists should take a leadership role administratively as well as clinically. Further, it is imperative that psychiatrists define their professional responsibilities to include advocacy for improving mental health service in jails and prisons.

* Source: American Psychiatric Association Task Force on Psychiatric Services in Jails and Prisons, 1990.

Figure 10-4. Advantages of Intermediate Care Units

- safety of patients

- humane living conditions for patients

- relief from burdensome and difficult inmates

- reduction in cost, frequency, and length of hospitalization

Safety of patients. Harsh and hostile prison environments tend to exacerbate mental illness. Patients become anxious and frightened and quickly decompensate. They may injure themselves. They also behave in annoying ways. Other prisoners hurt them and take pleasure in taunting them. Regrettably, even some officers have taken part in "buzzing up" patients.

Humane living conditions for patients. There are two very different approaches to keeping mental patients safe. One involves extensive use of segregation, isolation, deprivation, restraint, and punishment. Most prisons and jails at one time or another have tried this method. Inmates have been housed naked in their cells without clothing or bedding for weeks at a time, kept in four-point restraints for many days to keep from hurting themselves, or even strapped in baskets for extended periods. A more humane and progressive approach to managing patients creates a therapeutic environment which is safe, comforting, reassuring, and encouraging. Here it is possible to bring out what is good in a person, in other words, to nurture mental health, rather than to provoke the person's worst and sickest responses.

Relief to the correctional facility from burdensome and difficult inmates. Institutions cannot easily make distinctions in the way rules and regulations are applied and enforced. Consequently, mentally disordered inmates who do not fully comprehend the rules or who are unable to control their behavior often get into trouble and are punished even when they clearly have diminished responsibility, comprehension, or self-control. In a special living unit, the individualized treatment plan sets goals for behavior. Staff have specific training to understand and work effectively with these inmates.

Reduction in cost, frequency, and length of hospitalization. Most community psychiatric hospitals have a policy requiring discharge of patients as soon as "maximum hospital benefit has been achieved." This essentially means that the patient is well enough to go home in the care of a loving family member or to go to a group home or foster care facility. It is not realistic to characterize the general population setting of a prison or jail in this manner. Some effort might be made to persuade the hospital to discharge based on a criterion of "stability and current level of functioning"[7] rather than "achieved maximum hospital benefit," but this may be difficult to negotiate.

A realistic appraisal of the per diem costs of acute psychiatric hospital care often serves as a powerful incentive to develop the much more cost-efficient therapeutic environment[8] on-site, which can serve as a step-down program for patients being discharged from a psychiatric bed in the community. Each day of care in a psychiatric hospital typically costs well over $600. This is expensive. An average daily census of eighteen patients will cost around four million dollars a year. But a good intermediate care program can significantly reduce the number of costly hospital admissions and also allow some patients to be discharged sooner.

Spectrum of Mental Health Care

As Figure 10-5 illustrates, the spectrum of intermediate care extends from a subacute unit to part-time programming. In other words, the intensity of care decreases along the horizontal axis from left to right. At the left-hand margin are the

---

[7] This approach is recommended by B. Jaye Anno, *Prison Health Care: Guidelines for the Management of an Adequate Delivery System* (Chicago, Ill.: NCCHC, March, 1991): 128.

[8] Although there are some desirable features which can be designed into a newly constructed intermediate care unit, in most cases, a therapeutic environment does not require new construction. Initial focus should be on establishing an appropriate program in a portion of an existing facility.

hospitalized patients. At the right-hand margin are those inmates with mental illness who can adjust to the general population. Our focus here is on the intermediate-care setting, which can embrace several levels.

FIGURE 10-5. SPECTRUM OF INTERMEDIATE CARE LEVELS

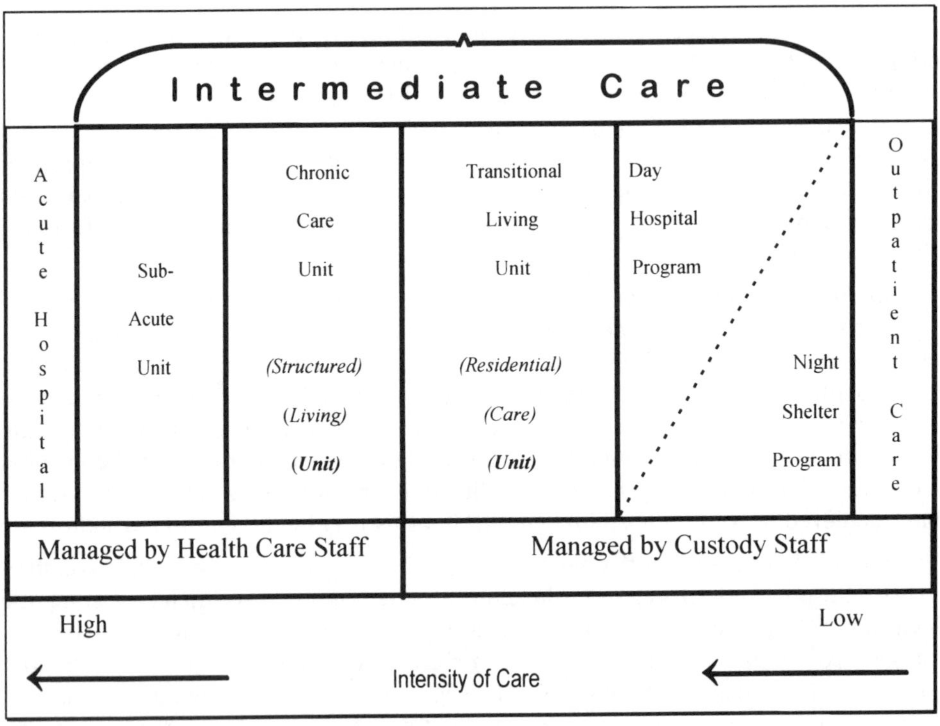

The *subacute unit* resembles a hospital setting, though its staffing and programming are somewhat less intensive. Its availability permits avoidance or significant shortening of the typical hospital stay. It requires nursing and attendant care staff around the clock, and includes a fairly comprehensive schedule of structured and closely observed therapeutic activities. Each inmate should have contact with a psychiatrist one or more times a week. An on-site subacute unit may be cost effective for large correctional systems.

A *chronic care unit* (or structured living unit) affords long-term placement for inmates whose illness is both chronic and severe, or who suffer irreversible brain damage, which permanently affects their ability to function. This sheltered living area requires twenty-four-hour attendant staff, adequate supervision, structured and supervised therapeutic activities, and availability of assistance with activities of daily living. There will be at least monthly contact with a psychiatrist as well as weekly contact with a primary therapist.

A *transitional living unit* (or residential care unit) may be viewed as a temporary placement for those inmates who have been hospitalized and who now need to be observed and prepared for transfer to the general population. It also may house, on a longer-term basis, persons who have demonstrated an inability to cope with the negative and harsh aspects of the general population, but who do not require all of the structure of the higher levels of care. A sense of safety, daily reminders to comply with medication, and ready access to a sympathetic staff person can make major differences for their well-being.

Day hospital program. Some inmates may be able to handle the general population setting for short periods, possibly each evening and night, as long as they are able to return to a more therapeutic environment during the active hours of the day and be among sympathetic staff and other patients. Each day will include an appropriate mix of individual (formal or informal) counseling time, group therapy, structured activities, and leisure time.

A variation of this also is possible. The inmate may sleep in the special housing unit, but spend much of each day with the general population. He or she might hold an institutional job in the kitchen or yard, attend regular classes, and eat meals in the prison meal hall, but always has a safe place to return in the evening.

There are no rigid boundaries among any of these units just described. Each might be defined more broadly or more narrowly. Much depends on the size of the population and the level of care needed. Units also can be specialized in their focus. Large systems may prefer to create a similar unit for mentally retarded inmates, rather than attempting to mingle them with mentally ill patients.

Strategies and Issues for Implementation
Observation Cell

A small jail, without enough mentally ill inmates to warrant setting up a special unit, will nevertheless need to house persons with serious mental illness away from the general population. Possibly they can be referred to a mental hospital or forensic center, [9] to remain there until recompensated adequately for assignment to the general population of the jail, or until they are free to return to the community and be followed by the community mental health program. A major concern for the small jail will be to identify a safe observation area affording close supervision for a suicide-prone or severely mentally ill inmate during the few hours pending evaluation and transfer. A cell with a solid door and a small window or food slot (characteristic of what are sometimes inappropriately termed "observation cells") does not permit adequate observation and should not be used for this purpose.

Malingering

Some argue that prisoners will feign mental illness in order to be admitted to a comfortable therapeutic unit or to remain in it longer than necessary. They might

---

[9] A mental hospital typically operated by the state, which is concerned with the legal aspects of mental illness and the treatment of persons who have been charged with or convicted of a crime.

even engage in self-injury and suicidal gestures just to get into a more attractive setting. Perhaps some will do this. But it is the responsibility of clinical staff to evaluate all persons who are admitted and separate out the occasional malingerer. Moreover, most persons who cut themselves (even in a manipulative way) are mentally ill. The question is whether it makes sense to render the unit so harsh and antitherapeutic that it becomes less effective for those patients who really need it, just to prevent the occasional malingerer from inappropriately "enjoying" it.

Role of Security Staff

Attempts at joint management of these units by officers and mental health professionals do not always work out very successfully. This comes as no surprise, given the widely disparate backgrounds, training, and orientation of correctional officers and health care professionals and the traditionally divergent methods of managing mentally ill inmates. A more consistently therapeutic environment is possible with clearly defined, rather than comingled, areas of responsibility.

The ideal model places day-to-day management of acute, subacute, and chronic care inpatient units entirely in the hands of health care staff, including direct care workers supervised by nursing personnel. Perimeter security, control of contraband, and emergency back-up constitute the extent of involvement by custody personnel with the inmates on these units.

On the other hand, transitional living areas, residential care units, and daycare areas may be staffed appropriately by security personnel, and the patients would have access to health care staff on an outpatient basis. It is well to include the officers of these units as members of the treatment team because their observations of patient behavior are highly relevant, and they are the ones who must supervise and facilitate some of the planned therapeutic activities for the patients.

While other models may be employed, this paradigm maintains a clear separation between two very distinct approaches to inmate management and discipline. It does not try to mix the correctional and the therapeutic methods. By keeping them well defined and completely separate, the integrity and effectiveness of both can be optimized.

Length of Stay

How long an inmate should be kept in an intermediate care unit is determined, in part, by the nature of the facility. For example, a detention center primarily will be interested in keeping the inmate safe, and, therefore, may prefer to keep the patient in the intermediate unit for the duration of his or her brief term in the facility. On the other hand, a long-term prison probably would want to assess whether the patient can acquire sufficient coping skills to adjust to placement in the general population or, at least, to a less-intensive care setting. Such a patient would be progressively moved to less-intensive settings (assuming these are available) and observed carefully to determine his or her adequacy of coping.

Movement to a less-intensive setting should occur only when the primary therapist determines that this is appropriate, and the patient feels ready. Always, the patient should be assured that he or she can return, if necessary, and should be properly oriented to the new setting and informed how to seek help should this be required. Changing environments is especially troubling for mentally ill persons, and every effort should be made to ease the transition. It might even be feasible to allow a patient a day or a weekend to try out placement in the general population, assured that return to the protected setting is possible. Sometimes, after one or more trials, a permanent transfer to general population can be made successfully.

Not every patient will be adaptable for movement to the general population. Some are best kept in a psychiatric setting throughout their entire period of incarceration. However, from time to time, they may require movement among the acute, subacute, chronic care, or transitional living units. This should not be surprising. As indicated earlier, the deinstitutionalization process, while a blessing for many, was not successful for all. Many of the failures of deinstitutionalization now occupy our prisons and jails. We need not make the same mistake twice.

Decision to Admit, Transfer, or Discharge

The decision to admit, transfer, or discharge patients to or from the intermediate-care levels always must be made by clinical staff, but a representative of the security staff should be included in the deliberation. Each transfer out of a therapeutic unit requires a written discharge plan. In transfers from one therapeutic unit to another, the transfer note should specify any revisions to the current treatment plan. These remain in effect until again revised at the next level.

Effective Programming

Effective programming is a critical component of an intermediate mental health unit. It is not enough simply to identify the patients and assign them to a special living area. They need both care and supervision. They also need therapy. Ideally, there will be specially trained staff present in the living areas twenty-four hours a day. Observing patients only through a window is not adequate.

Use of Punitive Measures in a Therapeutic Setting

One area in which the principles and beliefs of correctional officials can come into direct conflict with the opinions and practices of mental health professionals is in the manner of enforcing rules in a therapeutic unit. The following case history illustrates this point.

A large correctional facility had an acute-psychiatric inpatient unit as well as an intermediate-care unit for mentally ill inmates. Although the units were quite well staffed, the mental health professionals rarely, if ever, entered the living or activity areas of the patients. Instead, it was their custom to have patients escorted across the hall to the mental health clinic for scheduled appointments with clinical staff. On a day-to-day basis, officers were assigned to observe the patients through windows and were the first responders whenever emergency situations developed in the living areas.

At first, the officers were applying the same disciplinary expectations, criteria, sanctions, and procedures as elsewhere in the institution, but at the urging of mental health staff, they agreed to modify this approach. Mental health professionals met with custody representatives and, through discussion and compromise, reached agreement on a set of special rules and sanctions for these units. In theory, these were to give consideration to the mental status of the inmates by requiring a psychologist or social worker to impose or approve the sanctions. The sanctions generally were more lenient than those applied in other parts of the institution, giving evidence of some degree of understanding and tolerance. Examples included: a maximum of three days top-lock for disobeying a direct order or talking back to an officer, three days top-lock for striking another inmate, and twenty-four hours top-lock for failing to clean one's own cell daily. The officers felt it was imperative to impose some disciplinary sanction whenever there was an infraction unless the therapist determined that the patient was not responsible for the behavior.

A careful review of disciplinary reports revealed that the sanctions were indeed punitive. Inmates were being "sentenced" to specified periods of punishment rather than just imposing restrictions until a behavioral change occurred. Sanctions were being applied in this fashion even for behaviors which were clearly a result of a psychotic process, where there were both diminished responsibility and diminished control over behavior. One man was sitting despondently on the floor of his locked cell. The officer explained that he was on lockdown status because he had refused to clean his cell that morning. Later on that same day, his psychosis became so evident that he was admitted to an intensive psychiatric unit at the hospital.

For mentally ill persons, therapeutic measures are much to be preferred over punitive sanctions to achieve compliance with rules and requirements. This point was overlooked in the compromise solution. Even had the special rules been fully and properly implemented, it would not have been sufficient for a mental health professional to screen each case for individual responsibility in light of the acute illness. Punitive measures are inherently antitherapeutic—in other words, in conflict with the methods and goals of treatment. This is not to say that the officers were wrong because they wanted to prevent dangerous, aggressive, or inappropriate behavior. However, what was fundamentally lacking was a pervasive therapeutic presence of treatment staff in the patient living areas (as is the standard practice in any community psychiatric inpatient unit or residential care facility). The presence and close familiarity of staff with patients would lead to early recognition of signs and symptoms of impending decompensation, disruptive behavior, or inadequate coping of a patient, permitting timely and effective intervention by the treatment staff. The result of this therapeutic approach would be fully in keeping with what the officers really wanted—a safe and orderly unit—but the means to that end are vastly different.

Staffing

Professional staffing must be sufficient to ensure that each patient admitted to an intermediate-care unit has an individualized treatment plan, prepared by the interdisciplinary team within the first ten days. A nursing evaluation is required upon admission and a physical and psychiatric evaluation within three days, thereafter. Also, a comprehensive assessment of the patient needs to be made by each discipline represented on the team. Nursing evaluations should be documented for each inmate on a regular basis.

In addition, a chronic care unit requires a cadre of direct care workers, preferably working under nursing supervision. These direct care workers are assigned to work within the inmate living areas and are trained to interact in a supportive and therapeutic manner. They also provide escort, when this is needed, for chronic inmates who are permitted to leave the confines of the therapeutic unit.

Suitable therapeutic modalities include group and individual therapy, structured activity therapy, and supervised informal activity, conducted or directed by appropriately trained clinicians. The activity therapy may include occupational therapy, recreational therapy, music therapy, and creative arts therapy. Some units successfully have employed the care of pets and of plants as a therapeutic activity for chronic inmates.

Staffing implications for maintaining a safe and therapeutic intermediate environment are greater than many, at first, would expect. Appropriate staffing levels for mentally disordered patients frequently meet with surprise and resistance from persons in correctional management, since custodial care of inmates is based on lower staffing ratios. Useful guidelines for staffing patterns, therapeutic programming and therapeutic interaction usually are specified in state mental health codes or other laws and regulations, and can be applied whether or not the unit is actually licensed. While many factors must be considered in determining staff levels for a given situation, minimum staffing for seven-day coverage of three shifts, including relief, for a twenty-four bed chronic care unit would include one-third psychiatrist, one-half psychologist, one-half social worker, one activity therapist, four nurses, and ten direct care workers. A transitional living unit of comparable size, on the other hand, would require a similar complement of psychiatrist, psychologist, and social worker staff, and one-fourth activity therapist, two nurses, and seven correctional officers. Staffing for a twenty-four-bed subacute unit would use a full-time psychiatrist, psychologist, social worker, and activity therapist, eight nurses, and nine direct care workers.

These mentally ill inmates are among the most difficult populations that a jail or prison has to manage. Many of them, a few years ago, would have been in a chronic ward of a state mental hospital. Suicides and lawsuits are extremely costly for the correctional agency, and in almost all cases can and should be prevented by adequate staffing by individuals with proper training and an understanding of programs for inmates. The appropriate deployment and use of intermediate-care units significantly can reduce the need for expensive acute hospital stays. Well-planned and well-managed therapeutic environments are not only possible in correctional facilities, but are well worth the effort and the cost involved.

THE ROLE OF PHYSICIAN ASSISTANTS AND NURSE PRACTITIONERS

11

This chapter was written by R. Scott Chavez, M.P.A., PA-C. Mr. Chavez is the Director and Associate Professor of Physician Assistant Studies, Midwestern University, Downers Grove, Illinois. He is the former Vice President of Professional Services of the National Commission on Correctional Health Care, Chicago, Illinois.

Jail and prison officials, facing an ever-increasing population and limited resources, are constantly challenged to provide quality health care services. Nurse practitioners (NPs) and physician assistants (PAs) working with physicians in a correctional setting can provide some of the solutions for correctional administrators. Physician assistants and nurse practitioners have been providing quality medical care for over a quarter of a century, and their use in corrections has helped to provide health services to prison and jail populations in a timely and cost-effective manner. This chapter focuses on the training and licensing of physician assistants and nurse practitioners and their use in a jail or prison health care system. It also presents the similarities and differences between these two health professions.

Origins of Physician Assistants and Nurse Practitioners

The first physician assistant program began at Duke University School of Medicine in 1965. Its focus was on training individuals who would "assist the doctor . . . in such a way as to facilitate better utilization of available physicians and nurses."[1] The concept of civilian trained assistants to the physician had emerged from two sociological events arriving simultaneously onto the American scene: the Vietnam War and a physician shortage. Experienced medics returning from Vietnam to civilian life

---

[1] Eugene Stead, "Conserving Costly Talents: Providing Physicians' New Assistants, " 198, *Journal of the American Medical Association* (1966): 1108-1109.

found no comparable or appropriate health careers in the United States. Simultaneously, there was a maldistribution of primary care physicians, and many areas of the country were without access to medical care.

As a result, our country recognized that experienced military hospital corpsmen were an underutilized resource that could (1) increase access to basic medical care, (2) enhance primary care physician services, (3) fill in geographic vacancies where there was no access to physicians, and (4) help control health care costs.[2] This social environment fostered the development of many new physician assistant programs in the 1970s and the matriculation of a considerable number of military veterans.

Consequently, the profession was dominated in the early years by male ex-military corpsmen. However, in the thirty years since the start of the Duke physician assistant program, the profession has undergone changes in its training and deployment. Today, 47.2 percent of the physician assistants are female.[3] As of February 1997, there were eighty-four accredited physician assistant programs in primary care and three physician assistant programs in surgical assisting. The Association of Physician Assistant Programs (APAP) reports that as of January 1997, there have been just under 35,000 graduates from physician assistant programs.

The nurse practitioner (NP) profession was created in the 1960s as a solution to the lack of health care access by communities in need. More recently, the nursing profession has adopted the title of "Advanced Practice Nurse" or "Advanced Registered Nurse Practitioner" (ARNP), which encompasses nurses who have obtained advanced education and clinical experience beyond the two to four years necessary to become a registered nurse (RN). Advanced practice nurses include clinical nurse specialists, nurse anesthetists, certified nurse midwives (CNM), and family nurse practitioners (FNPs). There are an estimated 200 advanced practice nurse programs that provide various training for each of the specialty areas. The advanced practice nurse receives training in specialty areas such as acute care, adult medicine, emergency care, family practice, gerontology, neonatal care, occupational health, pediatrics, school/college health, women's health, and psychiatric or mental health. According to 1992 data, there are approximately 58,000 clinical nurse specialists with master's degree preparation, 26,000 nurse anesthetists, 5,000 certified nurse midwives, and 27,000 nurse practitioners.[4] Approximately 75 percent of the nurse practitioners have received education and training, beyond their initial RN training, in certificate programs that range from nine to twelve months.

---

[2] P. Eugene Jones and James Cawley, "Physician Assistants and Health System Reform: Clinical Capabilities, Practice Activities and Potential Roles," 271, *Journal of the American Medical Association* (1994): 1266-1272.

[3] American Academy of Physicians, *1995 AAPA Membership Census Report* (Alexandria, Va.: American Academy of Physicians, April, 1996).

[4] Division of Nursing, Bureau of Health Professions, *National Sample Survey of Registered Nurses* (Washington, D.C.: Health Resources and Services Administration, U.S. Department of Health and Human Services, 1992).

Other Names

Some confusion is caused by the various names that have been used for physician assistants and advanced practice nurses. "Mid-level practitioners" is a title that has been used since the 1960s. This title is rejected by both professions since it infers that the services provided are less than, inferior to, or half the quality of physician care. Studies have demonstrated that physician assistants and advanced practice nurses provide high-quality patient care and that their services are not hierarchical, but often are the point of first and only contact with a patient. It has been estimated that 80 percent of patient visits can be managed by advanced practice nurses and physician assistants. Advanced practice nurses and physician assistants diagnose, treat, and discharge patients without a physician's oversight.

"Physician extender" was a title that was used in 1965 to describe both disciplines. The term is accepted by physician assistants, since by law, professional ethics and training, they are extensions of the primary care physician. However, advanced practice nurses reject the term since they do not view themselves as extending physician's services.

The federal government recently introduced a new title, "nonphysician practitioners" (NPPs). This title has not gained great support from either group because it often is expanded to include psychologists, social workers, chiropractors, naturopaths, and others. This becomes confusing, especially when discussing an expanded scope of medical practice and prescription-writing privileges.

Educational Standards

Physician assistant educational centers must conform to the "Standards of an Approved Educational Program for the Assistant to the Primary Care Physician" that were initially adopted in 1971 and revised in 1978, 1985, 1990 and 1997. The Standards set minimum quality outcomes and expectations to which accredited programs are held accountable. The Commission on Accreditation of Allied Health Education Programs (CAAHEP)[5] endorses the physician assistant educational standards which define physician assistants as

> academically and clinically prepared to provide health care services with the direction and responsible supervision of a doctor of medicine or osteopathy. Functions of the physician assistant include performing diagnostic, therapeutic, preventive, and health maintenance services in any setting in which the physician renders care, in order to allow more effective and focused application of the physician's particular knowledge and skills. [6]

---

[5] The Commission has representation of sixty national health organizations, including the American Medical Association, the American Academy of Family Physicians, the American College of Physicians, the American Academy of Pediatrics, the American Academy of Physician Assistants, and the Association of Physician Assistant Programs.

[6] Commission on Accreditation of Allied Health Education Programs, *The Standards and Guidelines for an Accredited Educational Program for the Physician Assistant* (Chicago, Ill.: Commission on Accreditation of Allied Health Education Programs, 1997).

The typical physician assistant training program requires its applicants to have completed a minimum of two years of undergraduate-level course work in the health sciences, which includes biology, chemistry, mathematics, English, and behavioral sciences. Admission into a physician assistant program has become extremely competitive, with some programs reporting over 1,000 applicants for a class. Once admitted, a typical physician assistant student will take nine to twelve months of preclinical courses in anatomy, physiology, clinical medicine, physical diagnosis, preventive medicine, and clinical laboratory procedures and another nine to fifteen months of clinical education that is supervised by physicians. The physician assistant student will gain experience in both clinic and hospital settings in either rural or inner-city areas. Many physician assistants complete portions of their clinical training in a correctional institution.

Physician assistants completing an accredited program will receive either a certificate of completion, a bachelor's degree, or a master's degree. Approximately 70.2 percent of physician assistants have a bachelor's degree, and 14.7 percent have a master's degree.

The American Nurses Association, Nurse Practitioner Groups, and the National League of Nursing are advocating a master's degree as a requirement for those seeking to work as an advanced practice nurse by the year 2000. A typical nurse practitioner educational program focuses on comprehensive clinical skills for primary care in a twelve-month curriculum. Qualifications for entry into a nurse practitioner program vary with each specialty area. Nurse practitioners receive a theoretical and empirical foundation that is added to the clinical and technical skills necessary to provide the services needed for an advanced nursing practice. The nurse practitioners curriculum includes many of the skills and training that would be useful in a correctional setting:[7]

- Health promotion and disease prevention

- Comprehensive health assessment and screening techniques

- Diagnosis of problems of health and disease of all body systems

- Treatment and management of problems of health and disease of all body systems using pharmacologic and nonpharmacologic interventions

- Psychological processes

- Personal, cultural, spiritual, and developmental context of health and disease

- Interpersonal communication skills and counseling techniques in nurse/client relationships

- Application of group dynamics in leadership, negotiation, and conflict resolution

---

[7] American Academy of Nurse Practitioners, *Position Statement on Nurse Practitioner Curriculum* (Austin, Tex.: American Academy of Nurse Practitioners, 1997).

- Concepts of case management and managed care

- Principles of risk management

- Principles of bioethics

- Environmental concepts of care

- Community assessment skills

- Skills in critical diagnostic reasoning and decision making

- Skills in critiquing and using research in health care delivery

- Credentialing, public education, and mentoring of those in an advanced nursing practice

- Health policy and its application to nurse practitioner practice

Certification and Licensure

Upon completing an accredited program, a physician assistant is eligible to take a national certifying examination administered by the National Commission on Certification of Physician Assistants (NCCPA). The NCCPA examination is a nationally standardized two-day written examination. Individuals who successfully complete this comprehensive examination are entitled to use the credentials Physician Assistant-Certified (PA-C). PA-Cs must be recertified by obtaining 100 hours of continuing medical education every two years and take a recertification examination every six years.

Most states require graduation from an accredited training program as a condition for awarding of a license or certificate to practice medicine as a physician assistant. In forty-eight states, certification from the National Commission on Certification of Physician Assistants is required for state approval to practice medicine. Physician assistants must work under the supervision of a physician. The state medical boards authorize (either through certification, registration, or licensing) physician assistant practice and are responsible for monitoring physician assistant activities. Figure 11-1 provides a listing of states that are either delegatory (allowing the physician to delegate tasks) or regulatory (approving all aspects of physician assistant practice) in nature.

Entry into nursing practice requires a diploma and licensure from the state nursing board. Diploma nurses can come from either a two-year community college (AD-RN) or a baccalaureate-degree institution (BSN-RN). State nursing boards license and monitor the nursing practice of licensed practical nurses (LPNs) and registered nurses (RNs). Entry into a specialty area of advanced nursing (APN) requires no more than a license to practice nursing; however, some nursing practice acts are being amended to regulate the use of specialty titles and credentials. States may require certification based on specialty training, graduate education, and/or a national certification examination.

FIGURE 11-1. SUMMARY OF STATE PHYSICIAN ASSISTANT'S SCOPE OF PRACTICE

States that define scope of practice as authorized by the board of medical examiners.	8	Alabama, Arizona, Idaho, Iowa, Ohio, South Carolina, South Dakota, Wisconsin, and the District of Columbia
States that have delegatory statutes where medical diagnosis and treatment is permitted within the scope of practice of the supervising/collaborating physician.	41	Alaska, Arkansas, California, Colorado, Connecticut, Delaware, Florida, Georgia, Hawaii, Illinois, Indiana, Kansas, Kentucky, Louisiana, Maine, Maryland, Massachusetts, Michigan, Minnesota, Missouri, Montana, Nebraska, Nevada, New Hampshire, New Jersey, New Mexico, New York, North Carolina, North Dakota, Oklahoma, Oregon, Pennsylvania, Rhode Island, Tennessee, Texas, Utah, Vermont, Virginia, Washington, West Virginia, Wyoming
States that have no statutory law for physician assistant practice	1	Mississippi

Source: American Academy of Physician Assistants

Distribution

Where do physician assistants practice and why? The American Academy of Physician Assistants reports from its 1996 census that 37.2 percent of the physician assistant population practices in family practice, 7.7 percent in general internal medicine, 2.9 percent in obstetrics and gynecology, and 2.5 percent in general pediatrics.[8] Approximately 20.8 percent of the physician assistant population works in cities

---

[8] American Academy of Physicians, *1995 AAPA Membership Census Report* (Alexandria, Va.: American Academy of Physicians, April, 1996).

greater than 1,000,000; and 24.7 percent in towns of 250,000 to 1,000,000. Geographically, 25.1 percent works in the Northeast, 24.2 percent in the Southeast, 19.4 percent in the North Central, 17.5 percent in the West, and 13.8 percent in the South Central.[9]

In a recent study, physician assistants choosing nonprimary care specialties did so because of intellectual stimulation, technical orientation, and income; while physician assistants choosing primary care reported the opportunity to practice prevention, the opportunity for an academic appointment and activities, reduction of debt, scholarship and intellectual content, and peer influences as factors influencing their decisions.[10] According to the American Academy of Physician Assistants, 1.5 percent of 14,045 respondents to the annual physician assistant survey indicated that they work in corrections, while 1.2 percent indicated that they are employed by a department of corrections.[11]

Where do nurse practitioners practice? Approximately 94.4 percent of nurse practitioners work in metropolitan and suburban areas, and 75 percent work in primary care specialties. There is no breakout of the number or percentage of nurse practitioners who are employed in corrections.

Salary

According to the 1996 American Academy of Physician Assistants Census, the median total income for physician assistants who work full-time was $60,687, the mean was $65,125 with a standard deviation of $20,637. For physician assistants graduating in 1995 or after, the median income was $52,116, the mean was $56,318 with a standard deviation of $19,064.[12] Studies have not been done to determine the national salary mean of physician assistants working in corrections.

According to recent studies by the American Academy of Nurse Practitioners, the national mean salary for advanced practice nurses is "estimated to be over $50,000 with a range from the $40s to the $80s."[13] In some states, advanced practice nurses are permitted to establish independent practices and be directly reimbursed for their services. Again, there is no breakout of the salary for those nurse practitioners who work in corrections. However, it is obvious that it costs less to employ either physician assistants or nurse practitioners than medical doctors. For this reason alone, the number of individuals in both professions who are working in corrections should increase.

---

[9] *Ibid.*

[10] *Ibid.*

[11] *Ibid.*

[12] *Ibid.*

[13] American Academy of Nurse Practitioners, Published Memorandum, January, 1997.

Physician Assistant and Nurse Practitioner—Scope of Practice

The tasks that physician assistants can do vary according to the physicians who supervise them. In general, physician assistants take medical histories, perform physical examinations, order and interpret laboratory tests, interpret x-rays, treat illnesses, handle follow-up visits, share telephone call responsibilities, and provide preventive health services. Physician assistants are licensed or certified in forty-nine states, the District of Columbia, and Guam. Mississippi has no legislation authorizing the practice of physician assistants. Physician assistants are authorized to take histories, perform physical exams, order and/or perform diagnostic and therapeutic procedures, formulate a working diagnosis, develop and implement a treatment plan, monitor the effectiveness of therapeutic interventions, assist in surgery, offer counseling and education, and make referrals.

According the American Academy of Nurse Practitioners, nurse practitioners "provide nursing and medical services to individuals, families and groups, emphasizing health promotion and disease prevention, as well as the diagnosis and management of acute and chronic diseases." Nurse practitioners have a collaborative practice whereby, consulting with a physician, the nurse practitioner will provide primary care services from health maintenance and counseling for minor health problems to intervention in chronic health problems. The nurse practitioner is to consult with a physician when the patient's medical condition requires treatment beyond the nurse practitioner's experience and/or knowledge.

Prescriptive Authority

Some states permit limited prescriptive authority for physician assistants and nurse practitioners. Exercising the medical judgment to select the drug of choice still rests with the physician responsible for the patient's care.

Physician assistants have prescriptive authority in forty states, the District of Columbia, and Guam. In addition, California allows physician assistants, as of January 1995, to write "transmittal orders" for prescription drugs. The physician assistant may administer or provide medication to a patient, or transmit orally or in writing on a patient's record or in a transmittal order, a prescription from a supervising physician based on protocol or on a patient-specific order. Figure 11-2 provides a state analysis of physician assistant prescriptive authority (see page 193).

Nurse practitioners either have an integrated or a collaborative practice with physicians. In either case, it is expected that the nurse practitioner and the physician will discuss and review patient care, as appropriate. In 1996, the American Medical Association surveyed its state medical associations to establish a database of current legislation and regulation on advanced practice nurse prescriptive authority. Figure 11-3 provides a summary of state legislation on the scope of practice for advanced practice nurses (see page 194).

FIGURE 11-2. SUMMARY OF STATE PRESCRIPTIVE AUTHORITY FOR PHYSICIAN ASSISTANTS

States permitting physician assistants to prescribe or dispense noncontrolled drugs only	5	Delaware, Missouri, New York, Tennessee, Texas, and the District of Columbia
States that allow prescribing/ dispensing by physician assistants from board-approved formulary	8	Alabama, California, Florida, Idaho, Oklahoma, Pennsylvania, Virginia, West Virginia
States that allow full prescriptive authority for noncontrolled and schedule III to V drugs (controlled substances)	27	Alaska, Arizona (II to V), Colorado, Connecticut (IV-V), Georgia, Iowa, Kansas (II in emergencies only), Maine, Massachusetts, Michigan, Minnesota, Montana (II-V), Nebraska (II-V), Nevada, New Hampshire, New Mexico (II-V), North Carolina (II-V), North Dakota, Oregon, Rhode Island (V only), South Carolina (V only), South Dakota (II-V), Utah (II-V), Vermont, Washington, Wisconsin, Wyoming

Source: American Academy of Physician Assistants

The Controlled Substances Act of 1970 categorized controlled substances according to the potential for abuse of a drug. Category or Schedule I has the highest potential for abuse and no accepted medical use. Schedule I drugs include experimental drugs. A Schedule II drug has a high potential for abuse and can lead to severe physical and/or psychological dependence. Schedule II drugs are tightly controlled and renewals are not allowed. Schedule III drugs have some potential for abuse, leading to low-to-moderate physical/psychological dependence. Schedule IV drugs have a low potential for physical/psychological dependence. Schedule III and IV drugs may be renewed five times in up to six months. Schedule V drugs are classified as having a very low potential for abuse, and may not require a prescription.

FIGURE 11-3. SUMMARY OF STATE LEGISLATION ON SCOPE OF PRACTICE FOR ADVANCED PRACTICE NURSES

States where statutes require physician collaboration for advanced practice nurses integrated practice	25	Alabama, Arizona, Arkansas, California, Delaware, Florida, Georgia*, Idaho, Kentucky, Louisiana*, Maryland, Massachusetts, Mississippi, Missouri, Nebraska, Nevada, New York, North Carolina, Pennsylvania, South Carolina, South Dakota, Tennessee*, Vermont, Wisconsin, Wyoming *state has no additional prescriptive statutes
States where statutes require physician collaboration for advanced practice nurses prescribing	37	Alabama, Arizona, Arkansas, California, Colorado**, Connecticut**, Delaware, Florida, Hawaii**, Idaho**, Indiana**, Kansas**, Kentucky, Maryland, Massachusetts, Michigan**, Minnesota**, Mississippi, Missouri, Nebraska, Nevada, New Hampshire**, New Jersey**, New York, North Carolina, North Dakota**, Pennsylvania, Rhode Island**, South Carolina, South Dakota, Texas**, Utah**, Vermont, Virginia**, West Virginia**, Wisconsin, Wyoming **state requires supervision for prescribing only
States where advanced practice nurses can practice and prescribe without any physician involvement	7	Alaska, District of Columbia, Iowa, Maine, New Mexico, Oregon (Schedule III-V), Washington (Schedule V only)
States where advanced practice nurses can prescribe with minimal physician involvement	4	Arizona, Montana, New Hampshire, Vermont
States requiring physicians for quality assurance programs for advanced practice nurses	3	Montana, Pennsylvania, Vermont
States where advanced practice nurses prescribe (except controlled substances) with physician involvement	13	Alabama, California, Florida, Hawaii, Idaho, Kansas, Michigan, Missouri, Nevada, New Jersey, Tennessee, Texas, Virginia
States where advanced practice nurses prescribe all drugs including some or all controlled substances with physician involvement	33	Alaska, Arizona, Arkansas, Colorado (pending), Connecticut, Delaware, District of Columbia, Indiana, Iowa, Kentucky (pending), Maine, Maryland, Massachusetts, Minnesota, Mississippi, Montana, Nebraska, New Hampshire, New Mexico, New York, North Carolina, North Dakota, Oregon, Pennsylvania (pending), Rhode Island, South Carolina, South Dakota, Utah, Vermont, Washington, West Virginia, Wisconsin, Wyoming

Source: American Medical Association, Board of Trustees Report, June 23, 1996, p. 14

What is the Difference Between Physician Assistants and Nurse Practitioners?

In spite of the differences in training, licensing, and regulating of the careers, physician assistants and nurse practitioners have very similar jobs. The difference really narrows down to philosophy. Physician assistants are aligned with medicine. Physician assistants are accredited, trained, certified, and employed by physicians. Advanced practice nurses are aligned, trained, and rooted in the philosophy of nursing. Advanced practice nurses have a philosophical and educational perspective that encompasses a holistic approach to the patient. Physician assistants are more attuned to the medical and surgical approach to the diagnosis and treatment of patients. Advanced practice nurses are independent practitioners who work *alongside* the physician, while the physician assistant is a dependent practitioner working *for* the physician. The underlying philosophical differences may create a lot of conflict and friction between physician assistants and nurse practitioners over status, employment, credentials, and recognition.

The reality is that both the physician assistant and nurse practitioner augment the health care delivery system. When the supervising or collaborating physician supports the concept of an interdisciplinary or integrated health care team, the physician assistant and nurse practitioner can provide exceptional care. Both can work autonomously from the physician. Studies on patient satisfaction demonstrate that physician assistants and nurse practitioners provide good patient care and are accepted by the patients they treat. [14]

Physician Supervision and Collaboration

The American Medical Association (AMA) supports the use of physician assistants and advanced practice nurses. In June 1996, the AMA adopted the following principles for advanced practice nurses in an integrated practice. [15]

1. Physicians must retain authority for patient care in any team-care arrangement, for example, integrated practice, to assure patient safety and quality of care.

---

[14] Office of Technology Assessment, *1986 Nurse Practitioners, Physician Assistants, and Certified Nurse-Midwives: A Policy Analysis*. Health Technology Case Study 37 (December, 1986), Washington, D.C.; W. O. Spitzer, D. I. Sackett, J. C. Sibley, et al. "The Burlington Randomized Trial of the Nurse Practitioner," *New England Journal of Medicine* (1974) 290:251-256.

[15] American Medical Association, Board of Trustees Report 23. *Principles Guiding AAL4 Policy Regarding Supervision of Medical Care Delivered by Advanced Practice Nurses in Integrated Practice*, Chicago, Ill. (June, 1996).

2. Medical societies should work with legislatures and licensing boards to prevent dilution of the authority of physicians to lead the health care team.

3. Exercising independent medical judgment to select the drug of choice must continue to be the responsibility of physicians.

4. Physicians should recognize physician assistants and advanced practice nurses under physician leadership as effective physician extenders and valued members of the health care team.

5. Physicians should encourage state medical and nursing boards to explore the feasibility of working together to coordinate their regulatory initiatives and activities.

6. Physicians must be responsible for initiating and implementing quality-control programs for nonphysicians delivering medical care in integrated practices.

The American Medical Association guidelines for physician/physician assistant practice are as follows:

1 . Health care services delivered by physicians and physician assistants must be within the scope of each practitioner's authorized practice as defined by state law.

2. The physician is ultimately responsible for coordinating and managing the care of patients and, with appropriate input of the physician assistant, ensuring the quality of health care provided to patients.

3. The physician is responsible for the supervision of the physician assistant in all settings.

4. The role of the physician assistant(s) in the delivery of care should be defined through mutually agreed upon guidelines that are developed by the physician and the physician assistant and based on the physician's delegatory style.

5. The physician must be available for consultation with the physician assistant at all times either in person or through telecommunication systems or other means.

6. The extent of the involvement by the physician assistant in the assessment and implementation of treatment will depend on the complexity and acuity of the patient's condition and the training, experience, and preparation of the physician assistant as adjudged by the physician.

7. Patients should be made clearly aware at all times whether they are being cared for by a physician or a physician assistant.

8. The physician and the physician assistant together should review all delegated patient services on a regular basis, as well as mutually agree on guidelines for practice.

9. The physician is responsible for clarifying and familiarizing the physician assistant with his or her supervising methods and style of delegating patient care.

Figure 11-4 contains a summary of the supervision provided to the physician assistant.

FIGURE 11-4. SUMMARY OF PHYSICIAN ASSISTANT SUPERVISION

States that define supervision as oversight and direction but not direct, on-site physician supervision. Supervising physician must be readily available.	44	Alabama, Alaska, Arkansas, California, Colorado, Connecticut, Florida, Georgia, Idaho, Illinois, Indiana, Iowa, Kansas, Kentucky, Louisiana, Maine, Massachusetts, Michigan, Minnesota, Missouri, Montana, Nebraska, Nevada, New Hampshire, New Jersey, New Mexico, New York, North Carolina, North Dakota, Ohio, Oklahoma, Oregon, Pennsylvania, Rhode Island, South Carolina, South Dakota, Tennessee, Texas, Utah, Vermont, Washington, West Virginia, Wisconsin, Wyoming, and the District of Columbia
States that require physician on-site supervision	2	Hawaii, Maryland

Source: American Academy of Physician Assistants

Physician Assistant/Nurse Practitioner Use in Correctional Systems

Both the American Correctional Association and the National Commission on Correctional Health Care (NCCHC) have standards that address the use of physician assistants and nurse practitioners and provide guidance to correctional administrators.

American Correctional Association Standard 3-4334 for Adult Correctional Institutions [16] states:

> Appropriate state and federal licensure, certification, or registration requirements and restrictions apply to personnel who provide health care services to inmates. The duties and responsibilities of such personnel are governed by written job descriptions approved by the health authority. Verification of current credentials and job descriptions are on file in the facility.

The comment on this standard by the American Correctional Association Standards Committee is that:

> Only qualified health care personnel should determine and supervise health care procedures. Written job descriptions should include the required professional qualifications and the individual's specific role in the health care delivery system. Verification of qualifications may consist of copies of current credentials or a letter from the state licensing or certifying body regarding current credential status. Nursing services are performed in accordance with professionally recognized standards of nursing practice and the jurisdiction's Nurse Practice Act.

NCCHC Standards J-22 and P-19 also concern job descriptions for the physician assistant and nurse practitioner. These should be developed by the jail administrator and responsible health authority. They include discussion of the role and responsibility of patient care and the level of physician supervision/collaboration that is expected. Although it is the individual physician's responsibility to ensure that he or she provides adequate supervision, certain guidelines should be incorporated into the job description or contract of the physician. This assures the jail administrator and the responsible health authority that the physician-nurse practitioner/physician assistant team have a clear understanding of what is expected. Note that NCCHC also has standards on credentialing (J-17 and P-17).

The American Correctional Association standard for Adult Correctional Institutions on administration of treatment, 3-4335, contains special mention of nurse practitioners and physician assistants:[17]

---

[16] American Correctional Association, *Standards for Adult Correctional Institutions,* Third Edition (Lanham, Md.: American Correctional Association, 1990). Similar standards exist for jails, as well.

[17] Ibid.

Written policy, procedure, and practice provide that all treatment by health care personnel other than a physician, dentist, psychologist, optometrist, podiatrist, or other independent provider is performed pursuant to written standing or direct orders by personnel authorized by law to give such orders. Nurse practitioners and physician's assistants may practice within the limits of applicable laws and regulations.

Comment: Standing medical orders are orders written for the definitive treatment of identified conditions and for the on-site emergency treatment of any person having such a condition. Direct orders are those written specifically for the treatment of one person's particular condition.

Inmates who are frail, elderly, pregnant, chronically ill, physically handicapped, psychotic, or developmentally disabled require special attention by the physician or his or her designee. Nurse practitioners and physician assistants should have clear practitioner guidelines on the care and disposition of inmates with special health needs. Both the American Correctional Association and NCCHC have standards concerning communication on special needs patients. NCCHC Standards J-07 and P-07 provide guidance to jail staff on maximizing communication and cooperation between the custody and the health staff.

Health administrators should check with state regulatory agencies to ensure appropriate levels of credentials are maintained for their physician assistants and nurse practitioners. Correctional administrators should know the legal limitations and responsibilities of their nonphysician providers.

Continuing education for maintenance of competency is addressed in American Correctional Association Standard 3-4082 on specialist employees.[18] This standard requires that medical personnel and other specialists, whose backgrounds include considerable training for their positions, should receive specific training in their field as it relates to the institutional setting. This includes forty hours of training in addition to the orientation training during their first year of employment and forty hours of training each year thereafter. NCCHC Standards J-18 and P-18 require that health staff annually obtain a minimum of twelve hours of continuing education that are "appropriate to their positions." This standard does not specifically address clinical competency of physicians, physician assistants, and nurse practitioners, who require additional hours of continuing medical education (CME) to maintain their licenses. The appropriate state regulatory agency should be consulted when drafting prison and jail policies on continuing medical education for physician assistants and nurse practitioners.

Standards on preliminary health screenings and examinations specify what must be done for all new arrivals at the facility (American Correctional Association Standards ACI 3-4343 and 3-4344[19]; NCCHC Standards J-30 and P-32) and full health

---

[18] Ibid.

[19] Ibid.

appraisal (American Correctional Association Standard ACI 3-4345 [20]; NCCHC Standard J-33 and P-34). These standards provide considerable guidance to nurses, physician assistants, and nurse practitioners in the care and treatment of inmates.

The hands-on physical examination may be performed only by a physician assistant, nurse practitioner, physician, or appropriately trained RN.

The American Correctional Association standard on sick call (ACI 3-4353) [21] requires that it be conducted by a physician and/or other qualified personnel. The NCCHC standards on sick call (J-35 and P-38) provide clear guidance that a patient who reports the same complaint twice in a month should be referred to the physician. Depending on their training, certain elements of the patient's assessment will be performed at different levels by the physician assistant or nurse practitioner.

It is the use of *clinician guidelines* that provide the greatest aid to communication between the supervising physician and the physician assistant/nurse practitioner. Clinician guidelines outline specific therapeutic modalities and prescriptions that are preapproved by the medical director. Certain state practice acts require the supervising physician and physician assistant to have guidelines established for their practice. Clinician guidelines are specifically written for the individualized practice of the supervising physician, who has identified preferences in the treatment of common medical problems. Through clinician guidelines, the medical director establishes the standard of care expected in the prison or jail setting. Clinician guidelines are not verbal orders, standing orders, or assessment protocols. The latter mainly are used as instructions to health personnel that "specify the steps to be taken in appraising a patient's physical status."

Recruitment strategies should consider the level of autonomy and patient care that the individual physician assistant or nurse practitioner will be able to exercise once hired. This requires the medical director, responsible health authority and jail/prison administrator to clearly define the role and responsibility of the physician assistant or nurse practitioner before they are recruited and hired.

Systems which have not used physician assistants or nurse practitioners might wish to consider contacting a local nurse practitioner or a physician assistant educational program and ask to sponsor a student. By taking on a student, the correctional administrator, medical director, and health staff will have an opportunity to see how a physician assistant and/or nurse practitioner can be assimilated into the health care system. Studies have shown that the physicians most resistant to the use of physician assistants and nurse practitioners are those who have not worked with them. [22] To find a physician assistant or nurse practitioner training program closest to your jail or correctional institution, contact either the National Organization of Nurse Practitioner Faculties or the Association of Physician Assistant Programs, both of which are listed at the end of this chapter.

---

[20] Ibid.

[21] Ibid.

[22] S. Lutz. "Practitioners are Filling in for Scarce Physicians," 21:19, *Modern Healthcare* (May 13, 1991): 24-30.

Conclusion

The future of health care in the United States is a topic of much discussion during the 1990s. Concerns include how health care will be paid for, how it will be organized, and who shall provide it. The future of correctional health care is equally of interest. Nurse practitioners and physician assistants work extremely well with physicians in a correctional setting. Studies have shown that nurse practitioners and physician assistants are well trained to provide high levels of care.[23]

The problem of access to and delivery of health care services to an ever-increasing population is a real priority for jail and prison officials, especially when the treatment of the increased number of inmates must be performed with dwindling resources. This chapter has provided a description of the history, training, and use of physician assistants and nurse practitioners. It has explained the similarities and differences between these two health professions. Based on their background and training, nurse practitioners and physician assistants are qualified to provide health care services and their use should be considered to ease the maldistribution of physicians in corrections.

FOR MORE INFORMATION:

American Academy of Nurse Practitioners
Capitol Station
P.O. Box 12846
Austin, TX 78711
512-442-4262

American Academy of Physician Assistants
950 N. Washington Street
Alexandria, VA 22314
703-836-2272

Association of Physician Assistant Programs
950 N. Washington Street
Alexandria, VA 22314
703-836-2272

National Organization of Nurse Practitioner Faculties
One Dupont Circle, Suite 530
Washington, DC 20036
202-463-6930

---

[23] G. D. Wozniak, "Physician Utilization of Non-physician Practitioners," *Socioeconomic Characteristics of Medical Practice* (1995). Published by the American Medical Association, Center for Health Policy Research; S. Crane, "PAs/NPs: Forging Effective Partnerships in Managed Care Systems," 1.21:10, *Physician Executive Magazine* (October, 1995).

12 QUALITY IS ALSO IMPORTANT

Monitoring the quality of health care services is more than just a desirable or beneficial activity. It is a legal and moral obligation. "It is by now well-established that hospitals and other health care providers have a legal, as well as a moral, duty to monitor the quality of health care which they provide, as well as the qualifications of medical staff members, to protect the public from substandard care and from unqualified physicians. This duty is presently fulfilled, in part, by qualify assurance activities such as peer review."[1]

Quality control is important for any program—particularly one as complex and sensitive as delivery of health care in a correctional setting. In a managed care context, quality control is absolutely essential. A good quality improvement program lowers risk and may lower cost, though in the short run, it may involve some increase in costs.

Quality Management

Early quality assurance (QA) efforts in the health care field encountered at least two shortcomings. Some legal experts raised concerns about promising what could not be delivered. No one could assure quality. A guarantee should not be implied, since failure always can occur. Secondly, and more fundamentally, quality assurance efforts were directed primarily toward discovering any failure to comply with standards. Criteria were determined in advance—for example, that each patient was to receive the medication prescribed for that patient in the dosages and frequency prescribed. Then, a sample of records would be checked to determine the percentage of cases in which this criterion was not met. When an unacceptable noncompliance rate was encountered, the employee(s) responsible for the errors were counseled, and it was hoped that the behavior would be corrected. Many, however, disliked quality

---

[1] Arthur F. Southwick and Debora A. Slee,"Quality Assurance in Health Care: Confidentiality of Information and Immunity for Participants," 5:3, *The Journal of Legal Medicine* (1984): 396.

assurance activities precisely because of this negative focus. Others pointed out that quality assurance was directed primarily to the few outlying cases of error, while completely ignoring the fact that the vast majority of events may be all right.

A better approach has arrived from an unexpected source. Quality control approaches in U.S. industrial applications abounded between the 1920s and the 1970s. Yet, it became increasingly apparent that the quest for quality control in manufactured products was elusive, and that American products were consistently inferior to those produced in Japan. This was clearly evident, for example, in automobiles, computers, cameras, and electronic appliances. U.S. industrialists began to study Japanese industry and techniques to learn their secret. The improvements in quality were impressive, and were attributed to the introduction of a method known by various names, including Total Quality Management (TQM) and Continuous Quality Improvement (CQI). This approach has been adopted with some appropriate modification as a key component of a program endorsed by the Joint Commission on Accreditation of Health Care Organizations (JCAHO).

Continuous Quality Improvement is essentially a positive approach, in contrast to quality assurance. It focuses on improving quality through an ongoing, never-ending process. It does not seek to identify and blame the employees who fail to comply with predetermined criteria. Instead, it assumes that the employees are doing their best, but the system is deficient and can be improved. All staff become involved in the process, from the highest to the lowest level. It becomes, at least in theory, a matter of pride for employees to improve product quality.

Continuous Quality Improvement directs the efforts of the agency toward quality improvements affecting the majority of the services or product that it delivers. Rather than emphasizing elimination of the occasional error, it strives for overall excellence. Moreover, it seeks to improve the processes of production. Most problems occur because the system needs improvement, not because one or more employees need correction.

Each employee, as also each unit of the agency, is to view itself as both an agent serving customers or clients and as a customer of other agents. Some supply a service, while others are consumers of that service.

An Example

Studies of performance and quality are conducted regularly, and when criteria are not met, staff discuss how this can be improved. Staff may find, for example, that an unacceptably high rate of refused clinic appointments is occurring in the jail. The Continuous Quality Improvement approach likely would involve a meeting in which nursing staff, housing unit officers, command officers, clerical staff who schedule appointments, and medical record staff all are represented. The group would map out the entire process for making appointments, which includes appointing of the date and time, notifying inmates of appointments, notifying housing unit officers, calling out inmates, issuing passes, escorting inmates to the clinic, and so forth. Also, a sample of inmates who recently have refused appointments would be interviewed, and their reasons would be recorded. Suppose, for example, that this process revealed the following:

- Inmates generally are not aware of the reason for their clinic appointment. They do not know whether it is for medical or dental care, whether it is for follow-up care, a periodic health screening, a physical examination, or in response to a sick-call request

- No effort is being made to pass the word to another housing unit if the inmate has been moved after the call-out list was prepared.

- Officers, anxious to comply with the policy which provides a mechanism for inmates to refuse a clinic appointment, have been observed calling inmates to the control station and telling them: "You're scheduled for a medical appointment today. If you want to refuse, sign right here!"

- Inmates describe their strong objection to being called out at 7:00 A.M. on the date of a clinic appointment and having to sit in a holding area all day and not be able to return to their housing unit until 4:00 P.M., just to get to see the doctor or nurse.

The group should discuss the problem in all its detail and consider the information which they have been able to gather. No one should try to point the finger of blame at any individual or group. All should look for ways to improve clinic attendance for scheduled appointments. Ultimately, the group might decide to take all or some of the following steps:

- Inmates with chronic illness should receive a "return to clinic" appointment slip at the end of each clinic visit.

- Housing unit officers, upon receipt of the callout list for a given day, should call the clinic immediately to advise concerning inmates no longer on the unit, who had a court appointment, or otherwise were not available for clinic that day.

- Officers should be instructed to notify inmates about their clinic callout in a manner which encourages, rather than discourages, attendance.

- The clinic schedule should be subdivided into two-hour blocks of time, so that clinic appointments could be assigned to a short time-period rather than to the entire day.

Findings and decisions then would be reported to the Continuous Quality Improvement committee. An instrument would be prepared for monitoring the refusal/attendance rate each week over a three-month period, and staff would be informed of progress made in improving this rate.

Note: no one was blamed. All parties cooperated in identifying the source of the difficulty and in devising creative solutions. They were resolving system problems. They also built in a method to monitor the effectiveness of the remedies selected.

This is an example of the Continuous Quality Improvement approach. To be effective, it must involve essentially all staff. It cannot be accomplished adequately by a "CQI Coordinator" whose job it is to review a sample of records each month. The time invested by staff in learning how the quality improvement process works and how to do it right is well worthwhile.

Accreditation (ACA, NCCHC, JCAHO)

Accreditation is the process whereby an outside agency objectively certifies that a program demonstrates satisfactory compliance with a set of standards of excellence. The establishment, promulgation, and acceptance of standards is a complex process. [2]

Organized concern about the need to reform prisons in the U.S. was the articulated purpose of the formation of the American Correctional Association (then known as the National Prison Association) in 1870. At various points in the history of the American Correctional Association (ACA), the need to address the condition of health and of health care for prisoners was discussed. But little, if any, concerted and effective effort was undertaken until the ACA accreditation process began in 1978, [3] applying a set of standards which specified minimum requirements for environmental health and for health care services.

The American Correctional Association established a Commission on Accreditation for Corrections (CAC), an independent body which administers the accreditation process and is responsible for all accreditation awards. The standards themselves are established and updated by the American Correctional Association Standards Committee, whose membership is made up of persons appointed by the American Correctional Association and by the Commission on Accreditation for Corrections.

Well before this occurred, the American Medical Association (AMA), at its very first annual meeting in 1848, adopted the following resolution:

> Resolved, That the Committee on Public Hygiene be requested to investigate the effects of confinement in prisons and penitentiaries, and of the discipline in general, in those institutions, on the health of their inmates, and report to the next meeting of the Association. [4]

However, there is no subsequent evidence that this study was ever completed. Over the years, occasional reference was made to principles which should apply to health care in correctional institutions, but there was no determined effort until a

---

[2] Interesting accounts of the early history of accreditation in corrections can be found in Paul W. Keve, *Measuring Excellence: The History of Correctional Standards and Accreditation* (Lanham, Md.: American Correctional Association, 1996): 37-40; in Anthony P. Travisono and Mary Q. Hawkes, *Building a Voice: 125 Years of History* (Lanham, Md.: American Correctional Association, 1995): 97-99 *et passim*, and B. Jaye Anno, *Prison Health Care: Guidelines for the Management of an Adequate Delivery System* (Chicago, Ill: NCCHC, 1991): 16-21.

[3] The first facility accredited by the American Correctional Association was a halfway house, in May 1978. Personal communication, ACA staff (March 25, 1997).

[4] "The Transactions of the American Medical Association," (Chicago, Ill: American Medical Association, May, 1848): 44.

resolution was adopted in 1952 expressing disapproval of the participation of inmates in scientific experiments. [5] The earliest tangible action of the AMA with respect to correctional health care took place in 1977 when the American Medical Association published its first set of health standards for jails. These standards were revised in 1978 and 1979, and a set of standards for prisons was also published in 1979. The American Medical Association process of accreditation for jails began in August 1977, later to be continued under the auspices of the National Commission on Correctional Health Care. [6]

---

[5] Minutes, AMA House of Delegates. Chicago, Ill: American Medical Association (December 1952): 90-92.

[6] The board of directors of the National Commission on Correctional Health Care (NCCHC) is comprised of persons named by the following organizations:

American Academy of Child and Adolescent Psychiatry
American Academy of Family Physicians
American Academy of Pediatrics
American Academy of Physician Assistants
American Academy of Psychiatry and the Law
American Association of Osteopathic Specialists
American Association for Counseling and Development
American Association of Public Health Physicians
American Bar Association
American College of Emergency Physicians
American College of Healthcare Executives
American College of Neuropsychiatrists
American College of Physicians
American Correctional Health Services Association
American Dental Association
American Diabetes Association
American Dietetic Association
American Jail Association
American Health Information Management Association
American Medical Association
American Nurses Association
American Osteopathic Association
American Pharmaceutical Association
American Psychiatric Association
American Psychological Association
American Public Health Association
American Society for Adolescent Psychiatry
John Howard Association
National Association of Counties
National Association of County Health Officials
National Council of Juvenile and Family Court Judges
National District Attorneys Association
National Juvenile Detention Association
National Medical Association
National Sheriffs' Association
The Society for Adolescent Medicine

Standards for juvenile correctional facilities were published by the NCCHC in 1979, and subsequently revised in 1984, 1992, and 1995.[7] Accreditation by the NCCHC requires compliance with all of the essential standards and at least 85 percent of the important standards.[8]

With the health care scene growing more complex every day, few people really are able, on their own, to evaluate the quality of a facility and its programs. Hospitals as well as prisons, therefore, look to appraisal by experts in the field who have taken the time to make a careful inspection and review through a recognized accreditation process. In a typical accreditation, the facility submits an application requesting an evaluation and pays the required fees. Then, the facility completes a self-survey, designed to identify areas requiring attention. On a scheduled date, a survey team visits the facility and inspects all areas and programs relevant to the purpose of the assessment. During the exit conference, at the conclusion of the survey, preliminary findings are described. Surveyors then file their written report with the accrediting body. After the accrediting body meets and reviews these findings, typically from a blinded report which does not identify the facility, a decision is made to accredit, defer accreditation pending evidence of compliance with specific requirements, or deny accreditation.

Many correctional facilities are accredited by the American Correctional Association (ACA) which publishes various sets of specific standards.[9] Some of the American Correctional Association standards apply to health care services. The American Correctional Association accreditation process allows a waiver of the health care items when the facility has a current accreditation by the National Commission on Correctional Health Care or by the Joint Commission on Accreditation of Health Care Organizations.[10]

Some facilities are hesitant to seek accreditation because of the effort involved in preparing for the survey. On the other hand, facilities that have gone through the process typically seek reaccreditation on a regular basis. These facility administrators

---

[7] NCCHC, *Standards for Health Services in Juvenile Detention and Confinement Facilities.* (Chicago, Ill: NCCHC, 1995): viii.

[8] The most recent edition of the *Standards for Health Services in Prisons* is in press at the time of this writing. *Standards for Health Services in Prisons* contains thirty-seven essential standards and thirty-five important standards, while the 1996 *Standards for Health Services in Jails* contains thirty-three essential standards and thirty-six important standards, and the 1995 *Standards for Health Services in Juvenile Detention and Confinement Facilities* contains thirty-six essential standards and thirty important standards.

[9] For example, *Standards for Adult Correctional Institutions*, Third Edition (Lanham, Md.: American Correctional Association, 1990); *Standards for Adult Local Detention Facilities*, Third Edition (Lanham, Md.: American Correctional Association, 1991); *Standards for Juvenile Detention Facilities*, Third Edition (Lanham, Md.: American Correctional Association, 1991); and *1996 Standards Supplement* (Lanham, Md.: American Correctional Association, 1996).

[10] *1996 Comprehensive Accreditation Manual for Ambulatory Care* (Chicago, Ill: The Joint Commission on Accreditation of Health Care Organizations, 1996).

realize that much of the work involved in preparing for an accreditation survey is simply what proper management must do to ensure that all systems are in good order.

Accreditation requires that there be policies and procedures that embody the intent of each standard. They also require evidence of compliance with each of the standards. The emphasis on policy and procedure ensures a degree of permanence and institutionalization of the standards. Even if the survey were to find that actual practice conforms to the standard, it would be insufficient unless there were also a policy and procedure formally requiring compliance. Similarly, policy alone, without evidence of compliant practice, is insufficient. Evidence of compliance is typically found through review of documentation, interviews with staff and inmates, and visual inspection during an on-site visit by a team of experienced official surveyors.

The American Correctional Association *Standards for Adult Correctional Institutions* (January 1990) contains a total of 463 standards, of which 38 are mandatory and 425 are nonmandatory. To be accredited, all mandatory standards and 90 percent of nonmandatory standards must be met. Included are 54 health care standards,[11] of which 11 are mandatory and 48 are nonmandatory.

The Joint Commission on Accreditation of Health Care Organizations (JCAHO) does not have a separate set of standards for correctional facilities, but employs the standards of the 1996 *Comprehensive Accreditation Manual for Ambulatory Care*, which also are used in the community.

When the American Public Health Association (APHA) published a set of standards for correctional health care in 1976, it was the first document of its kind. These standards were revised in 1986.[12] Although these standards were never accompanied by an accreditation process, they continue to serve as a thoughtful and valuable reference manual for facilities interested in achieving quality health care.

Why Be Accredited?

Accreditation is voluntary.[13] A jail or prison or youth facility does not need to be accredited. Certainly, accreditation is not a factor by which prospective correctional

---

[11] There are several other ACA standards which address health care topics but are not carried in the section on health care. These include, for example, Standard 3-4244 requiring a mental health review of segregated prisoners, Standard 3-4246 requiring a daily visit by a qualified health care official to each segregated inmate, Standard 3-4387 requiring comprehensive counseling and assistance to pregnant inmates, and Standard 3-4388 requiring substance abuse programs for inmates with drug and alcohol addiction problems. Others, addressing such issues as exercise, hygiene, sanitation, safety and nutrition, are also relevant to health concerns.

[12] Nancy N. Dubler (ed.), *Standards for Health Services in Correctional Institutions*, Second Edition (Washington, D.C.: American Public Health Association, 1986).

[13] In some situations, accreditation may be mandated pursuant to a court order or a consent decree, which requires accreditation as partial evidence that the facility has achieved the level of care demanded by the court. Some jurisdictions which choose to contract with a private vendor for provision of health care services also require accreditation as one measure that the facility has achieved a satisfactory quality of health care services.

inmates will choose one institution over some other. Besides, there will be some cost involved in instituting the policies and programs required. So, why would any correctional administrator want to get accredited? Many do. As of March 1997, 994 programs currently were accredited by the American Correctional Association, including prisons, jails, juvenile facilities, parole and probation programs, electronic monitoring programs, and correctional training academies.[14] As of the same date, 165 prisons, 200 jails, and 32 juvenile facilities were accredited by the NCCHC.[15] Figure 12-1 displays some of the reasons for seeking accreditation.

FIGURE 12-1. SOME REASONS FOR SEEKING ACCREDITATION

- Matter of pride and honor

- Learning experience

- Reassurance to funding source

- Aid to recruitment of good health professionals

- More favorable outcome in court

One reason to seek accreditation is related to prestige. It is an honor, a matter of pride, to know that one's institution is well managed and has successfully met the scrutiny and approval of a national monitoring agency. Accredited facilities know that they are numbered among the very best. They have earned the "Seal of Good Housekeeping." They have the distinction of having been measured and certified by nationally accepted standards.

Accreditation can be looked upon as a process as well as an end point. The process itself can be educational for management and staff. By preparing for accreditation, an institution may discover weaknesses or deficiencies in a number of areas. Facility staff will study the standard and want to revise their policies to correct any problems. The surveyors themselves are often a source of excellent technical assistance during the site visit, and the national accrediting organization can provide a wealth of helpful suggestions by phone, especially when a situation is unique or poses a difficult problem. Though preparing for accreditation is hard work for staff, their morale is boosted through knowledge that they are making progress and that their efforts will be recognized.

Another reason may have to do with assuring the legislature or county commissioners that their money is being spent wisely. The accreditation certificate serves as a testimonial to the competence and dedication of the program staff.

---

[14] Personal communication with American Correctional Association staff, March 25, 1997.

[15] Personal communication with Michael Wohlke, NCCHC staff, on March 24, 1997.

A fourth reason is that a good quality program (along with the certification award to prove it) can be a factor in recruitment and retention of good health care professionals. Not many years ago, most doctors who worked in prisons belonged to one of two categories: the impaired physician with drug, alcohol, competency, performance, or moral problems who could not get a job anywhere else, or the "missionary" doctor who saw this as a calling to serve the least fortunate. The latter were few, and the former gave the name "prison doc" a stigma which few health professionals were willing to add to their curriculum vitae.

Fortunately, this image has been changing over the past twenty years, so that today, very many excellent physicians, as well as nurses, technicians, and other health professionals, are prison health care providers. In fact, the National Commission on Correctional Health Care offers a certification for individual correctional health professionals who have met certain stringent requirements. They are entitled to wear a special pin and add the letters CCHP [16] after their name.

A fifth reason relates to improving one's chances of a favorable outcome in court. This is, of course, by no means a guarantee. Accredited facilities have been found unconstitutional or liable. It is possible to "fool" the surveyors, or to fail to maintain the high standards, which were in evidence at the time of accreditation. But the fact of accreditation may help. It offers prima facie evidence that the facility has made an effort to excel. Even better, meeting accreditation standards should help to keep a facility out of court in the first place.

How to Survive Accreditation

While important and helpful, accreditation alone is an insufficient testimonial to adequate quality of services. It is possible to achieve paper or superficial compliance and yet be deficient in substantive areas. It also is possible to deceive the surveyors, despite their exercise of due diligence. Some of the privatized contracts for health services impose significant monetary penalties should the facility fail to obtain or maintain accreditation, or make continuance of the contract contingent upon being accredited successfully. While this, unfortunately, might lead an unscrupulous contractor (or an employee of a contractor) to perpetrate fraud to pass the survey, the accrediting agencies have built in reasonable safeguards.

Sometimes surveyors will miss deficiencies. They do the best they can, but there are many things to evaluate in a very limited time. It is relatively easy to verify the existence of a policy and procedure which addresses the content of a standard. But it is also expected that staff whose duties relate to a given standard will be aware of the policy and will have received training in its interpretation and application. Likewise, evidence should confirm that the policy is being followed. Finally, accreditors are less impressed with policies on which the ink is not yet quite dry, than they are with policies that have been in place six months or a year or longer. In other words, there should be a track record of compliance over time. But no one expects or requires 100 percent compliance, day in and day out, with each and every standard.

---

[16] Certified Correctional Health Professional.

Accreditation is concerned with systematic behavior. An occasional aberrance does not necessarily indicate that the whole system has broken down. Surveyors are not looking for the outlier case, but for the day-to-day pattern. However, there are certain areas which need to be regarded as "zero tolerance zones," such as failure to train officers about suicide prevention. But the finding of a single clogged shower drain, an overflowing trash container, or an unsigned or undated progress note, ordinarily would not be viewed as a serious deficiency or result in a missed standard.

Accreditation is not a trial. When the surveyors come, you should be able to tell your employees: "Be courteous, polite and helpful to the surveyors, but just keep doing your job like you always do." This is not the time to "put on a show." The best advice is to prepare as well as possible to achieve the intent and spirit of each standard in a way that makes sense for your facility. Be sure your policies include what the standards require. Be sure staff know the policies. Be sure supervisors encourage and enforce implementation of the policies. Develop your own Continuous Quality Improvement or monitoring program to ensure compliance. Then, on the day of the audit, tell your staff (as Eric Jacobson [17] used to say to his employees just prior to an accreditation or licensing survey), "Just do today the same as you do every day, and don't be nervous about the auditors."

Auditors do not want the facility to fail. When they find a concern, staff should listen carefully to what they say. They will offer suggestions on how to achieve compliance. After the surveyors have left, staff should sit down and carefully devise a plan to remedy each of the areas indicated as probable deficiencies. Even while awaiting the official ruling of the accrediting agency, the facility should submit any new evidence or documentation that it has implemented specific corrections.

The American Correctional Association standards address all aspects of corrections and meticulously spell out minimum requirements for indoor air quality, [18] number of toilets [19] and showers [20] per inmate population, quality and hygiene aspects of food service, [21] and compliance with local building codes. [22] The standards address such diverse health-related topics as a requirement that each inmate be offered three

---

[17] For many years until his retirement, he was the administrator of Duane L. Waters Hospital, a ninety-three-bed licensed and JCAHO accredited acute care hospital within the State Prison of Southern Michigan.

[18] American Correctional Association, *Standards for Adult Correctional Institutions* (1990), Standard 3-4144.

[19] American Correctional Association, *Standards for Adult Correctional Institutions* (1990), Standard 3-4132.

[20] American Correctional Association, *1996 Standards Supplement,* Standard 3-4134.

[21] American Correctional Association, *Standards for Adult Correctional Institutions* (1990), Standards 3-429/3-4298, 3-4300, 3-4303, 3-4305, and American Correctional Association, *1996 Standards Supplement,* Standard 3-4306.

[22] American Correctional Association, *Standards for Adult Correctional Institutions* (1990), Standards 3-4120 and 3-4121.

complete sets of clean clothing per week,[23] that there be appropriate policies for the management of serious and infectious disease,[24] and they set the minimum requirement for exercise and recreation space.[25]

NCCHC standards originally focused on delivery of care issues, in other words, basically on what happened within the confines of the clinic. Beginning in 1992, a new dimension was added to the standards, namely a "public health" concern for inmates, staff, and visitors. In other words, the new language and new standards indicated that the health authority and/or the medical director at the institution is to serve as a public health officer for the facility, concerned about safety and sanitation, hygiene, exercise, effects of tobacco products, ventilation, rodent and vermin control, hazardous waste disposal, TB screening for officers, and nutrition.

The standards add a significant concern for the health and safety of the public at large. This is especially true of jails and youth facilities with their rapid turnover, but also for prisons which house persons near the end of their sentences. The NCCHC standards recognize that this is a most opportune situation in which to provide education for health promotion and disease prevention. Tuberculosis, hepatitis B virus, human immunodeficiency virus, and venereal disease transmission can be minimized significantly by altering specific behaviors and adopting certain precautions. Life expectancy and the risk of costly illness can be profoundly affected by changes in lifestyles and behavior—such as the use of alcohol, drugs, tobacco, exercise, diet, stress reduction, and dental hygiene. This may be a "once-in-a-lifetime," very low-cost opportunity to show videos and hand out literature during the few hours, days, or weeks that many inmates will spend in jail. It never again may be this easy to get these people to sit still for this kind of education. Yet, these are the very people who come from (and will return to) high-exposure behavior and settings where altered behavior and correct information may have the greatest impact and benefit—such as prostitution, IV drug abuse, crowded and TB-infested housing, abusive families, and so forth.

Issues Often Emphasized During Surveys

Following are a few instances of issues emphasized by accreditation surveyors and the reasons which support their concern. Other examples can be found throughout this manual.

Importance of Officer Training

Officers, in most instances, will be the first responders in instances of first aid, cardiopulmonary resuscitation (CPR), universal precautions, and nonviolent intervention with the mentally ill. Their knowledge and skill can save lives, prevent serious

---

[23] American Correctional Association, *Standards for Adult Correctional Institutions* (1990), Standard 3-4319.

[24] American Correctional Association, *Standards for Adult Correctional Institutions* (1990), Standard 3-4365.

[25] American Correctional Association, *1996 Standards Supplement,* Standards 3-4147 and 3-4148.

injury, and avoid risk of infection. Their training must be current, and updated periodically. It is not enough to train them once in a new employee school.

Often, the wrong intervention can be worse than no intervention at all. Improperly trained officers can cause spinal cord injury by moving an inmate who has an apparent back or neck injury, can unnecessarily escalate an agitated mental patient, and can risk infection through unprotected interventions.

Officers need to be trained to recognize signs and symptoms of serious illness and to make prompt referrals. Alert, well-trained officers can recognize signs of illness among inmates who do not seek or may be unable to seek help on their own initiative. Early recognition and appropriate timely intervention permits more successful and less costly treatment.

Exercise

Out-of-cell movement of high-security prisoners, many of whom may be assaultive and dangerous, is understandably avoided, whenever possible. It is very labor-intensive to supervise out-of-cell activity for these inmates. Yet, experts indicate that exercise is necessary for good health. One can become "stir-crazy" from being kept confined in a small space, particularly when there is little opportunity for social interaction or communication with others. So, the standards established by the accrediting bodies uniformly stress the importance of regular out-of-cell exercise.

The American Correctional Association standards state that "both outdoor and covered/enclosed exercise areas for general population inmates are provided in sufficient number to ensure that each inmate is offered at least one hour of access daily,"[26] and "inmates in segregation receive a minimum of one hour of exercise per day outside their cells, five days per week, unless security or safety considerations dictate otherwise."[27] Moreover, the American Correctional Association standard explains that "Exercise/recreation spaces are not the same as dayrooms, although dayrooms can provide added opportunities for some exercise and recreation activities."[28]

The NCCHC standards require "an exercise program in which each inmate is offered exercise involving large-muscle activity a minimum of one hour a day, three times a week."[29] The discussion makes it clear that this standard is intended to apply to inmates in all custody classes, especially those who are in segregation.[30] The juvenile standards require that the minimum one-hour daily exercise occurs on a planned, supervised basis.[31] The newly revised prison standard specifies that it must be "a

[26] American Correctional Association, *1996 Standards Supplement op. cit.*, Standard 3-4147.

[27] ACA Standard 3-4258. Note that reasons for imposing limitations should be documented.

[28] American Correctional Association, *1996 Standards Supplement*, Standard 3-4147.

[29] NCCHC, *Standards for Jails, op. cit.*, Standard J-46

[30] NCCHC, *Standards for Prisons, op. cit.*, Standard P-47.

program of recreational exercise" to indicate that, for example, janitorial work or labor in the fields does not meet the requirement, and further clarifies that "permitting in-cell exercises does not constitute compliance with standard." Aside from the fact that most prison cells are small and cramped, the reason for these stipulations is that all human beings need an occasional change of pace—a break in the routine. Therefore, out-of-cell recreational exercise is required.

Clearly, none of the standards should be interpreted as requiring an inmate, who on a specific day is demonstrating particularly aggressive and dangerous behavior, to be offered out-of-cell time. But these exceptions should be made for individual cases with justifying cause, not routinely for a whole class of inmates.

Hygiene

Soap, toilet tissue, sanitary napkins, tooth brushes, toothpaste, combs, and towels are to be made available to inmates, either through purchase in the commissary, or without cost for indigent inmates. Also, new inmates upon arrival should be provided these kinds of supplies until they reasonably can be expected to acquire them on their own. [32]

The opportunity for showering, receiving a haircut, and shaving also is required, though not all standards agree on the requisite frequency for bathing. [33] Often, it is difficult for high-security institutions with large numbers of inmates in maximum custody and segregation to facilitate daily access to showers. Some facilities creatively have scheduled for prisoners on lock-down status one and one half hours each day for out-of-cell time, allowing one hour for recreational exercise, followed by a half-hour for shower and phone call, thus minimizing the number of times each cell door must be opened.

Sexual Assault

Sexual assaults do occur in many correctional settings. This situation poses several concerns for correctional administrators, among them some health-related issues. The victim may sustain physical injury as well as psychological and emotional trauma. Moreover, the victim as well as the perpetrator may have been exposed to a communicable and possibly fatal disease. Immediate response is imperative. Consequently, prisoners should be encouraged to report sexual assault and seek assistance

---

[31] NCCHC, *Standards for Juvenile Facilities, op. cit.,* Standard Y-55

[32] Cf. NCCHC Standards J-47, P-49, and Y-57

[33] Cf. American Correctional Association Standard 3-4322 and NCCHC Standards J-47, P-49, Y-57. Note that the ACA standard requires: "sufficient bathing facilities in the housing areas to permit inmates in the general population to shower at least three times per week," and adds the comment that "Inmates in special jobs, such as food, medical, sanitation, or mechanical services, should be encouraged to bathe daily, and ideally each inmate should be permitted to shower daily." The NCCHC Juvenile standard requires the facility to "permit regular bathing at least every other day" and to "permit daily bathing in hot weather in facilities without air temperature control."

promptly. Correctional staff should be trained in the proper response to these situations, including maintenance of a chain of evidence, protection of the reporter from retaliation, and prompt referral for medical attention. Medical staff also need to be trained properly regarding treatment and counseling of rape victims. Proper response is described in the standards. [34]

Risk Management

Closely allied both to quality improvement and to cost reduction is risk management. There is an old adage: "An ounce of prevention is worth a pound of cure." It will cost a lot less to repair the broken step than to fix the broken leg or broken neck and also respond to a lawsuit (or pay for convalescent leave) when an inmate or an employee trips and falls. [35]

Issues in risk management include the following:

- infectious disease surveillance, monitoring, and control

- surveillance and monitoring of the occurrence of accidents and injuries

- problem solving (now, not tomorrow)

- seeking expert advice from experts in sanitation, fire prevention, disease prevention, diet and nutrition, occupational and industrial safety, and so forth

- follow-up

- documentation

Occupational Safety and Health Administration fines can be costly. Facilities should take steps to avoid them. Prison industries and maintenance areas should install adequate safety devices which are "idiot-proof." For example, each hand must simultaneously push both "on" buttons before the press or stamping machine will function, effectively ensuring that fingers will not be cut off. The price of a periodic consultation and inspection from a good industrial safety engineer could avoid costly workers' compensation payments, lawsuits, lost time, medical bills, and fines. This is "risk management."

Some Examples

Suppose a "sick call list" is posted in each housing unit or kept at the officer's desk. To be seen by a nurse, doctor, or dentist, the inmate must sign the list and indicate the nature of his or her complaint. A nurse retrieves these lists daily from the officer and schedules follow-up appointments. This seems to work quite well, and

---

[34] NCCHC, op. cit., Standards J-55, P-57.

[35] Besides having still to fix the broken step!

inmates generally are seen in a reasonable amount of time. Emergencies are handled appropriately by requesting officer intervention. But one day there is a slip-up. An inmate goes into diabetic coma on Wednesday and dies. A lawsuit is filed, and the jury is shown the Monday morning sick call list containing this inmate's name alongside a note asking for urgent attention because his medication supply had run out. The nursing triage of this list is dated Wednesday evening, about six hours after the inmate had died. Testimony reveals that the slip had been locked in the officer's desk and that the officer was busy and not available on Monday evening and Tuesday evening when the nurse was collecting slips from the housing units. Plaintiffs allege that officers deliberately interfered with this inmate's access to health care. A simple mechanism which enables inmates to send a request directly to the nurse without intervention or involvement of officers would avoid the risk of this kind of lawsuit.

Or, in a similar scenario, the sick call list is presented as evidence in court. Although the inmate's name is clearly visible on the list, it has been crossed off. Plaintiffs allege that an officer must have crossed it off, insinuating that it was because of a grudge against that particular inmate. Some inmates testify that the deceased recently had been engaged in a loud argument with the officer and had called the officer some insulting names. Or, plaintiffs allege that another inmate crossed the name off and that the facility did not adequately protect the deceased inmate's right to have access to the health care system. Defendants might suggest that the inmate may have crossed out his or her own name. But they cannot easily prove this, because officers are "in the loop," and because other inmates have had ample opportunity to subvert the system. The facility has not protected itself against either of these possibilities.

What if sick call slips are used, but the officer collects and holds them for the nurse? How does a facility show that the officer did not divert or throw away a particular medical request slip? Most officers surely would never do such a thing. There even may be a policy clearly prohibiting such behavior. But the use of a locked box to which only the nurse possesses a key, and into which the inmate drops his or her own slip, gives powerful support to the defense's claim that there was no plausible possibility of an officer's interference with access.

Another example might apply, especially to prisons and large jails with chronically ill patients, such as diabetics and renal patients. It probably is cost effective to have a dietitian come on-site regularly to provide technical consultation to food service staff for therapeutic diet preparation, and to instruct patients on the importance of diet compliance. Besides enhancing the quality of care, this greatly can improve benefits derived from care which doctors are prescribing. Moreover, the cost of intensive care to rescue one or two patients who experience avoidable diabetic or renal crises due to faulty diet compliance would more than pay for the cost of hiring the dietitian.

A good Continuous Quality Improvement program also will identify numerous areas in which risk-management approaches are useful. Especially when the cost of mistakes (damage repair, litigation, investigation, and so forth) is high, risk-management strategies are all the more beneficial.

If the inmates sign a sick call sheet, there is no medical request slip, which can be filed in the health record. When an adverse outcome occurs, it is very tedious, perhaps impossible, to go through lists, logs, charts, and other documentation to establish when the sick call request was made, when it was reviewed or triaged, what the triage decision was, when an appointment was scheduled, and when it actually took place. Also, from the monitoring point of view, it is nearly impossible to track the length of time it routinely takes to be seen after filing a request for care. A good CQI program may want to monitor this parameter regularly as an early-warning indicator of access problems.

Some institutions have a program of fines, environmental safety, fire safety, and sanitation—but have no involvement or participation from the health care staff. Other facilities have an excellent infection control program—totally within the confines of the clinic, but without involvement with or impact upon the institutional environment. It makes a lot of sense to link these activities—perhaps through overlapping committees and reporting. Both groups have a lot to learn from each other, and both are concerned with the same objective—to minimize health and safety hazards for inmates, staff, and visitors. As a matter of fact, it is probably a good idea to rotate the physician(s) on occasion through the assignment of checking out the kitchen, showers, laundry, and housing areas for environmental sanitation and safety issues. While admittedly this work may be accomplished as well or better by less costly employees, there is value in the physician becoming closely aware of the conditions in which the inmates live, just as it is possible that the physician may observe a potential health hazard overlooked by others.

Every facility has a disaster plan to prepare for emergency situations. It is important that the health care response to each type of disaster also be thought out carefully before the emergency actually occurs. Disaster drills, involving the health care staff, should be conducted a minimum of once a year[36] on each shift[37] and should be followed by a documented critique by key participants and observers. It is well to include the facility training coordinator in the planning and critique of these drills, so that deficiencies can be addressed promptly in future training sessions.

The Courts

The courts are a strong guarantor of minimally acceptable quality. The incarcerated person is no longer free to seek health care services on his or her own, and must rely on the correctional agency to provide it. In the free world, once licensing and laws have ensured the basic minimum requirements of quality, patients are left to choose among a variety of providers. They can select their dentist, physician, hospital, or drug store. Patients in the free world often do so based on past experience or the recommendation of a friend.

Free-world patients can terminate their relationship with a given provider at any time and are free to seek another who is more to their liking. At a minimum, they desire good technical skills, coupled with a decent bedside manner, at a reasonable price. But a prisoner cannot choose, and must take what is provided. Therefore, the correctional agency has an obligation in law to ensure minimal acceptable standards of quality.

---

[36] American Correctional Association, *Adult Correctional Institutions*, Standard 3-4209 requires fire drills to be held at least quarterly in each institutional area, including administrative areas. NCCHC Standards on this are P-06, Y-06, and J-06.

[37] NCCHC Standard P-06

The Eighth Amendment's prohibition of cruel and unusual punishment has been interpreted by the Supreme Court [38] as prohibiting deliberate indifference to the serious medical needs of a prisoner and specifically forbidding interference with a doctor's order or denial of access to care. Lawyers have debated for years about the definition of the minimum level of care guaranteed by the U.S. Constitution. Loosely translated, the courts have indicated that the Constitution requires a prisoner to have ready access to the health care system where a determination of need can be made by a qualified health care professional, and also that the prisoner be provided the care which is prescribed for treatment of serious illness.

Sometimes, a case is brought in a state court alleging "malpractice" or "tort liability," rather than a constitutional violation. Here, the concern is breach of an implied contract between provider and patient, alleging that the doctor (hospital, and so forth) did not adhere to contemporary professional standards of care in providing the service. The two issues may be brought together in a consent agreement, whereby the plaintiffs and defendants commit to a certain plan of correction, which embodies the constitutional minimum and establishes a structure for delivery of contemporary quality care.

While the first response of a correctional agency in a lawsuit is to defend itself, a prolonged and overly defensive posture can prove costly. It is true that the majority of suits brought by prisoners lack merit, and often can be dismissed on technical grounds. However, some cases do have merit. It may be a class action suit filed in federal court. Defendants naturally want to avoid a judgment. So, their lawyers advise negotiation with plaintiffs. At this point, along with the required posturing, the best course may be for the defendants to be a little less defensive.

There are times when it is well even to assume the offensive, so to speak. A carefully developed plan of correction submitted by the defendants probably will find acceptance by the court, provided that it, in fact, addresses the alleged deficiencies in a reasonable manner. It should be a sensible and workable plan. Surprising though it may seem, generally the medical experts of the defendants and the medical experts of the plaintiffs frequently will not differ widely about the essentials of a well-developed remedial plan. But sometimes when lawyers are involved who misunderstand some of the clinical issues, the result is a distortion—both costly and difficult to implement. [39] A good remedial plan is important. The defendants certainly do intend to provide good health care, and should not find it difficult to say so. A good CQI system is essential for risk management and to assure the court that the defendant intends to maintain compliance.

---

[38] *Estelle v. Gamble*, 429 U.S. 97 (1976), 59 L. Ed. 2d 251, 97 S.Ct. 285.

[39] Some years ago, the author was assigned to assist the court monitor in negotiating an agreement between the parties of a class action case. After several days of unsuccessful bickering, the author asked the court monitor if it would be possible for him to meet with only the medical experts of the parties, with no lawyers present. At first, there was some resistance to this suggestion. But since it was apparent that no progress was being made, the parties reluctantly agreed. At the end of the following day, the lawyers were pleasantly surprised when they were called in to review the list of items on which the medical experts had found themselves in full agreement.

In other words, the defendants should set about complying, so as to get it "over and done with." Of course this sounds reasonable. But, rarely does it work this way in practice. What often happens is a thoroughly counterproductive and horrendously costly dance. The theme is: "Keep the Feds out of our territory." "Stay off of my ranch." Such provincial attitudes lead to legal maneuvers, political posturing, and bureaucratic barriers which delay progress sometimes for years. Defendants do the minimum that they can. They make slow progress, kicking and screaming all the way. But it only takes longer and costs more in the end. They make excuses that "We can't get staff." (But upon closer scrutiny, the salaries are excessively low, or the attempts to recruit are only half-hearted). Defendants should consider making an all-out effort, from the top down, to comply as quickly as possible with all reasonable requirements.

Agencies should be open and honest with their funding or appropriations committee, describing what is needed to comply with the court requirements and be able to explain the rationale. They also should show how the costs are derived. Perhaps improvements need to be phased in over several years, but litigation is exceedingly costly, and overall costs are kept to a minimum by quickly achieving compliance and giving evidence of sincere intentions. An effective CQI program is important. Court surveillance should be terminated as soon as possible. Attorneys can make fortunes in prolonged cases.

13

ISSUES IN HEALTH PROFESSIONAL ETHICS: SOME PRACTICAL CONSIDERATIONS

The author is greatly indebted to William J. Rold, Esq. for his thoughtful comments and suggestions, particularly on legal aspects of this chapter.

Ethics

There is a subtle but important difference between what is legal and what is right. Our system of courts and legislatures defines for us what is legal and illegal. Under most circumstances,[1] we hold that it is right to obey the law and wrong to disobey it. Some actions, however, are wrong even though not illegal—in other words, they are wrong in and of themselves, regardless of whether prohibited by a legislature. Thus, murder would be wrong even if no law prohibited it. Wanton disregard of another person's dignity and feelings, though not illegal, also would be wrong.

In expressing judgment about ethical or unethical behavior, the author is aware that good and wise persons may hold contradictory opinions. Nevertheless, the explicit reasoning presented here can provide a model for thinking about these difficult situations. Also, slight differences in the circumstances of each individual case could lead to differing assessments. The study of ethics offers a framework for defining what behavior is right and what behavior is wrong in a given set of circumstances.

---

[1] Except for laws which are intrinsically and patently evil. Nazi Germany's laws to exterminate Jews and other classes of persons clearly fall into this category and ought not to have been obeyed.

Virtually every profession has a set of ethical standards. So, for example, lawyers and clergy, as well as medical,[2] dental[3], nursing,[4] psychiatry[5], psychology[6], and social work[7] professionals are ethically bound to protect the confidentiality of

---

[2] Typical of principles of medical ethics are those promulgated by the American Medical Association for its members:

"Preamble: The medical profession has long subscribed to a body of ethical statements developed primarily for the benefit of the patient. As a member of this profession, a physician must recognize responsibility not only to patients, but also to society, to other health professionals, and to self. The following Principles adopted by the American Medical Association are not laws, but standards of conduct which define the essentials of honorable behavior for the physician.

   I. A physician shall be dedicated to providing competent medical service with compassion and respect for human dignity.

  II. A physician shall deal honestly with patients and colleagues, and strive to expose those physicians deficient in character or competence, or who engage in fraud or deception.

 III. A physician shall respect the law and also recognize a responsibility to seek changes in those requirements which are contrary to the best interests of the patient.

 IV. A physician shall respect the rights of patients, of colleagues, and of other health professionals, and shall safeguard patient confidences within the constraints of the law.

  V. A physician shall continue to study, apply and advance scientific knowledge, make relevant information available to patients, colleagues and the public, obtain consultation, and use the talents of other health professionals when indicated.

 VI. A physician shall, in the provision of appropriate patient care except in emergencies, be free to choose whom to serve, with whom to associate, and the environment in which to provide medical services.

A physician shall recognize a responsibility to participate in activities contributing to an improved community."

American Medical Association, Council on Ethical and Judicial Affairs, *Code of Medical Ethics: Current Opinions with Annotations* (Chicago, Ill., 1997): xiv.

[3] "Dentists are obliged to safeguard the confidentiality of patient records. Dentists shall maintain patient records in a manner consistent with the protection of the welfare of the patient . . ." Council on Ethics, Bylaws and Judicial Affairs of the American Dental Association, *Principles of and Code of Professional Conduct* (Chicago, Ill: American Dental Association, 1997).

[4] "Nurses in general are committed to respect for human beings. This commitment cannot be altered by the fact that the individuals being cared for are in a correctional institution and not in a health care setting. The philosophy and ethics, responsibilities, functions, roles, skills, and legal authority that guide the practice of nurses in general also guide the practice of nurses in corrections." *Standards of Nursing Practice in Correctional Facilities* (Kansas City, Mo.: American Nurses Association, 1985).

private matters entrusted to them by their clients/patients. Even if these and similar items are not covered in law or regulation, professional persons have a duty to observe them. Frequently, ethical codes are compiled and promulgated by professional associations, which can and do revoke membership for flagrant violations.

Ethical principles are taught by the professional disciplines. Familiarization with these principles and with their intent and applicability is an integral component of the acculturation and socialization which occurs during formal academic preparation for the professions. Thus, a lawyer, doctor, priest, or psychologist learns not only the cognitive and technical skills of the respective profession, but also the moral and behavioral expectations and obligations of its practice.

The code for nurses, published by the American Nurses Association,[8] expresses clearly the intent of a professional code of ethics:

> Upon entering the profession, each nurse inherits a measure of both the responsibility and the trust that have accrued to nursing over the years, as well as the corresponding obligation to adhere to the profession's code of conduct and relationships for ethical practice. The Code is thus more a collective expression of nursing conscience and philosophy than a set of external rules imposed upon an individual practitioner of nursing. Personal and professional integrity can be assured only if an individual is committed to the profession's code of conduct.

---

[5] "Respect for the individual's right of privacy and the maintenance of confidentiality are major concerns of the psychiatrist performing forensic evaluations. The psychiatrist maintains confidentiality to the extent possible given the legal context. Special attention is paid to any limitations on the usual precepts of medical confidentiality. An evaluation for forensic purposes begins with notice to the evaluee of any limitations . . ."

[6] "(A) Psychologists disclose confidential information without the consent of the individual only as mandated by law, or where permitted by law for a valid purpose, such as (1) to provide needed professional services to the patient or the individual or organizational client, (2) to obtain appropriate professional consultations, (3) to protect the patient or client or others from harm, or (4) to obtain payment for services, in which instance disclosure is limited to the minimum that is necessary to achieve the purpose.

(B) Psychologists also may disclose confidential information with the appropriate consent of the patient or the individual or organizational client (or of another legally authorized person on behalf of the patient or client), unless prohibited by law." American Psychological Association, "Ethical Principles of Psychologists and Code of Conduct," 47:12, *American Psychologist* (December, 1992): 1597-1628.

[7] "The social worker should respect the privacy of clients and hold in confidence all information obtained in the course of professional service." National Association of Social Workers, *Code of Ethics*, 1993, at II. H.

[8] *Code for Nurses with Interpretive Statements* (Kansas City, Mo.: American Nurses Association, 1985): iii-iv.

It serves to inform both the nurse and society of the profession's expectations and requirements in ethical matters. The requirements of the code may often exceed those of the law. The state nurses' associations, in fulfilling the profession's duty to society, may discipline their members for violations of the code. Loss of the respect and confidence of society and of one's colleagues is a serious sanction resulting from violation of the code.

The American Academy of Psychiatry and the Law has issued ethical guidelines for the practice of forensic psychiatry. One of these guidelines addresses the issue of confidentiality:

Respect for the individual's right of privacy and the maintenance of confidentiality are major concerns of the psychiatrist performing forensic evaluations. The psychiatrist maintains confidentiality to the extent possible given the legal context. Special attention is paid to any limitations on the usual precepts of medical confidentiality. An evaluation for forensic purposes begins with notice to the evaluee of any limitations on confidentiality. Information or reports derived from the forensic evaluation are subject to the rules of confidentiality as applied to the evaluation, and any disclosure is restricted accordingly.[9]

Another guideline addresses informed consent:

The informed consent of the subject of a forensic evaluation is obtained when possible. Where consent is not required, notice is given to the evaluee of the nature of the evaluation. If the evaluee is not competent to give consent, substituted consent is obtained in accordance with the laws of the jurisdiction.[10]

Correctional officials also subscribe to ethical obligations which in some cases also are codified in law, regulation, or policy. The American Correctional Association promulgates an ethical code for its members.[11]

People have a right to expect that a police officer will help rather than harm them; that a priest will not betray their confidence; that a teacher will not knowingly mislead them; that a doctor will not intentionally injure them; and that a correctional official will not abuse the power which he or she possesses.

Clearly, not every conceivable situation can be covered explicitly in a code of ethics. Application of ethical principles to individual situations is an ongoing, daily task. It sometimes can be a difficult challenge to choose among apparently conflicting

---

[9] *Ethics Guidelines for the Practice of Forensic Psychiatry* (Bloomfield, Conn.: American Academy of Psychiatry and the Law, 1995): 1.

[10] *op. cit.*: 2.

[11] American Correctional Association, Code of Ethics, revised August, 1994.

obligations in a specific circumstance. The correct solution is not always obvious. Even good and intelligent people legitimately may disagree on the interpretation or application of these principles. And what might at first appear to be a minor or scarcely relevant circumstance significantly may affect the analysis.

As was noted in Chapter 2, the health professions and the criminal justice professions have different starting points, objectives, philosophies, methods, and standards. Some policies or practices of a correctional institution may place a health care professional in a situation which is (or at least appears to be) in conflict with the principles of medical ethics. The doctor, nurse, or psychologist may question or object to the procedure or decline to follow it. This can be troublesome for the correctional supervisor in a system which is tightly managed by detailed policy manuals that all employees are expected to observe.[12]

In most cases, the health professional who objects to an established or proposed correctional policy on ethical grounds is not a troublemaker or an unruly person. He or she is a conscientious employee facing a real dilemma. Perhaps the dilemma can be resolved by a simple clarification. At other times, a policy directive may need to be changed, possibly resulting in actual benefit to the system. A highly principled, honest, and capable employee who thoughtfully and respectfully challenges a system to rethink some of its policies should be viewed as an asset, and is far better in the long run than a "go along to get along" employee who never questions anything. The following pages illustrate this with examples, and attempt to explore some boundaries of these ethical principles.

Correctional professionals regard their duty to safeguard the public through confinement of legally detained inmates as a sacred trust. They also subscribe to the maintenance of good order of the institution and the humane and safe management of inmates.

Physicians are bound by a fundamental principle that they will render service to a patient only when this intervention is deemed to be in the patient's best interest and for his or her well-being, and not for any other purpose. The physician is taught "primum non nocere"—"above all, inflict no harm." The Hippocratic Oath states: "I will use treatment to help the sick according to my ability and judgment, but I will never use it to injure or wrong them."[13] The World Medical Association holds out the

---

[12] An excellent discussion of such differences and of the resulting ethical concerns, from the perspective of psychologists working in corrections, can be found in Stanley L. Brodsky, "Ethical Issues for Psychologists in Corrections," in: John Monahan (ed.), *Who is the Client?: The Ethics of Psychological Intervention in the Criminal Justice System* (Washington, D.C.: American Psychological Association, 1980): 63-92. For example, Brodsky states on page 63: "While psychologists come from backgrounds of scientific discipline and helping concerns, correctional administrators are a part of the justice process . . . The law, from the courts through corrections, holds to the principle that truth arises from the adversary presentation of opposing views. Psychology and other helping professions assume that cooperation and collaboration are the essence of finding truth, through research endeavors and therapeutic procedures. Psychology tends to value trust; corrections values control . . ."

[13] Tom L. Beauchamp and James F. Childress, *Principles of Biomedical Ethics*, Fourth Edition (New York: Oxford University Press, 1994): 189.

following pledge: "A doctor shall preserve absolute secrecy on all he knows about his patient because of the confidence entrusted to him." [14] Other health professionals subscribe to similar principles.

In recent years, economic realities have required recognition of legitimate interests outside of what long had been widely regarded as a dyadic relationship [15] between physician and patient. Third-party payers (government, employers, and insurance companies) now have an active voice in doctor-patient decisions to prevent an unreasonable escalation of costs. Sometimes, there are circumstances in which the need for access to a particular treatment by other patients also must be considered in allocating scarce resources.

Most of the time, the issues will not be clear "all or nothing," "black and white" dilemmas in which the medical professional or the correctional professional must choose between two conflicting or opposing principles. Usually, concerns of both sides require open and candid recognition and discussion, so that decisions can be made which balance in a reasonable manner the legitimate demands of both. [16]

Often, it is helpful for decision makers to seek the advice of thoughtful persons from outside the agency who may bring a greater objectivity and fresh insight to the deliberations concerning sensitive and complex ethical issues. The Michigan Department of Corrections during the late 1980s added a medical ethicist from the community to its Health Care Advisory Board. The Florida Department of Corrections has had a Bioethics Committee since 1993, with a majority of its members being ethicists from outside the field of corrections. This Bioethics Committee has regular meetings, considers ethical problems within the correctional system, consults on individual cases, and proposes positions and policies.

Code of Ethics for the Correctional Health Care Professional

The American Correctional Association's Task Force on Health Care in Corrections was chaired by Kenneth P. Moritsugu, M.D. Its report, *Public Policy on Correctional Health Care* of June, 1996, merits careful study and attention by institution heads and others who are responsible for arranging and providing various aspects of health services to inmates of correctional institutions. While this twenty-five page document is not reprinted here, a few excerpts have been selected by the author (see Figure 13-1, pages 225-228). These are inserted (in italicized type) to illustrate the detail with which the report addresses some important provisions mentioned in the *Policy Statement.*

---

[14] International Code of Medical Ethics, cited in Beauchamp and Childress, *op. cit.*: 419.

[15] E. Haavi Morreim, *Balancing Act: The New Medical Ethics of Medicine's New Economics* (Boston: Kluwer Academic Publishers, 1991): 1.

[16] Readers interested in pursuing this topic further profitably may read some case examples in which both sides of the ethical deliberations are presented articulately, for example, Chris Hansen and Gordon C. Kanska, "Ethical Problems: Cases and Commentaries," 1:2, *Journal of Prison Health* (Fall/Winter, 1981): 97-104.

FIGURE 13-1. AMERICAN CORRECTIONAL ASSOCIATION PUBLIC CORRECTIONAL POLICY ON CORRECTIONAL HEALTH CARE*

Introduction:

Incarcerated individuals, or those in the custody of criminal justice agencies, have a right to adequate health care under the Eighth Amendment to the Constitution. Correctional jurisdictions must use a comprehensive, holistic approach to providing health and mental health care services which are sensitive to the cultural, subcultural, age and gender specific needs of a growing and diverse population. All services provided must be consistent with community health care standards. To ensure accountability and professional responsibility, these services should follow the policy guidelines set forth below, as well as the health and mental health care standards of the American Correctional Association.

Policy Statement:

Health care programs for offenders include comprehensive health, medical, dental and mental health services. Such programs should:

A. Be delivered by qualified and appropriately credentialed health care professionals;

> *Inmates or other individuals in the custody of law-enforcement agencies, shall never be used in the provision of direct patient care . . . . Treatment shall be provided and/or supervised by competent, appropriately credentialed health care professionals.*

B. Include a comprehensive health promotion and disease prevention program designed to meet the specific health maintenance needs of the specific residential population, which includes health, nutrition, and safety education programs;

> *The current practices in the contemporary correctional medicine field fall short of the proactive interventions that deal specifically with the issue of lifestyle behavior and health promotion and disease prevention . . . . The Task Force identifies the following as targeted areas for intervention through innovative program development:*
>
> - *Taking responsibility for one's own health*
> - *Tobacco-free correctional facilities*
> - *Violence prevention*
> - *Alternative conflict resolution*

---

* This policy was ratified by the American Correctional Association Delegate Assembly at the 117th Congress of Correction in New Orleans, Louisiana, on August 6, 1987 and reviewed and amended at the Congress of Correction in Nashville, Tennessee, August 23, 1996. The italicized paragraphs are excerpts from the report of the Task Force on Corrections.

- *Healthy nutrition*
- *Reducing risks for communicable diseases*
- *Elimination of substance/chemical abuse*
- *Exercise for life*
- *Good oral hygiene/plaque control*
- *Classroom education to address the disease entity*

C. Employ a stratified system of service delivery to maximize the efficient use of health and mental health care resources;

D. Include corrections officers who work in health and mental health care units as active participants in the multidisciplinary treatment team;

E. Create community linkages which will facilitate the continuation of the treatment plan by community health and mental health care agencies for persons being released from incarceration;

The unplanned cessation of mental health treatment upon release dramatically increases a person's chances of rearrest, either through criminal recidivism or technical violations of release conditions. This causes unnecessary loss of freedom for the individual and expense to the public. Thus, efforts must be made to plan and deliver aftercare with the full and mandated cooperation of community mental health agencies.

F. Establish appropriate classification, program and housing assignments for the chronically ill and elderly offender. Health and mental health programs must be developed which address the unique needs of geriatric populations

The most effective and efficient service delivery model is an adaptation of the community mental health model to prisons and jails. This model requires the availability of an array of services at varying levels of intensity within the community (i.e. the prison or jail) in addition to the need for occasional transfers to inpatient hospital settings.

The program must include:

- *A classification system that identifies the special needs of the chronically ill inmate, the elderly inmate, and inmates with serious mental illnesses, to include innovative programming, housing ranging from nursing homes to skilled nursing facilities (SNF), and adequate medical staff*

- *An early release mechanism for those elderly or chronically ill inmates who no longer represent a threat to society*

G. Establish hospice services for terminally ill offenders supported by a compassionate release program for those who qualify;

The program must include:

- *A formal process for the early release of offenders with terminal illnesses into appropriate community settings*

- *The requirement to provide on-site hospice care for those terminally ill inmates who are not qualified for early release*

- *Specific guidelines for the use of medications which relieve pain and provide comfort to terminally ill patients*

H. Establish comprehensive health, mental health, housing, and substance abuse programs that are specifically designed for the special needs of female offenders;

I. Upon intake screening, provide all offenders with oral and written information concerning access to health and mental health care services, followed by more formal instruction during the institution admission and orientation program;

J. Provide continuous, comprehensive services commencing at admission, including effective and timely screening, assessment and treatment, and appropriate referral to alternate health care resources where warranted;

K. Establish a system to provide access to emergency treatment twenty-four hours per day;

L. Establish a formal process to screen for, identify, treat and manage inmates with infectious diseases;

Correctional environments provide an opportunity to identify infectious diseases and educate offenders about these diseases to an extent that is possible only in this setting. Many of these offenders have not been exposed to adequate health education and prevention because of their social and/or economic status, or because of the lack of these services in the community. It is also noted that the vast majority of these offenders will eventually be released back into the public and hopefully they will carry with them the lessons learned while incarcerated. It therefore becomes incumbent upon correctional systems to provide for health education and disease prevention while there is the opportunity to do so.

[The Task Force recommended that] the planning and design of correctional facilities must include collaboration by custody and health services management to ensure that the physical environment supports infection control measures and practices recommended by local and federal public health entities.

All pregnant females should be tested for HIV so that positive testers may be treated aggressively to reduce the chance of transmission of the virus to the newborn.

HIV must be considered a disease and not a stigma and must be treated as such. There must be adequate and appropriate education on HIV disease for all offenders coming into correctional facilities.

Adequate and appropriate treatment must be offered for sexually transmitted diseases (STDs). Appropriate education on STD must be provided to all offenders.

Universal precautions must be practiced in all correctional facilities by all staff who are at potential risk.

M. Provide appropriate health care training programs that are cognizant of cultural, subcultural and gender issues for all correctional and health care staff, and allow for continuing professional and medical education programs;

[The Task Force recommended] parenting training as a necessary component of services for both women and men. In addition, policies for visitation with minor children and in jail nurseries for newborns must be considered.

[There is a] need to identify and properly diagnose mental health problems stemming from physical or sexual abuse.

Speaking the primary language and having an understanding of subcultures are important for accurate assessment and the provision of appropriate mental health and other services.

Mental health evaluations must be performed by well-trained clinical staff, who are experts in women's issues to ensure an appropriate diagnosis and to identify less disruptive, but serious mental illnesses, such as depression.

[Prisons should] utilize extensive peer support programs for women with substance abuse issues and histories of physical and sexual abuse.

N. Provide a medical records system to document diagnosis and treatment programs to facilitate treatment continuity and cooperation between health care professionals, consistent with privacy, confidentiality and security requirements;

O. Restrict physicians to prescribing medications from an established formulary and provide a pharmaceutical distribution system that conforms to applicable state and federal laws;

P. Provide a continuing quality improvement program using risk management programs; pre-certification, concurrent, and utilization review; and peer review activities to monitor and evaluate the health care services delivered;

Q. Establish a Patient Bill of Rights;

Upon entering custody of a correctional institution or law enforcement agency, each individual shall be evaluated for any emergency medical needs and be informed of the availability of continuing health, mental health, medical and dental care and the process by which these services can be requested.

The provision of withholding of medical care shall never be used as a form of punishment to the incarcerated person.

Medical treatment, including medication, may be given against the patient's will only when in the opinion of a physician immediate treatment is necessary to protect the patient, or others, from a physical condition threatening to cause death, damage or impairment of bodily functions or disfigurement, and the individual is incapable either physically or mentally of giving consent.

R. Provide a system for medical and administrative review of grievances relating to any health care offered, provided, or denied;

S. Provide screening for dual-diagnosis and substance abuse; and

T. Provide all new inmates given prescriptions with oral counseling or written information about their medication. This information should ideally be provided by pharmacists.

U. Provide the opportunity to establish a living will.

Similarly, the American Correctional Health Services Association recently published a Code of Ethics for correctional health professionals. It is reprinted here in its entirety in Figure 13-2 (see page 230). Over the several years of its development, there was widespread involvement and discussion among many correctional health professionals, leading to its present formulation.

Some Ethical Issues

Confidentiality and Privacy

People rightly expect the "doctor-patient privilege" to safeguard in strict confidence whatever the health professionals have learned about them in the process of rendering health care. They do not want their personal secrets revealed at a cocktail party or over the back fence. This is analogous to the attorney-client privilege or the confidence between priest and penitent. The expectation that this confidence will be respected is essential to the trust required in any of these relationships. The various codes of correctional health care standards [17] [18] [19] [20] [21] require that the medical records of inmates be kept separate from the institutional records and that their contents be held in strict confidence, available only to those persons with a legitimate need to have access to the information. Health care personnel go to considerable length to protect patient confidentiality. Medical and mental health encounters with patients should take place in relative privacy. Health record files should be kept locked and inaccessible to officers and inmates.

It is not hard to imagine areas of potential conflict, even in a well-managed correctional system. Inmates who are known to be dangerous should not be left alone with a health provider. And it is axiomatic in corrections that officers need to know what is going on with inmates; secrecy and privacy are problematic. Suppose a maximum-security institution has a policy that all inmates in certain housing areas are to have an officer present in the examining room during all medical encounters, because the warden or other appropriate authority has determined this to be necessary for safety and security. Here, careful examination of the intent and the content of both conflicting requirements can lead to a satisfactory resolution. Medical ethics do not intend to create unsafe conditions for the practice of medicine. Neither does the

---

[17] NCCHC, *Standards for Health Services in Prisons* (Chicago, Ill., 1997), Standards P-61, P-62, P- 63.

[18] NCCHC, *Standards for Health Services in Jails* (Chicago, Ill., 1996), Standards J-59, J-60, J-61.

[19] NCCHC, *Standards for Health Services in Juvenile Facilities* (Chicago, Ill., 1995), Standards Y- 60 and Y-61.

[20] American Correctional Association, *Standards for Adult Correctional Institutions*, Third Edition (Lanham, Md., 1990), Standard 3-4377.

[21] Nancy N. Dubler, ed., *Standards for Health Services in Correctional Institutions*, Second Edition (Washington, D.C.: American Public Health Association, 1986): 111.

FIGURE 13-2. CODE OF ETHICS FOR CORRECTIONAL HEALTH PROFESSIONALS: AMERICAN CORRECTIONAL HEALTH SERVICES ASSOCIATION (ACHSA)

(ADOPTED FEBRUARY 1995, REVISED AUGUST 1996) [22]

PREAMBLE: Correctional health professionals are obligated to respect human dignity and act in ways that merit trust and prevent harm. They must ensure autonomy in decisions about their inmate patients and promote a safe environment. The following principles adopted by the American Correctional Health Services Association are not laws, but a code of conduct which defines the essentials of honorable behavior for correctional health professionals.

PRINCIPLES: The correctional health professional shall:

1. Respect the law and also recognize a responsibility to seek changes in those requirements which are contrary to the best interest of the patient.

2. Evaluate the inmate as patient or client in each and every health care encounter.

3. Render medical treatment only when it is justified by an accepted medical diagnosis. Treatment and invasive procedures shall be rendered after informed consent.

4. Afford inmates the right to refuse care and treatment. Involuntary treatment shall be reserved for emergency situations in which there is grave disability or immediate threat of danger to the inmate or others.

5. Provide sound privacy during health care services in all cases and sight privacy whenever possible.

6. Provide health care to all inmates regardless of custody status.

7. Identify themselves to their patients and not represent themselves as other than their professional license or certification permits.

8. Collect and analyze specimens only for diagnostic testing based on sound medical principles.

9. Perform body cavity searches only after training in proper techniques and when they are not in a patient-provider relationship with the inmate.

10. Ensure that all medical information is confidential and that health care records are maintained and transported in a confidential manner.

11. Honor custody functions but not participate in such functions as escorting inmates, forced transfers, security supervision, strip searches, or witnessing use of force.

12. Undertake biomedical research on prisoners only when the research methods meet all requirements for experimentation on human subjects and when individual prisoners or prison populations are expected to derive benefits from the results of the research.

---

[22] Reprinted with permission of t⅃ American Correctional Health Services Association, Dayton, Ohio.

correctional concern for security intend to breach the doctor-patient privilege. Perhaps, the officer could stand just outside the door and observe the doctor and patient through a window. If the patient does not behave appropriately, the doctor should terminate the encounter at once. On the other hand, this may not always be adequate, and in extreme cases, good judgment may require the officer to be physically close during the encounter. At a minimum, each correctional agency should have a policy indicating that any officer who observes or overhears confidential or privileged information derived from the process of rendering health care to an inmate has a strict obligation to respect that confidence and is strictly prohibited from discussing or revealing this information to any other person. This is not a matter to be taken lightly, but neither should it present an insolvable dilemma.

The best solution may be a policy directing that an officer be present whenever there is reason to believe that a particular patient, on a specific occasion, is likely to present a security risk, rather than to require this precaution with every inmate in a certain security classification or housing unit. Then, the intrusion into privacy rests on a judgment regarding individual circumstances, and not merely because the person belongs to a particular class.

There are limits to confidentiality. Laws in most states require that doctors report gunshot wounds or signs of child abuse to the proper authorities, even when this information is obtained while giving medical care to the patient. Most states also require that certain infectious diseases be reported to the health department. These provisions are intended to prevent greater harm to the larger community. When a patient reveals an intent to inflict harm on a third party, and the mental health professional determines that disclosure of client information is necessary to protect the third party from a clear, imminent risk of serious injury or death, in most states there arises an obligation to warn the potential victim and the health professional is protected from liability in breaching the client's confidence.[23] Correctional officials have a need to know certain information to facilitate provision of care, for example, to escort a patient to a specific kind of provider, or to permit medications to be in a patient's possession. Also, when appropriate, they need to know the specific disease-prevention practices which are to be observed.[24] Information which indicates the likelihood of danger to self or to others must be shared with the institutional authorities, as, for instance, suicidal intent, possession of a weapon, or a plan for escape.[25]

---

[23] Jill Doner Kagle and Sandra Kopels, 19:3, *Health and Social Work*. National Association of Social Workers, Inc. (August, 1994): 217. See also *Tarasoff v. Board of Regents of the University of California*, 551 P. 2d 334 (1976).

[24] Clearly, however, this does not suggest that HIV-positive individuals should be identified for the protection of officers. The concept of *universal precautions* for blood-borne pathogens, if correctly understood and applied, offers far greater protection to the officers since those who are known to be infected represent only a fraction of all identified persons. Whenever there is potential exposure to blood and body fluids, the only safe course is to regard all persons as infected. Using "extra care" with known infected persons implies and promotes use of "lesser caution" with the others.

[25] Dubler, *APHA Standards, op. cit.*: 111.

Good facility design considerations can assist greatly in providing care in a *safe* as well as *confidential* manner. For example, doors to examination rooms should have windows which permit an officer to ascertain that all is secure. Alternatively, the solution might be a partition, which does not reach to the ceiling, and so allows loud cries or sounds to be heard easily. Generally, for mental health situations, privacy of sound is more important than privacy of sight. For certain medical procedures, the opposite is true.

Above all, the patient ought to be informed about any limits to the confidentiality she or he otherwise would have a right to expect. These limits of confidentiality should be explained by the mental health professional when interviewing a new patient.[26]

Informed Consent and Enforced Treatment

Medical and mental health practitioners justifiably are concerned to ensure that patients give informed consent for all therapeutic interventions. Ultimately, it is the patient alone who must determine what happens to his or her own body. Informed consent consists of communicating the risks and the benefits of a test or treatment in a way that allows the patient to decide whether to authorize the intervention. The practitioner who obtains the patient's informed consent generally will place a note to this effect in the patient's health record. For minor procedures, verbal consent or even implied consent usually is sufficient.

For invasive, intrusive, or risky procedures, a more formal process is required. An explanation is given to the patient concerning the advantages and disadvantages of the procedure, as well as the availability, benefits, and risks of alternative therapies or of no treatment at all, followed by a signed consent to treatment. Failure to obtain consent for treatment exposes the provider to tort liability for "unwanted touching." In other words, the patient can sue the doctor and win if consent were not granted.

An unconscious or incompetent person can be treated in an emergency under the presumption that the patient would give consent if able to do so. When time permits, surrogate consent is advised. Family members are often appropriate for this purpose. So also is the institution head. This procedure involves explaining the risks and advantages of the intervention to the patient's representative so that an informed decision can be made reflecting, as far as possible, the patient's own preferences and best interests.

Psychiatric treatment sometimes is administered involuntarily. The same principles and guidelines generally apply in a correctional setting as for a patient in the free world under similar circumstances. In the community, commitment to a mental hospital is a process involving many legal safeguards for the patient, in part because involuntary hospitalization deprives an otherwise free citizen of liberty. Some have argued that since this liberty already has been taken away from prisoners by a court

---

[26] See also John Monahan, (ed.), *Who Is the Client?: The Ethics of Psychological Intervention in the Criminal Justice System* (Washington, D.C.: American Psychological Association, 1980): 5-8.

of law, it is, therefore, within the authority of the head of the institution to assign the inmate to a mental health unit, even when the inmate does not wish to go, as long as no involuntary treatment is administered in the psychiatric unit. However, *Vitek v. Jones*[27] would disallow this interpretation, on grounds that the stigma attached to psychiatric commitment and the possibility of involuntary subjection to psychiatric treatment constitutes a deprivation of liberty requiring due process. This principle of *Vitek* was found applicable, even if the mental hospital is part of the correctional department.[28] While the exact language may differ, in most jurisdictions the decision to enforce treatment rests on a finding that the patient:

    a)   is mentally ill, and

    b)   as a consequence of the mental illness, is unable to care for his or her own bodily needs essential to the preservation of life or is imminently dangerous to self or to others, and

    c)   that no less invasive or less restrictive alternative will suffice.

In most states, a psychiatrist who makes such a determination may treat only in an emergency and may continue the treatment for a period not to exceed forty-eight hours. When prolonged involuntary treatment is determined to be necessary, a court order should be obtained or other due process followed, according to the established procedures in the jurisdiction.

The Supreme Court ruled[29] that, although prison inmates have a liberty interest in resisting unwanted psychotropic medications, due process can be satisfied by a competent physician's deciding to protect the inmate or others as long as the doctor's decision can be challenged in an administrative proceeding. The treating physician, however, may not be included in this proceeding.[30]

Policies in some correctional systems inappropriately may condone enforced medical treatment. Such a policy might state, in effect, that any medication or treatment prescribed by the doctor must be taken by the inmate as directed, or the inmate will be ticketed and subject to punishment. The reasoning (of at least one correctional system) was that each able-bodied prisoner is required to work in the fields every day. Remaining sick longer than necessary is not tolerated. Hence, if the doctor orders medication to cure the illness, the institution regards compliance as an issue of good order and discipline. Whether there is a legitimate state concern justifying enforced treatment under these circumstances is a matter which ultimately must be decided by a court. However, it would seem that the inmate's fundamental right to privacy—which involves the right to take or to refuse medication—would take precedence.

---

[27] 445 U.S. 480, 494-96, 100 S.Ct. 1254 (1980).

[28] *Baugh v. Woodard*, 808 F.2d 333, 335 n. 2 (4th Cir. 1987) and *Witzke v. Johnson*, 656 F.Supp. 294, 297-98 (W.D. Mich. 1987).

[29] *Washington v. Harper*, 494 U.S. 210 (1990).

[30] "Forced Psychotropic Medications Reviewed by Courts," 8:2, *CorrectCare* (May, 1994): 4, 6.

Most correctional facilities allow an inmate to refuse treatment. Most also provide a form for signing an "informed refusal," such as refusal to follow medical advice. This gives some protection to the provider and the facility from liability for adverse consequences suffered by the patient. Care must be taken, however, to ensure that the inmate is aware of the service being refused. When, for example, the inmate signs a refusal slip in the presence of an officer, stating as his reason that he no longer needs to see the dentist because his tooth is feeling better, this is not an informed refusal if the callout was for an intake physical examination or a blood pressure check.

Some institutions will not allow an inmate on a special diet to take both a diet tray and a regular tray for the same meal. This is acceptable. Other institutions inform the physician each time an inmate with a special diet order instead elects to take the regular meal. Should this occur frequently, the doctor is justified in advising the inmate that the special diet order will be discontinued. But, the inmate later should be able to ask for reinstatement of a medically necessary diet on condition of promised compliance—with some expectation that the promise will be kept.

Hunger Strikes

Hunger strikes pose a difficult situation for both the facility administrator and the health care staff. They quickly can become media events with far-reaching political ramifications. A hunger strike may be an attempt to attract attention or to get one's way. Often, it is a protest against real or perceived wrongs. Most hunger strikers are mentally competent persons acting in a purposeful and reasoned manner, perhaps even for a high and worthy cause.[31] Less often, the individual may be psychotic and acting on the command of hallucinatory voices.

Several alternative policy decisions are possible in these situations. The correctional authority should consider granting some or all of the hunger striker's demands, if they are not unreasonable and if this is likely to be successful. Attempts also should be made to persuade the hunger striker to redirect his or her protest efforts to a more acceptable mode. When such efforts have failed, and the inmate appears determined to continue the hunger strike, essentially two courses of action are possible, depending on the agency policy.

(1) Advise the inmate that the agency's no-rescue policy will be strictly followed. In this case, encourage the inmate to eat. Do not rescue. Be willing to allow the hunger striker to die if refusal continues.

(2) Intervene with forced feeding. It may be prudent to seek a court order for this intervention. Otherwise, such use of force on a competent person may be judged to be an assault.

---

[31] Outside of the correctional scene, the hunger strike has been employed by such respected persons as Mohandas Gandhi and Cesar Chavez, as a nonviolent but effective means of seeking support for the cause in which they deeply believed.

If forced feeding is the choice, it should be done at a relatively early stage. It is not advisable to wait until the inmate has become unconscious or is too weak to offer resistance. Intervention should take place before permanent or irreparable organ damage has occurred. Should serious irreversible damage be allowed to occur, very costly and ongoing medical care expenses will be the likely result.

The following strategies are recommended:

(1) Ascertain the nature of the complaint and the stated purpose of the protest. Have a talk with the inmate.

(2) Arrange for a competency examination by a psychiatrist or psychologist. If the inmate is deranged, incompetent, or mentally ill, consider seeking a court order for enforced nutrition.

(3) Monitor all materials brought into the cell of the inmate.

(4) Monitor all food and liquid intake and output if the strike continues beyond a few days. Accurate monitoring requires a cooperative subject, but some information is better than none.

(5) Transfer the inmate to a medical area—such as an infirmary bed where close observation is facilitated—when the inmate becomes debilitated or exhibits medical need.

(6) If it is determined that the inmate is competent and appears to be making a reasoned and purposeful choice, advise him or her that the facility has a "no rescue" policy. If he or she becomes unconscious or comatose or too weak to resist, life-saving emergency procedures will not be instituted to force-feed. Ask the inmate to sign a release stating that he or she has been advised of the consequences of continuing the fast, understands that there is a "no rescue" policy, and, in fact, does not want last-minute desperate rescue efforts.

(7) If it is determined that the inmate is incompetent or unreasonable, advise him or her that a court order will be sought for involuntary nutrition. If this is the decision, it should be implemented before the inmate becomes weakened or comatose.

(8) Continue to serve three appetizing meals a day. Measure (or estimate) fluid and solid intake and output. Keep up the contact by concerned visitors. Inform the inmate of the results and significance of the various medical tests being conducted. Encourage intake of liquids and vitamins even if food is being refused, since this will delay the onset of serious or irreversible health problems. Also, remind the hunger striker of the no-rescue policy decision.

(9) If the inmate has access to commissary items (or other food sources) and presumably eats them, while ignoring the food

which is served, perhaps the incident should be classified as other than a "hunger strike."[32]

(10) If it is possible to accede to the inmate's legitimate or reasonable demands, consider doing so as early as possible.

(11) Arrange visits to the hunger striker by a physician, psychiatrist, psychologist, social worker, nurse, chaplain, and family members. The physician should advise both the inmate and the visitors clearly and truthfully concerning the short-range and long-range consequences to health from dehydration or prolonged malnutrition.

(12) In a prolonged situation, hold a conference with the physician, psychiatrist, psychologist, nurse, warden, custody officer, central office representative, attorney, and chaplain, as appropriate, to review what has taken place and to discuss alternatives.

Forensic Use of Medically Obtained Information

General Principles

The ethical standards of correctional health care professionals forbid them to obtain specimens or perform tests to obtain information which may be used in prosecuting or punishing the inmate. This is an area related to (a) *confidentiality* and *privacy*, (b) *informed consent*, and (c) *therapeutic relationship*, and derives from the medical principle that above all else a doctor should inflict no harm on a patient. Forensic tests, for example, include blood, urine and tissue samples for DNA, or paternity determination, or the presence of alcohol or drugs; body cavity searches for contraband; evaluation of competency to stand trial or to submit to punishment; and evaluations for parole board decisions.

As indicated, several ethical principles may be involved. Suppose a prosecutor needs a blood or tissue sample from a prisoner to assist in convicting or clearing the prisoner of a crime. This action is not directed towards the delivery of health care services to the prisoner. It even may do some harm, although perhaps the "harm" is itself lawful and even has a noble purpose. The patient also may withhold consent for the procedure. Note that the concept of informed consent requires that the true reason for the test be explained in advance to the inmate.

In a recent case which the author encountered while surveying a correctional facility, the laboratory technician had been requested by the internal affairs investigator to draw blood from an inmate, but was not told the purpose of the test. It would be a violation of professional ethics to draw the blood without informing the inmate of the purpose and intended use of the specimens, and consent would be obtained

---

[32] Some facilities take steps to prevent access to all other sources of food except that served on the tray. This is not unreasonable.

deceitfully if the inmate were led to believe that this was just a routine medical procedure. This, of course, could be remedied by a court order requiring the inmate to supply the specimen. The court order also would override any conflict with confidentiality and the doctor-patient privilege. However, another principle still may stand in the way. Regular health care staff at the facility must be regarded by inmates as persons who always can be counted on to act in their patients' best interest. A trusting relationship arises between clinician and patient, which is termed a "therapeutic alliance." Effective medical and mental health care for patients requires this continued trust. A patient who does not trust his or her doctor is likely to withhold relevant symptoms and history or may fail to comply with prescribed treatment. Confidence in one's doctor has been shown to be important to the healing process itself.

Participation in the unconsented collection of blood or tissue specimens for the purpose of prosecution and eventual punishment of the inmate is inconsistent with the role of a trusted healer, particularly in a correctional setting where the inmate is given no real choice among providers. Thus arises the recommendation of the National Commission on Correctional Health Care [33] that tissue specimens for forensic uses ought to be obtained by a qualified health professional not employed as a regular health care provider for the prison or jail. While somewhat more costly, the reasons underlying this precaution are important and should be respected. These cases typically only should occur rarely, and, consequently, the cost would not be prohibitive. Hair samples for DNA or substance use testing and urine tests for drugs or alcohol should not be an issue since they can be obtained by officers at a location apart from the clinic setting and do not require the intervention or skills of the health care staff.

DNA Testing

Medical tests conducted for forensic purposes ought not to be carried out by correctional health care staff since it confuses the role of the health care provider who should be seen and respected as a caregiver, acting completely on behalf of and in the best interests of the patient. The health care provider should not be expected to use medical skills to perform actions which can lead to prosecution or punishment.

In cases where the testing must be accomplished, it is best carried out by an outside person, in other words, by a qualified health care professional who does not have, and is unlikely to have, a provider/patient relationship with the inmate.

It is important to distinguish among the following situations:

(a) the inmate who freely consents to (and perhaps even desires) the testing

(b) the inmate who does not give free consent, but acquiesces and does not actively resist

(c) the inmate who not only withholds consent, but actively resists the procedure

---

[33] NCCHC, *Standards for Prisons, op. cit.*, Standard P-68; *Standards for Jails, op. cit.*, Standard J- 66; and *Standards for Juvenile Facilities, op. cit.*, Standard Y-66.

There is generally no problem with the situation described in (a). Here, the test itself is perceived by the informed inmate as beneficial, or at least not harmful, and, consequently, the health provider is not placed in a position antagonistic to the well-being of a patient.

In situation (b), the health professional who bears a provider-patient relationship to the inmate ought not participate in obtaining the specimen for forensic purposes against the patient's will. However, when legally required, it may be performed by a qualified health professional who does not bear a provider-patient relationship and is not likely to do so.

The situation described in (c) can pose serious problems and ought to be performed only in cases of the greatest necessity, preferably with a court order and by a qualified provider who does not have a patient-provider relationship. The risk of causing physical injury to the patient weighs heavily against performing the procedure unless it is urgently required.

An increasing number of state laws are requiring DNA testing of all inmates.[34] Under these circumstances, the cost of arranging for separate staff to obtain the specimens could be excessive. A reasonable case[35] can be made for allowing a portion of the blood routinely drawn for intake medical screening of new inmates to be used for legislatively mandated DNA testing. The argument here is that the specimen is obtained routinely for all (or a large number of) inmates, does not involve a separate invasive procedure, and the possibility of an eventual forensic use of this information is remote from the act of collecting the specimen. This situation is distinguished from drawing a specimen from a particular inmate for a legitimate medical purpose and with the express intention of using the data in a current prosecutorial application.

Some state laws specify that the DNA testing shall be performed by health care staff of the institution. Even this need not be interpreted as requiring that the regular staff, with established or potential provider/patient relationships, must do the testing procedures. The institution might hire (such as by contract) outside providers on a part-time basis for this sole purpose. On the other hand, these special arrangements may be extremely costly. Faced with this situation, medical staff should take care to avoid interfering with the therapeutic relationship by appropriately informing the inmate prior to the procedure as to the purpose and the reason for its being done, and clearly distinguishing this from a medical procedure undertaken for the prisoner's health. Staff also should be alert to occasions when this appears in any way to undermine or compromise patient confidence in the health care staff.

Body Cavity Searches

A sure way to engender a lively discussion in many jurisdictions is to raise the subject of body cavity searches in the mixed company of corrections officers and

---

[34] Or of a subset of inmates, such as sex-offenders.

[35] There is a dispute concerning permissibility of making other (unconsented) use of discarded specimens when patient identifiers are kept.

medical staff.[36] The standards of both the National Commission on Correctional Health Care[37] and the American Public Health Association[38] clearly prohibit the conducting of body cavity searches by health care staff who routinely are assigned to provide medical care at the facility.

The concern is twofold. First, because body orifice searches are invasive procedures,[39] they would require informed consent if performed for medical reasons. If the consent is freely given (as may be the case with an inmate anxious to demonstrate his or her innocence), the nurse or doctor ethically may proceed unless it were judged that doing so would impair the doctor-patient relationship. Often, consent can be obtained by the proper attitude of the health care worker and a careful explanation.

The second concern is that the health care professional who routinely provides care for the inmates is not acting in the patient's best interest when conducting a search for concealed evidence which can lead to the inmate's punishment. This activity makes the health care staff appear to the inmates to be "police." Nurses and physicians work hard to achieve and maintain a therapeutic alliance with their patients. To perform an invasive search for contraband in a body cavity against the inmate's wishes is a breach of this trust.

Some experts, including the National Commission on Correctional Health Care[40] and the American Public Health Association[41] have suggested that body cavity

---

[36] Of course, this intensity of feeling usually is lacking in those settings in which medical staff have acquiesced to performing these procedures, or where the incidence of requiring a body cavity search is so rare as almost to be a nonissue.

[37] NCCHC, *Standards for Jails, op. cit.,* at Standard J-66 states that "correctional health care personnel are prohibited from participating in the collection of forensic information." The discussion to the standard adds: "The role of the health care staff is to serve the health needs of inmate patients. The position of its members as neutral, caring, health care professionals is compromised when they are asked to collect information from inmates to be used against them." The language of Standard P-68 for prisons and Standard Y-66 for juvenile facilities is similar. The discussion of P-68 adds: "Body cavity searches conducted for reasons of security should be done in privacy by outside health care providers. Alternatives to body cavity searches are available to institutions, such as the use of a dry cell."

[38] "Participation in this purely custodial function [strip and body cavity searches] compromises the ability of the health provider to relate to the health needs of the inmate population." Dubler, APHA *Standards, op. cit.*:112.

[39] In terms of invasiveness, body cavity searches for contraband fall midway between obtaining blood or tissue samples on the one hand, and collection of urine or hair specimens on the other.

[40] NCCHC, *Standards for Jails, op. cit.,* at Standard P-66 and *Standards for Juvenile Facilities, op. cit.,* at Standard Y-66 states: "Body cavity searches conducted for reasons of security should be done in privacy by outside health care providers (as noted above) or by correctional personnel of the same sex as the inmate [juvenile] who have been trained by a physician or other health care provider to probe body cavities (without the use of instruments) so as to cause neither injury to tissue nor infection." Note, however, that similar language has been omitted from the 1997 prison standards.

[41] Dubler, APHA *Standards, loc. cit.*

searches be performed by corrections officers who have received training by health care staff in how to explore body cavities with a gloved finger. At best, this is an unsatisfactory compromise. No single officer is likely to perform the procedure frequently enough to maintain the required skills to avoid causing injury or infection. There is also at least the appearance of impropriety when health care staff train officers in how to perform a procedure which is, by definition and intent, contrary to the well-being of their patients. In view of these considerations, the National Commission has omitted this recommendation from the 1997 prison health care standards.

These same experts also advise employment of health care professionals not associated with the provision of health care at the institution. This can be quite costly and inconvenient. Also, the inmate may not comprehend the subtle distinction in the nature of the health professional's employment contract, so that it still may appear that this procedure is being inflicted on him or her by a member of the institution's health care staff. Moreover, exploration of bodily orifices of an inmate who is not only unwilling, but is actively and aggressively resisting can be extremely difficult. In this situation, the trained correctional officer is at great risk of inflicting injury, while the highly skilled health professional simply may refuse to proceed under such circumstances.

Legislation permitting nurses and doctors to perform body cavity searches will make the procedure legal, but not necessarily ethical. Any facility or system which seeks to attract and retain good staff and respects the professional integrity of its medical staff will not ask them to compromise their ethical principles. What remedies remain?

Each agency should review its policy and practice regarding body cavity searches. How necessary are the searches which are currently being performed? Are they being ordered only when probable cause exists and when other, less invasive or potentially harmful methods, have been exhausted?[42] Is the specific order signed by a high-level authority, such as a warden or a jail administrator? Is each body cavity search carefully documented and reported to a higher authority, such as the director of corrections or sheriff, for retrospective review and monitoring to prevent abuse and overuse? If all of these safeguards are in place, the actual use of body cavity searches may become so rare that they easily can be handled by outside medical personnel without a major cost burden.[43]

Protection of the inmate from risk of serious harm in the event that a balloon filled with drugs were to burst within the body cavity is not sufficient justification for a body cavity search. Instead, the inmate should be advised of the serious consequences of a ruptured balloon and be encouraged to have it removed voluntarily.

---

[42] Some correctional agencies, for example, place an inmate who is suspected of having inserted contraband into the rectum, in a dry cell (without sink, toilet, or drain) with a "potty" bucket, under observation, until the contraband, if any, is excreted naturally.

[43] A very interesting discussion of ethical issues related to strip searches, body cavity searches, and religious beliefs is found in Peter C. Williams and Joan Hirsch Holzman, "Ethical Problems: Cases and Commentaries: Health vs. Safety: Receiving Needed Care," 1:1, *Journal of Prison Health* (Spring/Summer, 1981): 44-54.

The necessity of the search should be called into question in places where they occur frequently but produce very little yield. Strict standards and careful monitoring can minimize abuse. There should be probable cause, and each search should require written authorization of the warden or jail administrator (not of a "designee"). Further, a report of each instance, the rationale, the alternatives considered, and the outcome, should be made to the higher-level authority on a regular basis for retrospective monitoring.

Body cavity searches should be ordered only when there is good reason to believe that contraband is there, and when no satisfactory alternative can be found. A court order is not required, as long as there is an order signed by the appropriate authority, but in cases of determined and aggressive resistance, when the procedures must be done by force, a court order is advisable. This ensures that the special circumstances, rationale, and alternatives all have been considered and weighed by a disinterested party.

Evaluation of Competency

Two important steps in the judicial process, often employed when a question is raised about the sanity of a defendant, is to determine whether the defendant was mentally competent when the crime was committed, and whether the defendant is currently competent to stand trial.

A psychologist, psychiatrist, or other mental health professional who is responsible for the treatment of mentally ill inmates should not be assigned to make either of these determinations, nor should the record of treatment for mental illness be employed in reaching such a determination. There needs to be a clear and evident separation between the process of treating mentally ill patients and that of rendering evaluations of these patients that may result in adverse legal consequences to them.

Concept of Predicted Dangerousness

There is no satisfactory test for predicting whether a person is (or will become) dangerous. Psychiatrists and psychologists are not experts at foretelling future events. [44] While past behavior of an individual is the best available predictor of future actions, it is far from reliable. Despite this, parole boards, judges, and others continue to call upon a psychiatrist or psychologist to advise whether an inmate is or will become dangerous or will harm someone if released. They really are asking behavioral experts to make an "educated guess" about the credibility of a person's stated intent and the relevance of past behavior to the likelihood of some future event. While their best guess may be "better than nothing," it is not a prediction.

From an ethical perspective, a psychiatrist or psychologist who has been treating a patient and subsequently uses the clinical insight obtained through the process of treatment to prepare a prediction of dangerousness may be violating patient

---

[44] J. Monahan, "The Prediction of Violent Behavior," 141, *American Journal of Psychiatry* (1984): 10-15; H. Steadman, "The Right Not to Be a False Positive: Problems in the Application of the Dangerousness Standard," *Psychiatric Quarterly* (1980): 84-99.

confidentiality and privacy. Moreover, if the opinion/recommendation of the health professional might result in harm to the patient, such as failure to grant parole, this could be an unethical gathering and use of forensic information by a health care provider.

Two comments are in order. First, when such a "prediction"or recommendation is needed, it should be sought from a source not engaged in providing treatment to the patient. Often, this is done at a forensic center or a center for forensic psychiatry. An independent expert (psychologist, psychiatrist) also may be called in for this purpose. The forensic (legal) purpose of the evaluation should be made clear to the inmate at the beginning of the interview.

Second, it is a quite different situation when the treating health professional is not being asked to make a recommendation or prediction of dangerousness, but rather to offer advice on the kind of treatment which would be required under a different set of circumstances. For instance, if this inmate were to be paroled, would she or he require long-term/short-term care for an acute/chronic physical/mental condition? Would she or he require hospitalization? Outpatient treatment? Assistance with activities of daily living? To provide this information is an appropriate application of the principle of continuity of care and does not present an ethical concern, as long as there is at least presumed patient consent, and as long as the health professional is not led into predicting dangerousness or recommending for or against release.

Medical Clearance for Punishment

To question the ethical propriety of medical clearance for disciplinary segregation at first may appear puzzling. After all, is it not the purpose of such a practice to avoid unintended harm to a sick or debilitated inmate? But the health professional is guided by the principle "above all, do no harm." The practice of medicine (or psychiatry, psychology, nursing, dentistry, and so forth) and the role of healer are inconsistent with approving the imposition of punishment.

Still, many enlightened correctional systems have policies requiring formal input or clearance of health care professionals in classification decisions affecting housing and work assignments. In fact, the NCCHC requires [45] communication between correctional officials and health care staff prior to disciplinary measures for patients who are diagnosed as having a significant medical or mental illness or disability to ensure that these problems are considered and the prisoners' health and safety is protected. The rationale is to avoid unintended harm to inmates whose medical or psychiatric condition would contraindicate such an assignment.

Medical *clearance* for classification affecting housing or work assignments is appropriate, up to the point that the assignment is punitive in nature, or can reasonably be perceived to be punishing or harmful to the inmate. But there is a problem with medical *clearance* for segregation, for use of mace, [46] or for movement from

---

[45] NCCHC, *Standards for Prisons, op. cit.*, Standard P-07; *Standards for Jails, op. cit.*, Standard J-07; and *Standards for Juvenile Facilities, op. cit.*, Y-25.

[46] Mace and other toxic sprays may be especially harmful to an inmate with chronic obstructive pulmonary disease (including asthma), heart problems, or certain skin conditions.

lesser security to higher security with consequent restriction on activity and privileges. Health care professionals certainly should be asked to review and comment before all such assignments are initiated. But this process should not be called "medical clearance" or "approval."

This is not a trivial distinction. The doctor is not giving approval for punishment, regardless of whether she or he personally regards the assignment to disciplinary segregation as appropriate. In fact, the doctor is not even involved in the decision process, and should not be made to appear as if she or he were. Instead, the doctor simply is being asked to advise whether this inmate has a medical or mental health condition that will require specific safeguards, precautions, or treatments, or which makes him or her particularly susceptible to adverse consequences in the segregation setting (or, for example, from mace). Having so advised, it is up to the corrections officials to decide whether to make special arrangements and accommodations to ensure provision of all prescribed treatment and other medical precautions, to find another method for dealing with the behaviors of this inmate, or to accept the risk after due warning about possible adverse consequences.

For example, assume that an inmate who is dependent on supplemental oxygen is to be placed in a segregation unit where smoking by inmates and staff is permitted. The doctor, by asserting (a) the patient's need for supplemental oxygen, (b) the likely consequences of its prolonged deprivation, and (c) the hazards of smoking in the vicinity of oxygen in use, has done all that is required. At no time does the doctor "approve" or "disapprove" the punishment or "clear the inmate for segregation." The doctor simply has evaluated the patient and the circumstances of confinement and accurately described to correctional officials the probable outcomes, on a need-to-know basis and for the welfare of his or her patient.

A somewhat related situation also needs to be distinguished. Suppose an inmate, unobserved by correctional officers, makes obscene remarks to a nurse or touches her inappropriately, or intentionally damages medical equipment, or acts in a disorderly manner in the clinic. There is no ethical problem if the health professional reports the behavior, even to the point of filing a formal complaint, knowing that this may lead to prosecution or punishment of the inmate. How does this square with *primum non nocere*? Reporting the incident under these circumstances reasonably cannot be perceived as an act of medical treatment. Medical professionals clearly are entitled to a safe working area. Were such behaviors to occur in a free-world hospital or emergency room, the nurse would summon hospital security staff and possibly also the police. Staff would file formal charges. It is no different in a correctional institution. The doctor or nurse immediately should disengage from the provision of care to that patient, until and unless the behavior is corrected and controlled.

On the other hand, behavior which does not threaten the safety or security of the institution, such as swearing at staff, should not be "written up" by health care staff. Health professionals are not police, and should not behave as such. [47]

---

[47] Anno, *op. cit.*: 63.

Witnessing the Use of Force

American Public Health Association standards[48] explicitly prohibit health care staff from serving as witnesses to the use of force. So also does the American Correctional Health Services Association Code of Ethics. Again, such practices may have well-intentioned origins, namely to ensure by the presence of a presumed humane and caring individual, that excessive use of force or wanton brutality will not occur. The inmate, however, is likely to perceive that the health care professional condones and supports the unwanted use of force and the violation of his or her liberty.

This is not to be confused with the application of medically ordered physical restraint, such as in the treatment of a severely disturbed psychotic or manic patient. Health care staff appropriately may participate in the application of restraints under these circumstances since their purpose is therapeutic and to prevent harm to the patient.

It is common in many states for policy to require health care staff to check restraints that have been applied without health care direction. The American Correctional Association prohibits application of restraints as punishment.[49] Moreover, a mandatory standard of the American Correctional Association requires the health authority to be notified to assess the inmate's medical and mental health condition whenever an offender is placed in a four/five point restraint. The health authority is to "advise whether, on the basis of serious danger to self or others, the inmate should be placed in a medical/mental health unit for emergency involuntary treatment with sedation and/or other medical management, as appropriate."[50] It is not objectionable for health care staff to check the health status of restrained prisoners. The purpose of this periodic monitoring is to ensure that the restraints are not constricting circulation and that other factors are not threatening the inmate's health.

Participation in Executions

Participation in any aspect of capital punishment presents an extreme case of ethical conflict for a physician or other health professional. In this activity, the skills and knowledge of the healer are directed toward causing the death of a person. The vast majority of physicians and other health professionals recognize this as an intrinsic conflict. Thus, the American Medical Association strongly condemned physician participation in executions in its resolution of 1992.[51] The American Public Health Association standards state:

> Medical and mental health personnel have a professional obligation to utilize their training and expertise to maintain the health and wellness of the patients . . . Medical personnel must

---

[48] Dubler, APHA *Standards, op. cit.*: 113.

[49] ACA *Standards, op. cit.*, Standard 3-4183.

[50] American Correctional Association, *1996 Standards Supplement*, Standard 3-1483-1.

[51] Brian McCormick, "Ethics Panel Spells Out Physician Role in Executions," *American Medical News* (December 28, 1992): 6.

not participate in any aspect of the execution process. Medical and mental health personnel must not participate in the planning or carrying out of executions. They must not prepare medications to induce death or certify competency of the inmate for death.[52]

Numerous health care associations oppose participation by clinical staff in capital punishment.[53][54][55]

The clinical appearance of the lethal injection chamber used in some jurisdictions, with a stretcher or gurney, intravenous apparatus, and monitoring equipment, belies the stark contradiction between the healing process and the killing process.

Thus, the American Medical Association has included in its compendium of ethical directives for physicians the prohibition of participation in any way with capital punishment. This is separate and apart from the individual practitioner's own sentiments and personal convictions regarding capital punishment. Employment of the healing arts to inflict death on a condemned inmate is a direct contradiction of the code of conduct of the health professionals. This applies to examination for competency to undergo execution, treatment to restore competency to undergo execution, determination and advice on the amount of lethal force or material which will be required to inflict death to this person, positioning a target over the prisoner's heart, acquisition of, preparation, or supervision of preparation of the lethal injection or other means of execution, inserting the needle, or activating the injection mechanism,

---

[52] Dubler, APHA *Standards, op. cit.*: 114.

[53] "Health Groups Oppose A.G. on Executions," 7:1, *CorrectCare* (January/February, 1993): 3, 7.

[54] "Health Care Associations Join to Oppose Participation in Executions," 8:2, *CorrectCare* (May, 1994): 5.

[55] "In the course of our research, we found that physicians are involved in all methods of executions, especially ones performed by lethal injection, in violation of professional ethical guidelines. Physicians continue to consult on lethal dosages, examine veins, start intravenous lines, witness executions, and pronounce death. The threat posed to the moral standing of physicians, and to the public trust that physicians hold, is great. It warrants immediate and decisive action to assure the public, and each patient, that physicians will not use their skills to cause immediate and irreparable harm.

"We also discovered that state law and regulation are in direct conflict with established ethical standards regarding physician participation in executions. The majority of death penalty states define a role for physicians in the execution process, from witnessing in an official capacity to monitoring vital signs and pronouncing death. Although many states declare execution methods are not medical acts, they seek to involve physicians to make the process more 'humane'; this is contradictory and a distortion of the physician's role in society." *Breach of Trust: Physician Participation in Executions in the United States.* American College of Physicians in Philadelphia; Human Rights Watch in New York; National Coalition to Abolish the Death Penalty in Washington, D.C.; and Physicians for Human Rights in Boston (1994).

and advising when death has been accomplished and further lethal attempts are no longer necessary.[56]

The high court in Louisiana ruled that involuntary medication to render an inmate competent for execution was unconstitutional, stating that such medication constitutes punishment, not therapy, and violates state statutes against "cruel, excessive use of punishment."[57] Further,

> The National Commission on Correctional Health Care standards require that the determination whether an inmate is "competent for execution" should be made by an independent expert and not by any health care professional regularly in the employ of, or under contract to provide health care with, the correctional institution or system holding the inmate. This requirement does not diminish the responsibility of correctional health care personnel to treat any mental illness of death row inmates.[58]

Given the express objection to participation by members of the health care staff in any aspect of the capital punishment process, precisely the same reasoning should indicate the incongruence and inappropriateness of locating the execution chamber within (or adjacent to) the health care unit. As with physicians and other health care staff, the clinical area itself must be indisputably recognized as a location for healing activities.

Use of Medication for Behavior Control

Some medications are very effective for altering mood or behavior. Some can render a person unconscious or, at least, debilitated and unable to resist or be aggressive. It is unethical for these medications to be prescribed simply to control behavior. Their use requires (a) informed consent (sometimes by a surrogate) and (b) a decision by a qualified provider that the patient has an illness for which this is the appropriate treatment. Thus, a mentally ill patient whose aggressive behavior is a consequence of psychosis can be treated with a tranquilizer, but an assaultive, angry inmate without a diagnosis of mental disorder should not be treated with medication in this way. This is the reason for the third standard of the American Correctional Heath Services Association's Code of Ethics: "The correctional health professional shall [R]ender medical treatment only when it is justified by an

---

[56] On a related issue, the American Medical Association has issued a statement regarding organ donation by condemned prisoners. This practice "is permissible only if (1) the decision to donate was made before the prisoner's conviction, (2) the donated tissue is harvested after the prisoner has been pronounced dead and the body removed from the death chamber, and (3) physicians do not provide advice on modifying the method of execution for any individual to facilitate donation." American Medical Association, July 1980. Cited in American Medical Association: Council on Ethical and Judicial Affairs, Code of Medical Ethics. (1997): 12.

[57] *Perry v. Louisiana*, 610 So. 2d 746 (La. Ct. App., 1992).

[58] "Competency for Execution Policy Adopted by NCCHC," 3:1, *CorrectCare* (January, 1989): 1.

accepted medical diagnosis."[59] Every penal institution should have a policy which clearly prohibits the prescribing of medication except when appropriate for the treatment of illness.

Medical Restraint

Physical restraint, which is ordered for medical or mental health reasons, always should be carried out in a medical setting, with adequate nursing supervision. A segregation cell is not suitable for this purpose. A facility without an acute psychiatric inpatient unit or at least a medical infirmary under full-time nursing direction should not attempt to employ medically ordered physical restraints or enforced psychotropic medication. Instead, these patients should be transferred to a hospital or other suitable medical setting where the procedures can be monitored safely. In some cases, it may be necessary to restrain or medicate as part of the process of transferring a patient to the hospital.

Soft leather or plastic restraints are preferable to metal restraints when used in a medical context. They should be ordered only when it is documented in the health record that less restrictive measures are inadequate, and should be employed for no longer than necessary. The order for application of restraints should state the condition for which the restraint is deemed necessary as well as the behavior or condition of the patient which will warrant removal of the device. Restraints should be ordered only by a psychiatrist, physician, or psychologist, or as consistent with the state mental health code.[60] Likewise, an order for restraints should not be valid for longer than three to four hours, or as consistent with the state mental health regulations in this regard. When possible, ambulatory restraints should be used in preference to restraining the patient to a bed.

Food Loaf

Some correctional institutions have adopted a creative approach to managing inmates who throw their food at officers or visitors in the segregation unit. The regular portion of food and drink normally served to inmates on that day is mixed together and baked into a loaf to be eaten with the fingers and without table utensils. While purportedly the food loaf is as nutritious as the regular menu, it is decidedly less tasty and palatable.

Many consider the food loaf to be a humane as well as practical way to feed the type of prisoner for whom it was originally designed, a segregation inmate who

---

[59] American Correctional Health Service Association, *Code of Ethics, loc. cit.*

[60] The mental health statutes of various states contain regulations governing use of restraint, seclusion, and forced medication. These often are found in the section which deals with recipient rights. If there is no formal mental health code in a particular state, an acceptable guide may be found in the policy directive of a state mental hospital. Adherence to these local requirements will provide evidence that the facility is following the accepted community standard of practice.

habitually throws (or threatens to throw) his or her food out through the bars at any-one who passes by. However, some jurisdictions have broadened its usage to all inmates in disciplinary segregation, or to a food thrower for a specified period, such as thirty days, ninety days, and so forth, and not merely until he or she makes a credible contract not to repeat the objectionable misuse of food. Deprivation of palatable nourishment is not an appropriate punishment. [61] Over a prolonged period, poor nutrition may have adverse consequences on health. Physicians and health care professionals should not become involved in developing or prescribing food loaf since this cannot be regarded as a medical diet.

Directly Observed Treatment (DOT)

Directly observed treatment (DOT) is the recommended mode of medication distribution for treatment and chemoprophylaxis (medical prevention) of tuberculosis (TB). This is because premature discontinuance or intermittent taking of antibiotic medications for tuberculosis can result in selecting strains of bacteria that are resistant to treatment. These organisms, then, can infect other persons, and cause illness which is untreatable or more difficult to treat effectively. Directly observed treatment is not to be confused with forced treatment. An inmate who previously had given informed consent but is now refusing to take the tuberculosis medication should be counseled by medical staff, reminded of the risks of intermittent or interrupted compliance, and told that if refusal continues, the treatment will be stopped.

Inmates may be required to ingest other medications in the presence of a nurse (or officer) who gives them a drink of water, orange juice, or some other drink and watches them swallow. This is an acceptable practice, and its purpose is to prevent the accumulation of quantities of medication, either for sale in the yard or for later ingestion of a large and possibly fatal dosage. A clinical purpose may be verification of ingestion so as to determine if failure to achieve the expected results of treatment is due to faulty compliance or to an inadequate dosage.

Some places also require the inmate to open his or her mouth and roll the tongue around to show that he or she has not "cheeked" the medications. This is somewhat of an indignity, and it takes the time of an officer or nurse, but is not wrong in principle. In fact, this practice is recommended if abuse of medication is a problem with an inmate.

Crushing of Medications

A number of correctional institutions require all medications to be crushed prior to administering them to inmates. The reason given is to ensure that the medications are ingested, and not saved for later overdose or for sale to other inmates. While there is a legitimate interest in preventing these abuses, the means chosen may not be

---

[61] The American Correctional Association standard states that food is not to be used as a disciplinary measure. It explains that food should not be withheld, nor the standard menu varied, as a disciplinary sanction for an individual inmate. *Standards for Adult Correctional Institutions* (1990), Standard 3-4301.

appropriate in certain cases. Particularly with enteric coated, slow-release, and sub-lingual forms of medication, crushing of medications is ill-advised. The manufactur-er may have coated or specially formulated a product for any of several reasons, such as to mask an unpleasant taste, protect components from atmospheric degradation, prevent contact with a compound which is an irritant, separate reactive ingredients, protect the teeth, control the site of medication release, slow or delay absorption of the medication, and for other reasons.[62]

Good medical practice seeks to encourage compliance by patients with their pre-scribed treatment program. "A spoonful of sugar helps the medicine go down," as Mary Poppins sang in the familiar musical. Many persons find the taking of medicine to be unpleasant. Requiring ingestion of crushed medications further exaggerates this association of unpleasantness with the taking of medicine. This is especially prob-lematic for psychiatric patients, for whom faithful compliance with their treatment regimen is necessary to prevent decompensation and aggravation of their illness. Unless a facility is experiencing widespread and persistent problems with misuse of medications, the routine practice of crushing medications should be employed with caution, if at all. While somewhat more costly to purchase and more time con-suming to administer, use of liquid forms of medication, when available, is preferable to crushing tablets when there is a problem of abuse and when compliance is to be encouraged.

Treating or Diagnosing under Less than Satisfactory Conditions

Some circumstances and environmental arrangements simply are not acceptable for medical or mental health evaluation or treatment. Of course, in emergencies doc-tors and nurses may have to work under less than satisfactory conditions. But to do so routinely or when it is avoidable cannot be justified and could represent a breach of professional ethics by the health care practitioner who continues to provide health care under these conditions. Unfortunately, this concern is sometimes overlooked in correctional settings, where certain practices are rationalized under the rubric of "security" and may be tolerated or accepted without question by the medical staff. The following examples are posed for discussion, keeping in mind the original premise that there should be no real contradiction between a legitimate security requirement and a legitimate medical need.

Patient Assessment through Closed Door

In some facilities, nursing or mental health rounds of segregated or maximum-security prisoners are conducted by shouting to the inmate through a closed cell door that has a tiny Plexiglas window. In others, both inmate and staff must crouch down to talk through a food slot in the door. Shouting out one's medical or psychiatric symp-toms for the world to hear is an inexcusable breach of privacy and confidentiality. Miscommunication is also a very real possibility, given the difficulties posed by the

---

[62] Robert Hilton,"Crushing Medications," 7:4, *CorrectCare* (November, 1993): 12.

muffled and distorted voice and by other background noises. This is not the kind of information exchange which is customarily found in a physician's office. It would be an outrage if our own private physician were ever to confer with us in that fashion.

Seeing and observing patients, noting the skin color, tremors, eye movement, and nonverbal body language often communicates more to a skilled medical or mental health professional than do the words of the patients themselves. This kind of observation is impossible through a small security window or a food slot in a solid steel door. It is also uncomfortable and undignified for the inmate as well as for the staff person, who likely hurries along and does not take the time that is really warranted. Lighting is usually inadequate for proper clinical observation, even if the patient can be seen. Taking vital signs of pulse, temperature, and blood pressure, or listening to the chest, or looking at the throat are not possible, nor can injuries, wounds, or signs of trauma be observed and evaluated. Besides, the patient does not feel as if she or he has been properly evaluated, consequently is not satisfied, and will likely file a kite or stop the next nurse who passes by to try to tell the same story all over again. [63]

A different design of the doors is one solution, and certainly should be a consideration for any new facility or in any major renovation. At the very least, medical staff should be instructed never to hesitate to insist that the door be opened or that the inmate be taken to a different area whenever this is deemed to be necessary to resolve a doubt about the patient's condition. When this is done, additional security staff may have to be summoned to ensure that it can be accomplished safely.

The American Correctional Association requires that inmates in segregation [64] receive daily visits from a qualified health care official and also that a psychologist or psychiatrist personally interview and prepare a written report on any inmate remaining in segregation for more than thirty days. [65] The National Commission on Correctional Health Care requires that inmates in disciplinary segregation be evaluated by qualified health personnel daily "to determine the individual's continuing health status," and further states that "the daily evaluations should include notation of bruises or other trauma markings, comments regarding the inmate's attitude and outlook (particularly as they might relate to suicide ideation), and any health complaints." [66]

---

[63] It clearly would be unacceptable for any health professional to attempt to diagnose and treat a patient through a closed door. The level of assessment, which typically occurs during segregation rounds, however, is closer to a triage function. The nurse, for example, is attempting to learn whether the segregated inmate is expressing a medical complaint, or whether there appears to be a medical concern, that requires a face-to-face evaluation. The nurse also is making a determination concerning the urgency of the problem and the particular health discipline to which the inmate should be referred.

[64] Note that this ACA standard does not distinguish between administrative or disciplinary segregation.

[65] ACA *Standards, op. cit.,* Standards 3-4246 and 3-4244.

Undue Noise

Busy corridors can be very noisy. Because of a decision to subdivide a large prison into separate areas with fencing, a new clinic was created to serve one of the new subdivisions and thus reduce the amount of inmate traffic to the main clinic. Soon after opening the clinic, it was apparent that the numerous carts (wagons) pulled by inmate porters through the corridor alongside the new clinic, carrying food, laundry, waste, supplies, and so forth, made such a racket that medical staff could not satisfactorily listen to a heartbeat or hear lung sounds on their stethoscopes. After some discussion and problem-solving—since otherwise this was an ideal location for the clinic—someone suggested that pneumatic tires replace the steel-rimmed wheels on the wagons. This accomplished, the problem disappeared. Not to have taken effective action to solve this problem would have resulted in an unacceptable quality of care.

Risk to Safety of Health Care Staff

Safety is an important concern for all health care staff—female or male. The clinic of a minimum-security correctional camp was in a structure located furthest from the administration building. It routinely was not staffed by officers. While no unfortunate incident had occurred, staff were uncomfortable—especially when there was only one health care provider in the clinic. There was a potential for physical abuse or hostage taking. At first, these concerns were dismissed by the superintendent on grounds that (a) it was a minimum-security camp, and (b) officers are often alone with prisoners in this setting. But it was pointed out that medical staff are not able to remain fully attentive to security concerns, since the very nature of their work (such as listening to a chest, examining a patient, reading a medical chart, or viewing an x-ray or laboratory test result) temporarily distracts the clinicians from the requisite security alertness and renders them vulnerable to any prisoner who would wish to take advantage. The result was a decision by the superintendent to assign an officer to be in the clinic whenever there was only one health care employee present. Staff also were given personal alarm devices and required to wear them whenever on duty in the clinic.

No Sink or Running Water

From time to time, one still can find, even in some not very old correctional buildings, a medical or dental clinic without a sink and running water. Therefore, the dentist, physician, or nurse has to (a) rely on moist towelettes to cleanse hands between patients, (b) walk considerable distance and lose valuable time to go to a bathroom between each patient (also unsatisfactory if there are one or more doors en route which must be opened by hand), or (c) see patients without washing hands. None of these solutions is satisfactory, though option (a) is probably the best temporary solution. A sink with running water, paper towels, soap dispensers, and adequate lighting are essential for any medical or dental clinic area. Suitable plumbing and fixtures should be installed, or the clinic should be relocated.

Defective Equipment

Timely replacement or repair of defective medical equipment should be a priority if the responsible health authority presents this as a critically needed item. For example, in a clinic without a functioning autoclave (sterilizer) for medical instruments and supplies, certain medical procedures and most dental procedures cannot be performed safely.

Defective x-ray equipment can leak dangerous radiation, exposing patients and especially staff (because of prolonged presence in the area) to the risk of cancer. Defective equipment also can produce misleading results.

It is important that clinical staff promptly report defective or malfunctioning equipment and arrange for its repair or replacement. A program of preventive maintenance can avoid costly repairs and downtime. Often, with expensive and highly complex equipment, it is wise to negotiate a maintenance contract with the vendor, specifying an acceptable time frame for repair, including, when feasible, provision of loaned equipment while repairs are being performed.

Inadequate Lighting or Poor Visibility

One large county jail had constructed a new addition. Overlooking each two housing units was an officer station, fitted with large unbreakable windows. Shortly after opening the unit, at the suggestion of officers, amber-colored transparent plastic film was affixed to the interior of the windows in the officers' stations. As a result, as long as lighting was of higher intensity in the housing unit than inside the officers' station, the window served as a one-way mirror, permitting the officers to see the inmates, but preventing the inmates from watching the officers. There were small-slotted openings through which a voice could be heard and a narrow opening below the windows through which small items could be passed (such as pieces of paper).

The problem with this arrangement was that three times each day the nurse would wheel a cart into the officers' station to conduct nurse sick call and to distribute medication. The prisoner could not see the nurse. Both parties needed to shout to be heard, with the result that officers and other inmates were privy to the conversation. Third, the colored plastic as well as the poor lighting made it difficult to see clearly enough to evaluate the patients' appearance. When deemed necessary, though with considerable inconvenience and delay, officers would admit an inmate to a small anteroom (sally port) adjacent to the housing unit and there the nurse could take inmates' temperature, pulse, blood pressure, or observe the patient. Even here, the lighting was not adequate, and it was so inconvenient for the officers that nurses only rarely were requesting that this expedient be employed.

Physicians and nurses are justified in insisting on lighting which is adequate for them to perform their duties. Not to do so is an unacceptable and an unethical breach of the requisite standard of care.

Methods of Preventing HIV Transmission

Over the past few years, a number of prisons and jails have attempted some bold steps to reduce transmission of HIV and other bloodborne pathogens. In addition to educational efforts, some facilities have provided (or permitted inmates to purchase) condoms. While homosexual contact was clearly prohibited in their institutions, the authorities decided to encourage safer sex practices for those activities which would occur despite their efforts to enforce the rules. At one large metropolitan jail, a bowl of condoms was located on the physician's desk and inmates were permitted to help themselves to a small quantity. The facility established a policy that an inmate would not be charged with possession of contraband if he had three or fewer condoms at any one time. For similar reasons, a few facilities also have made small quantities of diluted household bleach available to inmates for disinfecting their intravenous drug equipment. These approaches recognize the seriousness of HIV as well as the reality of behaviors which occur among some of the inmates, and were adopted as public health measures. On the other hand, studies have not been conducted which demonstrate the effectiveness of these measures in prison settings.

Undoubtedly, more facilities will follow suit over the next few years. Policies like these, however, are highly responsive to political pressures. No department head or elected official wants to see a policy ridiculed in the headlines. Consequently, decision makers hesitate to make policies which could convey the impression that the agency condones illegal or immoral behavior.

Reporting Abuses by Staff

Inmate abuse by staff is often difficult for supervisors to discover and prove. A "conspiracy of silence" prevails, resulting in insufficient evidence to conclude the investigation in a satisfactory manner. An implied "code of conduct" deters employees from informing on their colleagues. In a correctional setting, this bond can be very strong, since these same coworkers must be counted on for protection in a disturbance or inmate-initiated attack.

Persuasive as these considerations may be, a higher ethical responsibility applies to situations in which the misconduct is abusive to inmates. An employee who is aware of the activity, but fails to report its occurrence or to take appropriate action to prevent its occurrence, becomes a responsible party and shares in the blame for the injury or abuse inflicted.

Thus, a nurse must report to the proper correctional authority any evidence which suggests that an inmate has suffered a trauma inflicted by an officer, or when observing any abusive behavior. Similarly, a worker on a mental health unit is obliged to report to the proper authority any staff abuse of the rights of patients.

Only in this way can the abusive behavior pattern be stopped. Supervisors, of course, have an obligation to protect the informant from retaliatory action. By the same token, false reporting or frivolous accusations should not be condoned. The responsibility to report abusive behavior of other employees should be taught to new employees and regularly encouraged by supervisors.

A Note of Caution

Despite their initial strong commitment to ethical principles, many health professionals after some time in corrections begin to experience a lessening of sensitivity and a blunting of these ideals. The erosion is a gradual process, and often appears to be proportionate to the degree of direct contact with inmates. The erosion also will be greater the more the professional is isolated from his or her peers.

Sometimes, the first signs are a growing tendency or willingness to deal punitively with inmates, such as, putting "no shows" last on the list for rescheduled appointments, if at all, or identifying "malingerers" (those who report to sick call without a legitimate medical problem) to correctional staff for punishment. Another sign may be the feeling that the inmates already are getting more than they are entitled to, given the nature of their crimes. Singling out socially disapproved behaviors as being less deserving of treatment reflects social prejudices rather than logic.[67] Other evidence of the erosion may be reflected in the tone of voice with which nurses or doctors address inmates. It is not customary in doctors' offices, outside of correctional institutions, for the nurse or receptionist to open the door to the waiting room and shout the patient's last name to summon him or her into the examination room. Insistence on habits of courtesy and respect, just as in community practice, will serve as reminders to staff and will earn the reciprocal respect of inmates, as well.

Contact with fellow health professionals, regular attendance at professional conferences, and periodic discussion among health care staff of ethical considerations, therefore, are to be encouraged. Coworkers also can be a strong source of support in maintaining and sharpening the awareness of medicine's lofty principles.

---

[67] Lawrence McCullough and Richard Stubbs, *Ethical Challenges of Physician Executives* (Tampa, Fla.: The American College of Physician Executives, July, 1995): 22.

EPILOGUE

Overall, this book has been about the intercept between the noble healing profession and society's outcasts. Their meeting takes place in a context managed by correctional professionals. An immense concentration of clinical pathology can be found among the inmates of almost any correctional institution. Few health professionals ever studied about correctional medicine during their school days, or even dreamed about a career in corrections. Much about the correctional environment is (or has been) antithetical to the healing process, although there are some welcome signs that this is beginning to change. Similarly, few correctional professionals have studied about health care.

As correctional administrators better appreciate the mission and involvement of the health professionals who enter their domain and as they come to understand the reason for some of their requests and requirements, the possibility opens for constructive collaboration.This book strives to reach across the gulf and share some of the "secrets" of caring for the confined with the correctional officers and administrators, who are the necessary partners of the doctors and nurses in this endeavor. The author hopes that this small offering will provoke much debate, dialog, discussion, research, and—especially—cooperation and understanding.

BIBLIOGRAPHY

Alexander, Elizabeth. 1991. *Wilson v. Seiter:* A Second Look: Case Did Not Change the Standard for Proving an Unconstitutional Denial of Medical Care. *CorrectCare.* October, p. 4, 13.

Amboyer, Donald J. 1993. Michigan County Requires Inmates to Defray Cost of Incarceration. *Corrections Today.* Vol. 55, No. 6, p. 88.

American Academy of Nurse Practitioners. 1997. *Position Statement on Nurse Practitioner Curriculum.* Austin, Texas: American Academy of Nurse Practitioners.

———. 1997. Published Memorandum. Austin, Texas: American Academy of Nurse Practitioners.

American Academy of Physician Assistants. 1996. *1995 AAPA Membership Census Report.* Alexandria, Virginia: American Academy of Physician Assistants.

———. 1997. *1996 AAPA Membership Census Report.* Alexandria, Virginia: American Academy of Physician Assistants.

American Academy of Psychiatry and the Law. 1995. *Ethics Guidelines for the Practice of Forensic Psychiatry.* Bloomfield, Connecticut: American Academy of Psychiatry and the Law.

American Bar Association. 1990. Guidelines Concerning Privatization of Prisons and Jails. Washington, D.C.: Prison and Jail Problem Committee, Criminal Justice Section, American Bar Association.

American Correctional Association. 1991. *Standards for Adult Local Detention Facilities, 3rd Edition.* Lanham, Maryland: American Correctional Association.

———. 1991. *Standards for Juvenile Detention Facilities, 3rd Edition.* Lanham, Maryland: American Correctional Association.

———. 1996. *Directory of Juvenile and Adult Correctional Departments, Institutions, Agencies, and Paroling Authorities.* Lanham, Maryland: American Correctional Association.

————. June 1996. Public Policy on Correctional Health Care. Lanham, Maryland: American Correctional Association.

————. 1996. *Standards for Adult Correctional Institutions, 3rd Edition.* Lanham, Maryland: American Correctional Association.

————. 1996. *1996 Standards Supplement.* Lanham, Maryland: American Correctional Association.

American Correctional Health Services Association. 1996. *Code of Ethics for the Correctional Health Care Professional.* Dayton, Ohio: American Correctional Health Services Association.

American Dental Association, Council on Ethics, Bylaws and Judicial Affairs. 1997. *Principles of Ethics and Code of Professional Conduct.* Chicago, Illinois: American Dental Association.

American Health Consultants. 1994. Elderly: Regular Inmates, or Nursing Home Residents? *Correctional Health Care Management.* April.

————. 1994. Facility for Inmates with AIDS Aims to Lower Costs, Improve Care. *Correctional Health Care Management.*March.

————. 1994. War on Crime Results in Casualties to Correctional Health Care Budgets. *Correctional Health Care Management.* April.

American Medical Association. The Transactions of the American Medical Association. (May, 1848:44). Chicago, Illinois: American Medical Association.

————. December, 1952. Minutes, AMA House of Delegates. Chicago, Illinois: American Medical Association.

————. June, 1996. *Board of Trustees Report 23: Principles Guiding AMA Policy Regarding Supervision of Medical Care Delivered by Advanced Practice Nurses in Integrated Practice.* Chicago, Illinois: American Medical Association.

————. 1997. *Code of Medical Ethics: Current Opinions with Annotations.* Chicago, Illinois: American Medical Association.

American Nurses Association. 1985. *Code for Nurses with Interpretive Statements.* Kansas City, Missouri: American Nurses Association.

————. 1985. *Standards of Nursing Practice in Correctional Facilities.* Kansas City, Missouri: American Nurses Association.

American Psychological Association. *1992.* Ethical Principles of Psychologists and Code of Conduct. *American Psychologist.* Vol. 47, Number 12.

Anno, B. Jaye. 1991. *Prison Health Care: Guidelines for the Management of an Adequate Delivery System.* Chicago, Illinois: National Commission on Correctional Health Care.

Anno, B. J., K. L. Faiver, and J. K. Harness. 1996. A Preliminary Model for Determining Limits for Health Care Services. *Journal of Correctional Health Care.* Volume 3, No. 1.

Axelson, G. L. 1987. *Psychotic vs. Non-psychotic Misdemeanants in a Large County Jail: An Analysis of Pre-trial Treatment by the Legal System.* (Doctoral Dissertation) George Mason University. Cited in Patricia A. Griffin. 1990. The Back Door of the Jail: Linking Mentally Ill Offenders to Community Mental Health Services. In Henry J. Steadman, ed. *Jail Diversion for the Mentally Ill: Breaking through the Barriers.* Washington, D.C.: National Institute of Corrections.

Barthwell, Andrea G. and Cynthia L Gibert. 1993. *Screening for Infectious Diseases Among Substance Abusers.* Rockville, Maryland: U.S. Department of Health and Human Services.

Beauchamp, Tom L. and James F. Childress. 1994. *Principles of Biomedical Ethics, 4th Edition.* New York: Oxford University Press.

Benenson, Abram S., ed. 1995. *Control of Communicable Diseases Manual, 16th Edition.* Washington, D.C.: American Public Health Association.

Boston, John. 1994. Court Rules on Smoking Case. *CorrectCare.* Vol. 8, No. 2, pp. 7, 14.

Breach of Trust: Physician Participation in Executions in the United States. 1994. American College of Physicians in Philadelphia; Human Rights Watch in New York; National Coalition to Abolish the Death Penalty in Washington, DC; and Physicians for Human Rights in Boston.

Brecher, Edward M. and Richard D. Della Penna. 1975. *Health Care in Correctional Institutions.* Washington, D.C.: U.S. Government Printing Office.

Brodsky, Stanley L. 1980. Ethical Issues for Psychologists in Corrections. In John Monahan, ed. *Who Is the Client?: The Ethics of Psychological Intervention in the Criminal Justice System.* Washington, D.C.: American Psychological Association.

Bureau of Justice Statistics. 1982. Prisoners 1925-81. In *Bureau of Justice Statistics Bulletin.* Washington, D.C.: U.S. Department of Justice.

———. 1994. *Correctional Populations in the United States, 1993.* Washington, D.C.: U.S. Department of Justice.

———. 1995. Prisoners in 1994. In *Bureau of Justice Statistics Bulletin.* Washington, D.C.: U.S. Department of Justice.

———. 1996. Prison and Jail Inmates, 1995. In *Bureau of Justice Statistics Bulletin.* Washington, D.C.: U.S. Department of Justice.

———. 1996. *Sourcebook of Criminal Justice Statistics 1995.* Washington, D.C.: U.S. Department of Justice.

Carter, James H. 1988. The Chronic Mentally Ill in the Criminal Justice System. *CorrectCare.* Vol. 2, No. 1, p. 10.

Centers for Disease Control and Prevention. 1988. Changing Patterns of Groups at High Risk for Hepatitis B in the United States. In *Morbidity and Mortality Weekly Report* (July 22, 1988). Atlanta, Georgia: U.S. Department of Health and Human Services.

———. 1993. *HIV/AIDS Prevention Bulletin* (April 19, 1993). Atlanta, Georgia: U.S. Department of Health and Human Services.

———. 1996. Prevention and Control of Tuberculosis in Correctional Facilities: Recommendations of the Advisory Committee for the Elimination of Tuberculosis. In *Morbidity and Mortality Weekly Report* (June 7, 1996). Atlanta, Georgia: U.S. Department of Health and Human Services.

———. 1997. Update: Trends in AIDS Incidence, Deaths, and Prevalence—United States, 1996. In *Morbidity and Mortality Weekly Report* (February 28, 1997). Atlanta Georgia: U.S. Department of Health and Human Services.

Chavez, R. Scott. 1991. Achieving Risk Management Through Accreditation of Health Services. *American Jails.* September-October.

Commission on Accreditation of Allied Health Education Programs. 1997. *The Standards and Guidelines for an Accredited Educational Program for the Physician Assistant.* Chicago, Illinois: Commission on Accreditation of Allied Health Education Programs.

Corrections Cost Control and Revenue Report. August 1995. Gaithersburg, Maryland: Aspen Publishers, Inc.

The Corrections Professional. 1996. Inmates Have No Privacy Claim Against HIV Disclosure. Horsham, Pennsylvania: LRP Publications

Cotton, G. 1995. Privatization of Jail Health Care Services. *American Jails.* January- February.

Crane, S. 1995. PAs/NPs: Forging Effective Partnerships in Managed Care Systems. *Physician Executive Magazine.* Vol. 21, Issue 10.

Daneluk, Rochelle and Daniel T. Welihan. 1997. The Management of Hepatitis in the Correctional Environment. Presentation delivered at American Correctional Association Winter Conference, Indianapolis, Indiana, January 28, 1997.

DeGroot, Anne S., Theodore M. Hammett, and Rochelle Scheib. 1996. Barriers to Care of HIV-Infected Inmates: A Public Health Concern. *The AIDS Reader.* May/June, pp. 78-79.

Division of Nursing, Bureau of Health Professions. 1992. *National Sample Survey of Registered Nurses.* Washington D.C.: Health Resources and Services Administration, U.S. Department of Health and Human Services.

Douglass, Richard L., Mary Lindemann, William Lovett. 1991. *Oldtimers: Michigan's Elderly Prisoners.* Lansing, Michigan: Michigan Office of Services to the Aging and the Gerontological Society of America.

Dubler, Nancy N., ed. 1986. *Standards for Health Services in Correctional Institutions, 2nd Edition.* Washington, D.C.: American Public Health Association.

Dvoskin, Joel A. 1990. Jail-Based Mental Health Services. In Henry J. Steadman, ed. *Jail Diversion for the Mentally Ill: Breaking through the Barriers.* Washington, D.C.: National Institute of Corrections.

Eichold, Samuel. 1995. HIV Care in Correctional Facilities. *Journal of Correctional Health Care.* Vol. 2, No. 2, p. 111.

Elliott, Lawrence J. 1995. Presentation of a Pilot Study of Hepatitis B Vaccinations in Michigan Correctional Facilities (August 1995). Lansing, Michigan: Michigan Department of Public Health.

Faiver, Kenneth L. 1984. Epidemiologic Review of Deaths in a Prison Setting. Conference on Suicide Prevention in Michigan Jails, Lockups and Holding Centers (April 1984). East Lansing, Michigan: Michigan State University.

———. 1997. Perspective from the Field: Golden Years and Iron Gates. In Anthony Walsh. *Correctional Assessment, Casework, and Counseling, 2nd Edition.* Lanham, Maryland: American Correctional Association.

Faiver, Kenneth L. and B. Jaye Anno. 1991. Cost Considerations: Financing, Budgeting and Fiscal Management. In B. Jaye Anno. *Prison Health Care: Guidelines for the Management of an Adequate Delivery System.* Chicago, Illinois: National Commission on Correctional Health Care.

Faiver, Kenneth L. and Robert S. Ort. 1994. Managing the Mentally Ill in Correctional Settings: Creating Therapeutic Environments. Eighteenth National Conference on Correctional Health Care (September 27, 1994). San Diego, California.

———. 1996. Strategies to Manage the Mentally Ill in Jails. Twentieth National Conference on Correctional Health Care (October 29, 1996). Nashville, Tennessee.

Famighetti, Robert, ed. 1996. *The World Almanac and Book of Facts.* New York: Press Publishing Co.

Federal Medical Center. July, 1995. *Hospice Program Procedures.* Rochester, Minnesota: Federal Medical Center.

Fiske, Donald. 1994. Pennsylvania Department of Corrections Joins with Local Hospice to Meet Needs of Dying Inmates. *CorrectCare.* Vol. 8, No. 3, p. 4.

Fogel, Catherine Ingram. 1995. Pregnant Prisoners: Impact of Incarceration on Health and Health Care. *Journal of Correctional Health Care.* Vol. 2, No. 2, pp. 169-90.

Gipson, Frances T. and Elizabeth A. Pierce. 1996. Current Trends in State Inmate User Fee Programs for Health Services. *Journal of Correctional Health Care.* Vol. 3, No. 2. p. 165.

Gottula, Roderic. 1996. The Importance of Defining Medical Necessity. *CorrectCare.* Vol. 10, No. 4.

Haddad, Jane E. 1991. Management of the Chronically Mentally Ill within a Correctional Environment. *CorrectCare.* Vol. 5, No. 1, pp. 5, 7.

Hammett, Theodore M. and Lynne Harrold. 1994. *Tuberculosis in Correctional Facilities.* Washington, D.C.: National Institute of Justice.

Hammett, Theodore M., Rebecca Widom, et al. 1995. *1994 Update: HIV/AIDS and STDs in Correctional Facilities.* Washington, D.C.: National Institute of Justice.

Hansen, Chris and Gordon C. Kanska. 1981. Ethical Problems: Cases and Commentaries. *Journal of Prison Health.* Vol. 1, No. 2, pp. 97-104.

Harper Perennial. 1996. *The Real War on Crime.* Cited in "Prison Care," *Modern Maturity.* March/April 1997, p. 33.

Harrison, Bernard P. 1996. In the Matter of Charging Prisoners for Health Services. *Journal of Correctional Health Care.* Vol. 3, No. 2, p. 114.

Hartstone, Eliot. 1990. The Mentally Ill and the Local Jail: Policy and Action. In Henry J. Steadman, ed. *Jail Diversion for the Mentally Ill: Breaking through the Barriers.* Washington, D.C.: National Institute of Corrections.

Hayes, Lindsay M. 1995. *Prison Suicide: An Overview and Guide to Prevention.* Mansfield, Massachusetts: National Center on Institutions and Alternatives.

Hilton, Robert. 1993. Crushing Medications. *CorrectCare.* Vol. 7, No. 4, p. 12.

Huskey, Bobbie L. 1995. Think Twice Before Abolishing Inmate Privileges. *Corrections Today.* June.

Jemelka, Ronald. 1990. The Mentally Ill in Local Jails: Issues in Admission and Booking. In Henry J. Steadman, ed. *Jail Diversion for the Mentally Ill: Breaking through the Barriers.* Washington, D.C.: National Institute of Corrections.

The Joint Commission on Accreditation of Health Care Organizations. 1996. *1996 Comprehensive Accreditation Manual for Ambulatory Care.* Chicago, Illinois: Joint Commission on Accreditation of Health Care Organizations.

Jones, P. Eugene and James Cawley. 1994. Physician Assistants and Health System Reform: Clinical Capabilities, Practice Activities and Potential Roles. *Journal of American Medical Association.* 271:1255-1272.

Jones, Robert. 1996. In Search of a Definition of Medical Necessity. Twentieth National Conference on Correctional Health Care (October 28, 1996). Nashville, Tennessee.

Journal of Correctional Health Care. Fall 1996. [Entire Issue]

Kagle, Jill Doner and Sandra Kopels. 1994. *Health and Social Work.* Vol. 19, No. 3, p. 217.

Kaminer, Anita. 1992. Women in Prison: Study Looks at Life Maternal Feelings. *CorrectCare.* Vol. 6, No. 3, p. 14.

Keve, Paul W. 1996. *Measuring Excellence: The History of Correctional Standards and Accreditation.* Lanham, Maryland: American Correctional Association.

Lakeland Correctional Facility. 1996. *Job Duties: Prisoner Assistants for Disabled Prisoners.* Coldwater, Michigan: Lakeland Correctional Facility.

Levens, Steve. 1995. Telemedicine as Dial-an-Expert Tool Misses Point of Technology. *Telemedicine and Telehealth Networks.* December, p. 12.

Linton, Larry. 1996. Alabama's Solution to an Old Dilemma. *Corrections Forum.* November/December.

Long, Ray. 1993. Increase in AIDS Burdens Prisons. *Chicago Sun Times* (December 6, 1993).

Lopez, M., and K. Chayriques. Billing Prisoners for Medical Care Blocks Access. *National Prison Project Journal.* 9(2), 1-2, 17. Cited in William J. Rold. 1996. Charging Inmates for Medical Care: A Legal, Practical, and Ethical Critique. *Journal of Correctional Health Care.* Vol. 3, No. 2, p. 137.

Lovett, William W. et al. 1992. *Report on Michigan's Elderly Prison Population.* Lansing, Michigan: Michigan Department of Corrections.

Lutz, S. 1991. Practitioners are Filling in for Scarce Physicians. *Modern Healthcare.* Vol. 21, No. 19, pp. 24-30.

McCormick, Brian. 1992. Ethics Panel Spells Out Physician Role in Executions. *American Medical News.* December 28, 1992, p. 6.

McCullough, Lawrence and Richard Stubbs. 1995. *Ethical Challenges of Physician Executives.* Tampa, Florida: American College of Physician Executives.

McDonald, Douglas C. 1995. *Managing Prison Health Care and Costs.* Washington, D.C.: National Institute of Justice.

McKinley, Jr., James C. 1995. Isolation Ends for Prisoner Who Refused Testing for TB. *New York Times.* August 22, 1995. p. B5. Cited in Karen Wilcock, Theodore M. Hammett, Rebecca Widom, and Joel Epstein. 1996. Tuberculosis in Correctional Facilities 1994-95. *Research in Brief* (July 1996). Washington, D.C.: National Institute of Justice, U.S. Department of Justice.

Mentally Ill Inmates: Better Data Would Help Determine Protection and Advocacy Needs. Washington D.C.: General Accounting Office (April 1991). Cited in National Commission on Correctional Health Care Position Statement on Mental Health Services in Correctional Settings. *Journal of Correctional Health Care.* Spring 1995, p. 85.

Modern Maturity (January/February 1996). American Association of Retired Persons, p.32 ff.

Monahan, J. 1984. The Prediction of Violent Behavior. *American Journal of Psychiatry.* 141:10-15.

Monahan, John, ed. 1980. *Who Is the Client?: The Ethics of Psychological Intervention in the Criminal Justice System.* Washington, D.C.: American Psychological Association.

Moore, J. 1986. Prison Health Care: Problems and Alternatives in the Delivery of Health Care to the Incarcerated (Part I and Part II). *Florida Medical Association.* Vol. 73, No. 8 (531- 535), No. 9 (615-620).

———. 1986. Privatization of Prison Health Services. *The Privatization Review.* 2(4).

———. New Jersey Department of Corrections Master Plan Medical Services, presented October 25, 1995.

Morreim, E. Haavi. 1991. *Balancing Act: The New Medical Ethics of Medicine's New Economics.* Boston, Massachusetts: Kluwer Academic Publishers.

Morton, Joann B. 1992. *An Administrative Overview of the Older Inmate.* Washington, D.C.: National Institute of Corrections.

National Association of Social Workers. 1993. *Code of Ethics.* Washington, D.C.: National Association of Social Workers.

National Commission on Correctional Health Care. 1989. Competency for Execution Policy Adopted by NCCHC. *CorrectCare.* Vol. 3, No. 1, p. 1.

———. 1991. U.S. Supreme Court Redefines "Deliberate Indifference." *CorrectCare.* Vol. 5, No. 3, pp. 1, 14.

———. 1991. *Wilson v. Seiter, et al.*: What the Court Did. *CorrectCare.* Vol. 5, No. 3, p. 15.

———. 1993. Health Groups Oppose A.G. on Executions. *CorrectCare.* Vol. 7, No. 1, pp. 3, 7.

———. 1994. Forced Psychotropic Medications Reviewed by Courts. *CorrectCare.* Vol. 8, No. 2, pp. 4, 6.

———. 1994. Health Care Associations Join to Oppose Participation in Executions. *CorrectCare.* Vol. 8, No. 2, p. 5.

———. 1994. *Position Statement: Women's Health Care in Correctional Settings.* Adopted by the NCCHC Board of Directors (September 25, 1994). Chicago, Illinois: National Commission on Correctional Health Care.

———. 1995. *Standards for Health Services in Juvenile Detention and Confinement Facilities.* Chicago, Illinois: National Commission on Correctional Health Care.

———. 1996. *Standards for Health Services in Jails.* Chicago, Illinois: National Commission on Correctional Health Care.

———. 1997. *Standards for Health Services in Prisons.* Chicago, Illinois: National Commission on Correctional Health Care.

Nevada Department of Prisons. 1996. *Correctional Health Care: A Provider Review.* Carson City, Nevada: Nevada Department of Prisons.

Newsweek. Justice, Texas Style. October 6, 1986, p. 50.

New York State Special Commission on Attica. 1972. *Attica: The Official Report of the New York State Special Commission on Attica.* New York: Bantam Books.

O'Neal, Donna. 1993. Prison to House Inmates with AIDS. *Orlando Sentinel.* August 24, 1993.

Office of Technology Assessment. 1986. *1986 Nurse Practitioners, Physician Assistants, and Certified Nurse-Midwives: A Policy Analysis.* Health Technology Case Study 37 (December 1986). Washington, D.C.: Office of Technology Assessment.

Pitre, Renee. 1994. Jail Introduces Healthy Start Project. *CorrectCare.* Vol. 8, No. 1, p. 1.

Ringler, Tim. 1992. Consideration of Mental Health Factors in Inmate Discipline. *CorrectCare.* Vol. 6, No.2, pp. 4ff.

————. 1995. Monitoring Compliance. Presentation at National Commission on Correctional Health Care Conference, Washington, D.C. (November 1995).

Rold, William J. 1996. Charging Inmates for Medical Care: A Legal, Practical, and Ethical Critique. *Journal of Correctional Health Care.* Vol. 3, No. 3, p. 134.

Rowan, Joseph R. 1991. *Suicide Prevention in Custody: Intensive Study Correspondence Course.* Lanham, Maryland: American Correctional Association.

————. 1997. Suicide Prevention in Adult and Juvenile Institutions. Presentation at American Correctional Association Winter Conference (January 27, 1997). Nashville, Tennessee.

Rowan, Joseph R. and Lindsay M. Hayes. 1988. *Training Curriculum on Suicide Detection and Prevention in Jails and Lockups.* Mansfield, Massachusetts: National Center on Institutions and Alternatives.

Santamour, Miles B. 1989. *The Mentally Retarded Offender and Corrections.* Lanham, Maryland: American Correctional Association.

Sekscenski, E. S., S. Sansom, C. Bazell, M. Salmon, and F. Mullan. 1994. State Practice Environments and the Supply of Physician Assistants, Nurse Practitioners, and Certified Nurse-Midwives. *The New England Journal of Medicine.* 331:19:1266-1271.

Singer, A. and R. Hooker, 1996. Determinants of Specialty Choice of Physician Assistants. *Academic Medicine.* 71(8):917-9.

Snell, Tracy L. 1993. *Correctional Populations in the United States, 1991.* Washington, D.C.: U.S. Department of Justice, Bureau of Justice Statistics.

Southwick, Arthur F. and Debora A Slee. 1984. Quality Assurance in Health Care: Confidentiality of Information and Immunity for Participants. *The Journal of Legal Medicine.* Vol. 5, No. 3, p. 396.

Spitzer, W.O., D. I. Sacket, J. C. Sibley, et al. 1974. The Burlington Randomized Trial of the Nurse Practitioner. *New England Journal of Medicine.* 290:251-256.

Start, Armond H. 1996. Physician Recommends Format for Determining Necessity. *CorrectCare.* Vol. 10, No.4, pp. 4, 7.

Stead, Eugene. 1966. "Conserving Costly Talents: Providing Physicians' New Assistants." *Journal of the American Medical Association.*198: 1108-1109.

Steadman. H. 1980. The Right Not to Be a False Positive: Problems in the Application of the Dangerousness Standard. *Psychiatric Quarterly.* 52: 84-99.

TB Monitor. July, 1994. Inmate Screening Process Helps Identify Active Cases. Atlanta, Georgia: American Health Consultants.

———. August, 1994. Maintaining Negative Air Pressure Requires Vigilance. Atlanta, Georgia: American Health Consultants.

———. August, 1994. Multi-agency Effort Results in Testing of Correctional Workers. Atlanta, Georgia: American Health Consultants.

———. November, 1996. New TB Guidelines Could Save Prisons Money. Atlanta, Georgia: American Health Consultants.

Teplin, Linda A. 1990. Policing the Mentally Ill: Styles, Strategies, and Implications. In Henry J. Steadman, ed. *Jail Diversion for the Mentally Ill: Breaking through the Barriers.* Washington, D.C.: National Institute of Corrections.

Texas Department of Criminal Justice. 1987. *Manual Policies and Procedures,* No. 3- 12D (August 1987). Huntsville, Texas: Texas Department of Criminal Justice.

Torrey, E. Fuller. 1997. *Out of the Shadows: Confronting America's Mental Illness Crisis.* New York: John Wiley & Sons.

Travisono, Anthony P. and Mary Q. Hawkes. 1995. *Building a Voice: 125 Years of History.* Lanham, Maryland: American Correctional Association.

U.S. Senate Special Committee on Aging, American Association of Retired Persons, Federal Council on Aging and Administration on Aging. 1986. *Aging America: Trends and Projections.* Rockville, Maryland: U.S. Department of Health and Human Services.

Walsh, Anthony. 1997. *Correctional Assessment, Casework, and Counseling, 2nd Edition.* Lanham, Maryland: American Correctional Association.

Weinstein, Henry C. 1990. Psychiatric Services in Jails and Prisons: Who Cares? *CorrectCare.* Vol. 4, No. 1, p. 7.

Wess, G. 1996. Inmate Health Care, Part 1: As New Commitments Climb, Health Care Budgets Follow. *Corrections Compendium.* Vol. II, No. 10.

Wilcock, Karen, Theodore M. Hammett, Rebecca Widom, and Joel Epstein. 1996. Tuberculosis in Correctional Facilities 1994-95. *Research in Brief* (July 1996). Washington, D.C.: National Institute of Justice.

Williams, Peter C. and Joan Hirsch Holzman. 1981. Ethical Problems: Cases and Commentaries: Health vs. Safety: Receiving Needed Care. *Journal of Prison Health.* Vol. 1, No. 1, pp. 44-54.

Wishart, Margaret D. and Nancy N. Dubler. 1983. *Health Care in Prisons, Jails and Detention Centers: Some Legal and Ethical Dilemmas.* Bronx, New York: Montefiore Medical Center.

Wozniak, G. D. 1995. Physician Utilization of Non-physician Practitioners. *Socioeconomic Characteristics of Medical Practice.* Chicago: American Medical Association, Center for Health Policy Research.

INDEX

Dental services, 108, 220, 225
Depression
    suicide indicator, 158
    in women inmates, 138
Developmental disabilities of
        inmates, 145-46, 150
Diabetes
    standard for management of, 71
    women inmates, 138
Diagnostic related groups (DRGs), 2
Diets, medically necessary, 234
Directly observed treatment (DOT), 248
Disabled inmates
    ADA requirements, 129
    aging, applicability of discussion of, 123
    assistance of other inmates with, 130-31
    copayment exemption, 120
    developmental disabilities of, 145-46
    mental illness, See Mental health of
        inmates
    mental retardation, 145-46, 150
    nurse practitioners and physician
        assistants, guidelines for, 197
Disaster preparedness, 30, 31, 216; See also
        Emergencies and acute conditions
Discharge, See Release or discharge of
        inmates
Discipline of inmates
    medical clearance for, 242-43
    mentally disordered inmates, 162-64,
        179-80
    withholding medical care as form of, 76
Discrimination
    appropriate and necessary care, reasons
        for granting or withholding, 75, 76
Diseases, communicable and infectious,
        See Communicable and infectious
        diseases
Diversion programs for mentally ill
        inmates, 166
DNA testing, 237-38
Do not resuscitate (DNR) orders, 129
Doctors, See Physicians
DOT (directly observed treatment), 248
DRGs (diagnostic related groups), 2
Drug abuse, See Substance abuse
Drugs, medicating, See Medication
Due process
    copayment notification and appeal, 119
    involuntary treatment, 173, 233
Duke University
    nurse practitioners and physician
        assistants program at, 183

E

Ectoparasitic control, 30
Education
    health education, See Health education
    mental health of inmates, education for
        staff members regarding, 165
    nurse practitioners and physician
        assistants, 185-87, 197

Eighth Amendment rights
    Estelle v. Gamble, 19
    Newman v. Alabama, 19
    quality of care, 217
Elderly inmates, See Aging inmates
Elective procedures defined, 73
Emergencies and acute conditions
    appropriate and necessary care,
        defining, 77
    mental health of inmates, 149-51
    preparedness for, 25, 216
    treatment access, 227
Enforced treatment, See Involuntary
        treatment
Entry screening of inmates, See Intake
        health screening
Equipment, defective
    less than satisfactory conditions, treating
        or diagnosing under, 251-52
Estelle v. Gamble, 19-20
    challenges to, 21
    Eighth Amendment rights established
        by, 19
    medical autonomy doctrine, 32
Ethical considerations, 25, 219-54
    abuse of inmates by staff, reporting, 253
    American Correctional Association Code
        of Ethics, 25
    American Correctional Association Task
        Force on Health Care in
        Corrections, 224-28
    ACHSA ethics code, 229, 232
    AIDS and HIV transmission,
        preventing, 252-53
    bill of rights for inmate-patients, 228
    bioethics committee, 224
    blood and tissue specimens, taking, 236-38
    body cavity searches, 238-41
    closed-door assessments, 249-52
    communicable and infectious diseases
        American Correctional Association
            policy, 227
        AIDS and HIV transmission,
            preventing, 252-53
        directly observed treatment (DOT) for
            TB patients, 248
    competency evaluations, 241
    condemned prisoners, 244-46
    confidentiality, 229-32
    correctional activities performed by
            health care professionals
        behavioral problems, reporting, 243,
            253-54
        blood and tissue samples,
            taking, 236-38
        body cavity searches, 239
        competency evaluations, 241
        discipline, medical clearance
            for, 242-43
        DNA testing, 237-38
        executions, participating in, 244-46
        force, witnessing use of, 244

Index

students, using, 198
supervision by physicians
American Medical Association
guidelines, 193-95
state requirements, 195
terminology, 185
Vietnam War, positions arising
from, 183-84
Nurses
abuse reporting, 253
assessment of inmates in segregated
housing, 105-06
as cost containment strategy, 16
earnings of, 1
ethical code for, 220, 221-22
Nursing home care, 129
Nutritional issues, 225
food loaf, 247-48

O

Obesity in women inmates, 137-38
**Occupational Safety and Health
Administration (OSHA)**
fines, 214
standards, 59
Observation cells
mental health of inmates, *See* Mental
health of inmates
**Ohio Department of Rehabilitation and
Correction**
privatization by, 46
special units for elderly in, 130
Older inmates, *See* Aging inmates
On-call arrangements, 112-14
**Organ donations by condemned
prisoners**, 246
Organizational issues
centralization, *See* Responsible health
authority
models, organizational, 35
and outside agencies, 36-37
privatization, 38-40
responsible health authority, *See*
Responsible health authority
RFP, describing organizational
requirements in, 62
training needs, coordinating, 27, 29-31
Osteoporosis in women inmates, 140
Outsourcing
organizational issues, 36-37
privatization, *See* Privatization
specialists, requirements regarding
outside trips to, 66-67
Overweight women inmates, 137-38

P

Pap smears, 136
Parenting issues, 138, 139
training in, 228
Peer observers to prevent suicide, 160
Pelvic inflammatory disease (PID), 135

Pennsylvania
health service contracts in, 45-46, 47, 53
partial contractual model, 64
performance guarantees in, 67
Performance bonds, 65
Pharmacy, *See* Medications
Philosophical issues
belief systems of correctional and
medical institutions, 27-28
care and custody of inmates as
correctional aim, 25
coercive practices, medical versus
correctional attitudes towards, 27
consistency between correctional policies
and good health care, 25-26
divergence between correctional and
medical aims, xv, 26, 223, 255
ethics, *See* Ethical considerations
Hippocratic Oath, 223
methodologies of correctional and
medical institutions, 26-27
primary clients of correctional and
medical institutions, 26
protection of public as main aim of
correctional facilities, 25
punishment as main aim of correctional
facilities, xv, 26-27
purpose of correctional and medical
institutions, 26
training, medical versus correctional
attitudes towards, 27
Physical abuse, *See* Abuse, physical or sexual
**Physician assistants and physician
extenders**, *See* Nurse practitioners
and physician assistants
Physicians
earnings of, 1
Hippocratic Oath, 223
medical director, role of, 34
shortage of, positions arising from, 183-84
time, effective use of, 16
Pill line, 109-10
Point-of-entry health screening, 106-07
Population of correctional facilities
aging inmates
baby boom, effect of, 123-24
growing number of, 10
life expectancy of population at large,
general increase in, 5-6
Michigan's elderly offenders, profile
of, 125-27
baby boomers and the aging inmate
population, 123-24
cost-control issues raised by growing
numbers, 11
increasing number of inmates, 8, 9, 41
juveniles, growing number of, 10-11
mentally ill inmates, growing number
of, 143-46, 169, 170
Michigan's elderly offenders, profile
of, 125-27

V

Vaccinations

Hepatitis B, 93-94

Vermont

privatization of health care in, 47

Vietnam War

nurse practitioners and physician
assistants, 183-84

prison reform, effect on, 18

Virginia

privatization in, 46

special units for elderly in, 130

Victimization, 138-39

Visibility, poor

less than satisfactory conditions, treating
or diagnosing under, 252

W

War on Poverty Campaign

prison reform, effect on, 18

Water

health care professionals' access to, 251

Weight-lifting, 6, 7

Wellness programs

aging inmates, 131-32

cost control, 3-4

trends in health care, encouraging use
of, 6-7

West Virginia

privatization of health care in, 47

special units for elderly in, 130

Wilson v. Seiter, 21

Wisconsin

special units for elderly in, 130

Women inmates, 133-41

American Correctional Association public
policy statement on needs of, 134

aging inmates, 139-40

AIDS and HIV, 136-37

background of abuse among, 138-39

boot camp placement for, 141

breast cancer screening of, 136

cervical cancer screening of, 136

chaperones for, 137

children of

care needs of, 135-36

stress of separation from, 138

chlamydia infections, 97

as consumers of health care, 9

contraception for, 139

cosmetic concerns, addressing, 140

court-ordered requirements for, 134

depression in, 134, 138

diabetes in, 138

economic reasons for crimes committed
by, frequency of, 133

gender issues of, 227

gynecological care on premises, need
for, 137

health education, 140

high number of health care needs
compared to male inmates, 133-34,
137

hormonal replacement therapy, 139-40

human papilloma virus in, 136

increasing number of, 9, 133-34

intake health screening, 135-37

menopause, 139-40

menstrual irregularities, 136

mental health problems of, 138-39

numbers of, 9

obesity, 137-38

osteoporosis, 140

Pap smears, 136

pelvic inflammatory disease, 135

poverty, background of, 133

pregnancy, *See* Pregnant inmates

screening requirements,
specialized, 135-37

sexually transmitted diseases, screening
for, 135, 136-37

as single mothers, 135-36

syphilis, 135

violence suffered by, 138-39

work activities for, 141

Work activities

of aging inmates, 131-32

of pregnant inmates, 141

of women inmates, 141

World Medical Association

ethics code, 223-24

Wyoming

privatization of health care in, 47, 64

special units for elderly, 130

ABOUT THE AUTHOR

Kenneth L. Faiver, a respected leader in the field of correctional health care, served for sixteen years as Associate Director of Health Care for the Michigan Department of Corrections and more recently as Chief Medical Coordinator for the Puerto Rico Department of Public Health. Currently, he is President and Chief Executive Officer of Correctional Health Resources, Inc., a company which recruits and supplies health care professionals for correctional facilities. He also is active as a consultant and court expert in correctional health care matters.

Faiver holds a master's degree in public health (MPH) from the University of Michigan, a master's degree in labor and industrial relations (MLIR) from Michigan State University, and a licentiate in sacred theology degree (STL) from the Catholic University of America. He has completed the course work towards a doctorate in public health (DrPH) from the University of Michigan.